CHROMOGRAPHIA

D1285060

Chromographia

American Literature and the
Modernization of Color

NICHOLAS GASKILL

University of Minnesota Press
Minneapolis | London

The University of Minnesota Press gratefully acknowledges the generous assistance provided for the publication of this book by the Rutgers University Research Council and the Department of English at Rutgers.

Every effort was made to obtain permission to reproduce material in this book. If any proper acknowledgment has not been included here, we encourage copyright holders to notify the publisher.

Excerpts from "Spring and All" by William Carlos Williams from *Imaginations* (New York: New Directions Publishing Corporation, 1971); copyright 1970 by Florence H. Williams. Reprinted by permission of New Directions Publishing Corporation.

A different version of a portion of chapter 2 was published in "The Articulate Eye: Color-Music, the Color Sense, and the Language of Abstraction," *Configurations* 25, no. 4 (December 2017): 475–505; copyright 2017 The Johns Hopkins University Press. Different versions of portions of chapter 3 were published in "Of Primitives and Primaries," *Cabinet* 61 (Spring–Summer 2016): 34–41, and in "Learning to See with Milton Bradley," *Bright Modernity: Color, Commerce, and Consumer Culture,* ed. Regina Lee Blaszczyk and Uwe Spiekermann (Palgrave Macmillan, 2017): 55–73; the latter reprinted with permission of the publisher. Different versions of portions of chapter 4 were published in "Red Cars with Red Lights and Red Drivers: Color, Crane, and Qualia," *American Literature* 81 (December 2009): 719–45.

Published by the University of Minnesota Press
111 Third Avenue South, Suite 290
Minneapolis, MN 55401-2520
http://www.upress.umn.edu

Printed in the United States of America on acid-free paper

The University of Minnesota is an equal-opportunity educator and employer.

25 24 23 22 21 20 19 18   10 9 8 7 6 5 4 3 2 1

Library of Congress Cataloging-in-Publication Data
Names: Gaskill, Nicholas, author.
Title: Chromographia : American literature and the modernization of color / Nicholas Gaskill.
Description: Minneapolis : University of Minnesota Press, 2018. | Includes bibliographical references and index. |
Identifiers: LCCN 2018001932 (print) | ISBN 978-1-5179-0348-0 (hc) | ISBN 978-1-5179-0349-7 (pb)
Subjects: LCSH: Color in literature. | American literature–20th century–History and criticism.
Classification: LCC PS228.C585 G37 2018 (print) | DDC 810.9/005–dc23
LC record available at https://lccn.loc.gov/2018001932

Contents

Introduction
How Color Became Modern

Milton Bradley worried about color chaos. In the decades following the success of his 1860 board game the Checkered Game of Life (now simply LIFE), he saw thousands of new tints and tones flood the market, packaged under wonderful names: ashes of roses, magenta, Styx, baby blue, Nile green, eminence, elephant's breath. As a longtime believer in the stimulating power of well-placed hues, Bradley welcomed the increased use of color in commercial goods. But he feared that manufacturers were disseminating the synthetic dyes pouring out of industrial chemistry labs so quickly and haphazardly that the visual environment had become littered with discordant arrangements. And since color terms were proliferating at the same dizzying rate as colorants themselves, it seemed impossible to establish a language of color standards capable of curbing the chaos. What did "elephant's breath" look like anyway?[1]

To clarify this confusion, Bradley devised a pack of colored papers (Plate 1). Available in six standardized colors—red, orange, yellow, blue, green, and violet—along with their intermediate hues, Bradley's papers promised to bring order by providing a common reference point. "Red" meant the same thing for anyone who owned a set of the papers; all one had to do was consult the red sheet. For elephant's breath and the other changeable hues of fashion, the procedure was almost as easy: arrange the component colors on a Milton Bradley Color Wheel in a specified ratio and then crank the handle to turn the wheel (Figure 1). The spinning papers mixed in the eye, and *voilà,* elephant's breath. Bradley delighted in demonstrating how the incomprehensible names attached to modern colors could be translated into fixed formulas for producing the hues. He revealed that Styx, for example, comprised ten parts red (R), twenty-one parts white (W), and sixty-nine parts black (N), written "R.10, W.21, N.69." Using this precise nomenclature, Bradley and his employees used

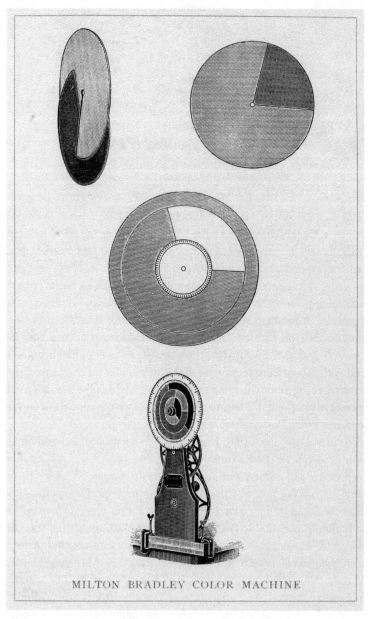

MILTON BRADLEY COLOR MACHINE

FIGURE 1. Milton Bradley Company Color Wheel for optical color mixing. Users would place disks of colored paper on the wheel in specified proportions and spin. Emily Noyes Vanderpoel, *Color Problems: A Practical Manual for the Lay Student of Color* (New York: Longmans, Green, 1902), Plate 27. RB 710255, Huntington Library, San Marino, California.

to "telephone colors" between the office and the factory, speeding up production times and ensuring that each edition of the Checkered Game of Life had the same red on its board.[2] For manufacturers, Bradley's papers and the nomenclature they supported offered a handy way to harness the potential of new industrial colors without getting overwhelmed by their intimidating number and uncertain names.

Yet Bradley wanted to beautify the products of manufacturing as well as streamline their production, and here he took the long view: he put his papers at the center of an ambitious program of color education aimed at training the hands and eyes of the next generation of designers. In the 1890s he wrote several books on why and how children should learn color, the most famous of which was *Elementary Color* (1895). All of them touted the benefits of his systematic nomenclature and offered exercises and activities based on his colored papers. Bradley trusted that with the right instruction, students could learn to attend to their own responses to chromatic stimuli, to discern when an arrangement pleases and when it unsettles, and to carry this knowledge into the production of colorful products that refresh sensation rather than exhaust or confuse it. What he pitched to both factory owners and teachers as "The Bradley Educational Colored Papers," then, aimed at an intensive training of color perception to counter the motley discords daily thrown up on billboards and shop windows and even, with chromolithography and printed wallpapers, pressing into the home.

In the decades around the turn of the twentieth century, when cultural interest in color reached an unprecedented height, Bradley's papers circulated far and wide. Their travels map the astounding range of pursuits devoted to color in this period. In addition to responding to the alarm over synthetic dyes and helping make color an unquestioned part of early education, the Bradley papers made an early contribution to the projects of color standardization that resulted in classification systems like Pantone, and as such they were a fixture of scientific investigations into color perception. Their merits were discussed in the pages of *Science* and *Nature,* where such luminaries as Herbert Spencer joined the debate.[3] Moreover, both the papers and the color wheel were part of the basic equipment of the first psychology labs in the United States. William James and Hugo Münsterberg stocked them at Harvard, where Gertrude Stein, then a student at Radcliffe, adjusted the spinning colored disks to test the perception of color saturation (Figures 2 and 3). In particular, she spun Bradley's wheel to specify the conditions under which red starts to look redder, just as others used it to test a broad range of color phenomena, from afterimages and simultaneous contrast to the influence of sound or fatigue on color sensitivity. Their combined inquiries raised fundamental questions about what color is and where it is located. Is it in the eye that registers a sensation, the mind that processes it, the wheel that spins, or in the entire activity that pulls these factors together into a single, colorful event?

In the same years that psychologists shuffled Bradley's papers to puzzle over the nature of color, some of the earliest ethnographers packed them on expeditions to test the "color sensitivity" of indigenous peoples. Most notably, W. H. R. Rivers based his conclusions about "primitive color vision"—the idea that the islanders of the Torres Strait perceived colors

FIGURE 2. Among the items on display in this photograph of the Harvard Psychology Lab in the early 1890s are a Milton Bradley Color Wheel and several color disks for testing color perception. "Interior of a Laboratory Room," from Hugo Münsterberg, *Psychological Laboratory of Harvard University* (Cambridge, Mass.: Harvard University Press, 1893), 16. Image from ECHO: Cultural Heritage Online, Max Planck Institute for the History of Science, Creative Commons CC-BY-SA, http://vlp.mpiwg-berlin .mpg.de/vlpimages/images/img31116.jpg.

differently than did white Europeans—on experiments partly conducted with the Bradley papers in the late 1890s.[4] And the game manufacturer's standards were still fueling research thirty years later. Franz Boas's student Melville J. Herskovits equipped his assistants with Milton Bradley Color Tops, miniature versions of the color wheel, to measure the skin tone of African Americans for *The Anthropometry of the American Negro* (1930) (Figure 4). Here too a famous student researcher joined in the effort: Herskovits assigned Zora Neale Hurston the task of turning the top to record the skin pigmentation of the "well-to-do and professional portion" of Harlem.[5] So in the same years that Hurston invoked intense color perceptions to convey "How It Feels to Be Colored Me" (1928), as her essay title has it, she encountered a tradition of parsing people according to their sensitivity to chromatic stimuli. Where psychologists spun Bradley's wheel to question the nature of color, ethnographers wielded the same equipment to claim that color experience discloses human differences, manifested in varying degrees of responsiveness to the sensory world.

The far-flung travels and diverse occupations that characterize the

FIGURE 3. Two Milton Bradley Color Wheels *(bottom right and left),* along with several color disks of various sizes. There are also apparatuses for testing the perception of afterimages, luminous color, color blindness, and "appreciation of color." "Instruments for Experiments on Sight," from Hugo Münsterberg, *Psychological Laboratory of Harvard University,* 8.

career of Bradley's papers thicken our intuitive sense, gathered from exhibitions and catalogs of modern art, that in the early twentieth century
color emerged as a privileged sign of modernity. The new synthetic dyes
that unleashed chromatic and linguistic chaos altered the very stuff of
color, its materials no less than the economic networks that brought it to
consumers. Educational and scientific endeavors to organize these brilliant, chemical colorants generated dynamic accounts of color perception
that unseated long-held philosophical beliefs about the feeling body and
the sensory world. Color at once changed the perceptual feel of modernity and provided a paradigm for its most distinctive philosophical and
artistic formulations. Bradley's papers bring into view the multiform and
overlapping concerns that made color an essential part of what it meant
to feel and be modern—or, by contrast, "primitive"—in the United States
in the decades between 1880 and 1930.

With Bradley in mind, let us turn to the larger cultural practices that
mobilized his papers and modernized color. We will look at three major

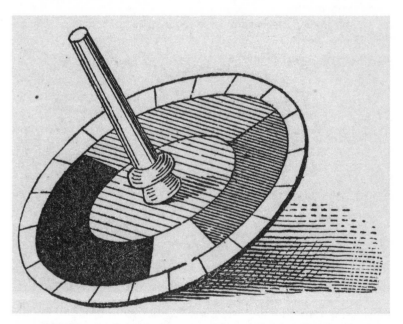

FIGURE 4. Milton Bradley Color Top, a portable version of the Milton Bradley Color
Wheel, handy for desk activities or fieldwork. Milton Bradley, *Elementary Color,* re-
vised edition (Springfield, Mass.: Milton Bradley, 1895), 32. RB 603471, Huntington
Library, San Marino, California.

topics: the emergence of a relational model of color experience, made explicit in psychology and philosophy but on display in a range of color practices; the proliferation of synthetic dyes and their impact on the materials and meanings of color; and the formulation of a distinctive "color sense" that could be enhanced through training or diminished through neglect, a distinctive faculty for feeling colors that many believed marked a perceiver as "primitive" or "civilized." These historical developments combined to make color modern.

The chapters of this book focus on specific sites and problems that took shape against this broader backdrop and will pay particular attention to how U.S. writers engaged modern color—what they did with it, how it figures in their work. So while printed and painted images will be important in what follows, my primary concern will be with inscriptions of color in writing: *chromographia*. I take this approach because literature, as a borderland between history and philosophy, registers both the social worlds within which chromatic technologies emerged and the ideas about perception, language, and the sensory environment that accompanied their proliferation. The activity of narrating color experience, of giving form to feeling, involves writers in a task at once historical and metaphysical, and this full story of color is vividly captured in the literary record. Stein and Hurston handled Bradley's standards directly, but many more authors worked with the meanings of color that those papers helped produce. The results of these engagements show the language of modern color to be more fantastic even than the fashionable names that irritated Bradley, more imaginative and far more complex than "elephant's breath" or "eminence" or, for that matter, "R.10, W.21, N.69."

Color and Its Problems

"Colors spur us to philosophize," wrote Ludwig Wittgenstein.[6] Nowhere does this dictum ring truer or reverberate through a wider array of cultural practice than in the diverse inquiries into color experience at the end of the nineteenth century. Together, these practices facilitated a remarkable shift in the metaphysical status of color. Whereas traditional empiricism cast chromatic qualities as deceitful overlays cloaking the real world, the combined efforts of psychologists, philosophers, dyers, and paint manufacturers promoted a view of colors as relational phenomena that cut across the reigning categories of subject and object, inside and outside, nature and culture. Practical and scientific investigations into color experience fostered a novel understanding of experience in general. Sometimes this colorful spur found voice in professional philosophy, most notably in the process-driven empiricisms of C. S. Peirce, William James, and Alfred North Whitehead. More often, and more spectacularly, it manifested in the array of attempts to describe, name, theorize, and arrange color that unfolded at the turn of the twentieth century.

For instance, observe Stein mixing Bradley's papers on the color wheel in James's lab at Harvard. She and Leon Solomons, her supervisor and the man whose name appears on the 1896 paper that reported their results in the *Psychological Review,* began with the assumption that the more red they put on the wheel, the redder the spinning assembly would appear. Not so. What they in fact found was that there is no one-to-one relation between the physical stimulus and the perceptual quality, no primal color "out there" that perceivers then registered in vision. Rather, the amount of red saturation "depends only on the ratio of the color to the white" on the wheel, as well as on background illumination conditions.[7] Against an intuitive sense that color is a property of objects, or the view that it is instead located entirely in the perceiving subject, Stein and Solomons arrived at an account of color experience as fundamentally *relational* in at least two ways: first, in that it requires both a seer and something to be seen; second, in that what is seen is not a single thing but instead a complex field of ratios and relations, such that perception is less a process of passively registering the world and more one of making active calculations about it. Yet these calculations are imbued with a felt quality. The feeling of red may result from a process of mediating relations, but it is experienced as a paradigm of immediacy.

Stein's research exemplifies the more general interest in color perception among psychologists, who embraced color as a discrete domain through which to investigate larger questions about how the body senses its environment and the physiological basis of aesthetic response. Her conclusions are revealing not because they were groundbreaking but because they expressed a developing scientific consensus. The major nineteenth-century studies of color—including Hermann von Helmholtz's *Treatise on Physiological Optics* (1856, 1860, 1867) and Ogden Rood's *Modern Chromatics* (1879)—all demonstrate a shift from the Newtonian emphasis on light to a focus on the relations among stimulus, eye, nerves, and brain, a shift from physics to psychology. Likewise, the French chemist Michel Eugène Chevreul's influential theory of simultaneous contrast insisted that our perception of any one color necessarily involved its relations to the colors that surround it, thus formalizing the practical knowledge that had long passed between dyers and weavers.[8] Color, in other words, could no longer be presented as a simple sense impression. As Peirce observed, staking out his own space in the scientific debates about sensory experience, "Color is sometimes given as an example of an impression. It is a bad one; because the simplest color is almost as complicated as a piece of music. Color depends upon the *relations* between different parts of the impression."[9]

Another upshot of the numerous studies of chromatic sensory perception—studies of the subtle influence of color on judging time or perceiving distance, of chromatic illusions, of the effects of various forms of distraction on color sensitivity, and so on—was that color came to be regarded as a distinctive force with identifiable effects on the body and the emotions.[10] This idea of course has a long pedigree, from ancient beliefs about gems to Ishmael's quest in Herman Melville's *Moby-Dick* (1851) to isolate the "innermost idea" of whiteness from its cultural associations.[11] But when Gustav Fechner, Wilhelm Wundt, and their many American students reported the sensory and affective responses that both human and nonhuman subjects exhibited in the presence of particular hues, the once-mystical search for a "language of color" received an empirical grounding that pushed it into a variety of cultural domains: advertising, interior design, civic planning, and postimpressionist painting (where it was mystified all over again). By the end of the nineteenth century this way of thinking about color was so entrenched that a writer in the *Arena* could assert, "It can hardly be doubted that color may produce within us certain feelings which arise independently of any principle of association, although these feelings may be of a very vague character."[12] As we will see throughout this book, the prospect that colors could affect people without their knowing raised the question of how the relations between seer and seen revealed in color might be managed, a question answered in tones both sinister and utopian.[13]

Within philosophy and the sciences, the relational character of color provoked two distinct interpretive responses, loosely corresponding to two models of empiricism and reality. First, German physiologists such as Helmholtz concluded that if colors depended on the perceiving subject, then they could not be communicated between researchers and so were barred from scientists' pursuit of objective reality. The data suggested that because of the "personal equation," slight variations in how perceivers process stimuli, one person's sensation upon looking at Bradley's standardized blue would be minimally yet measurably different from another person's. As Lorraine Daston and Peter Galison argue in *Objectivity* (2007), the ensuing concerns about the radical privacy of color sensations pushed philosophers such as Gottlob Frege and mathematicians such as Henri Poincaré to bar color, and indeed all sensory experience, from objective reality.[14] Color by these accounts was too variable, too slippery, too resolutely subjective to find a place in the neutral universe assumed by physicists and logicians.

This dismissal of color from the world updates the materialist view that had gained prominence in seventeenth-century natural philosophy and had made chromatic sensations both epistemologically and morally suspect. I mean the notion that, in Melville's vivid phrasing, the world's colors "are but subtle deceits, not actually inherent in substances, but only laid on from without; so that all deified Nature absolutely paints like the harlot, whose allurements cover nothing but the charnel-house within."[15] Color experience didn't always seem so suspect. The ancient Greeks and medieval scholastics treated colors as properties of things. It was only in the seventeenth century that philosophers began to dismiss one of our most salient sensory experiences as ancillary to reality. How did this happen? As Mazviita Chirimuuta explains in *Outside Color* (2015), color only becomes a problem "when theoretical emphasis is placed on physical reality abstracted away from the presence of perceivers."[16] Within such a framework, the senses are given the impossible task of representing an inert reality explicitly defined as separate from sensation—that is, a world as it exists apart from human experience.

Think of John Locke's well-known distinction between primary and secondary qualities in *An Essay Concerning Human Understanding* (1690). For Locke, the *qualities* of objects have the power to produce *ideas* in us, but not every quality can be trusted to give accurate information about the world. He thus distinguishes between *primary* qualities, which are "utterly inseparable" from their objects and include "Bulk, Figure, Texture, and Motion," and *secondary* qualities, which "are nothing in the Objects themselves" but only "Powers to produce various sensations in us by their *primary Qualities*"—for example, sounds, tastes, and colors. According to Locke, ideas of primary qualities resemble their objects and indeed "really exist" in them, whereas the ideas of secondary qualities—like my sensation of red—in no way resemble the physical properties that produce them.[17] As a consequence, he reasons that our ideas of secondary qualities tell us nothing about the world; rather, they tell us only of our own experiences of objects that, at bottom, are bundles of primary qualities (physical properties that cause phenomenal experience). Such is the great swindle of modern thought: the reward of secure knowledge comes at the price of embodied experience and the colorful world it reveals. From this perspective, the alluring hues of the world amount to pleasing distractions at best, dangerous illusions at worst: deified nature, made up like a harlot.

The second interpretation of the relational nature of color perception avoids this skeptical conclusion by refusing to kick the observing subject outside of reality. J. W. Goethe leads the way here. His monumental *Theory of Colours* (1810) argues that Newton's physical account of the refraction of white light into the spectral hues covers only a fraction of the ways color appears to us and that a comprehensive theory would also encompass afterimages, color contrasts, hallucinations, and other phenomena inextricable from the human observer. Goethe classed these latter cases as "physiological colour," those that "belong altogether, or in a great degree, to the *subject*—to the eye itself."[18] Importantly, though, this link to the subject does not make them merely subjective, for the seeing eye cannot be disentangled from what is seen; in fact, as Goethe explained, "The eye may be said to owe its existence to light, which calls forth, as it were, a sense that is akin to itself" (xxvi). Combine this with his earlier comment that "nature as a whole . . . manifests itself" through both light and color as they appeal to "the sense of sight," and we can see how far we are from Locke (xvii). Nature here does not exclude color in favor of light, nor does knowledge of reality require a self-imposed color blindness. Instead, Goethe proposed that colors attune us to the relational, dynamic processes that, by his account, define the natural world. In the name of a more robust notion of reality, then, one that refuses to denigrate our qualitative experiences, Goethe sought to save color phenomena from the fumbling of mechanistic philosophy and "to awaken the conviction that a progressive, augmenting, mutable quality, a quality which admits of alteration even to inversion, is not fallacious, but rather calculated to bring to light the most delicate operations of nature" (xxx).

The view of nature that emerged from Goethe's investigations into colors found philosophical expression at the end of the century in the radical empiricism of William James. James too refused to separate human activity from nature and famously insisted that relations are as real as objects. And like Goethe, who attempted to describe all the myriad conditions under which colors appear in our experience, he set the ontological question of how reality is made over the epistemological question of how we come to know it (Locke's question). Indeed, one way to understand James's project, especially as it has been elaborated by Whitehead, John Dewey, Brian Massumi, and Isabelle Stengers, is to see it as an attempt to reframe our metaphysical categories to make color as real as anything else we encounter in experience. As Whitehead wrote in *Science and the Modern World* (1925), "If we are to include the secondary qualities in the common world, a very drastic reorganization of our fundamental concept is necessary," starting with the way we account for our own embodiment.[19] The studies coming out of James's lab at Harvard had supported Goethe's general intuitions about the affective and bodily components of color experience. The radical empirical response was to treat such findings as an invitation to frame a picture of cognitive life in which feelings play a constitutive part, inseparable in the stream of consciousness from reason or thought.[20]

Ultimately the view of color as a relational quality that depends on the active imbrication of self and world found more footing in the many domains of color practice emerging in the nineteenth century than in professional philosophy.[21] And this practical grounding entrenched the experiential challenge of color more than any essay or treatise. That is, painters, designers, textile dyers, manufacturers, and educators—all those who made it their business to work with color—developed a vernacular metaphysics that opposed the persistent dichotomies of subject and object, body and mind, interior quality and exterior matter that made color a "problem" for philosophers. For instance, in a popular book on house painting, the New York paint and varnish manufacturer John W. Masury invoked the relational view against the position that "the many colors, and hues, and tints, which we see around us, have no existence but in the brain." He asked his readers to consider the rainbow: ephemeral, yes, but the result of a definite arrangement of relations. "When the sun, eye, and the rain-drops shall again find themselves in the same relative positions," he wrote, "the colored bow will reappear."[22] Masury's rainbow illustrates how the relativity of eye and color entailed a concomitant emphasis on the relations within the perceived scene, since the observer takes in an interrelated composite (sun-and-drops), not a collection of self-identical entities or hues. The house painter could bypass the theoretical problem of color by engaging the intricate and shifting relations involved in the act of seeing.

In the late nineteenth and early twentieth centuries, the habits of perception involved in attending to color insinuated themselves into all manner of tasks, distributed across the social and professional spectrum. In 1880 Henry T. Finck informed the readers of *Littell's Living Age* that the previous two decades had witnessed such a remarkable number of investigations into chromatic experience that "in the history of science they might be alluded to as the Age of Color."[23] The insights of these studies were then packaged for popular consumption, sometimes literally mailed to people's doors. An 1890 advertising card from paint manufacturer H. W. Johns presented viewers with a "miniature color chart" suitable for "schools & families" and illustrative of the fundamental tenets of color mixing, with a few points about harmonies to boot (Plate 2). When the company ran a slightly modified version of the ad three years later, it had multiple East Coast offices and branches in Chicago, Atlanta, and London—and that was just one of the companies disseminating such knowledge.[24] By 1930, according to *Scientific Monthly,* "the accurate description of color" had become "the business of everyday life," from

> the physician searching through his microscope for the tints which distinguish the eosinophile from the polymorphonuclear, to the housewife matching scientifically dyed thread to scientifically dyed fabric, to the rancher's daughter isolated beyond the last filling station nervously ordering a spring dress from Sears Roebuck or Montgomery Ward, to the very tot in school studying a color chart arranged according to the discoveries of physics.[25]

And of course there were those Bradley colored papers, moving through kindergartens and psychology labs to facilitate right thinking about color.

These everyday acts of analyzing color facilitated a regard for sensory experience in all of its ephemerality and subtlety, all the ways it calls attention to the feeler's embeddedness in the world. Not that all Americans grew into mini-pragmatists; but the rapid advance of color technologies at

the end of the nineteenth century brought out the relational, active qualities that traditional empiricism handled so clumsily and that figures like
James and Whitehead put front and center. In other words, the psychological theories of color perception that upended the subordinate position
of color, as well as the metaphysical divisions that made color a problem,
circulated through the discourses and practices devoted to chromatic
experience and united, as Goethe put it, "to bring colour again to credit"
(xxx). The result was a tacit yet formidable picture of the world and our
place in it modeled on the relational structure of color experience and the
powerful, often imperceptible influence of colors on the mind and body.
This picture was formulated through historically specific materials and
a particular understanding of the social value of sensory responsiveness.
To understand the full meaning of modern color, then, let us move from
its general relational character to the poles it relates.

The Mauve Decades

In 1930, the literary critic and soon-to-be-novelist George R. Stewart Jr.
predicted that "when the perfect history of English literature is written"
it will list "W. H. Perkin's discovery in 1856 of phenylphenosafranine
$(C_{27}H_{25}N_4Cl)$"—the organic compound for mauve dye—as "one of the
most important events in the history of poetry during the nineteenth
century" (71). I think he's right, even more than he says, and for reasons
more numerous than he lists. Mauve and other synthetic dyes not only
added new words to the English language (Stewart's primary point) but
also transformed the visual landscape and remade the very meanings
and materials of color. Their effects were impossible to miss. Moreover,
because they incited concerns about the sensory and emotional influence
of the newly vibrant commercial environment, chemical colorants of the
sort that bothered Bradley endowed the relational character of color
experience with a historically distinctive significance. Just as important
as the dynamic of chromatic perception was the materiality of the colors
perceived.

   In 1833, the German chemist Friedlieb Ferdinand Runge, one of
Goethe's scientific interlocutors, isolated an aromatic, oily liquid called
aniline $(C_6H_5NH_2)$ from the oozy black refuse of coal refinement. The compound had been encountered earlier in indigo ("aniline" comes from the
ancient root word for the indigo shrub), but once Runge pulled it from coal

tar it became a mainstay of mid-nineteenth-century organic chemistry, an inexpensive and readily available material used as a building block for more elaborate synthetic compounds. Runge mixed it with chlorine powder to make a beautiful blue colorant—the first aniline dye.[26] But it was not until Perkin accidentally produced a deep and lovely purplish liquid when trying to synthesize antimalarial drugs from aniline—or rather, not until he collaborated with the dye works at Perth, Scotland, to produce it on a large scale—that the craze for aniline dyes took hold in Europe and America. The initial colorants, like mauveine, consisted of entirely artificial molecular compounds that had not existed prior to their synthesis in the lab. Some version of mauve may have been seen by human eyes before 1856, but Perkin's compound was a genuinely novel entity. Soon, however, the craze for mauve and magenta (another new color) made dye production the most lucrative branch of professional science. Chemists began to map the properties of natural dyestuffs like indigo and cochineal in order to re-create them at home, cutting out the burdensome work of traveling to distant lands, negotiating with foreign dye makers, and paying princely sums for materials that took many workers and several months to produce. By the 1890s, every shade and tint that had previously been derived from organic matter was being made to order in chemistry labs on both sides of the Atlantic. From the black refuse of industry, organic chemists wrought a vibrant, unearthly spectrum more varied, adaptable, and intensely brilliant than any other palette in history.[27]

Whereas Bradley fretted that the invention of hundreds of new color names to match this expanding catalog hampered business and muddled communication, Stewart saw the imaginative terms accompanying modern chemical colors as an engine of literary advance. His essay argued that modern poets were the unknowing beneficiaries of three centuries of scientific research devoted to distinguishing, naming, and recording color phenomena. If Newton had not squinted at the rainbow and put "violet" into circulation as an abstract color term, then, as Stewart noted, Edwin Arlington Robinson could not have "described his Isolt of the violet eyes, which, so often mentioned, give to her at once the touch of romance and of individuality" (74). Likewise, we might add, had Perkin not turned a French flower name into an English color term, Claude McKay could not have imagined his jazz pianist in *Home to Harlem* (1928) as "curiously made up in mauve."[28] For Stewart, such examples showed that the "color richness of English poetry" resulted from a long line of scientists whose writing had vastly expanded the linguistic resources for chromatic description (73).

Yet Stewart, ingenious as his argument is, does not go far enough, especially not with mauve. For that matter, neither does Thomas Beer, who christened the 1890s "the Mauve Decade" not in reference to Perkin's discovery but as a nod to James McNeill Whistler's quip—"Mauve? Mauve is just pink trying to be purple"—which for Beer captured the pretentions of the fin-de-siècle U. S. Culture.[29] A full account of why the synthesis of mauve counts as an "important event" in literary history requires us to look not just at the addition it made to the English language but to the practices that produced it, the meanings it assumed, and the visual and literary aesthetics it helped create. So rather than discuss the Mauve Decade, *Chromographia* details the mauve *decades,* understood as the years between 1880 and 1930 when the innovations in synthetic colorants initiated by Perkin defined the character of modern color experience.

Aniline dyes fueled what historian Regina Lee Blaszczyk terms the "color revolution," the remarkable proliferation of chromatic richness and variety across the United States in the late nineteenth and twentieth centuries.[30] Billboards, posters, and advertising cards spangled visual space during the day, and electric signs shone with multicolored flashes by night. Everything from textiles and building materials to candy and tin-can labels displayed a brighter glow, and starting in 1897 the color section of the Sears Catalog brought multihued images of these multicolored goods to homes all along the Transcontinental Railroad. Objects that in 1850 were sold in only one or two hues were available in a dazzling array of colors by the early twentieth century. "Today color is the modern note everywhere," one commentator wrote in 1930; "we have special color effects in bathrooms, kitchens, cooking utensils, house furnishings, and even at night some of us climb into bed between colored sheets."[31] These colors were "new" not only in the sense that many of them derived from original molecular compounds but also because they appeared in new locations and through different media. As David Batchelor notes, the history of colors comes in the way they are "delivered to us." "We may not see in an illuminated advertisement any colours that we haven't seen before in a stained glass window," he explains, "but we see those colours in different ways: on different scales, in different places, at different times of day and night and with different levels of frequency and intensity."[32] In the aniline era, colors previously expensive and precious became cheap and ubiquitous. Pigments that once had a textured depth derived from organic matter were replaced with "pure" versions that eliminated all but the coloring molecules, producing a flat and intense chromatic character. We are accustomed to thinking of the experience of modernity in terms of speed, disruption, and overload, but none of those qualities would have been as salient without the colorful materials that exaggerated the sensory appeal of urban spaces and commercial goods. The shock of modern life required the brilliance of aniline.

The color revolution tinted print culture as well. In 1896, William Randolph Hearst's *New York Journal* announced the addition of its colorful Sunday supplement with an enthusiasm characteristic of the age: "EIGHT PAGES OF POLYCHROMATIC EFFULGENCE THAT MAKE THE RAINBOW LOOK LIKE A LEAD PIPE."[33] Indeed, one of the stars of those splendid pages, R. F. Outcault's the Yellow Kid, gave the journalism of that era its distinctive name: after a high-profile bidding war over Outcault's comic between Hearst and Joseph Pulitzer, the sensational style shared by the two newspapers came to be called "yellow-kid journalism"—"yellow journalism" for short.[34] Magazines too showed brighter hues after the 1890s. The chic covers of the magazine *Every Other Week* in William Dean Howells's novel *A Hazard of New Fortunes* (1890), like the one "in black and brick-red" on "delicate gray" paper that graces the inaugural issue, depend on contemporaneous advances in color printing, not to mention the buzz around color itself.[35] Charlotte Perkins Gilman described the turn-of-the-century newsstand as a garden "bloom[ing]" with hues that "flame" and "blaze," such that visual and verbal elements of magazines melted together into a lively picture language:

> So bright the cover-colors glow,
> So clear the startling stories show,
> So vivid their pictorial scenes,
> That he who runs may read.[36]

Children's books glowed just as brightly, with similar innovations in mixing image and text. And we need only recall the "pink and yellow books" that Sir Claude picks up from the train station at the end of Henry James's *What Maisie Knew* (1897) or the "bright covers of the books" in Helga's room in Nella Larsen's *Quicksand* (1928) to see how color printing came to enclose novels in a variety of hues.

In addition to modifying the material of print culture, aniline dyes—

along with the techniques that produced them and the markets that distributed them—reorganized the social relations around color. Following Perkin's success, each new patent pushed the color business further from its origins in international trade routes and deeper into the emerging associations between science and industry now known as the research and development division.[37] The fate of empires hung in the balance: indigo markets in India and the Caribbean collapsed once chemists reproduced the relevant molecules, and it took only a few years for the French production of madder root to grind to a halt after the German chemist Adolf von Baeyer synthesized the molecular agents responsible for the dark-red pigment.[38] To be sure, the demand for eye-catching hues at the end of the nineteenth century also stimulated improvements in natural dyes, but after aniline the center of gravity in the economics of color forever shifted from the colonies to the laboratory.

These economic shifts ushered in concomitant changes in the social connotations of color. In previous centuries richly saturated hues had been a prerogative of power, tools used by the church, the court, and the military to inspire awe and flaunt wealth, but over the course of the nineteenth century they came instead to be associated with the lower classes.[39] In particular, bright colors—aniline and otherwise—came to stand for the vivification of the modern sensory environment and the disruptions to the social order threatened by mass culture and the rowdy populations who thrilled to its chromatic charms. When E. L. Godkin, editor of the *Nation,* bemoaned the decline in national morals signaled by the sex scandal around Rev. Henry Ward Beecher, he called the essay "Chromo-Civilization" (1874), linking the popularity of chromolithographic prints to a general cheapening of tastes and standards.[40] And when Howells, in *The Rise of Silas Lapham* (1885), told the story of a Vermont farmer who briefly mingles with the patrician circles of Boston, he picked paint as the means of dramatizing the difference between the nouveau-riche Lapham and the aristocratic Bromfield Corey. "I will tell you plainly," Corey says to his son Tom when the latter expresses interest in one of Lapham's daughters, "I don't like the notion of a man who has rivaled the hues of nature in her wildest haunts with the tints of his mineral paints."[41] For Corey, Lapham's ubiquitous outdoor advertisements sully the natural world with garish hues in the same way that Lapham's drawing room, with its "parti-colored paint," represents an "unnatural" assault on the social order (189). Indeed, for many genteel observers, chromo-civilization was no civilization at all but just the opposite: a degenerate eruption within polite society.

The long history of color in the West has always involved a productive tension between what Batchelor calls "chromophilia" and "chromophobia," between utopian figurations of chromatic ecstasy and buttoned-up fears of colorful excess, and the aniline era was no exception.[42] At the same time that people like Godkin worried that mass-produced hues threatened to wreck civilization, others celebrated the liberation of color in commerce as a sign that white Americans were ready to throw off their Puritan heritage. *Fortune* magazine announced in 1930 that the flood of colorful consumer goods had "released" the "Anglo-Saxon" from "chromatic inhibitions." "Certainly color has fitted the tempo of the times," the editors asserted, and "in this post-war period of broken precedents, of weakened traditions, it is not surprising that old chromatic inhibitions should be shaken off and that the American people should gratify its instinct for color by bathing itself in a torrent of brilliant hues."[43] Aniline dyes and the commercial revolution they sparked amplified the convoluted manner in which vivid color could signify the primitive and the modern in the same stroke. Without them, it is difficult to grasp the rhetorical space within which the various figurations of color experience in U.S. literature took shape, from the detailed evocations of progressive and degenerate color perception in Gilman and Hamlin Garland to the effulgent celebrations of modern color in novels about 1920s Harlem, the stark hues of modernist poetry, and the chromatic aesthetic based on childlike vision that developed in picture books.

There remains one final way in which the synthesis of mauve counts as a literary historical event. Beyond its material and social effects, Perkin's discovery also implied the dissolution of any meaningful distinction between human and natural activity, with important implications for the understanding of language. Once the same molecular compound found in indigo could be derived from coal tar, what did "natural" indigo mean? For that matter, what did "nature" mean, and how could it be distinguished from the artifices of laboratory science? As Charlotte Ribeyrol argues, this radical blurring of natural and synthetic substances in aniline dyes explains why the decadent and aestheticist obsession with artificiality so often coincided with an interest in glittering, superficial colors.[44] Jacques Le Rider goes even further, casting the spread of aniline dyes as an enabling condition for the emergence of symbolist poetics.

Just as mauve detached color from natural materials, so too did Stéphane Mallarmé and Arthur Rimbaud attempt to fashion a language isolated from the naturalized conventions of the tribe.[45] To put it starkly, after aniline the referent of "color" changed: where it once referred to a sensory property of natural objects, by the end of the nineteenth century it invoked the artificial means of manipulating and exaggerating chromatic quality as an abstract entity with its own rules, even its own language.

In perhaps the best-known invocation of mauve in U.S. literature, Thomas Pynchon made this nature-conquering aspect of aniline dyes an emblem of the scientific hubris that reached a horrific apotheosis in the Nazi death camps. In a séance scene early in *Gravity's Rainbow* (1973), the German foreign minister Walter Rathenau speaks from beyond the grave to reveal the "invention of mauve" as more than a mere industrial process. At once an emblem of the "passed over" refuse of coal tar being redeemed as color and of the growing reach of "structures favoring death," the "meaning of mauve" as "the first new color on Earth" becomes inseparable from the growth of the totalizing systems that are the novel's main concern.[46] As Pynchon's title reminds us, the mass destruction represented by the arc of the rocket overlapped with the German dye industry. During the war, the chemical company IG Farben, whose name enshrines its origins as a dye manufacturer, produced the poisonous gas Zyklon B for use at Auschwitz.[47]

Not all writers approached the procedures that produced aniline dyes from this grim vantage point; in fact, for writers living through the color revolution, the strategies of intensification through extraction modeled in mauve offered a fitting figure for the aesthetic itself. Dewey, writing at the end of this period in *Art as Experience* (1934), invoked synthetic colors to illustrate his central thesis that aesthetic experience results from "the clarified and intensified development of traits" that belong to ordinary living. Once we "discover how the work of art develops and accentuates what is characteristically valuable in things of everyday enjoyment," then the art product will "be seen to issue from the latter . . . as dyes come out of coal tar products when they receive special treatment."[48] Mauve here testifies to the ability of artistic techniques to give experience a "special treatment" that heightens a viewer's awareness of the qualities pervading everyday life. Its intensifications are neither celebrations of artifice nor sinister control tactics but clarifications of our embodied relation to a shifting environment, a relation that always belies the nature–culture split since it makes human activities inseparable from an evolving world. From this perspective, William Carlos Williams's characterization of the imagination in *Spring and All* (1923) looks remarkably aniline: "To refine, to clarify, to intensify that eternal moment in which we alone live, there is but a single force—the imagination," whose goal is "experience dynamized into reality."[49] In U.S. modernism, the writer doubled as chemist, extracting and amplifying experiential qualities to then reassemble them in glowing compositions: a red wheelbarrow beside white chickens, clarified through language and rearranged through enjambment. The color revolution gave birth to an aniline aesthetic.

We can now see how Stewart's grand claims for the literary historical importance of mauve should be given an even more ambitious expression. Innovations in modern chemistry and fashion not only stretched the descriptive resources of writers; they also shifted the social meanings of color and influenced both the depiction of color perception in narrative and the modern understanding of literary representation—not to mention the way books were packaged and promoted. If modernist writers filled their poems with stark colors—Ezra Pound's "Petals on a wet, black bough," the "green" hurled in H. D.'s "Oread," the transformative hum of Wallace Stevens's blue guitar—if they even aimed at modeling their work on the power of bright hues, we can be sure that those colors were aniline.

The Color Sense

In 1898, when Bradley and other color educators were decrying the visual mess inflicted by the success of modern dyes, the ethnographer and neurologist W. H. R. Rivers joined the Cambridge expedition to the Torres Strait to test the color vision of aboriginal tribes. He packed a color wheel, some dyed bits of wool, and Bradley's papers—little tokens of the color revolution, taken far away from the factories that produced them (Figures 5 and 6). After months of observations and several struggles to get his subjects to understand the strange tasks he asked of them, Rivers drew a remarkable conclusion: the islanders did not see colors in the same way as he and his fellow Brits. He surmised that "primitive color vision" was less precise, less sensitive than "civilized" perception. His subjects could only detect very strong intensities of blue, often confused the hues at the cooler end of the spectrum, and used the same word

FIGURE 5. W. H. R. Rivers demonstrates the color wheel as part of his research into "primitive color vision" during the Cambridge expedition to Torres Strait. Mabuiag, 1898. CUMAA T.Str. Figure 7.1, page 162—P.754.ACH1, reference number N.23036.ACH2, Museum of Archeology and Anthropology, University of Cambridge.

to describe both "the brilliant blue of the sky" and the "darkest black"—a linguistic artifact of a perceptual shortcoming.[50] Precise color perception, Rivers and his team decided, was a badge of civilization.

Rivers's findings contributed to a cross-disciplinary effort, unfolding in tandem with the color revolution, to grasp the nature and development of a distinct perceptual faculty called the *color sense*. Not quite the same as color perception, "color sense" denoted a cultivated talent for seeing and feeling colors, both singly and in combination, that was thought to improve with training, decay with neglect, and vary across human populations based on cognitive and social attainments. It began its life as a concept rooted in philology, and as evidenced by Rivers's attention to the words his subjects used for the sky, it never lost this association with language. But the questions it posed about the history of perception propelled the idea of a trainable color sense into contemporaneous debates about evolution, racial difference, and—bringing Bradley's papers back

FIGURE 6. C. G. Seligman tests color vision with Frithiof Holmgren's set of colored wools during the Cambridge expedition to Torres Strait. Hula, Central District, British New Guinea, 1898. CUMAA Papua C.D. 252, Figure 6.4, page 144—P.2059. ACH1, reference number N.34989.ACH2, Museum of Archeology and Anthropology, University of Cambridge.

home, so to speak—the perceptual damage inflicted by the proliferation of manufactured hues. Mauve modernized the stuff of color, but it fell to the color sense, which linked the sensing body to civilization, to modernize the relational dynamics of color experience itself.

The story of how the very act of sensing color came to be considered something capable of being either modern or primitive begins not in the antipodes but in a work of literary scholarship. In his multivolume *Studies in Homer and the Homeric Age* (1858), published just two years after Perkin's synthesis of mauve, the British statesman William Gladstone observed that while no idea is "more definite to the modern mind . . . than that of colour," the philological record suggested that this had not always been the case.[51] How else to explain the confused use of color terms in the otherwise exemplary Homer? Gladstone listed several "signs of immaturity" in the colors of the *Iliad* and the *Odyssey,* including the "vast predominance" of black and white ("the most crude and elemental forms of colour"), the use of several distinct color terms to describe the selfsame object, and the use of a single color word for "colours which, according to us, are essentially different" (458). He puzzled over the poet's description of green honey, "smutty" thunderbolts, and "violet-coloured sheep"; he wondered at the total lack of color terms in the many "animated and beautiful descriptions" of horses; and like Rivers after him, he positively gasped at the fact that even though Homer "had before him the most perfect example of blue" in the Mediterranean sky, "he never once" managed to describe it so (487, 479, 483). We all know the epithet "the wine-dark sea"—but this familiar image, already odd when considered in terms of its color, seems even stranger once we learn that Homer applied the same adjective to an ox (472). Gladstone greatly admired Homer, and so he did not want to dismiss these linguistic peculiarities as bad poetry, either poorly expressed or weakly observed.[52] Instead, he reasoned that Homer and his fellow Greeks possessed a perceptual organ strikingly different from that of the "modern mind": where nineteenth-century Europeans saw color, Homer perceived modalities of light and dark. Thus, Gladstone concluded, "the perceptions so easy and familiar to us are the result of a slow traditionary growth in knowledge and in the training of the human organ, which commenced long before we took our place in the succession of mankind" (496). In short, color vision was a historical accomplishment.

In 1867, the German philologist Lazarus Geiger bolstered Gladstone's speculations by demonstrating that the same descriptive peculiarities in Homer appeared in many other ancient texts, and that these seeming anomalies followed a specific pattern. Drawing on the Vedic poems, the oldest Hebrew scriptures, and the Zend-Avesta of the Zoroastrians, Geiger claimed that after a primitive phase in which the only colors described are white and black (or light and dark), words for red appear, followed by words for yellow, green, and finally blue and violet. As he was quick to point out, this sequence exemplified Spencer's law of evolutionary development, in which "notions start from extremities"—like black and white—"and gradually pass on" to more nuanced distinctions.[53] What Gladstone had explained through a vague notion of perceptual education now seemed grounded in the very progress of nature.

Geiger called on physiologists to solve the riddle posed by ancient color terms, and in 1877 the ophthalmologist Hugo Magnus gave the philological sequence a Lamarckian explanation that briefly put the color sense at the center of nineteenth-century debates about human evolution. Magnus's *Die geschichtliche Entwickelung des Farbensinnes* (On the historical evolution of the color sense, 1877) argued that the human retina developed its sensitivity to various hues gradually, in response to the "stimulus produced by the unremitting pounding of the ether particles" which "continually refined the responsiveness of the sensitive elements of the retina, until they stirred the first signs of color perception."[54] In the late nineteenth century Jean-Baptiste Lamarck's view that evolution proceeded according to the use or disuse of particular organs had far more followers than Darwin's theory of natural selection, and the gene had not yet become the accepted vector of inherited traits. Instead, characteristics acquired in the life of an organism—the neck of the giraffe stretched long to reach the top leaves, the sensitive portion of the retina grown responsive to blue light—were thought to be passed on to subsequent generations. Magnus's theory cast the color sense as just such a trait, with the result that color perception and color terms were incorporated into the vast array of Lamarckian assumptions that, at the turn of the century, informed theories of human difference. Responsiveness to color began to function in the same way that "nervous sensitivity" or "impressibility" did, situating racial character within the nerves and impulses of the body.[55]

Magnus's theory drew comment from nearly all the major voices in nineteenth-century evolutionary thought and served as a battleground for hashing out competing theories. Gladstone championed it in a widely cited essay called "The Colour-Sense" (1877), in which he repackaged his earlier thesis in terms of "the laws of hereditary growth."[56] Echoing the recapitulation theory of Ernst Haeckel (who also supported Magnus),[57] Gladstone reasoned that just as "painters know that there is an education of the eye for colour in the individual," the historical record suggested that "this education subsists also for the race" (367). The Darwinians, however, objected, starting with Darwin himself, who voiced his doubts to Gladstone days after the essay appeared.[58] As Alfred Russel Wallace argued, sensitivity to color was crucial for both natural and sexual selection, from insects looking for food to peahens picking a mate, and this long evolutionary history suggested "that man's *perception* of colour in the time of Homer was little if any inferior to what it is now," even if the terms were less precise.[59] The science writer and novelist Grant Allen built on Wallace's work to mount a book-length rebuttal to Magnus in *The Colour-Sense: Its Origins and Development* (1879). Mustering evidence from the anatomical basis of color vision across species, ethnographic surveys of "primitive" peoples, and recent archeological findings about the chromatic designs of ancient statuary, including that of the supposedly stark-white Greeks, Allen insisted that basic color sensitivity had remained constant throughout human existence.

Like many spurious ideas, the notion of an evolved, physiological color sense proved too useful to be discarded, especially in the Age of Color. Two things in particular launched the color sense into public consciousness, where it found a ready home in the growing number of practices aimed at color perception. First, a series of spectacular train accidents in the 1870s and 1880s, supposedly caused by conductors failing to distinguish the red and green signals from station masters, made color blindness an object of popular, professional, and governmental concern. The publicity around the wrecks provoked a campaign for mandatory color-sense testing in professions involving a color-coded system of communication. In Europe, Frithiof Holmgren designed a test consisting of several dozen skeins of wool dyed different hues (the ones Rivers used on his expedition). In the United States, the Yale psychologist E. W. Scripture devised a "color sense tester" that improved on Holmgren's by using luminous hues, the better to mimic on-the-job perceptions (Figures 7 and 8). The momentum behind research into color blindness led to statistical studies at the end of the nineteenth century that revealed a higher incidence of color blindness in white males than in women, African Americans, or Native Americans—thus feeding the belief that color perception was somehow tied to "civilization," even if

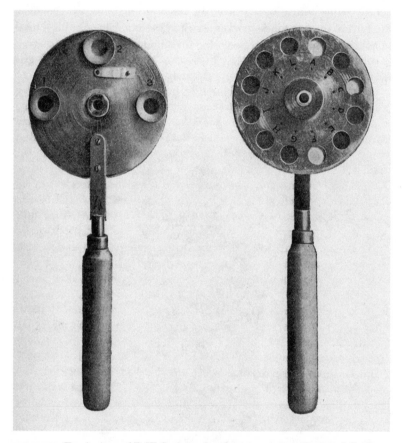

FIGURE 7. Two images of E. W. Scripture's color-sense tester (first model), showing both sides. The dial on the back has small panes of red, green, and gray glass that the subject looks at through the holes on the front, which filter the color either through a darkly smoked lens, a lightly smoked lens, or a clear one. The objective is to represent the viewing of a railway signal in various atmospheric conditions. Edward W. Scripture, "A Test of Safe Color Vision," in *Studies from the Yale Psychological Laboratory,* vol. 7 (New Haven: Yale University Press, 1900), 3, Olin Library, Cornell University, Ithaca, New York.

in different ways than Gladstone had proposed. Though color blindness was eventually distinguished from the color sense, the two were close enough that public interest in the one lent credibility to the other. Each connected color perception to heredity, and from there to sexual and racial difference.[60]

Second, the genteel reaction to the aniline era named a crisis in color sensitivity as both the cause and the result of the chromatic chaos at the turn of the twentieth century. As Bradley complained in his educational books, the discordant coloring in commercial spaces bespoke an underdeveloped sensitivity in American workers. And the products of this deficient sense served only to exacerbate the problem. According to one artist, the visual disarray fueled by the "hideously crude and brilliant

FIGURE 8. The color-sense tester could be attached to a semaphore in order to illuminate the colors. Scripture recommended this approach for laboratory use, as opposed to on-site examinations of workers. Scripture, "A Test of Safe Color Vision," 6.

dyes of civilization" threatened to dull the perceptual capacities of modern Americans, especially the young, leaving them "lacking in greater or less degree the power of seeing color."[61] By this logic, the explosion of modern color necessitated a concomitant effort to train color perception, lest sight be exhausted by the sensory barrage. Had the color revolution not provoked attention to the effects of chromatic environments, had it not cast the drama of modern color precisely in terms of savage tendencies and the fate of civilization, the idea of a trainable color sense may have remained an academic affair. Even after the so-called Gladstone debate seemed settled, it proved the perfect concept for discussing the increasing impingements of modern color.

These wider adaptations of the color sense, combined with the responses to the Darwinian criticisms, transformed color sensitivity from a strictly physiological phenomenon to a more nebulous matter of chromatic feeling. Initially located in the eye, the color sense moved to the mind. We will see notable exceptions to this rule—Rivers, for instance, could not shake the conviction that the Murray Islanders' descriptive practices resulted from an anatomical difference—but on the whole, after 1880 most discussions of color perception in the United States and the United Kingdom treated it as a complex mental act that varied according to a vague notion of intellectual sophistication. As the chemist A. H. Church wrote in a passage often cited at the turn of the twentieth century, "Individual sensibility to colour" is "susceptible to immense improvement," but "this cultivation of the sense of colour is . . . rather psychological than physiological, rather mental than physical. It is not that the organ of vision is improved, but our power of interpreting and co-ordinating the sensations which it transmits to the brain."[62] Thus reinterpreted, the color sense ceased to refer to an ability to register individual hues and instead indicated a cultivated talent for feeling color relations, a talent that also involved regulating one's own relation to the sensory world.

The more ambiguous, more psychological repackaging of the color sense proved useful in propping up ideas of racial difference in the face of mounting anatomical evidence for a physiology of vision shared by all humans at all times.[63] In short, a qualitative "feeling" of color—difficult to measure yet supposedly revealed in color preferences and design practices—proved a more malleable concept for invoking the distinction between civilized and savage modes of perceiving. In 1885 a writer for *Gentleman's Magazine* put the matter in plain terms, reasoning that because "the sensations of cultivated man are different altogether in kind from those of lower creatures, inasmuch as in his case they are associated with complex ideas and trains of thought," color perceptions will vary among human populations depending on their degree of "cultivation."[64] Even Magnus backed down from the strong version of his thesis. He conceded that a Congolese man could distinguish a blue object from a green one, but he held that the African probably experienced the difference between the hues less keenly than a European, who sensed it so strongly as to give the two sensations separate names.[65] Associations between bold colors and supposedly primitive people had been in continuous circulation since the beginning of colonialism; Goethe, for instance, claimed that "savage nations, uneducated people, and children have a great predilection for vivid colours" (30). Over the course of the nineteenth century, partly through the color-sense concept, such observations hardened into the racist libel that bright hues held a special appeal to those with emotion-prone bodies and unrefined nerves. How one felt colors came to indicate the kind of person one was.[66]

Racialized versions of color perception grounded in Lamarckian models of the sensing body intersected with late-nineteenth-century formulations of aesthetics, especially the aesthetics of "pure" color. Allen offers the clearest illustration early in *The Colour-Sense* when he narrates the dramatic emergence of a disinterested appreciation of color evolving from an ancestral ability to discern red fruit among green leaves: "Part of our business in this work," he explains,

> will be to trace out the slow steps by which the love of bright-coloured food led on to the choice of bright-coloured mates; and how this again brought about a liking for bright colours in general, which shows itself in the savage predilection for brilliant dyes and glistening pebbles; till at last the whole long series culminates in that intense and unselfish enjoyment of rich and pure tints which makes civilized man linger so lovingly over the hues of sunset and the myriad shades of autumn.[67]

Passages such as these abound in the popular literature on color. They link the liberation of color from figuration trumpeted by early-twentieth-century abstract artists to nineteenth-century ideas about a cultivated faculty of color sensitivity. The vibrant abstractions of Henri Matisse and Wassily Kandinsky may have been derided as primitive by the reviewers of their day, but for those attuned to color as a historical achievement, their canvases expressed the apex of perceptual evolution.[68]

As attempts to train people in how to see, modernist painting and writing held much in common with the diversity of turn-of-the-century endeavors launched to improve the color sense of Americans. As Susan Buck-Morss says of Walter Benjamin's writing on art, "The whole point of philosophical interest in 'aesthetics' in the modern era" is that "the senses can be acculturated," for better or worse.[69] From this perspective, *aesthetics* names the effort to understand and transform sensory perception, and Bradley's books on color education count as aesthetic undertakings no less than Stein's avant-garde poetry. The following five chapters track how these two cultural threads—color-sense training and modernist aesthetic education—emerged from shared debates about empiricism and modern painting and then diverged along distinct but overlapping lines. One perpetuated the overtly racialist account of perceptual style from color-sense discourse (Gilman's reform fiction, for instance); the other transformed it into a convoluted primitivism that celebrated the perceptual mode linked to bright hues while muting its affiliation with dark-skinned bodies (the painterly ideal of a child's view of color that grew from late-nineteenth-century child psychology). Yet even as their paths separated, these lines continued to intersect, and they clashed dramatically, tellingly, in the novelistic depictions of Harlem life that enjoyed a vogue in the late 1920s. Color became modernist only against a background of color perception becoming historical.

What's in a Color Word?

The three developments that modernized color—the relational theory of color perception, the success of aniline dyes, and the trainable color sense—not only provide the most salient contexts for understanding what color meant for U.S. writers; they also offer a perspective from which to grasp how colors, and for that matter sensory qualities more generally, appear in literature. Writing does not merely record historical color but inscribes it in unique and revealing ways.[70] Any study that uses literary analysis to reveal something about the history of perceptual experience therefore has to account for how writing mediates sensation. Yet the seemingly simple question, What's in a color word? contains a viper's nest of methodological quandaries. Within linguistics the answers have swung from one pole to the other, from the idea that perception determines language to the theory that language determines perception. Literary study requires a more subtle approach, one that balances a recognition of the material conditions for literary color—like those Stewart indicated when he praised Newton for giving poets "violet"—with an attention to literary performances that exceed any vision that arrives through the eye. The ideas tested in the color-sense debates provide all the components of this middle way, as well as vivid illustrations of the extremes it avoids.

The entire Gladstone controversy reads as a series of responses to the question of how color words relate to color sensations. Even after the ideas prompted by Geiger's sequence had migrated from philology to physiology, psychology, and aesthetics, scholars continued to treat the literary record as an excavation site for the archeology of the senses. In an influential essay, "The Colour-Sense in Literature" (1896), the English psychologist Havelock Ellis deemed it "fairly obvious that we may best ascertain and trace any evolution in colour preferences by the comparative study of imaginative writers who instinctively record the impressions they receive from the external world."[71] He went on to tally the instinctual impressions of William Shakespeare, the Romantics, Edgar Allan Poe, Alfred Tennyson, and several others, arranging the number and nature of their color terms in a series of charts (Figure 9). Others built on Ellis's findings, expanding his corpus to determine how color imagery provides "an instrument for investigating a writer's personal psychology."[72] Though no longer taken as an indication of "civilized" intellects, color perception and its translation into color words continued to offer a quantifiable metric of mental experience, as it varied across time, cultures, and individual writers.

Ellis and his followers chalked up color preferences to individual psychology; Rivers linked them to social groups arrayed along the continuum of civilization. But in the same decades Boas proposed a different framework through which to understand color perception: culture. As a PhD student Boas had attempted to formulate a metric for quantifying the color of water (wine-dark and otherwise), but like so many others he had been unable to establish a system on which everyone could agree.[73] Something seemed to be getting in between the sensory stimuli and the qualitative sensation. In his subsequent work, Boas called this mediating something "culture." In "On Alternating Sounds" (1889), a foundational text in the formulation of the culture concept, he cited the distance between a sensation of green and the word "green" to illustrate the ways that different language speakers experienced the same sensory

Colours of Predilection.		White.	Yellow.	Red.	Green.	Blue.	Black.	Predominant Colours.
Blue, black	Mountain Chant	28	13	3	...	19	37	Black, white.
Red	Wooing of Emer	34	3	48	...	...	14	Red, white.
Red	Volsunga Saga	14	...	71	...	14	...	Red.
Green, red	Isaiah, Job, Song of Songs	18	4	29	33	...	15	Green, red.
Black, yellow	Homer	21	21	7	2	...	49	Black, white-yellow.
White, yellow	Catullus	40	21	17	9	4	8	White, yellow.
White, red	Chaucer	34	10	28	14	1	13	White, red.
Yellow, purple, black	Marlowe	19	21	19	6	6	28	Black, yellow.
Red	Shakespeare	22	17	30	7	4	20	Red, white.
Brown, black, green	Thomson	9	...	18	27	9	36	Black, green.
Black	Blake	17	17	13	16	7	29	Black, white-yellow.
Blue, green	Coleridge	21	7	17	25	14	16	Green, white.
Blue, purple, gray	Shelley	17	19	11	21	21	11	Green-blue.
Yellow, green	Keats	14	23	24	29	8	1	Green, red.
Green, gray	Wordsworth	14	18	10	35	11	12	Green, yellow.
Yellow, violet, purple	Poe	8	32	20	12	4	24	Yellow, black.
Black, blue	Baudelaire	11	9	19	10	16	34	Black, red.
Purple	Tennyson	22	15	27	15	10	11	Red, white.
Yellow, white, gray	Rossetti	30	22	22	9	7	10	White, yellow.
Red, white	Swinburne	28	18	28	16	6	4	Red, white.
Brown, red, pink	Whitman	25	10	26	14	8	16	Red, white.
White, yellow, gray	Pater	43	19	11	11	9	7	White, yellow.
Gray	Verlaine	20	15	24	9	14	18	Red, white.
Blue, white	Olive Schreiner	38	12	25	3	19	2	White, red.
Red, blue, violet	D'Annunzio	15	11	46	7	14	6	Red, white.

FIGURE 9. Havelock Ellis's chart tracking the color sense as expressed in poetry from antiquity through the late nineteenth century. For each poet Ellis records the "predominant colours" and "colours of predilections" —that is, the most used colors and the ones used with "special frequency" in relation to other writers. Havelock Ellis, "The Colour-Sense in Literature," *Contemporary Review* 69 (1896): 718.

stimuli. Boas's approach came to trump Rivers's in U.S. anthropology departments (it was as a Boasian that Hurston spun her Bradley color top for Herskovits). As a result, by the 1930s color terms were offered as paradigmatic examples, along with words for snow and verb tenses, of how language shapes rather than reflects perception. Linguistic anthropologists relocated the color sense yet again: "'Color sense' is not given physiologically or psychologically," one scholar summarized, "but to a great extent depends upon language training and language tradition." Indeed, "the very interpretation of the sensation is a language function."[74] Associated with the Sapir–Whorf hypothesis that language radically constrains thought, this consensus continued well into the twentieth century, especially in literary and cultural studies. Cultural relativism turned the Gladstone thesis on its head.[75]

The Boasian perspective changed the set of questions raised by color terms: not, How did color vision evolve? but, What are color terms for? and, How does language mediate visual experience? To be sure, this position too led to excesses, including the strong version of the Sapir–Whorf argument, and significant counterevidence to the idea that language determines perception emerged in vision science and comparative anthropology throughout the twentieth century.[76] But at the turn of the twentieth century the attention to extrapsychological factors of color facilitated a nuanced investigation into the pragmatics of color words and their deployment within literature. Case in point: Robert S. Woodworth, student of William James and colleague of Boas, drew on his own tests of "more or less primitive peoples" assembled at the Louisiana Purchase Exposition in St. Louis in 1904 to conclude that color terms reflected the needs and activities of a language group rather than its naive perceptions.[77] From this perspective, the word "blue" implied a historically situated need for denoting blueness, rooted in practices such as dyeing. No wonder, then, that at the end of the nineteenth century, as aniline dyes created more and more commercial colors, the language for color expanded at such a dizzying pace. Stewart took up this line of thinking in his essay on the literary importance of mauve, countering the lingering adherents to the Gladstone thesis by arguing that if Geoffrey Chaucer's palette seemed childish compared to Amy Lowell's, it was only because the latter had the advantage of centuries of color technologies and their corresponding vocabularies (71–72).[78] For Stewart, the colors of Anglophone poetry bespoke the historical needs and chromatic practices of English speakers as much as the personality of individual poets.

Once color terms were seen as tools rather than mirrors, it became possible to ask what they did to chromatic perception without falling too far toward relativism. One of the most remarkable features of color discourse in this period was the conviction that language could improve color perception, that with more words and more linguistic resources humans would see more of the chromatic world. Stewart, for example, asserted that the expanded descriptive range resulting from modern colorants "has undoubtedly rendered us more sensitive to color" (77). Educators, writers, artists, and psychologists all gave voice to similar claims and so expanded the space between Gladstone's assumption that language reflects perception and Benjamin Whorf's claim that language determines it. For the major figures discussed in *Chromographia,* language has the power to augment the sensory encounter with the world, fixing attention, training memory, and facilitating an expansion of color experience through its transformation into a different medium. In this view, the terms "red" and "yellow"—or even better "magenta," "ashes of roses," and Bradley's "R.10, W.21, N.69"—prop up color perception without constituting it. They form essential factors in the ongoing fabrication of modern color experience.

This approach to the language of sensation departs from a prominent thread in twentieth-century writing that casts color as the opposite of words, an opponent of thought and systems. It is a venerable tradition, enfolding Walter Benjamin, Jacques Derrida, Roland Barthes, Michael Taussig, and many others, but I can illustrate it with two examples: Aldous Huxley high on mescaline, and Julia Kristeva high on Giotto.[79] Huxley explained the intensity of the colors in his drug-enhanced visions by reasoning that the world glowed brighter when seen in a state "free of language" and "outside the system of conceptual thought."[80] Habits, concepts, language—in short, anything that generalizes—could for Huxley only dim vision and distance us from the world. In "Giotto's Joy" (1980), a touchstone for theoretical work on color, Kristeva adopts a similar utopian register to proclaim that "it is through color—colors—that the subject escapes its alienation within a code (representational, ideological, symbolic, and so forth)" and approaches an unconstrained primeval condition able to upset discursive regimes.[81] The rhetorical function of color for Kristeva, as for Huxley, is to stand for all that escapes control: a brilliant rainbow at the outskirts of language and power.

To be sure, there *is* something unruly about color, something messy and bodily that frustrates attempts at rationalization. Just as certain is that a giant gap separates the millions of colors we distinguish with our eyes from the dozens we name with our tongues. In this regard Huxley and Kristeva testify to an important aspect of chromatic experience, one that occupied dozens of modern U.S. writers. Yet an exclusive attention to this opposition, especially when rendered in the grandiose terms of a subject escaping the alienation of a code, threatens to foreclose an analysis of what happens when a color is named or conjured in language, of what is involved when "red" is read. A literary analysis of color requires an appreciation not only of color's affective force but also of the linguistic performances that seek to harness or draw attention to it.[82]

In *Chromographia,* I treat color terms not as failed attempts to capture the chromatic world but as extensions and transformations of it. Such an approach aligns me with those thinkers at the turn of the twentieth century who approached language, systematization, and thought as ways of enhancing rather than diminishing the intensity of color experience. One of the central lessons of modern color discourse is that mediation facilitates immediacy. Stein saw as much when she apprehended color perception as a calculation and inference; the chemists proved it when their laborious processes of extraction and amplification raised concerns about the direct, bodily influence of aniline dyes; and educators and manufactures like Bradley practiced it when they recommended that systematic training would equip viewers to have more powerful emotional responses to color.

Radical empiricism helps us grasp the metaphysical implications of this practical approach to color. To trade the question of how color terms refer to a separate reality for the question of how the language of color extends what chromatic experience can be, we need both to embrace a process-driven picture of reality and to give up the ontological opposition between abstractions (language) and concrete realities (colors, sensations). In radical empiricism, relations are as real as individual things, and pragmatist aesthetics disposes of the idea that "only certain *special* things—those attached to the eye, ear, etc.—can be qualitatively and immediately experienced."[83] From this perspective Huxley gets it all wrong.

The mediations of language are not obstacles to the perception of color but a means of connecting with chromatic sensation, however imperfect (and nothing is perfect).

The Gladstone controversy made the complex ways that color appears in poetry and prose key considerations for literary scholars, but for almost a century now interest has dwindled to almost nothing.[84] Perhaps there is something in the idea of literary color analysis that invokes elementary exercises in decoding symbols: red means passion, green means nature. This book provides a more sophisticated way of reading color in literature that attends to the history of color and to what writers do with and to the chromatic phenomena of their day. I reveal color terms and images as compact expressions of the relation between self and world, perceiver and perceived, articulated through the resources of a given historical moment. For this reason I focus on color in general rather than on particular hues, though this choice sets *Chromographia* at odds with many like-minded books: Bruce R. Smith's *The Key of Green* (2008), Sabine Doran's *The Culture of Yellow* (2013), Carol Mavor's *Blue Mythologies* (2013), and Michel Pastoureau's studies of *Blue* (2001), *Black* (2008), *Green* (2014), and *Red* (2016). As important as hue is, it constitutes only one of the dimensions of color experience, and in fact one of Gladstone's mistakes was to have treated it as the most important category of color classification. Though English puts the weight on red, blue, green, and so on, other languages, such as ancient Greek, attend more to texture, luminescence, or intensity. "Wine-dark" is a weird description of the hue of the Mediterranean but a convincing one of its shine, shimmer, and movement. Likewise, aniline revolutionized the brightness and saturation of commercial color as much as it multiplied its hues. No doubt the analysis of how particular hues or even specific dyes have accumulated significance and changed connotation will continue to illuminate the history of art, color, and culture writ large, but for this study, which aims at a literary history of color experience and all it makes visible, I need the whole palette.

Color Scheme

The chapters that follow team a more detailed description of the discourses and practices that rendered color a sign of modernity with an analysis of how modern U.S. writers described, dramatized, and realized color experience in their fiction, criticism, and poetry. The marriage aims to be mutually enhancing. I establish aniline dyes and the color sense as necessary backgrounds against which to understand the course of literary production at the turn of the twentieth century, and I present literature as offering unique insights into the historical experience of modern color.

Chapter 1 elaborates a relational model of color perception—and its implications for writing and art—that subsequent chapters variously implement and revise. My central example is the American local color writer Hamlin Garland. Rather than situating him within the usual histories of regionalism, I present his criticism and fiction as important manifestations of a modern transatlantic aesthetic that invokes the perception and representation of color as indications of art's superior empiricism. This tradition, which stretches from Goethe's *Theory of Colours* and John Ruskin's *Modern Painters* (1843–60) to French and American impressionism, celebrates color as the site of the entanglement of perceiver and perceived—as the "place where our brain and the universe meet," as Paul Cézanne would later put it.[85] Garland, who worked in the decades after the phrase "local color" had passed from a technical term in art criticism to a generic designation in literature, embraced this chromatic aesthetic to redefine the local through color, to shift emphasis from rural folkways to the relational dynamic between an observer and an environment that unfolds within a specific moment in time. Learning how to attend to that moment, and how to realize it in writing, formed the basis for a program of aesthetic education that runs from Garland through modernism.

The tradition tracked in the first chapter resulted in an artistic valorization of "pure" color freed from form or figuration; chapter 2 specifies the cultural meanings and political uses of this modern notion of abstract color as they developed in interior design, social theory, and avant-garde attempts to create an art of colored light projections. To illuminate the neglected connections among these varied fields I turn to a writer who traversed them all, the social reformer Charlotte Perkins Gilman. Best known for her short story "The Yellow Wall-Paper" (1892), in which the degeneration of a neurasthenic woman is dramatized through her increasing obsession with the colors of her walls, Gilman illustrates how color perceptions came to be deemed "primitive" or "modern" and how design reformers worked within this intellectual matrix when advocating for abstract color. Crucial for Gilman's interest in color experience was the way it focused attention on the dynamic relation between people and their environment, a relation that, for Lamarckian thinkers like Gilman, formed the site of social change. From this perspective, the best method for reforming people's physical and cognitive capacities—including those marked as "masculine" or "feminine"—was to modify their environment. This fascination with the influence of chromatic surroundings brought Gilman surprisingly close to the champions of art for art's sake whom she claimed to detest, so much so that in the 1910s she published multiple stories praising the abstract art of "color music." Chapter 2 sets out to understand how and why such a strange affinity between progressive reform and modernist abstraction developed around color at the turn of the twentieth century.

Chapter 3 explains how children came to be associated with bright colors. Specifically, it argues that one of the most enduring tropes of modern art—the child's vivid and natural delight in color—has roots both in psychological studies of the juvenile color sense and in the related pedagogical efforts to cultivate the child's initial, unrefined perceptions. As such, the third chapter continues the work of the second, as it shows how a modernist aesthetic ideal emerged from beliefs about primitive color vision and the analogy between individual and racial development. To reveal how this transformation occurred, I give special importance to children's picture books, which combined visual styles pitched at the child eye with narrative scenarios that instructed young readers in how to consume the colors on the page. I focus in particular on the colorful first edition of L. Frank Baum's *The Wonderful Wizard of Oz* (1900) and its illustrations by W. W. Denslow and on the books they published in the years before and after *Oz*. These works demonstrate how children's books readied white audiences to enjoy a bold aesthetic of bright, lively hues without relinquishing the authority and bodily comportment that attended their whiteness. In short, Baum and Denslow instructed their readers in how to indulge a so-called primitive love for bright colors without becoming primitive themselves. As significant as this was for art, it was even more important for consumer culture, where the colorful enticements bred by the aniline revolution were wielded to activate the child eye latent in all adults.

While Gilman and Garland strained to capture the nuances of sensory perception and Baum synced his language to literal hues on his pages, writers such as Stephen Crane and Gertrude Stein set out to exaggerate the distance between colors perceived and colors imagined, specifically colors *read*. Chapter 4 focuses on these authors to investigate the types of color experiences facilitated by language alone. Starting with a review of Crane's *The Red Badge of Courage* (1895), which coined the phrase "lurid realism" to describe the novel's chromatic excesses, I argue that Crane's unconventional application of color terms to moods and speech acts (a "blue haze of curses" or a "red sickness of battle") aligns him both with symbolist poetry and with the visual strategies taking shape in art posters and storefront windows. I nominate Crane as an exemplary figure within the aniline aesthetic, a writer who followed the chemists in extracting chromatic qualities, intensifying them, and combining them into new imaginative compounds. His work thus clarifies the productive power of color terms within perception and so provides a framework for analyzing what at first seem to be two distinct phenomena: the flamboyant color figurations of the avant-garde (from Rimbaud to Stein) and the mundane yet no less inventive chromatic constructions of racial discourse in the era of *Plessy v. Ferguson,* when not only a man but also his speech or behavior could be designated "black" or "white." To demonstrate how these discursive domains were historically intertwined as well as structurally analogous, I analyze how the language of racial color in Stein's *Three Lives* (1909) sets up the experiment in linguistic construction that she conducts in the color-filled pages of *Tender Buttons* (1914).

Chapter 5 weaves together the major threads of *Chromographia* to analyze the all-important trope of color in the Harlem Renaissance. My first four chapters chart an increasingly complicated relationship between modernist style and racialized understandings of color sensitivity; this one investigates the moment in U.S. literary history when these two phenomena clashed as never before, throwing a bright light on the entwined aesthetic and political uses of color in modern fiction. Focusing on writing by Nella Larsen, Carl Van Vechten, Claude McKay, and Zora Neale Hurston, I demonstrate that the exuberant chromatic descriptions that run throughout novels about Harlem in the late 1920s constitute risky engagements with the rhetoric of modern color, especially its characteristic blend of cutting-edge technologies and riotous sensations—risky because, as Larsen shows in *Quicksand,* the performances of keen sensitivity and personal taste encouraged by commercial color discourse could always be folded back into the framework of primitive color vision. Yet even in the face of this threat, black writers cultivated what McKay called the "challenge" of color to white civilization: the way color experience gives the lie to the divisions of mind and body, self and world that underwrite the entwined histories of capitalism and colonialism and so provides a resource for reconstituting how the world is felt. In the end, then, the writers of the Harlem Renaissance articulate the political implications of the chromatic metaphysics developed throughout this book, as well as the abiding habits of perception that work to dampen its force.

A recurring yet subterranean theme of *Chromographia* is that in the period between 1880 and 1930 those who worked with or wrote about color long enough came to think like radical empiricists, because color experience makes vivid the relational, active, ephemeral qualities that traditional empiricism handled so roughly. My epilogue considers the moment when this connection became explicit: at Black Mountain College in the 1930s and 1940s, when Dewey's pedagogical principles melded with Josef Albers's experiential approach to color instruction. Albers's *Interaction of Color* (1963), based on earlier classroom exercises in cutting and arranging colored paper (alas, no longer Bradley's), demonstrates the aesthetic implications that follow from the pragmatist solution to the epistemological problem of color. Once colors and other sensory qualities are embraced as factors of the common world rather than mere psychic overlays, the question becomes how to work within the relational construction of reality to build new sensory environments—not, How can we know color? but, What can we do with it?

The Place of Perception
Local Color's Colors

"Local color" didn't always mean local culture. Before it named a narrative genre, and even before it designated the customs and characteristics usually taken as that genre's subject, the phrase belonged to theories of painting, where it often appeared in the plural—"local *colors*." These literal hues referred not to places in the world but to the local arrangements of pigments on a canvas that were required to achieve a convincing illusion of real-world objects. They named a technique for adjusting pigments to perception and so foregrounded the question of how art stands in relation to the reality it depicts. Say you want to paint a poppy. You might begin by picking out the shade of red that best matches the flower. But as soon as you situate that red within the larger compositional scheme, its character shifts, assuming a different tint in relation to the paints you have chosen for the green of the stalk, the black of the stamens, and the quality of light that falls on the petals. When you modify your initial red to account for these changes, you are adjusting what eighteenth- and nineteenth-century art critics called local colors, *local* because their place within the painting determined their appearance and thus their ability to depict an object.

By the 1880s, when writers such as Sarah Orne Jewett, Mary Murfree, and Hamlin Garland began publishing their stories of local life, this original definition had been entirely reworked: the locale had shifted from the pictorial space of the painting to actual regions of the world, the colors had lost their visual significance, and literary magazines had eclipsed art galleries as the designated venues for encountering this newly metaphorical mode of "color." What started as a term for the painterly relation between image and object had transformed into a term for the literary relation between writing and place. In the process, it seemed to shed its connection to visual hues—so much so that hardly anyone writing about the U.S. local color tradition has mentioned the term's roots in painting. What, at first blush, could be further from the quiet, rural scenes of Jewett and Murfree than European debates about color in art?

Yet despite apparent differences, the problems of artistic mediation that motivated the theorization of local colors in painting anticipate the most commented upon feature of local color fiction: the distance between the observing author or narrator and the observed characters and folkways. The local colorist has long been assumed to stand apart, either as a wide-eyed tourist or as a lofty artist. Critics have disagreed about the ideological import of this distance—some casting authors as complicit in the forces of capitalist expansion and national unification that linked these rural communities to urban readers, others insisting on the subversive nature of female and minority portrayals—but no one has challenged the assumption that a gap between observer and observed constitutes the distinguishing structural feature of local color and that this gap determines how its writers connect language and place.[1]

The long history of local color, as it moves across media and through a variety of meanings, provides a different purchase on this central concern. But to attain it we have to do what critics so far have thought unnecessary, even silly: keep our eyes trained on literal color. During the decades that local color drifted from the visual to the verbal, from the relative hues of painting to the absolute "color" of cultures, arguments about the reality of color and about the role of color in representations of reality made the *relational* aspects of color perception central to defenses of modern painting. Epistemological controversies had repercussions for painterly practice. If, as John Locke proposed, colors were "secondary" qualities that failed to correspond to the actual world, then the hues of a painting could do little more than entertain the eye. They could not reveal capital-T Truth. But if, as Goethe insisted, colors bodied forth the relational push and pull between subject and object that propelled the universe, then expert coloring revealed a sensitive grasp of nature's most essential dynamic. Over the course of the nineteenth century, in both science and art, Goethe's view won out. The major studies of color perception all emphasized its relational essence, not as ontological deficiency but as a window into our ways of processing—and therefore *realizing*—the natural world. In art, this metaphysical shift ousted the subdued tones of eighteenth-century classicism in favor of the fiery hues of J. M. W. Turner and the "pure colors" of impressionism, both treated as insights into our entanglement with the sensible world. The relational quality of chroma emphasized in eighteenth-century definitions of local color expanded to encompass the very rhythms of perception, with the result that color, no longer subordinated to line or form, came to indicate an artist's superior ability to perceive and communicate this dynamic vision of nature.

No local color writer kept as close to the aesthetic problems raised by modern color as Hamlin Garland. As both an early defender of impressionism in the United States and a staunch advocate of local color in fiction, he was poised between the decline of the term in painting and its popularization in literature. In his critical writing of the 1890s, he embraced the label "local color" more energetically than any of his contemporaries, yet his pleas for regional particularity invoke the shifting world of perceptual relations that occupied modern art more than the isolated bubbles of culture that concerned other local colorists. Where most nineteenth-century writers—like most twenty-first-century critics—treated the phrase as a dead metaphor, Garland took the *color* of "local color" seriously, at times even literally. He wove elaborate evocations of shifting hues into his stories of life in the Midwest, especially during the decade when he championed impressionism. His work illuminates the way the history of local color in painting—as a series of debates about the relationship between artistic vision and the empirical world—intersected with the history of local color in writing, understood less as a particular movement and more as a technique for tying writing to place, a technique that persisted long after the vogue for local color had faded.

In short, then, Garland's "veritism"—as he called his late-nineteenth-century approach to local color—frames the aesthetic issues that occupied writers in the era of the color sense. He interpreted modern painting in light of evolutionary theory and at times made explicit his belief that artistic innovation remade human sensation. As he said of the Hoosier Group of Midwest impressionists, "A group of men like these can transform the color sense of the whole west—or more truly awaken the unconscious color sense."[2] Garland too aimed at enlivening perception through color. Instead of describing the distinctive features of a setting, he explored the dynamic process of perceiving an environment, where perception marked a way of relating to or mingling with one's surroundings rather than presenting a convincing depiction of them. This different aesthetic aim produced new questions for artists and writers alike.

How do the mediations of art provide access to the empirical world, especially once that world is conceived as an evolving process rather than a static object? How do colors on the canvas relate to colors in experience? Which aesthetic techniques promise to transform or quicken perception, and to what end? Like William James's pragmatic theory of truth as "verification," veritist local color responded by situating the activities of knowing, feeling, and representing the world within the wider processes of nature. As a result, the "local," in Garland's hands, became more a mode of feeling than a particular region; it was a way of inhabiting *any* place and of having that place inhabit you.[3]

How Color Became Modernist:
Local Colors from the Claude Glass to Impressionism

The winding path that led local color from painting to prose is made all the more complicated by the fact that in the midst of this transition—and partly facilitating it—the term's visual meaning did an about-face. When the French art critic Roger de Piles first wrote of local colors at the turn of the eighteenth century, he meant the coloring practices used to create artistic images, but by the mid-nineteenth century the term denoted the "true" colors of physical objects considered apart from distorting influences such as atmospheric light, reflected colors from nearby objects, or the techniques of tinting and toning that, in de Piles's initial definition, were precisely the point. Once an attribute of representations, local color became a property of the objects represented. This reversal mirrored the general drift of nineteenth-century art criticism toward a new ideal of artistic vision, one in which the clear and accurate perception of nature counted as the all-important precondition to painting well. Yet to muddle matters further, this new ideal, after being aligned with contemporary physiological accounts of color, emphasized the relational activity of perception as the true locus of chromatic phenomena, such that the notion of local color as a quality of things-in-themselves fell out of favor almost as soon as it was formulated. All the while, color itself was feted more than ever. For modern artists and their advocates from the mid-nineteenth century on, vibrant hues surfaced as the privileged sign of art's superior ability to capture a reality wide enough to encompass both perceiver and perceived, both the colors on the painting and those in the landscape.

Throughout this tangled history, the idea of local colors maintained an intimate relation to the idea of modern art. Indeed, de Piles introduced his concept as an entry in the long polemic for aesthetic color that culminated in modernist painting. His goal was to valorize the practices of tinting and toning, which in early-modern disputes about the essence of art had been subordinated to the supposedly more rational and masculine principles of drawing. Against the idea that outline and form were painting's most powerful tools for picturing the truths of nature, he insisted that coloring methods dealt with the sensible properties through which reality is apprehended and thus held an epistemological priority that doubled as a painterly prerogative.[4] The category of local colors specified what these methods were and how they transformed the world into art. As de Piles wrote in *The Principles of Painting* (1708; first English translation, 1743), "Local colour, by its agreement with the place it possesses, and by the assistance of some other colour, represents a single object: as a carnation, linen, stuff, or any object, distinct from others."[5] Recall our painted poppy. Making it stand out, giving it "the character of truth," required modulating its red in relation to the neighboring hues. Its singularity as a depicted thing depended on a relational complex of artistic color. The initial definition of local colors thus turned on two features that, in subsequent versions, changed their meaning but never entirely went away: first, an insistence on the relational character of color (here confined to artistic practice); second, an attention to the mediations that connect nature and art (here figured as a transformation so complete as to make artistic colors wholly different from natural ones).

De Piles's plea for local color exhibited the fundamental distinction between the world as it appears in perception and the world as it appears transformed in art that characterized the aesthetics of the picturesque, a category rooted in eighteenth-century landscape painting and exemplary of the artistic principles that impressionists later rejected. Local colors were "artificial" rather than "natural," denizens of painting alone, in opposition to the empirical hues investigated by optics. Mastering local color involved modifying one's hues in relation to the artistic conventions governing composition. Rather than attempting a point-for-point correspondence with reality, as did their contemporaries in natural philosophy, painters sought to tone and shape the natural world into an image worthy of Art. The picturesque depended on exactly this process of modification, naming as it did the practice of seeing and appreciating nature for its aesthetic qualities. Thus William Gilpin, who coined the term "picturesque," distinguished beautiful scenes, which "please the eye in their *natural state,*" from picturesque ones, which "please from some quality, capable of being *illustrated in painting.*"[6] To see something as picturesque meant to see it through the prism of art, here understood as a realm apart from nature and bound by a set of established conventions.

The "prism of art" is of course a metaphor; to enjoy the picturesque, eighteenth- and early-nineteenth-century tourists actually looked into a *mirror*—specifically a black, slightly convex one (Figure 10). The Claude mirror, so named because it toned and adjusted the reflected landscape in the manner of the seventeenth-century painter Claude Lorrain, captures the historical configuration of vision that was later displaced by the

FIGURE 10. A black, slightly convex mirror known as a Claude mirror, 1775–80. Victoria and Albert Museum. Museum number P.18–1972. British Galleries, Room 120; Wolfson Galleries, case 10, http://collections.vam.ac.uk/item/O78676/claude-glass-unknown/.

optical advances energizing impressionism. Painters and tourists alike used it to condense the wide vistas of the natural world into a unified view suitable for translation into art. Rather than gazing upon raw nature, they literally turned their backs to the scene the better to enjoy its reflection in the Claude mirror. Gilpin praised the device as a metaphor for the artistic eye, a means by which even the most philistine travelers could see a landscape as a great painter might. In *Remarks on Forest Scenery* (1834), he suggested that with the help of a Claude mirror, "The eye examines the general effect, the forms of objects, and the beauty of the tints, in one complex view."[7] The mirror's convexity transformed a messy scene into a unified image, and its tone softened nature's vivid hues into a more manageable and coherent palette, aiding in the adjustment of de Piles's local colors.[8] In these operations, the device presupposed an observer detached from the landscape, one whose mechanisms of perception in no way participated in the formation of visual images, and a model of art that favored tradition and delighted in deliberate distortions.

In addition to the Claude mirror, visitors to the Lake District and other rustic locales could aestheticize the landscape with a collection of Claude glasses, variously colored monocles that tourists and painters placed over their eyes to render a scene more picturesque (Figure 11). The many available hues—"blue, green, red, yellow, orange, dark brown, and so on"—each cast a particular tone over the visible world and encouraged spectators to think of their prosthetically enhanced perceptions as approximations of particular painters.[9] James Plumptre offered a telling satire of these trends in his comic opera *The Lakers* (1798), when Miss Veronica Beccabunga gazes over a stretch of land in the Lake District:

Speedwell, give me my glasses. Where's my [Thomas] Gray? *(Speedwell gives glasses.)* Oh! Claude and Poussin are nothing. By the bye, where's my Claude-Lorrain? I must throw a Gilpin tint over these magic scenes of beauty. *(Looks through the glass.)* How gorgeously glowing! Now for the darker. *(Looks through the glass.)* How gloomily glaring! Now the blue. *(Pretends to shiver cold.)* How frigidly frozen! What illusions of vision! The effect is unspeakably interesting.[10]

In addition to lampooning the claims of users that the Claude glasses endowed them with painterly vision, Plumptre's scene shows that art, for these characters, constitutes a subjective overlay that occurs in the empty space between the perceiving eye and perceived world. Where the Claude mirror reinforced the imagined distance between the artist and the environment, the colored glasses offered a model of how artistic minds cast their unique hue over a world that remains unchanged in its empirical reality. After all, they are only "illusions of vision."

By the mid-nineteenth century, the central virtue of the artist was no longer the ability to create beautiful illusions but the power to see the world clearly. As a result, the popularity of the Claude mirror declined sharply, as did the prominence of the broader configuration of artistic

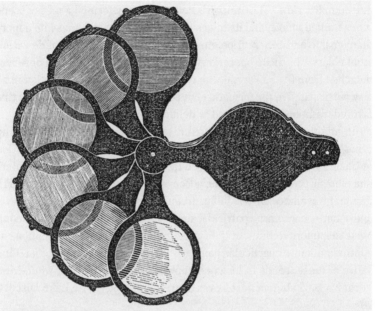

Claude Lorraine Glass.—(Fig. 709.)—This consists of a variety of different colored glasses, about one inch in diameter, mounted in horn frame and turning on one centre, for producing a great variety of colors and showing their combination; it also will be found both pleasing and useful for viewing eclipses, clouds, landscapes, &c.

Price, $1.50 to $3.00.

FIGURE 11. A set of variously hued glass lenses for viewing landscapes and exploring color effects, known as Claude glasses. Benjamin Pike Jr., *Pike's Illustrated Descriptive Catalogue of Optical, Mathematical, and Philosophical Instruments* (New York: published and sold by the author, 1856), 193. Science, Industry, and Business Library, New York Public Library, Astor, Lenox, and Tilden Foundations.

vision to which it belonged. John Ruskin delivered a direct blow in *The Elements of Drawing* (1857) when he derided the black convex mirror as "one of the most pestilent inventions for falsifying Nature and degrading art which has ever been put into an artist's hands."[11] What held for the Claude mirror held for its namesake; in the early volumes of *Modern Painters,* Ruskin never missed an opportunity to disparage Lorrain's carefully toned and conventionalized landscapes as affronts to nature's brilliant, shifting colors. Whereas classical painting valued the stylization of nature, Ruskin made perceptual accuracy art's foremost virtue, the grounds upon which he defended Turner's glowing hues against charges of exaggeration. Within this empirical ideal, artists were to strive for "fidelity to given facts" and so had to cultivate the powers of "observation and intelligence" until their "instrument"—meaning their vision—had been "perfected" by being "employed in a consistent series of careful observation."[12] As Ruskin later put it, "The whole technical power of painting depends on our recovery of what may be called the *innocence of the eye;* that is to say, a sort of childish perception" of the "flat stains of colour" that make up perceptual experience, "without consciousness of what they signify."[13] Strictly speaking, the picturesque could not exist under such conditions; it required an eye trained in aesthetic convention, not the innocent vision of a child. Furthermore, Ruskin's appeal to immediate perception as the locus of art ran counter to the mediations of the Claude mirror, just as the self-conscious embrace of artifice in eighteenth-century aesthetics contrasted with the commitment to careful observation preached in *Modern Painters.*

As artists made bold claims for their ability to register and record empirical reality, the definition of local color underwent a dramatic, yet silent, reversal that fit these new aesthetic ideals. No one announced the revision or made a case for it; yet by the time Ruskin took up his pen, local colors had been relocated from painting to nature, reclassified as "natural" rather than "artificial." What in the eighteenth century was a relative notion applicable only to art became in the nineteenth an absolute property of empirical objects. A typical description, from an 1823 painting manual, cast local color as "the colour of the object when seen in a full, clear light, and at a small distance"—that is, the color as perceived under idealized, almost laboratory-like viewing conditions.[14] As an object's "true" color—what a different manual called the "'self colour' of an object"—local color stood opposed to apparent color, the misleading hues that objects assume through reflection and illumination.[15] Though in line with the empirical ambitions that ousted the picturesque, this absolute version of local color widened the gap between the perceiver and perceived assumed by Gilpin by borrowing the scenography of empirical science to posit "real" hues that exist apart from being seen, as if color could be turned into a primary quality by detaching it from perceptual experience.

The idea of an absolute color, despite its deference to the rhetoric of science, was soon unsettled by experiments in the physiology and psychology of perception, which in turn caused it to be rejected by a subsequent generation of empirically minded painters. Studies such as Michel Eugène Chevreul's *De la loi du contraste simultané des coleurs de l'assortiment des objets colorés* (1839, translated as *The Principles of Harmony and Contrast of Colours* in 1854) and Ogden Rood's *Modern Chromatics* (1879) insisted that colors *always* depend on their relation to other colors for their particular quality and that the physical properties of the eye and brain are *integral* to the perception of objects. Individual hues and even individual observers could no longer be thought of as self-sufficient entities. Rather, they appeared as part of an ongoing relational process of perception, a drama of dancing light playing on the retina that undid any hard distinction between an object's purportedly real, substantive properties and the ephemeral qualities imposed by its surroundings. Before long, even painters and art critics derided the absolute notion of local color as being at odds with the truth of perception. "Scientifically speaking," proclaimed one such critic, "there is no such thing as 'local color'"; "what seems to be the general hue of the objects . . . is only the play of light upon their surfaces."[16] The painter Burleigh Parkhurst too denied that local colors existed, explaining in 1890 that "objects change continually with every change of atmospheric condition and every change of position of the sun" and that thus, "for the painter an object has no color of its own, but only such color as the varying conditions of things may for the moment give to it."[17] In place of the stable hues of a separate reality, late-nineteenth-century artists saw the play of light and atmosphere and recorded the perceptual encounters that belied the abstractions of "self colors." They pushed local colors out of visual art.

No style hastened this removal more than impressionism. Painters such as Claude Monet and Pierre-Auguste Renoir in France and Dennis Miller Bunker and Childe Hassam in the United States pitted their entire aesthetic technique against the premises of absolute local colors, and in the process they changed what it meant to have an innocent eye. Like Ruskin they rejected convention in the name of seeing nature clearly, but unlike Ruskin they incorporated contemporary knowledge of psychophysics and color relations to craft paintings premised on the perceptual transformations wrought on the world by the eye. Indeed, the essential point of these scientific studies—that the eye and mind play a constitutive role in producing color—underwrites the most distinctive features of impressionist practice. Only with a theory of how the human organism processes color stimuli could a painter such as Renoir, and later Georges Seurat, pair complimentary colors to produce gray or juxtapose unmixed hues to create a uniquely vibrant color in perception. Such techniques took for granted that, as the like-minded art critic Eugène Véron put it in *Æsthetics* (1879), "color is never absolutely self-contained," that it "is always more or less modified by its neighbor or neighbors."[18] By abandoning absolute local colors in the name of an artistic eye that sees only relational effects, impressionist painters not only freed artistic vision from tradition but also lodged it in the body and networked it to the environment.

Rejecting the nineteenth-century visual meaning of local color entailed redistributing the relational character of artistic colors stressed in the original definition to fit the late-nineteenth-century renovation of artistic vision. After all, de Piles also insisted on the way a color's "neighbors" contributed to its quality, but he confined these effects to the properties of painted representations. When the impressionists carried their easels out into the landscape, however, they relocated these relational effects to the interplay of self and world involved in the nature of *all* color. Many of the early commentaries on impressionism, including one by Garland, presented the open-air technique and the juxtaposition of "pure" hues that combined in the viewer's mind as the primary methods through which modern painting asserted its claim to empiricism. Because impressionists strove "to represent in color an instantaneous effect of light and shade as presented by nature," Garland explained in *Crumbling Idols* (1894), they worked "in the open air necessarily"—not as a preliminary step and not with the help of a Claude mirror but as a performance that captures a unique encounter between the artist and the landscape (98). Rather than "paint leaves, they paint masses of color; they paint the *effect* of leaves upon the eye," and this technique generated canvases that conveyed "unified impression[s]," moments of vision as they occur untainted by artistic convention (99, 97). The work of condensing, sorting, and unifying a landscape, once off-loaded to the Claude mirror, reappeared in modern art as the function of the artistic eye itself. No longer a passive instrument, the painter's perceptual apparatus acted as a constructive mechanism expressing a particular relation to its world. The goal of painting shifted from the creation of a picturesque image that presumed a distinction from natural vision to an empirical attempt to capture "the stayed and reproduced effect of a single section of the world of color upon the eye" (98). The Claude Lorrain mirror gave way to Claude Monet's eye.

The empirical mission of modern painting—the effort to see a vague reality—involved a pedagogical task aimed at sensitizing viewers to the colors of perception, a task nowhere more evident than in the invocation of colored shadows. "To most eyes," Garland noted, "the sign-manual of the impressionist is the blue shadow" (102). Even more so than the other glowing tones of modern painting, the presence of blues and purples where audiences expected to see grays and blacks caused a "shock," as well as a fair amount of ridicule (109). Yet for Garland, "To see these colors is a development," not only because they are "flags of anarchy" waved in the faces of tradition-bedazzled critics, but also because they mark a process by which artistic vision reveals an overlooked feature of the empirical world (102, 109). Here Garland joined Ruskin in invoking color perception as the mark of the artist's superior vision of what is. "The first great mistake that people make," Ruskin explained in the first volume of *Modern Painters,* "is the supposition that they must *see* a thing if it be before their eyes." In fact, "the truth of nature is not to be discerned by the uneducated senses" (3: 141). And just as Garland pointed to cool-colored shadows as an illustration of such trained perception, Ruskin announced that Turner's "most distinctive innovation as a colourist was his discovery of the scarlet *shadow*" (7: 413; emphasis in original). Like Monet's blues, Turner's scarlet was "offensive," even "inconceivable," to contemporary audiences, yet Ruskin insisted that it marked the kind of clear, empirical vision that elevated Turner above Claude and the old masters (it was a "discovery," after all) (7: 413). Over the course of the nineteenth century, tinted and toned shadows came to exemplify the empirical ideal of the artist's eye, the claim that artists above all others saw the world as it was. Philosopher C. S. Peirce, for instance, held that if an "ordinary man" and an artist were to survey a snow-covered field "on which the sun shines brightly except where shadows fall," the former would describe the landscape as "white, pure white, whiter in the sunlight, a little greyish in the shadow." The latter, however, would report "that the shadows are not grey but dull blue and that the snow in sunshine is of a rich yellow." Peirce accounts for this disparity by arguing that the "ordinary man" responds according to "his theory of what *ought* to be seen" rather than to "what is before his eyes"; his thoughts modify his perception of the presentness of the world and interfere with the immediate observation that marks the artist.[19] Yet many held out hope that we could all come to see as artists—not through the distortions of an apparatus such as the Claude glass but through an encounter with modern painting. As the author of an 1896 manual for color education put it, the success of Turner's techniques, which for the first time "illustrate[d] the fact that Nature is colored," promised that "in time the public will learn to see color."[20]

Turner was not the first painter to color his shadows, but he may have been the first to do so in the name of an immediate perception of nature rather than the technical mediations of art. Indeed, the elevation of colored shadows as a badge of perspicacity follows from the same movements that ousted absolute local colors from art by relocating color's relational dynamic from the painting to the act of vision. Earlier colorists, such as Rubens and Eugène Delacroix, had intensified the hue of their objects by tinting and toning the shadows they cast: a yellow lemon might have a purplish shadow, an orange vase a bluish one.[21] But these were surreptitious techniques, tricks of the trade to create a convincing illusion, not flamboyant gestures that caused disbelief in viewers. The blue or purple in such a shadow was *local* in de Piles's original definition, since "by its agreement with the place it possesses, and by the assistance of some other colour, [it] represents a single object." Yet just as the "place" of local colors shifted from the canvas to the world in the nineteenth century, so too did colored shadows move from the artist's handiwork to the natural landscape. All the major treatises on color science discussed them. Goethe analyzed them at length in *Theory of Colours* (1810), categorizing them as "physiological colors" bound to the perceiving subject. Subsequent researchers, such as Helmholtz, Rood, Ewald Hering, and G. Stanley Hall, argued over where exactly these colors appeared: in the retina, in the mind, or in the shadows themselves.[22] But all agreed that they were a feature of color experience, making it possible for modern painters to claim them as evidence of their innocent—and therefore discerning—eyes.

The case of colored shadows shows that the demise of local color in visual art was in fact its reorganization within a new paradigm of artistic vision, one that elevated color effects to an unprecedented prominence. When de Piles celebrated coloring techniques, when Ruskin championed Turner, when Garland defended impressionism's blue shadows, each fought against the subordination of color and attempted to fashion chromatic experience as a window into reality's deepest workings. The story of modern painting is at least in part the story of attempts to make color primary, to frame its relational dynamics not as a "problem" but as real features of the actual world. The difficulty of going all the way in this regard is evident from many half measures: de Piles maintaining the distinction between "artificial" and "natural" colors, for instance, or Ruskin invoking Locke to cast color as a "beautiful auxiliary" and "the least important feature of nature," precisely because of its dependence on a perceiving subject (3: 301, 3: 299–300). According to Garland, the "impressionist view of nature" had no such reservations. It constituted "a discovery, born of clearer vision and more careful study,—a perception which was denied the early painters, precisely as the force we call electricity was an ungovernable power a generation ago" (110). To see what Garland made of this discovery, we must follow the course of local color from painting to prose, pausing at the intersection he created between the visual and the verbal, between literal and metaphorical colors.

Garland and the Evolution of Local Color

"Local color—what is it?" (52). When Garland formulated his own definition in *Crumbling Idols,* he guarded it against its popular affiliation with the picturesque detail and the ways of seeing encapsulated by the Claude glass. "It means that the picturesque shall not be seen by the author,— that every tree and bird and mountain shall be dear and companionable and necessary, not picturesque." While "the tourist cannot write the local novel," he continued, the modern author cannot help but generate local color: "It must go in, it *will* go in, because the writer naturally carries it with him half unconsciously" (54). With this distinction, Garland confounded both his contemporaries' treatment of literary local color as something hunted, researched, or otherwise consciously sought after, and the most influential readings of the local color tradition by literary critics, which similarly assume a distance between the observing narrator or writer and the people or places observed. For Garland, such distance was anathema to local color. Instead, he aligned himself with the "impressionist view of nature" and the coloring methods that brought it forth into art. In the blue shadows and "fearless coloring" of the painters he admired, Garland found the means of making the color of local color modern. To resist the aspects of the picturesque aesthetic that followed the concept into literature, he launched a campaign for local color as a "necessary" and almost unconscious quality of artistic perception, a sign of the sensory openness modeled in the impressionists rather than of the outside interest epitomized in the tourist.

By the time Garland came to local color, it had long made its decisive pivot into writing. As Vladimir Kapor explains in *Local Colour: A Travelling Concept* (2009), the term entered literary criticism in early-nineteenth-century France as one of several metaphors drawn from the visual arts to discuss writing. To be precise, then, the act of transplantation occurred as a matter of *couleur locale*—which may account in part for why it has gone unnoticed by Anglophone critics.[23] As in de Piles's initial definition, literary local color made a particular thing "distinct from others," yet unlike the original formulation, and in step with the nineteenth-century one, it treated *place* as a specific location in the world.[24] At first these places were far away and exotic (the local color of Théophile Gautier and Prosper Mérimée); by the end of the century they were close and familiar (that of Gustave Flaubert and George Eliot). In each case the emphasis was on particularity against generality, such that the exemplary articulation of local color in American letters might well be the "real" grasshopper that William Dean Howells juxtaposed to the "ideal" one in his critical writings on realism. While the latter, according to Howells, had dominated fiction, it was a mere abstraction, a cardboard cutout "very prettily painted in a conventional tint." He called writers instead to look to the real, concrete grasshopper and the practices of description that could bring it into fiction.[25] Literary local color at the end of the nineteenth century was thus a matter of mustering details to create a feeling of veracity, supported by a sense of specificity. And in their endeavor to avoid the "conventional tint," local color writers embraced the fundamental conceit of absolute local colors: the notion that the groups they represented had a true color that existed apart from the perception that registered it or the representation that communicated it. The goal was to go out and find it.

By the early years of the twentieth century, the characterization of literary local color as the exotic details captured by an outside observer— the characterization Garland rejected—had become so common as to be the stuff of parodies. A representative article in the *Atlantic Monthly* declared that "the only requisites to" the study of local color were "an unfamiliar environment and a superior mind"—the very inverse of the "companionable" surroundings and "half unconscious" feelings that Garland invokes.[26] Likewise, Mary Austin's "The Pocket Hunter" in *The Land of Little Rain* (1903) takes the mining activities of its central character as a figure for the local colorists. "When he came to a watercourse," she writes, "he would pan out the gravel of its bed for 'colors,' and under the glass determine if they had come from far or near, and so spying he would work up the stream until he found where the drift of the gold-bearing outcrop fanned out into the creek."[27] Austin's image draws on the characterization of local color details as something to be hunted and tracked down, something that readers were meant to connect back to their source, and something that, if properly deployed, could mean literary gold. Like similar parodies, the story literalizes the "color" of local color to poke fun at a genre that was past its prime, in the hopes of opening a different path for writing about place.

Yet when Garland invoked the visual meaning of local color, he did so not to joke but to read the literary tradition back through the discourse of painting that gave it its name. He found in the premises and practices of impressionism a paradigm for reconfiguring place in literature as a matter of perception—not the toning and distancing perception of the picturesque but the immersive, embodied vision exemplified in modern color. Soon after arriving in Boston from Iowa in 1884, Garland befriended John Joseph Enneking, an American painter who had studied in Paris and adopted the open-air techniques of Monet, Camille Pissarro, and Renoir. Enneking introduced him to a number of local artists and to the styles and controversies of the day, and Garland carried this newfound enthusiasm for the visual arts into lectures, essays, and traveling exhibitions throughout the 1890s, eventually penning what has been identified as "probably the first all-out defense of the [impressionist] movement to be written in English."[28] "Impressionists are, above all, colorists," Garland wrote in that early essay (later collected in *Crumbling Idols,* where it sat side by side with adamant calls for local color writing); their technique "makes much of the relation and interplay of light and shade,—not in black and white, but in color" (99). Garland's paean to impressionist hues signals his strategy of adopting the relational aesthetic expressed in modern painting to combat the touristic aspects of late-nineteenth-century narratives about place.

The lesson impressionism offered to fiction was that all perception *localizes;* it unifies the landscape in an act of vision that bears the marks of both the observer and the environment. The hues of Monet's haystacks and cathedrals tag the canvases as emerging from a particular moment in a particular place—the light of the French countryside at dawn or at dusk, or the afternoon hues of Rouen. "The point to be made here is this," Garland wrote, "the atmosphere and coloring of Russia is not the atmosphere of Holland. The atmosphere of Norway is much clearer and the colors more vivid than in England. . . . This brings me to my settled conviction that art, to be vital, must be local in its subject; its universal appeal must be in its working out" (103–4). Yet capturing the "local" here means attending first and foremost to the immediate act of perception through which it appears: "The impressionist," Garland continued, "deals with the present" (104). Thus, when in Garland's short story "Among the Corn-Rows," Seagraves gazes at the landscape, the uniqueness of the time, place, and character follow a vivid description of the sea-like prairie in the spreading mist. "No other climate, sky, plain, could produce the same unnamable weird charm," the narrator notes, and Seagraves himself concurs: "'It is American,' he exclaimed. 'No other land or time can match this mellow air, this wealth of color, much less the strange social conditions of life on this sunlit Dakota prairie.'"[29] When artistic vision and activity involve opening oneself to feeling the landscape, neither the painter nor the writer can help but see local color—it goes in "half unconsciously." It is with this in mind that we must approach Garland's oft-quoted images of spontaneous literary production: local color writing offered "a statement of life as indigenous as the plant-growth" because the conduits of expression—the perceptual equipment of the author— worked in concert with the regional surroundings (*Crumbling Idols,* 54). The seer and the seen are coconstituents of the selective process by which the perceptual image is formed. For Garland, when art is "natural and unrestrained," the earth itself becomes articulate: "The corn has flowered, and the cotton-boll has broken into speech" (52).

Impressionism introduced Garland to a new sense in which writing could represent or reflect place, one in which reflection occurs on the model of *colors* rather than mirrors. To be sure, a canvas by Hassam or Mary Cassatt teems with reflection, but the colors that bounce between objects and people in no way model a transparent relation between image and reality. Rather, they present a world in which perceivers absorb, shape, and refract perceptual stimuli through their individuating selections, a reality in which the material composition of each object sorts through the range of potentials in white light to throw a particular hue back at the world. Such is the scene that opens "A Branch Road," the first story in *Main-Travelled Roads*. "The frost began to glisten with reflected color," Garland writes, and the "broad face and deep earnest eyes" of the young protagonist "caught and retained some part of the beauty and majesty of the sky" (6). The entire landscape—including the youth—glisten along with the frost on the grass, offering a play of reflected color that figures the ongoing perceptions that limn a life. With this scene in mind, we can return to the question with which this section began: "Local color—what is it? It means that the writer spontaneously reflects the life which goes on around him. It is natural and unrestrained art" (*Crumbling Idols*, 52). The writer reflects the environment in the same way that objects of vision reflect their colors—through a process of selection that absorbs some aspects, bends others back, and creates an image that changes the stimulus rather than simply representing it.

To arrive at these implications for local color writing, Garland extended the impressionist account of color perception by situating it within a late-nineteenth-century evolutionary framework. Indeed, evolution and impressionism were twinned in Garland's mind as dual expressions of the modern spirit. While in Iowa he cut his intellectual teeth on Hippolyte Taine, the French intellectual whose *History of English Literature* (1864; translated into English 1871) insisted on the importance of "environment" in the formation of national literature, and he discovered Spencer and Véron during his years of self-education at the Boston Public Library, at about the time he began promoting modern painting. "I read both day and night," he later wrote of that time, "grappling with Darwin, Spencer, Fiske, Helmholtz, Haeckel,—all the mighty masters of evolution."[30] From these writers, Garland learned more than the Spencerian theory of artistic and sociological progress; he gained an image of life as the constant interplay between creatures and their surroundings and a notion of art as emerging from—and looping back into—these dynamics.

As a quality of an interaction between an organism and its environment, rather than a property solely of the perceiving mind or the perceived object, color helped Garland resolve a tension in the nineteenth-century evolutionary thinkers he admired. To begin, his early allegiance to Taine and Spencer convinced him of the determining influence of the natural landscape on artistic expression. Such ideas bolstered the wider program of local color and led a few writers to embrace the literal hues of the environment as revelatory of regional character.[31] In the essay "Local Color" (1886) for the *Critic,* Kentucky writer James Lane Allen held that "the first general idea regulating the use of local color in literature" was that "the writer must lay upon his canvas those colors that are true for the region he is describing and characteristic of it." Though he admitted that such intense attunement to the visual world withdrew "attention from character, plot, incident, [and] motive" and "fixe[d] it upon skies, atmospheres, horizons, landscapes, sites, monuments," he insisted that it fed back into the depiction of human life by virtue of the Tainian principle that "the natural pictorial environment" has "manifold effects upon humanity."[32] Nearly forty years later, Austin adopted a similar premise in her arguments for regionalism. "Man is not himself only," she wrote in *The Land of Journeys' Ending* (1924); "he is all that he sees; all that flows to him from a thousand sources, half noted, or noted not at all except by some sense that lies too deep for naming." Austin's "half noted" influences recall Garland's local color, which goes in "half unconsciously." And like Garland, Austin gave color special weight: "If there is in the country of his abiding, no more than a single refluent color, such as the veiled green of sage-brush or the splendid wine of sunset spilled along the Sangre de Cristo, he takes it in and gives it forth again in directions and occasions least suspected by himself, as a manner, as music, as a prevailing tone of thought."[33] Environmental color sets the tone for artistic coloring.

As much as Garland embraced the idea that atmosphere and terrain condition artistic effort, he would not allow determinism to cancel the agency of the artist. He drew equally on Véron, whose *Æsthetics* sought to develop a naturalistic account of art against the conservative influence of the French Academy. On the first page of his copy of Véron's book Garland wrote, "This book influenced me more than any other work on art. It entered into all I thought and spoke and read for many years after it fell into my hands about 1886."[34] Véron taught Garland that what mattered in art was the individual's response to an environment: *how* that environment was felt rather than *what* it was. In *Æsthetics,* he insisted that all "truth as to facts" necessarily translates into the "truth of our own sensations," the "truth as we see it, as it appears modified by our own temperaments, preferences, and physical organs. It is, in fact, our personality itself" (389). "Personality," then, referred to an operation lodged in the body and situated in culture, and it accounted for why "there can be no art without selection" (360). But as Garland explained in his gloss of this passage, in which he tried to tip the balance away from the solitary individual, the artist's personality emerged as a *result* of these operations, rather than the other way around: "'There can be no art without selection,' and in this selection, in the arrangement of lines and colors, in the 'distribution of values,' the artist appears."[35] So too the place: the process of selection that engenders the artist does so only by instituting relations between the perceiver and perceived that, in turn, create the visible world. Art, for Garland, was a question not simply "of one man facing certain facts" but of an artist "telling his individual relations to" those facts (*Crumbling Idols,* 30). It occurred not through the substantives, but in the relations produced by selective perceptions, the relations indexed by impressionist color. "The higher art," Garland wrote, is "the art that perceives and states the relations of things, giving atmosphere and relative values as they appeal to the sight" (42).

For this reason, both Véron and Garland denied that photography, along with its pretentions to a colorless and nonrelational perspective, could be a model for artistic vision. The former proclaimed the photograph's presentation of "reality taken from a point of view without connection with us or our impressions" to be "the very negation of art"; its mechanical and nonselective capture of "all the features and details of an object or event" paradoxically produces images that "remain inferior to reality" (*Æsthetics,* 389, 105). The view from nowhere falls short because it subtracts an essential element of the empirical world: the relations formed through our perceptual activities. For Garland, the missed relations between perceiving self and perceived world marked both the literal and metaphorical realm of color that eluded nineteenth-century photography. A painting "will never be mere reproduction so long as the artist represents it as he sees it," he wrote; "the fact will correct the fantasy. The artist will color the fact" (*Crumbling Idols,* 63). "Coloring" here denotes the acts of selection that individuate artistic expression and embed the observer in nature, and Garland's comment explains why he thought that "veritism" was synonymous with local color. For color encompasses a field of empirical elements absent in photographic realism but present to the veritist, who writes not of bare facts but of "things *plus* his interest in them—things *plus* his selection of them and distribution of values," as emergent from "the position ascribed to him."[36]

Just as artistic color helped Garland square Spencer's determinism with Véron's individualism and thus reconcile two opposing endeavors to bring aesthetics in line with evolution, so too did evolutionary thinkers push him to radicalize the "view of nature" he found in painting. They emboldened him to push what were often seen as the epistemological claims of impressionism—the idea that their techniques revealed how nature is *seen*—into ontological claims about what nature in fact *is*. Darwin, Alfred Russel Wallace, and Grant Allen, provoked by Gladstone's suggestion that the human color sense had evolved within historical time, all speculated on the origins of color perception in the animal kingdom to make color a feature of the world itself. They situated human responsiveness to color within Darwinian evolution (a theory that Gladstone resisted) and arrived at a fully relational account of color's emergence in the organic world, an account that paralleled and indeed extended the impressionists' use of color.

Allen offered the most elaborate argument in *The Colour-Sense: Its Origins and Development* (1879), published two years after his more popular *Physiological Aesthetics* (1877) and emerging from that work's brief investigation into color perception. In what amounted to a rejection of the metaphysical dismissal of color as a subjective addition to the objective world, Allen argued for the gradual coevolution of colors (in fruits, flowers, and birds) and color vision (in insects, birds, and mammals). He hypothesized that the production of the color sense in animal life had, through the mechanisms of natural selection, generated much of the "objective" color in the world. Because some insects happened to be attracted to flowers with bright colors, the seeds of those plants were spread and their species flourished; likewise, animals able to detect the red fruit among the green leaves held a reproductive advantage over those who could not. And once this basic groundwork was in place, some animals began to favor brightly colored mates, promoting the development of vivid hues on male birds, for instance.[37] Allen's argument made it impossible to separate the perceiving organism from the colorful surroundings and, in the process, placed aesthetic color within evolutionary history.

Such was the lens through which Garland understood impressionist techniques and adopted them for literature: as evidence that the qualities of human perception point beyond the self without thereby standing as records of the "objective" world. Evolution prompted Garland to reject the notion of an unmediated or innocent eye that simply registers a reality waiting to be captured, which amounts to seeing the eye as a camera capable of full color. Instead, he placed artistic vision within the developmental lineage of the color sense and treated aesthetic mediations, including linguistic ones, as ways of linking perceiver and world rather than prying them apart. It's fitting, then, that when Garland discussed that epitome of modern artistic perception, the blue shadow, he invoked a scene of aesthetic instruction that begins not with painting or with his own naive eye but with the written word. "In my own case," Garland recounted, "I got my first idea of colored shadows by reading one of Herbert Spencer's essays." Only then did he "see blue and grape-color in the shadows on the snow" (*Crumbling Idols,* 102).

The essay in question, Spencer's "The Valuation of Evidence" (1853), takes this tangle of concepts and perception as its very subject, outlining the reciprocal ways in which scientific observations can be compromised: "the presence of hypothesis and the absence of hypothesis." After surveying a number of instances in which researchers recorded phenomena consistent with their expectations but, as later experiments showed, inconsistent with the data, Spencer offered the case of colored shadows as an example of clear perception requiring a fresh idea to break free of unreflective habit. "Ask any one who has received no culture in art, or who has given no thought to it, of what color a shadow is, and the unquestioning reply will be—black." Spencer spent much of his youth assuming this "creed of the uninitiated," even "quoting all of [his] experience" to deny the contrary claims of an amateur artist. But eventually he encountered "a popular work on Optics" proposing that "the colour of a shadow is always the complement of the colour of the light casting it," a variant of color contrasts. Once he had this principle fixed in his mind, the evidence of his experience changed: he saw not only blue shadows but also green, purplish, yellow-grey, and even multicolored ones. "Is it not clear,"

Spencer concluded in a remark that echoes Ruskin, "that to observe correctly is by no means easy?"[38] Colored shadows proved that the exact observation of nature involved more than just immediate perception—it required a proper interpretive mind-set, a "blue-shadow idea" (*Crumbling Idols,* 97).

Acquiring this mind-set involved training. As a writer for the *Nineteenth Century* noted in 1895, "We must go through a certain schooling before we can detect color-shadows in nature."[39] For Garland, such schooling occurred on the go. To enter the "world of frank color" promised by the "idea of colored shadows," Garland submitted himself to unusual positions and uncommon speeds (*Crumbling Idols,* 103). "By turning my head top-side down," Garland reported, "I came to see that shadows falling upon yellow sand were violet," and the visual effects of these contortions were then matched by those of horseback riding: "On my horse I caught glimpses of this marvellous land of color as I galloped across some bridge. In this world stone-walls were no longer cold gray, they were warm purple, deepening as the sun westered" (102). Far from the subjective overlay imposed by the Claude glasses, these hues arose from empirical practice and revealed a world of shifting relations and situated perspectives in which the rigid categories of subjective fancy and objective fact no longer applied. Unlike the conceit of the innocent eye, which pits accurate perception against conceptual intervention, Garland characterized color perception as a process of tuning one's concepts to the world, of finding ideas and forms that put the observer into active contact with the environment. He treated the colors of modern painting as akin to the exaggerated sizes and perspectives produced by microscopes and telescopes: they offer a strange yet empirical view into an otherwise-unseen corner of nature. In the end, "the change in method" that produces such "vivid and fearless coloring, indicates a radical change in attitude toward the physical universe" (109).

What blue shadows revealed to Garland, then, was a world in which the relations constitutive of color perception were as real and fundamental as anything else in the physical world. This metaphysical "attitude," in turn, supported a method of artistic production in which processes of mediation were treated as techniques for forming new relations within nature, where nature encompassed both human activity and its environments. When Garland spoke of "a whole new world of color . . . opening to the eyes of the present generation," he meant it literally, the product of aesthetic innovations.[40] In this way Garland squared the two "places" of artistic local colors at the turn of the twentieth century: he refused to separate artistic coloring techniques from the world's "true" colors, the contributions of the observer from the products of empirical observation—the way the world is felt from what the world is. He saw that the evolutionary perspective muddles the opposition of mediation and immediacy as thoroughly as it tangles subject and object, making literary constructions and painterly compositions equivalent efforts to fashion representational frameworks through which to view a newly colorful world.

We must therefore approach the dozens of colored shadows that weave throughout Garland's writing not only as ekphrastic portrayals of an impressionist eye but also as explorations of the constitutive role that language and writing play in the perception of nature's hues. From the "deep-blue shadows" that "stream like stains of ink" in "God's Ravens" to the "deep purple shadows" in "Western Landscapes" (1893) and the "peaks deeply shadowed in Tyrian purple" in *Wayside Courtships* (1897), Garland's hues act as linguistic aids to perception, attempts to energize the feelings of presentness that Peirce associated with the artist through his own literary medium.[41] "As I write this," Garland announced in his essay on impressionism, "I have just come in from a bee-hunt over Wisconsin hills, amid splendors which would make Monet seem low-keyed." He then set his own experience of the "brilliancy and sparkle of color" against the efforts of the painters, with liberal emphasis on the shadows:

> Amid bright orange foliage, the trunks of beeches glowed with steel-blue shadows on their eastern side. Sumach gleamed with marvelous brilliancy among the deep cool green grasses and low plants untouched by frost. Everywhere amid the red and orange and crimson were lilac and steel-blue shadows, giving depth and vigor and buoyancy which Corot never saw (or never painted),—a world which Inness does not represent. (*Crumbling Idols,* 103)[42]

Garland's attention to the mingling of word and vision doubles back onto his characterization of the impressionists: these artists "have added a new word to painting," Garland wrote, and that word "has made nature more radiantly beautiful. . . . Like the word of a lover, it has exalted the painter to see nature irradiated with splendor never seen before" (110).

The mediations of art, like complex blue-shadow ideas, make nature present, bringing out its colors by establishing new links between perceiver and world.

If veritism follows impressionism in revealing a surprising realm of marvelous hues, its burden—and the task of aesthetics conceived not only in the wake of evolutionary science but also as itself an empirical endeavor—is to communicate these visions to others. Garland makes this process of translating individual perspectives to a wider community a central feature of his writing, an expanded analogue to the work of helping others see shadows as colored rather than gray. The veritist "sets himself a most arduous task": "His art consists in making others feel his individual and distinctive comment on the life around him."[43] Literature requires not only the personal impressions that emerge through the localizing operations of consciousness but also a procedure by which these perceptions take hold in a reader, the analogue to the impressionist method of laying unmixed colors side by side to be blended in the act of seeing. The writer feels an environment from a particular vantage and then "make[s] his reader feel it through his own emotion" (*Crumbling Idols,* 54). At times, Garland described this process in words that recall a perspective prior to the "radical change in attitude toward the physical universe"; he says that veritism consists of "an individual impression corrected by reference to fact" or of an individual manner of writing "corrected by reference to life."[44] But "reference," "fact," and "life" must all be read under the sign of evolution. "Life is always changing, and literature changes with it"; therefore, facts are always "perceived fact[s]" and reference involves a prospective rather than retrospective maneuver (*Crumbling Idols,* 64). To reference the world is to jump into the flow of experience and to act according to an idea, to look for blue shadows through the corner of one's eye or from atop a galloping horse.

Veritism in its full sense thus entails a process of verification, one resonant with the pragmatist philosophy of William James. Garland reflected that he christened his style with "a word which subtended verification,"[45] and his future-oriented aesthetic grounded in readings of evolutionary theory and psychophysical research sets him squarely within James's intellectual domain.[46] In particular, James separated truth from correspondence and situated it within a world of process. "The truth of an idea is not a stagnant property inherent in it," he wrote in *Pragmatism* (1907). "Truth *happens* to an idea. It *becomes* true, is *made* true by events.

Its verity is in fact an event, a process: the process namely of its verifying itself, its veri-*fication*."[47] Likewise, the truths of veritism unfold along two processual paths: the acts of sorting, filtering, and registering the landscape that constitute the event of composition, and the acts of sorting, filtering, and registering the text that make up the moment of reading. The different stimuli allow for different experiences, but in each case a particular truth—entangled with a particular perspective—emerges through a transaction between a perceiver and an environment.

Pragmatism and veritism thus mark complementary attempts to embed thought and writing within the work of the world. In his critique of Spencer's correspondence theory of mind, James insists that "the knower is not simply a mirror floating with no foot-hold anywhere"; instead, "the knower is an actor, a co-efficient of the truth on one side, whilst on the other he registers the truth which he helps to create." Individual interests, proclivities, and hunches—all the messy elements of cognition that Spencer excludes but that a writer cannot help but engage—all "help to *make* the truth which they declare."[48] Garland's debt to Véron brought him in line with James's criticisms of Spencer, such that he embedded the writer as firmly as James embedded the thinker: "Born into a web of circumstances, enmeshed in common life, the youthful artist begins to think" (*Crumbling Idols,* 53). So positioned, the project of representing reality gave way to that of arranging, reworking, and condensing the material of experience in order to add to reality's stock. Works of art "excel the reality from which they spring; they condense and complete it," Véron wrote (102); but they also feed back into it.[49] Reality grows; new colors emerge in the shadows, and Garland's veritism installs itself in the midst of these developments, the better to direct the truths they produce.[50]

Situated Color: Garland's Sketches and Stories

As we have seen, Garland grasped the "radical change in attitude toward the physical universe" through the material hues of modern art. The localizing perceptions of impressionism, the empiricism of blue shadows, and the relational character of color identity all equipped him to recast local color aesthetics from the perspective of evolution's subtle transactions between embodied organisms and sensory environments. Yet when Garland spoke of the "whole new world of color . . . opening to the eyes of the present generation," he did not confine himself to the "violet shadows on the road." For him, the optical advances of the impressionists augured a wider range of perceptual progress: "I believe, also," he continued, "that there is the same wealth of color-mystery in the facts of our daily lives," ready to be revealed by a new generation of "dramatists and novelists."[51] From his earliest sketches to his most famous stories, Garland relied on precise and often-ornate color descriptions to convey the "color-mystery" of modern life in the Midwest, starting with the qualitative feel of the landscape and working up to the social conditions that determined how that feeling varied from observer to observer. In *Main-Travelled Roads* he embedded the vivid observations conjured in his color sketches within the lives of his characters and then set these various perceptions against one another in order to establish a middle ground between narrowly self-centered views and photographic claims of neutrality. To do so, his veritist local color folded the stylistic flourishes and impressionistic techniques associated with 1890s aestheticism into the Populist Party program for which he is best known.[52] Garland made "aesthetics" a matter not only of art but also of sensory perception, lodged in the body and situated in an environment and a culture. Through these techniques, he forged a vision of the nation as a relational network of evolving locales and of the individual as an entity at once singular and overflowing. He imagined America and its citizens on the model of color.

Garland began his literary career by sketching color. During his trek back to the Dakota Territory from Boston in 1887, the trip that provoked him to write his earliest short stories, he filled his travel notebooks with colorful accounts of the landscape, which he later integrated into his fiction.[53] One sketch comes under the title "A Feast of Color":

> The maples resplendent in all their vivid tints running from light green to the most gorgeous yellows and reds and orange tints. The green orchards shower gold and yellow as light green glows amid the dark green of the foliage. Here and there the dull rich red of the dog vine offsets the soft yellow or russet of the elms and the nut brown of the locust, the green of grass.[54]

The passage captures many of the features that characterize Garland's depictions of the visible world: the hues run and "shower" through the scene, tied to the ever-shifting light; the colors offset one another in relations of contrast and complementarity; and a parade of adjectives ("dull

rich red," "resplendent" and "vivid tints," "gorgeous yellows") bespeak
the author's strained efforts to capture the nuances of visual perception.
Garland almost never allowed color terms to stand on their own; whereas
his friend Stephen Crane limited himself to a stark palette of basic
colors—red, yellow, blue, black, and so on—Garland favored hyphenated
hues, such as "blue-black," "yellow-gray," "yellow-green," "blue-green,"
"yellow-brown," "purple-brown," "purple-black," "gray-green," "rose-pink,"
"whitish-yellow," "slate-blue," "deep-green," and several others.[55] Like
the mobile colors of perception, these terms transform under the reader's
eyes, marking a literary project aimed at communicating color experience in all its complexity.

These aspects of Garland's colors emerged from his efforts to immerse
himself in the landscape, to use his writing to connect to the scene and,
in so doing, to redefine local color as a quality of embodied perception.
Garland wrote his earliest color sketches to feel his way into a local environment, attuning himself to the present moment and composing a record of his presence that he could return to when crafting his narratives.
Yet he came to see these descriptive passages as stand-alone literary
units and published subsequent color-soaked sketches in venues such as
the *Atlantic Monthly* in the 1890s. In these texts, the life of the landscape
is tied to the play of luminous colors, presented as mere spectacle, a way
of revving up the sensory attunement required to bring readers closer to
perception and what it reveals. One sketch, "Washington State," presents
the American Northwest as a study in green: "Everywhere are greens,—
bronze-green of the firs, gray-green and emerald-green of the mosses,
the yellow-green of the ferns, the blue-green of the pines, the pea-green
of the little firs, and the tender timid grass blades. These are the colors;
nothing brighter, nothing gay."[56] Here and elsewhere Garland's color impressions attune us to a "now" that also includes a "here." They present in
concentrated form his blend of impressionist techniques and nineteenth-
century writing about place, his distinct way of altering the meaning of
the *local* by taking *color* literally.

To observe the landscape in this way, one must not only *see* but also
feel the surrounding colors; only then does the body take its place within
nature to register impressions. Indeed, Garland's hues have a texture as
well as a look: "velvety purples," "soft yellow[s]," "a fine purple," and a
"velvety-brown."[57] Many of Garland's characters come to feel these colors
only after undergoing an ordeal in which they are alienated from and

then reunited with their bodies. In "A Branch Road," Will's threshing leaves him with "a weird feeling of being suddenly deaf" and with legs "so numb that he could hardly feel the earth," and his jealousy and anger combine to blind him to his sensory surroundings until he returns to town to awaken new visions in Agnes (17). "God's Ravens" presents this process in even clearer terms. Rob, a writer who arrives in Wisconsin from Chicago to live the picturesque life, keeps the community at a distance, and this social detachment becomes literalized as physical dislocation when he falls ill on his way home from the post office: "He felt blind for a moment," and "the world of vivid green grew gray, and life receded from him into an illimitable distance" (*Main-Travelled Roads*, 208). When he awakens, nursed back to health by the townspeople, he "feel[s] his body as if it were an alien thing," and this newfound awareness of his physical self—of himself as physical—readies him to take in the visual world. The farmer William McTurg turns him toward the window, and "a new part of the good old world burst on his sight. The sunshine streamed in the windows through a waving screen of lilac leaves and fell upon the carpet in a priceless flood of radiance" (209). As stylized as such chromatic descriptions are, as much as they invoke the "pure" hues of aestheticism, they always point to an embodied and grounded interaction.

The evolutionary trends that placed perception in the body landed language there as well, and aestheticians such as Véron pursued the idea that words form connections with other sensations in the complex networks of the nervous system. This integrated image of language strengthened Garland's conviction that the constructions of literary art could intensify one's contact with the physical environment. As Véron argued, literary impressions achieve "a successful mingling of ideas and sensations" (350), and in Garland's hands this meant that writing should render the multifaceted aspects of social life in a linguistic form that, through reading, might be felt. In the evolutionary attitude expressed in impressionist method and echoed in veritism, even mediations can be immediately experienced; even intellectual operations are embodied. In "A Branch Road," Garland narrates "a strange and powerful feeling of the passage of time" that takes hold in Will as he returns home; the "vague feeling" combines with the rustling leaves and the song of the birds, and the ensemble pulses within the mind's recesses: "It was a feeling hardly to be expressed in words—one of those emotions whose springs lie far back in the brain" (26). Garland likened the process of conveying this aggregate feeling to the artistic technique of painting "the *effect* of leaves upon the eye." In his essay "Literary Prophecy," he proclaimed that the "novel of the future . . . will teach, as all earnest literature has done, by effect; but it will not be by direct expression, but by placing before the reader the facts of life as they stand related to the artist." This set of relations, perceived and communicated as an integrated impression, "will not be put in the explanatory notes" as in a social treatise; instead, it "will address itself to the perception of the reader" (*Crumbling Idols,* 42–43). It will be felt.

An impression so expanded changes the context and method of composition. After all, a writer does not capture the rhythm of conversation while holding a discussion nor render the drama of a political crisis from amid the rally. Literature is not written *en plein air,* and even though Garland incorporated his sketch work into his narratives, he did much of his writing away from the scenes of his stories. This insertion of distance has long occupied critics of regionalism and local color writing, and its presence in Garland's work has been variously treated as part of an imperialist logic, a cosmopolitan vantage, and an analysis of regional writing's complicity in exploitative markets.[58] But as the stories and journalistic writing make clear, Garland brings local views into contact with outsider standpoints to explore the workings of individual perceptions, which remain inaccessible to the perceiver. This method stays true to his veritism by keeping all perspectives embedded and at the same time uses the mode of one perception to gain purchase on another, and vice versa. In "Up the Coolly," Howard McLane's urbane detachment sees elements of the landscape invisible to his brother Grant; Rob's dinner preparations in "Among the Corn-Rows" prevent him from seeing the "wealth of color" Seagraves celebrates in the prairie; and Julia, in the same story, must break from her fieldwork before gazing at "the sea of deep-green" before her (*Main-Travelled Roads,* 100). In each of these cases, "hard life, toil, lack of leisure, have deadened and calloused the perceiving mind" and crippled the potential of local art (*Crumbling Idols,* 16). Garland the critic called for a literature immersed in the soil, but in his short stories he recognized the need for an outside perspective, one able to enter the landscape and open itself to the physical and social impressions of a region. Only then could the writer feel the world as it coalesces around a rural community, and only then might those feelings gain an articulation closed off to the laborer.

To this end, Garland's narrative voice jumps among the various perspectives presented in a story, dipping into free indirect discourse only to jerk back to a wider, yet always limited, viewpoint. This slippery mode of narration allows him to mine the felt experience of his characters without relinquishing the flexibility afforded by an aesthetic distance. The end of "Salt Water Day," Garland's journalistic report about the holiday crowds at the Jersey shore, suggests the rewards of such a technique: "What a picture to take back to their hot and ungracious farms! . . . That this scene sinks deep into their starved souls I know, for I have been a toiler in the harvest fields. . . . Their enjoyment is dumb, shy of expression, almost inarticulate; but they perceive the beautiful, after all, and its effects are as lasting as granite."[59] The beachgoers sense their surroundings with aesthetic delight, but they are unable to give their impressions voice. The veritist works by realizing these impressions in prose and presenting them as literary effects to be activated in the reading experience—linguistic lenses akin to the "blue-shadow idea" that lights up the gray landscape.

In "Homestead and Its Perilous Trades: Impressions of a Visit" (1894), another of his journalistic pieces, Garland directs his color descriptions toward sensitizing his readers to the harmful social conditions centered in the iron mills of western Pennsylvania. The article mixes aestheticized depictions of the furnaces (their "mighty up-soaring of saffron and sapphire flame" that strikes "a magnificent contrast to the dusky purple of the great smoky roofs below") and condemnations of the material and social damage wrought by the iron industry (which "lay like a cancer on the breast of the human body").[60] The aesthetic and the social are not kept separate here; instead, the "blushes of beautiful orange and rose amid the blue" in the sunset over Homestead facilitate a felt connection of presence with the environment, of being a body within the body of the world, that Garland saw as a source of both artistic achievement and social well-being. "Salt-Water Day" takes this tangle of self and world as its focus, detailing the "barbarism of color" that connects the clothing, sky, waves, and wares into one chromatic scene.[61] By focusing on a collective experience or set of impressions that are tied to a singular social experience, these reports occupy a middle ground between the color sketches, which concentrate on perception alone, and the short stories, which put many perspectives into play.

Garland's stories use narrative to reveal how perceptual modes are activated and arranged within a social context. When Howard in "Up the Coolly" comes back to Wisconsin after years working in the theater, he sees the landscape with the "dreaming eyes" of one who returns. The "greens [were] fresher, the grain more golden" to Howard "than to anyone else, for he was coming back to it all after an absence of ten years" (45). It is through these dreaming eyes that we see a sunset that could have been pulled right out of Garland's notebooks:

> A few scattering clouds were drifting on the west wind, their shadows sliding down the green and purpled slopes. The dazzling sunlight flamed along the luscious velvety grass, and shot amid the rounded, distant purple peaks, and streamed in bars of gold and crimson across the blue mist of the narrower upper Coollies. (49)

Howard's heart "swell[s]" at the sight—but the older man driving him home, who also gazes with "a far-off, dreaming look," is "silent": "He gazed at the scene which had repeated itself a thousand times in his life, but of whose beauty he never spoke" (49). Among other questions, the story asks what merit, if any, Howard's aesthetic perception has for those who live and labor in the land, and how, if at all, it might give voice to these "silent" observers. For Garland knew the dangers of presuming to speak for someone else. When Howard, in a later scene, remarks on the beauty of the country, the locals fall quiet: "There was only dead silence to this touching upon the idea of beauty" (74).

Grant, the brother who stayed on the farm, inhabits the countryside very differently than his aesthete brother. When Howard watches "the falling sun stream[ing] in broad banners across the valley" and enjoys "the pleasant tangle of sound" made by the cowbells and katydids, Grant trudges out in "ill-smelling clothes and great boots that chafed his feet" to "milk the cows,—on whose legs the flies and mosquitos swarmed, bloated with blood" (69). To imagine how these two views might intersect, or how the former could benefit the latter, Garland turns again to painting, this time to a scene of agricultural labor by Jean-François Millet. The image gives Howard an insight into the different conditions shaping his brother's life and demeanor, and it presents the reader with the first in a series of aesthetic mediations of the farmer's toil. At times such mediations seem as if they can only distort; Howard, watching Grant walk out to the pasture, muses that "the poet who writes of milking the cows does it from the hammock, looking on" (69). Yet Garland also insists that Grant's view is impoverished and that the mediating frameworks of aesthetics can be pathways to the real. "Up the Cooly" ties color perceptions to social positions to inquire after art's ability to contribute to the political reform projects that pushed Garland to write in the first place.

At the end of the story, Howard has yet to find the words that could give voice to the inarticulate material relations that dim the color vision of the Wisconsin farmers; the tragedy of the story is in no small part a tragedy of failed communication. In other texts, Garland framed this concern with what and how literature communicates by investigating *tone* as an important register in the expressive capacities of speech. His color sketches often betray an anxiety about casting vision into words. For instance, a notebook entry from 1886 records a sunset that generates "an indescribable color neither pink nor purple," and in *Rose of Dutcher's Cooly* (1895) a stirring scene appeals to Rose "with a power which transcended words."[62] Moments of "unnamable" vision weave throughout Garland's prose, and yet the very quality that defies description—color— lies open to language through the register of tone. The veritist, Garland wrote, "aims to be perfectly true in his delineation of his relation to life, but there is a tone, a color, which comes unconsciously into his utterance" (*Crumbling Idols,* 43). Here metaphorical color marks the felt relation of the perceiver to the perceived, the qualitative *how* of vision that the veritist-impressionist refuses to exclude. Garland's stories examine the affordances and limitations that tone introduces as a means of communication. For example, at the end of "A Branch Road," when Will asks Agnes to leave her life of toil and join him in the East, his "vibrant voice call[s] up" "emotion" through the submerged registers of tone that recall the blue shadows of Garland's color work: "Then she heard his words beneath his voice somehow, and they produced pictures that dazzled her. Luminous shadows moved before her eyes, driving across the gray background of her poor, starved, work-weary life" (41–42). Will's speech becomes a magic lantern, casting colorful visions onto the barren walls of Agnes's house—a figure for Garland's own blend of aestheticized local color and reform fiction.

Garland's fiction mobilized his impressionist method to draw out both the local colors that distinguished particular perspectives and the cultural forces that dimmed them, either through backbreaking labor or through the cultural homogenization bred by economic centralization. He wrote not only to register difference but to extend differences, and in so doing he formulated a vision of America that resists the unifying, essence-based version of the nation that critics of regionalist fiction have taken for granted. In Garland's work, America is an open and evolving network of fragmentary locales, a shifting composite that varies with the play of its parts. In this regard, only local color fiction could aspire to be truly national precisely because it alone eschewed the project of speaking for everyone in favor of crafting a localized perspective that embraced its finitude, its embeddedness, as the conditions under which it contributed to an emergent and fluctuating nation. Garland insisted that "local color means national character" (*Crumbling Idols,* 53). In fiction, it is "the native element, the *differentiating* element," the qualities of a style that forge an individual perception not from a pre-set difference but through a process of differentiation (49; emphasis mine). Such attunement to difference marked "the test of a national literature," a literature that would be borne not by "an over-topping personality" but by "a multitude of loving artists" whose efforts unfolded "the intimate social, individual life of the nation" (26, 62). Individual life is always social, Garland asserted; like a color, it involves more than itself. Therefore, not until "individualism" becomes "the coloring element of a literature" will there "be association of equals" (120). Democracy must be colorful.

We can now see why Garland clung to the phrase "local color," and why critics lose much when they abandon it for the anachronistic "regionalism." A writer attuned to the interplay of visual and literary concepts, Garland found in color a technique for addressing a knotty set of aesthetic and political problems about representation, identity, and the uses of a national literature. In his comments on impressionism, he praised the shifting, relational hues of Monet and Renoir as the visual indexes of our perceptual openness to the environment, and his stories investigate the complexities of this openness as it unfolds among the exigencies of a particular social space. They render the individuating colors of the Midwest in order to foster a national literature made up of interlocking perspectives and impressions. Throughout his early work, he inverts the absolute local color of nineteenth-century painting into a relational local color, in which place and identity alike are networked and singular, qualitatively distinct and yet not self-contained.

In grappling with the painterly problematic of the relation between artistic techniques and empirical reality, and specifically by channeling this question through evolution, Garland established a relational framework for understanding both color perception and its aesthetic figurations that holds, with modifications, for all the major figures in *Chromographia*. Even though contemporary criticism treats Garland as a minor player in the development of regionalist writing, his reconfiguration of the local through color shifted the course of early-twentieth-century writing about place toward his own interests in perceptual experience. As one critic wrote in 1907, "It is not really for the sake of describing a locality that local color is given, but for the sake of showing how that place or certain attributes of it can be impressed upon the consciousness of a beholder and transcribed by him."[63] "Color" remained a metaphor in such writing, but after Garland the tenor of that metaphor changed from denoting details of a particular locale to conveying the qualitative experiences that link those details to a perceiver: the "colors," for instance, of Theodore Dreiser's *Colors of a Great City* (1923), a collection of New York sketches that exhibit no special interest in sight over other senses. Likewise, Garland's investment in the perceptual processes that cocreate self and world found an echo in regionalists of the 1920s such as Austin, who made the task of expressing the distinct features of a regional environment inseparable from that of presenting "the intensity and solidarity of experience *while it is passing.*"[64] Even writers not classed as "regionalist" or "local colorist" per se but who nonetheless shared a commitment to communicating the unique feelings of a place and time—including many modernist poets and the novelists who sought to capture the energies of Harlem in the 1920s—inherited Garland's blend of literal and figurative color, his way of connecting to location through perception. When William Carlos Williams claimed to dispense with the "beautiful illusion" by stirring his reader's feeling of the "eternal moment in which we alone live," he may have had postimpressionist and cubist painters in mind, but he was extending a tradition of aesthetic education crystallized in Garland's appropriations of impressionism.[65]

Yet "place" need not be so big. Though Garland cared most for the colors of the landscape, and though his specific political concerns led him to emphasize the field and the factory more than the parlor, his understanding of the human as shaped through physical activities within an environment applied equally well to the closer spaces of the home. Just as geographical region affects perception, so too does the arrangement of a room, the floor plan of a house, even the color on a wallpaper. And because such environments can be easily and often modified—requiring only a fresh coat of paint and a day of redecorating—they encouraged the utopian hope that a remodeled domestic interior could produce a renovated psychological interior. Such dreams drove the design reform project at the end of the nineteenth century, in both its aestheticist and progressive incarnations. And so to follow the implications of Garland's literary hues, we must turn from local colors to household decoration, from the canvases of art to the walls on which they were hung, from Garland's unlikely mix of politics and aesthetics to the equally improbable conjunction of progressive reform and avant-garde abstraction in Charlotte Perkins Gilman.

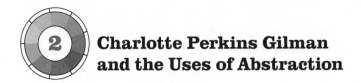

Charlotte Perkins Gilman
and the Uses of Abstraction

We know that Charlotte Perkins Gilman chafed under the label "literature." When William Dean Howells asked to reprint her story "The Yellow Wall-Paper" (1892) in what would become *The Great Modern American Short Stories: An Anthology* (1920), she consented, but with this caveat: the story "was no more 'literature' than my other stuff, being definitely written 'with a purpose.'"[1] Gilman here seems to draw a bright line between her own aesthetic efforts and the celebrations of "art for art's sake" associated with late-nineteenth-century figures such as Oscar Wilde and James McNeill Whistler, as well as their modernist descendants. Whatever techniques she employed, whatever narrative scenes she invented, whatever arts she admired were aimed at advancing her progressive project of reforming the unequal configurations of sexual difference that shaped women's lives and labor. What, then, are we to make of her excited notice, published in the *Forerunner* just a few years before the invitation from Howells, about a "color concert," a performance of colored lights projected onto a gauze curtain, with no figurative content and no obvious reference to the social or even the material world? What sort of "purpose" could Gilman have attached to an art of abstract colored lights?

The occasion for Gilman's enthusiasm was a 1915 performance in New York of Alexander Scriabin's modernist symphony *Prometheus: The Poem of Fire* (1910), a performance made notable by the debut of the Chromola, a type of color organ. This instrument, designed by Preston S. Millar of Edison Testing Laboratories specifically for the event, followed a special portion of Scriabin's score to produce "light harmonies" that bathed a curtain behind the orchestra with shifting, varying hues.[2] Novelty notwithstanding, the reviews of the concert were overwhelmingly bad—but you would never glean that from Gilman's notice. She fairly glows about the prospects of "color music" and even tries to position herself as the art's unsung founder. Her article opens, "At last it has come, the beginnings at least, of an art I have longed for and invented (on paper) since childhood." After quick mention of Scriabin and a prominent book on the topic by Alexander Wallace Rimington, she outlines her own recommendations for how this art should proceed, both with and without musical accompaniment:

> For piano music the color effect should be in rippling showers, like the fall of rocket lights. For the organ, in soft rushing waves, as of lit wind-driven clouds. Then it should be done by itself, in darkened theaters, on a whole proscenium curtain of deep gauze, with such dim form effects—sheets, flashes, drops, flickering waves and darts—as the composer called for. We shall have it yet![3]

We shall have it yet? Gilman's excitement adds a wrinkle to the usual accounts of color music. Histories of this art treat it as a moment in the development of nonfigurative painting, an experiment motivated by Whistler's visual "symphonies" and Walter Pater's dictum "All art constantly aspires to the condition of music."[4] They place *Prometheus* and Rimington alongside Kandinsky's forays into abstraction and Loïe Fuller's chromatically illuminated serpentine dance. Gilman, needless to say, is never invoked. Yet her obvious interest in color music—she incorporated it into two short stories and reasserted her claim to have invented it in her 1935 autobiography—prompts us to reconsider the politics and aesthetics of color in the Progressive Era, such that we can understand how a writer with a focused social purpose not only championed the aesthetic of supposedly "pure" hues but also incorporated them into her own work.[5] Accounting for Gilman's excited comments on color music, then, involves reassessing both the role of abstract color in modernism and the narrative setup for which Gilman is most widely known and to which she returned several times: a woman staring at moving colors on a flat surface.

Pursuit of the aesthetic possibilities of abstract color—color considered apart from particular objects or outlines—extended well beyond color music and the avant-garde to include the reform objectives of interior designers and home decorators. What mattered in each case was the potential for creating psychological effects through chromatic arrangements.

Despite their differences, U.S. designers and European aesthetes agreed that, as Wilde put it, "mere colour, unspoiled by meaning, and unallied with definite form, can speak to the soul in a thousand different ways." Under this dispensation the task of the artist or decorator was to manipulate color to influence "mood and temperament," often beneath the notice of observers.[6] Yet conjuring color responses required more than a well-tuned palette; for interior designers, it also depended on the inhabitant's ability to feel and be affected by a room—it demanded a quickened color sense. Home decorators warned that this sense had been so long neglected that people didn't even register the harmful effects wrought by the discordant colors marring their interiors. The introduction of cheap and brightly colored wallpapers, textiles, and furnishings to a buying public woefully uneducated in the principles of chromatic harmony threatened to create a dangerous spiral in which weak perceptual capabilities yielded poorly colored goods, which in turn crippled color sensitivity even more. Rimington, who saw color music as a tonic for this trouble, blamed audiences' resistance to his abstract compositions on their "general insensitiveness to colour" and emphasized the "urgent need for cultivation of the colour sense."[7] Wilde in his own way concurred, quipping that "a colour-sense is more important, in the development of the individual, than a sense of right and wrong."[8] During the decades of their emergence, the arts of pure color—those that aimed to use color alone as their primary aesthetic medium—made regular appeals to the color sense and its significance for individual, even national, improvement. "We shall have it yet!"

Gilman makes an excellent guide through the meanings and uses of pure color at the turn of the twentieth century. Like Wilde, she belonged to that signal moment in the history of Western art when color became detached from figuration and was deployed as a psychological stimulant in its own right. Yet in her opposition to aestheticism, the movement through which this history has almost always been written, she reveals an understudied but pervasive understanding of the political and aesthetic potential of pure color. For Gilman, as for the design theorists she would have encountered when training at the Rhode Island School of Design and for the color musicians she admired in the 1910s, color promised to stimulate the languishing color sense and to fix attention on the imbrication of self and environment theorized in Lamarckian social thought and exemplified in home decoration. If a color sense was indeed more important than a sense of right and wrong, it was not because aesthetics stood apart from morals but, rather, because the perception of color and other sensory qualities had an ethical valence: *how* one saw color—be it with subtle aesthetic feeling, overwhelmed awe, or an increasingly insane fixation on the particular tints of yellow on a wallpaper—expressed the sort of person one was. Color sensitivity bespoke psychological health, nervous strength, and mental character, all organized within a hierarchy of "civilization" that, for Gilman, made chromatic experience a ready tool both for dramatizing the forces that rendered white women "primitive" and for the reforms that might modernize them. The color sense gave pure color a purpose.

Gilman put this purpose to work in her fictional figurations of color perception, which embraced the same model of organism–environment relations that Hamlin Garland and the impressionists located in color, but with an added twist. Whereas impressionists struggled to present an accurate and objective rendering of the moment of perception, without refining or passing judgment on that perception, Gilman sought to convey the social conditions and cognitive habits that give a perception its unique quality. Her stories take up Garland's project of embedding the immediacies of the color sketch into a narrative, where characters' varied color perceptions indicate distinct and unequal positions within the social world (the worn-down farmer versus the East Coast dandy, the neurasthenic housewife versus the male doctor or female artist). She wanted to *change* environments and the impressions they made, not simply record them. Doing so meant turning from the natural to the "man-made world," as she put it in one of her titles; it meant joining decorators and color musicians, even painters like Whistler, in using color to create aesthetic atmospheres capable of organizing and directing sensory life.[9] Turning first to design discourse, and later to color music, Gilman enlisted the aesthetics of pure color to imagine how art intervenes in the tangle of activity and receptivity that links self and environment, inhabitant and house, reader and text. She transferred Garland's careful attention to the nuances of perception into the controlled spaces of domestic parlors and concert halls, where they registered not just the present moment but the acts of aesthetic construction that define and sustain how that moment is felt.

Primitive Color Vision

About two-thirds of the way through "The Yellow Wall-Paper," the narrator, who by this point is well on her way to madness, relates a discovery that she has made in the long hours of staring at the faded, peeling wallpaper lining the room of her confinement. "There is one marked peculiarity about this paper," she declares, "a thing nobody seems to notice but myself, and that is that it changes as the light changes."[10] Gilman's critics, too, have been slow to notice the changing colors on the wall, the way the yellow quivers between a greenish "sulfur" and a "lurid" yellow-orange as the sun and the moon cast their varying lights through the room's many windows. Instead of focusing on this play of light, most readings of the color in Gilman's famous story have attempted to tie the eponymous yellow to some historical or psychological referent. The array of yellows on offer is vast: cultural options include yellow journalism and the Yellow Peril; aesthetic alternatives range from the wallpapers of William Morris and the yellow-backed books of French Decadence to the sunflower in Oscar Wilde's lapel; and psychoanalytic possibilities include shades of "saturated urine" and of "a child's feces" that mark a "fear of motherhood."[11] This diversity of critical hues responds largely to Susan Lanser's 1989 argument that "in privileging the questions of reading and writing as essential 'woman questions,'" the feminist criticism that revived Gilman's story "has been led to the [wall]paper while suppressing the politically charged adjective that colors it."[12] And to be sure, elaborations of the various political and historical charges that energize the yellow have enriched Gilman scholarship by adding a recognition of her eugenic nationalism to the initial emphasis on feminist interpretation and textuality.[13] These critical efforts have nonetheless been limited by their monochromatic focus. Gilman's politics of color has always been treated as a politics of yellow.

Yet the marked peculiarity of the paper is that its colors shift with the light, or rather that the narrator's perception of these colors does not stay the same, that the quality of attention she brings to her surroundings changes as the story develops. The emphasis is less on a particular hue and more on the movements of perception. Gilman invests her yellow with a political charge not by using it as a symbolic stand-in for some cultural phenomenon but by figuring the debilitating conditions of the "rest cure"—and of the adherence to a thoroughgoing belief in sexual difference that made such a cure seem reasonable—through the narrator's increasingly vivid and unhinged descriptions of color experience. The question is not Why yellow?, but Why color perception? Why use a character's response to the colors of a room to dramatize the psychological effects of a particular social arrangement? To answer this question, we must situate the hues of the story within turn-of-the-century discussions about color perception in general, not just the historical meanings or uses of yellow. Such a broadened scope does not simply reveal the affinities that "The Yellow Wall-Paper" has to Gilman's other stories about color perception, stories that celebrate the therapeutic effects of colors properly arranged; it also attunes us to the Progressive-Era pursuit of capturing color's sensory force to diagnose as well as shape human perceptual capacities.[14]

Over the course of the nineteenth century, the perception and enjoyment of color came to bear an unprecedented moral weight as a sign of individual and national health. Two key ideas help explain this link. First, as psychologists and psychophysicists honed the procedures and instruments for measuring sensory responses, they detected a more significant variation from individual to individual than expected, leading them to accentuate the role of the "personal equation" in perception.[15] Color had been considered an observer-dependent quality since the seventeenth century—but the observers in question had been assumed to be largely uniform, without notable discrepancies from person to person. Modern psychology raised the specter of radically subjective color. Once measured, that is, the difference between Peter's red and Paul's red laid the groundwork for the serious consideration that perhaps Peter's red is actually Paul's green. Studies in color blindness and animal color vision further revealed the fascinating varieties of chromatic experience, such that by 1890 it seemed almost intuitive to suggest that each person enjoyed a unique relation to the world's colors.

Within this new pluralism, not all subjective color visions were considered equal. The variety implied by the personal equation was sifted through the categories of progress and degeneration that marked the nineteenth-century discourse on civilization. Here then is the second idea involved in making color perception a morally loaded activity: color experiences located an individual within hierarchies of race and sex, expressed as a matter of nervous organization. As Kyla Schuller argues in *The Biopolitics of Feeling,* Lamarckian thinkers in the nineteenth-century

United States held that sensitivity to environmental stimuli varied from race to race and that, as a consequence, one's ability to feel and respond to sensory impressions—one's "impressibility"—determined whether one was regressing from or progressing toward a civilized state. White bodies were held to be the most responsive to their surroundings and thus the most capable of evolutionary adaptation into the future; the bodies of "savages" and people of color were supposed to have sluggish or deadened sensitivity, a flaw that marked them as doomed for extinction.[16] Art historian Natasha Eaton has shown that nineteenth-century studies of color blindness and other forms of abnormal color vision perpetuated this framework through the belief that "the attentive examiner could discern the candidate's intelligence and moral character" by "detecting his chromatic sense." Indeed, the leading European authority on color blindness, Frithiof Holmgren, pursued his topic in the belief that color-blind persons were "*les viciés*—the polluted," a "dreamy, inattentive and effete" lot whose impaired responsiveness separated them from civilization's vanguard.[17] Not that all attributions of the color sense fell along this neat trajectory—color blindness was most common among white men, and Gilman was not alone in worrying that white women inhabited a "primitive" state—but nonetheless a supposed link between nervousness and civilization pervaded the period's thinking about chromatic experience. If, as one critic remarked in 1901, psychology had made "the sense of colour . . . a matter of nerves," then the concept of impressibility tied color sensitivity to the politics of sensation.[18]

When Gilman reached for a way to depict the disastrous effects of S. Weir Mitchell's rest cure for neurasthenic women, she landed on these links between color and character, understood variously in physiological, moral, and psychological terms. As a "matter of nerves," color was also a matter of nervousness. The French neurologist Jean-Martin Charcot used colored disks in his experiments with hysterical female patients, finding that the "highly sensitive and pathological state of the nervous system" in his subjects made them acutely responsive to the emotional force of colors.[19] At around the same time, physicians attempted to harness the power of color exhibited in Charcot's patients to cure those suffering from nervous disorders. Dr. Ponza, director of the asylum at Alessandria in Italy, proposed treating insanity with a bath of blue light, and in the 1870s periodicals as diverse as *Scientific American, Forest and Stream,* and *Harper's Bazaar* weighed in on the "blue-glass craze."[20] Similarly, in *The Principles of Light and Color* (1878) Edwin Babbitt claimed to have reinvigorated a "worn out man of business" using red light and eased digestion troubles with yellow, all by implementing his discovery that some colors "animate" the nerves while others "cool" them.[21] Variations on chromotherapy persisted into the 1910s, when doctors placed shell-shocked soldiers from the Great War in the "colour-cure ward" (and even today a quick internet search will turn up dozens of websites advising readers on which colors to use in their homes to soothe their stressed-out nerves).[22] Whether as a sign of nervousness or its cure, color promised physicians, quacks, and neurologists alike access to a patient's mental health.

Nineteenth-century art critics made analogous claims about color in painting, drawing on the same concepts of nervous degeneration. In his influential screed *Degeneration* (1892), Max Nordau attributed the pathological sensitivity that Charcot located in hysterical women to modern artists. Whereas Garland praised impressionists for "paint[ing] with nature's colors—red, blue, and yellow," Nordau treated this restricted palette as a symptom of a color sense reduced to its most basic receptors.[23] He wrote off the blurry scenes on Monet's canvases as the result of "*nystagmus,* or trembling of the eyeball"; he invoked "clinical observation" to align "color mysticism" with "mental decay"; and he quoted Italian criminologist and social-Darwinist Cesare Lombroso to nominate "the colour-sense" as the "predominate attribute" of modern painters, not as a term of praise but as a way of bemoaning the withering of rational content in art.[24] Less strident, perhaps, but no less insistent, Ruskin warned readers of *The Elements of Drawing* (1857), "Your power of colouring depends much on your state of health and balance of mind; when you are fatigued or ill, you will not see colours well." What holds for the individual, he continued, was doubly true for the nation: "Though not infallibly a test of character in individuals, colour power is a great sign of mental health in nations; when they are in state of intellectual decline, their colouring always gets dull."[25] The tonalist painter Charles Walter Stetson, best known as Gilman's first husband, echoed Ruskin in an article published three months before "The Yellow Wall-Paper": "In the decay of the artist's color sense you must always find inevitably recorded the decay of his mind and the weakening of his soul," he proclaimed; "color is an angel who records with pitiless exactness any change in us."[26]

Stetson's comments could serve as an epigraph for Gilman's tale of the degeneration brought on by the rest cure. In "The Yellow Wall-

Paper," the "decay" of the narrator's mind is presented through the contortions of her color sense, rendered through the "marked peculiarity"
of the paper: the way it changes with the light. "When the sun shoots in
through the east window . . . it changes so quickly that I never can quite
believe it," the narrator remarks; "by moonlight . . . I wouldn't know it
was the same paper" (139). Her fascinated attention to a shifting display
of sensory particulars—and her increasing inability to separate herself
from them—provide the material for her fabrication of the imprisoned
woman behind the paper's pattern: "At night in any kind of light, in twilight, candlelight, lamplight, and worst of all by moonlight, [the pattern]
becomes bars!"; "by daylight [the woman] is subdued"; "in the very bright
spots she keeps still, and in the very shady spots she takes hold of the
bars and shakes them hard" (139, 141). Her narrative grows out of her
overly sensitive mode of perception.

Lest we mistake such acute attention for the "pure perception" of an
artist—something akin to the habitless eye thrilling to "strange dyes,
strange colours" and every little "stirring of the senses" that Pater celebrates in the conclusion to *The Renaissance*—Gilman describes the
movement that draws light and observer together as *creeping*. As literary
critic Dana Seitler has argued, the term is loaded with connotations of
atavism.[27] While watching the moonlight creep "so slowly" on "that un-
dulating wallpaper," the narrator takes on the qualities of the interaction:
she watches "till [she] felt creepy" (138). By the story's end, the creeping
light infuses not only the pattern and the imagined woman behind the
wallpaper's design but also the narrator herself, as she circles the room
"creep[ing]" over her collapsed husband. Gilman connects this atavistic reversion to the intensification of color: each round of creeping adds
to the "smooch" that transforms the patterned paper into a murky color
field, and when the journal conceit collapses, signaling the breakdown
of the self, the narrator's madness manifests as a fixation on hue. She
justifies her fear of being taken outside by explaining, "Outside you have
to creep on the ground, and everything is green instead of yellow" (144).
Like Charcot's patients or Nordau's aesthetes, Gilman's narrator loses
her mind as she slips into color.

Yet we would be amiss to think that Gilman eschewed the aesthetic
enjoyment of colors or thought that responsiveness to chromatic effects
posed an inherent threat. The problem, instead, had to do with the difference between an appreciation of color as a *general* quality and the

immersion in its sensory particularity. What Pater regarded as a fault—the tendency "to form habits" and make mental generalizations that organize perceptual experience—Gilman valorized as a mark of the civilized, enshrined in language. In *Women and Economics* (1898), she illustrated her idea that "it is easier to personalize than to generalize" by analyzing the vocabulary of "savages":

> There are savages who can say "hot fire," "hot stone," "hot water," but cannot say "heat," cannot think it. Similarly, they can say "good man," "good knife," "good meat"; but they cannot say "goodness," they cannot think it. They have observed specific instances, but they are unable to collate them, to generalize therefrom.[28]

Gilman's reasoning rehearses the two premises of the ethnographic color sense: that language offers a transparent window into perceptual experience, and that the quality of that experience varies along the continuum of civilization. Like other social-evolutionary thinkers, including Herbert Spencer, E. B. Tylor, G. Stanley Hall, and Lewis Henry Morgan, she arrayed racial groups along a single trajectory from primitive to civilized and marked progress through facility with—and delight in—generalizing thought.[29] And while Gilman used "heat" and "goodness" to prove her point, others appealed to color terms. Grant Allen speculated that "primitive man in his very earliest stages [would] have no colour terms whatsoever," for such a person would instead speak only of "concrete objects."[30] And Albert Gatschet of the U.S. Geological Survey reported observing this phenomenon among the Klamath Indians, who had only one word to designate the hue of a local plant, even though "the plant passes from the green of spring time and summer into the faded yellow of autumn."[31] The color term remained tightly tied to the object.

On the basis of linguistic differences, especially the presence or absence of words designating hue, ethnographers at the end of the nineteenth century speculated on what it might be like to see like a savage. The jump from words to sensitivity had been a central part of color-sense discourse since William Gladstone's readings of Homer, but at the turn of the twentieth century the burgeoning field of anthropology tackled these philological questions using a combination of visual and linguistic tests on non-Westerners. The Cambridge ethnographer and neurologist W. H. R. Rivers, who later specialized in treating the damaged nerves of British soldiers during the Great War, joined the discipline-defining expedition to the Torres Strait to settle the Gladstone controversy. And though he found that the tribesmen of Papua New Guinea could, when asked, make perceptual distinctions as well as any European, he could not shake the belief that because his subjects used the same term for "blue" and "dark"—because "the brilliant blue of the sky received from [them] the same name as the deepest black"—they must not experience the perceptual difference in the same way or with the same salience as civilized observers.[32]

The ambiguity packed into the phrase "color sense" allowed the locus of what Rivers termed "primitive color vision" to shift from a difference in discriminating power ("sense" denoting sensation) to a difference in how such chromatic discriminations are *felt* ("sense" denoting sensibility). In this context the ability not only to see colors but to enjoy them *for their own sake,* with the intensity attributed to aesthetic experience, served as a defining feature of advanced color sensitivity, the culmination of its evolution from food detector to a source of the most refined pleasures. For Grant Allen (as well as for such like-minded Spencerian thinkers as Gilman), "The purest form of disinterested love for mere colour" was exhibited only by observers with sufficient powers of generalization to pull color away from its objects (249). The narrator of "The Yellow Wall-Paper," of course, is anything but disinterested, and when Gilman set out to convey the mental qualities of a mind ruined by Mitchell's treatment she broke color from its pure visual modality to emphasize this dissolution of sensory boundaries: the yellow is tactile and material (it "stained everything it touched"), as well as olfactory and diffuse (as a "yellow smell" it pervades the house) (140, 141). No less than Rivers or Allen, Gilman turned to chromatic quality to imagine how it feels to be savage.

Or rather, she turned to color to imagine how it feels to be *made* savage. For unlike the ethnographers, Gilman wanted not only to identify sensory differences but also to reform them. Color offered her an aesthetic tool capable of picturing the social conditions that, in her words, reduced women to a station more "primitive" than that of men (*Women and Economics,* 330–31). Her primary target was the middle-class household. In *The Home: Its Work and Influence* (1903), she argued that turn-of-the-century domestic arrangements restricted women "to a primitive, a savage plane of occupation," which also manifested in "an equally savage plane of aesthetic taste."[33] Such comments support what Seitler and other critics have argued at length: that Gilman advanced her feminism by embracing whiteness, along with the social-evolutionary schema that put it on top.[34] The reason for sexual equality, by this logic, was that white women needed to be healthy if they were to give birth to the next generation of the race. And healthiness entailed an organized nervous sensibility: a generalizing mind and a body able to master sensations. But as Gilman detailed in book after book, the demands of domestic chores stripped the housewife of such powers. "As a common law of mental action," Gilman wrote in *Women and Economics,* "the power to observe and retain an individual impression marks a lower degree of development than the power to classify and collate impressions and make generalizations therefrom" (81). The problem with housework was that it forced women to attend to a range of distinct tasks, each of which required minute attention to detail, with the result that their ability to extract themselves from immediate sensory experience was curtailed. Working within such circumstances, the housewife had to "adjust, disadjust, and readjust her mental focus a thousand times a day; not only to things, but to actions; not only to actions, but to persons; and so, to live at all, she must develop a kind of mind that does *not object to discord.*"[35]

In "Through This," an 1893 short story that critics have called the "prequel" to "The Yellow Wall-Paper," Gilman vividly renders this "kind of mind."[36] The narrative returns to the scene of shifting colors on a wall to illustrate the "primitive" conditions of domestic labor—but this time Gilman figures color not as a direct indication of the narrator's sensory conditions but as a perceptual balm for tired nerves. The story presents a day in the mental life of a housewife as she prepares meals, mends clothing, buys groceries, tucks in the kids, and—most notably—begins and ends her day by watching the sun's colors "creep" along her "bedroom wall." The narrative is tightly focalized through the unnamed protagonist, tracking her thoughts as they jerk from task to task and as they repeatedly attempt—and fail—to imagine the place of her labor within the wider social world. (Several times the narrator begins to formulate the larger significance of her actions—"through this I might . . ."—and each time her thoughts are interrupted.)

The most striking formal feature of this short text, however, is not the abruptness of its transitions, the shortness of its sentences, or the other techniques used to convey the narrator's tottering interiority; rather, it is the nearly symmetrical descriptions of the dawn and dusk colors that bookend the bustle of the day. The story begins, "The dawn colors creep up my bedroom wall, softly, slowly. Darkness, dim gray, dull blue, soft lavender, clear pink, pale yellow, warm gold—sunlight" (35). The almost liturgical tones of these sentences yield to casual descriptions of the day's chores before returning in the story's final lines:

> I'll go [to bed] now, if it is before dark—then get up early to-morrow and get the sweeping done. How loud the crickets are! The evening shades creep down my bedroom wall—softly—slowly.
>
> Warm gold—pale yellow—clear pink—soft lavender—dull blue—dim gray—darkness. (37)

Taken together, these two passages provide a rather self-conscious—even clumsy—frame for the narrative, clumsy because the tone of these sentences contrasts so sharply with what comes between them. Yet this clumsiness is precisely the issue: the narrator's daily routine has dulled her perceptual and cognitive faculties through the constant, chaotic strain of domestic work, and these meditative visions of the sun's shifting hues constitute desperate attempts at self-therapy. After all, with so many things to do (and with such an optimistic outlook on doing them), we would expect the narrator to rise early and work until her husband returns; instead, she seeks out these moments to bathe her eyes in the sunset, as if the regular progression of hues from outside the home might give order to her jumbled sensory life. Judging by the punctuation difference between the opening and the conclusion, her prospects are not good. Where the dawn colors come in ordered segments, separated by commas, the dusk comes in a rush, with the hues connected by the same dashes that elsewhere in the story signify interruptions and breaks. Very soon her ability to manage impressions will crumble; she will no longer object to discord.

Shifting yellows, creeping colors: Lamarckian social thought and the idea of an evolving color sense gave Gilman a framework for using the perception of abstract colors to indicate character. But her aim was not simply to diagnose pathologies. She sought instead to reveal the complicated imbrication of mental quality with social milieu, the subtle ways that physical space conditions movement and thus shapes the sensations, perceptions, and "kinds of mind" that an environment allows. Not yellow, not pure color, not even color response but color as a sign for the unnoticed yet momentous transactions between people and the material of their sensory surroundings is finally what motivated Gilman's depictions of chromatic experience. To model these relations, she turned to the hues of home decorating.

Interior Designs

The design reform movement drew directly from the discourse of civilization. If progress in social evolution meant replacing the so-called primitive fixation on individual things with a facility with generalizations, the reasoning went, then the Victorian interior, cluttered as it was with bric-a-brac and other objects, threatened to mire inhabitants in an insufficiently civilized state. What was needed was a style that promoted abstraction, one that offered visual support for "civilized" thinking. And so in place of the detailed and deceptive ornamentations popular in the previous century—lamps shaped like ostriches, wallpapers depicting classical views—reformers promoted stylized compositions of form and color as the proper domain of the decorative arts: conventionalization rather than illusionistic representation. The very well-being of inhabitants was at stake. "We do not want a soup-plate whose bottom seems to vanish in the distance," Wilde explained to American audiences during his 1882 lecture tour; "one feels neither safe nor comfortable under such conditions."[37]

Wilde's emphasis on how interior designs make people *feel* indicates the social ambitions of modern design that most appealed to Gilman: the hope that arrangements of abstract hues might facilitate healthy bodies and calm minds, that tired nerves might be rejuvenated and mental powers enhanced. Color here acts as a sign of the shifting seam that connects self to world, a figure for the relational entanglement of room and inhabitant no less than a tool for reconstructing it. Even as Gilman resisted the drive toward abstraction championed by Wilde, preferring instead to fold modernist techniques into realist narratives, she found in the colors of modern design a way of imagining how her literary writing could participate in her broader efforts at social reform. Her stories make tangible the subtle influence of environments, in the hopes that they could then be more easily manipulated.

Gilman's early training set her squarely amid the overlap of design reform and social-evolutionary thought. While at the Rhode Island School of Design (RISD) in the 1870s, she learned to treat decorative schemes as expressive of national or racial character through the study of "historical ornament," which presented students with the characteristic motifs and color preferences of ancient and Eastern civilizations.[38] And as an advertising artist for her cousin's soap company and an interior-design consultant for the Pasadena Opera House, she created chromatic compositions at the same time that design theorists began to celebrate abstract forms and colors for their ability to work directly on impressible nerves.[39] By the turn of the century, these two threads—color as sign of character and color as sensory force—had been twisted together in the discourse of modern design. As painter and scholar Denman Ross explained in a RISD lecture in 1903, design is "not the ornamentation of things" but a "mental activity," not "prettyfying things" but the creation and enjoyment of "order in human feeling and thought and in the many and varied activities by which that thought and feeling is [sic] expressed."[40] For Ross no less than the Gilman of "Through This," design reform meant sweeping away the disorder that crowded the mind in favor of filling the walls with clear and restful hues.

In his modernist polemic "Ornament and Crime" (1908), Austrian architect Adolf Loos gave spirited formulation to this gesture of moving forward by clearing out, making all too evident the way that design as "mental activity" drew on the affiliation of generalization and civilization. Loos's central claim, that *the evolution of culture is synonymous with the removal of ornamentation from objects of everyday use,"* is a direct extrapolation of the ethnographic theories of Tylor and Morgan.[41] Ornament must go, he reasoned, because it appealed to a "lower" fascination with sensory particulars. Likewise, the "lack of ornamentation" in modern design stood for him as "a sign of intellectual strength," proof that both designer and consumer were operating "on the cultural level of today" (175, 173). Loos even rehearsed Hugo Magnus's Lamarckian theory of color-sense evolution to support his correlation of design and civilization, stating that the human child began life with "sense-impressions . . . like a new-born dog's," and then recapitulated subsequent stages in "the development of humanity":

> At two he sees with the eyes of a Papuan, at four with those of a Germanic tribesman, at six of Socrates, at eight of Voltaire. At eight he becomes aware of violet, the color discovered by the eighteenth century; before that, violets were blue and the purple snail was red. (167)

Lest Loos the European modernist seem too remote from Gilman the American progressive, we should note that he offered an earlier formulation of his ideas about ornament in the essay "Ladies' Fashion" (1902), where he called women to abandon "velvet and silk, flowers and ribbons, features and paints" in favor of streamlined, modern fashion; thirteen years later Gilman issued a very similar call in *The Dress of Women* (1915), and she clothed the women of *Herland* (1915) in "simple," "comfortable," and unadorned garments that would have easily won Loos's blessing.[42] In the early twentieth century one did not need to be a modernist to push for shedding ornament and embracing pure color; one might simply be a Lamarckian.

The shift to abstract color schemes in design informed a concomitant shift in how writers portrayed the relation between characters and their environments, heightening the emphasis put on sensitivity as the century drew to a close. To illustrate, let's look at two rooms depicted by Gilman's contemporaries that, taken together, demonstrate this general change and clarify Gilman's particular position within it. The first is the eponymous paint manufacturer's drawing room in William Dean Howells's *The Rise of Silas Lapham* (1885). Lapham, who has "crude taste in architecture," plans to build a new house on Beacon Street, and his architect convinces him to decorate it in the modern, all-white style. The drawing room in Lapham's current house, in contrast, is a motley mess:

> The Lapham drawing-room in Nankeen Square was in the parti-colored paint which [Silas] had hoped to repeat in his new house: the trim of the doors and windows was in a light green and the panels in salmon; the walls were a plain tint of French gray paper, divided by gilt moldings into broad panels with a wide stripe of red velvet paper running up the corners; the chandelier was of massive imitation bronze; the mirror over the mantel rested on a fringed mantel-cover of green reps, and heavy curtains of that stuff hung from gilt lambrequin frames at the window; the carpet was of a small pattern in crude green, which, at the time Mrs. Lapham bought it, covered half the new floors in Boston.[43]

Howells's rambling sentence conveys the crowd of mismatched colors and gaudy furnishings that cause the aristocratic Bromfield Corey and his wife to squirm during their visit to the Laphams. The novel employs a straightforward semiotic of taste based on the idea, popularized in Clarence Cook's *The House Beautiful* (1881), that a "room ought to represent the culture of the family"—indeed, that it not only "ought to" but "will and must represent them, whether its owners would let it or no."[44]

For Howells, writing at a moment when design norms were in flux, Silas's fixation on particular items and pictorial furnishings ("stone-colored landscapes," two "allegories of Faith and Prayer"), his old-fashioned interest in *things* rather than their relations, signals his pedestrian taste as much as the fact that those items are tacky (190).

Harold Frederic's *The Damnation of Theron Ware* (1896) rewrites Howells's scene for an era of aestheticism, with its dual emphasis on mere color and nervous sensitivity. Ware, a Methodist minister recently relocated to a small town in upstate New York, spends the novel flirting with the intellectual and cultural trends of modernity, only to find that what he "took to be improvement was degeneration."[45] Though the temptations he faces are many—Catholicism, the anthropology of religion, evolutionary science—Frederic establishes the blue-and-yellow music room of the beautiful aesthete Celia Madden as the site where Theron's "degeneration commences."[46] The scene begins when Theron meets Celia during a night stroll; he is recovering from a "collapse of the nerves," and she invites him back to her room, where she will play Chopin for him, "the real medicine for bruised and wounded nerves" (186–87). Once inside, Theron "look[s] about him with frankly undisguised astonishment." Lanterns with "half-opaque alternating rectangles of blue and yellow glass" cast their glow on sculptures and paintings arranged along the walls, setting the keynote for the rest of the room. But Theron misses the pattern.

> A less untutored vision than his would have caught more swiftly the scheme of color and line in which these works of art bore their share. The walls of the room were in part of flat upright wooden columns, terminating high above in simple capitals, and they were all painted in pale amber and straw and primrose hues, irregularly wavering here and there toward suggestions of white. Between these pilasters were broader panels of stamped leather, in gently varying shades of softest blue. These contrasted colors vaguely interwove and mingled in what he could see of the shadowed ceiling high overhead. They were repeated in the draperies and huge cushions and pillows of the low, wide divan which ran about three sides of the room. Even the floor, where it revealed itself among the scattered rugs, was laid in a mosaic pattern of matched woods, which, like the rugs, gave back these same shifting blues and uncertain yellows. (191–92)

A "scheme of color and line" orders the room, subordinating individual items to its overarching pattern, and Theron's failure to sense this

organization—like Lapham's inability to employ one—marks him as un-
couth. But where Howells represented that uncouthness through the affiliation between one's room and one's character, Frederic portrayed it
through Theron's *response* to someone else's room, placing the emphasis
on nervous sensitivity and the worrying way bodies can "degenerate" if
they cannot manage their impressions. Once Celia begins to play, the
minister responds to the mix of music and color like a puppet to the tugs
of a puppeteer: he is "drawn resistlessly to his feet" (196). The sensations
stir him in ways he hardly understands and cannot control ("it could not
be helped") (199).

In its portrayal of the potentially damning effects of interior design,
the scene in Celia's music room could have come directly out of a manual on home decoration. Practically all such manuals in the period insisted that domestic spaces had an unperceived but decisive influence
on the mental and physical health of their inhabitants. Many factors were
cited—pattern, furnishings, images—but the rhetorical emphasis fell on
color, whose long associations with emotional and sensory life proved
suited to figuring the vague influences central to design discourse.
"When we enter certain houses," reported the *New York Times* in 1901,
"we are immediately affected by their air. This pleasant or disagreeable
impression in the tone of the physical surroundings results from this or
that color, or combination of colors, on the walls." Housewives and hosts
were called to take note: for "it is not by wine alone that a dinner party
can be set in good humour"; "that is a coarse method compared with
the action of colors on the unconscious subjects of a properly managed
interior."[47]

Yet as Theron's degeneration shows, the subtlety with which colors
affected "unconscious" subjects meant that the average person rarely noticed their influence. As a result, as a correspondence course in decoration explained, "sensitive women have been known to pay the price of one
headache a week for a red wall paper."[48] Candace Wheeler, an influential proponent of design reform in the United States, placed the mingled
threat and promise of color at the heart of her approach to decoration. In
"The Philosophy of Beauty Applied to House Interiors" (1893), she wrote
that when furnishing interiors, "the first and most important necessity
is harmony and effect of color; in fact, without this all effort is vain, all
expenditure futile." She continued,

Color is the beneficent angel or the malicious devil of the house. Properly understood and successfully entreated, it is the most powerful mental influence of the home; but if totally disregarded or ignorantly dealt with, it is able to introduce a level of unrest, to refuse healing to tired nerves and overtaxed energies, to stir up anger and malice and all unseen enemies that lie in wait for victims of weakness and fatigue.[49]

The sly agency that designers attributed to decorative colors demanded an insistence that those influences be managed through an organizing scheme. Decorative advice amounted to techniques for bringing sensitive housewives and their children into restorative balance with their surroundings.

The attention paid to colors *felt* more than *seen* makes modern design, no less than modern painting, a participant in what Douglas Mao has identified as the widespread tendency at the turn of the twentieth century to think of life as "a series of transactions between an organism and its environment."[50] But whereas impressionist artists sought to capture these perceptual transactions as they unfolded within the natural landscape, designers attended to surroundings more easily renovated. The more controlled space of the domestic interior provided opportunities not only to observe life's transactions but also to *change* them. Reformers focused their efforts on children, the most impressible of a house's inhabitants. Wheeler, for instance, advised that kids living in a well-designed home "grow up with the knowledge of form and color, a sense of beauty and fitness—in short, with a standard of taste" that in later life endows them with "unconscious superiority" (14). Similar statements linking decoration to civilization litter modern design discourse, and as Mao demonstrates, they spilled into aestheticism: Wilde too worried about the effects of wallpaper on growing children in "The Decorative Art in America," and Whistler—whose "symphonies" and "nocturnes" offer an alternative route into "pure color" from that of Monet—stood accused of giving his canvases "the sort of beauty which porcelain has, rather than the sort of beauty which pictures have."[51] (As the designer of the Peacock Room, a blue-and-gold interior designed to showcase the owner's porcelain collection, Whistler would have taken this insult as a compliment.) Throughout what Mao calls "aestheticism in its socially interventionist mode," both in practical design and in painting, the effects of chromatic environments concentrated attention on "the operations of unregistered experience" and the aesthetic techniques that manage them.[52]

At times the power to mold character invested in the "harmony and effect of color" smacked of determinism, as if the right combination of hues would universally foster healthy and relaxed inhabitants. Mao notes that "anxiety about freedom in various senses almost inevitably attends serious reflection on aesthetic experience's power to shape the soul," especially when this experience is occasioned by an all-encompassing interior.[53] Frederic channeled this anxiety in his depiction of Theron overtaken by the music room; Celia, referring to the way the blue-and-yellow scheme complements her fiery red hair, describes the room as "mak[ing] up what I hope Whistler would call a symphony" (193). The scene casts aestheticism as the artistic expression of late-nineteenth-century materialism: in each case, human agency withers in the face of strong environmental forces. The spirit of Spencer, given voice in the novel by Dr. Ledsmar, lives also in Celia.

Gilman skirted the deterministic implications of modern design by reading pure color and form through her Lamarckian allegiances.[54] She didn't begin at this position: her first book, *Art Gems for the Home and Fireside* (1888), presented reproductions and narrative analyses of forty-nine paintings and advised mothers to hang them up in the home, where they would have a "strong and lasting influence" on the children.[55] The sentiment here fits the common fare of decorative discourse at around the time Gilman went to RISD. But as she immersed herself in the social-evolutionary thought of Lester Frank Ward, Gilman came to believe that a creature's milieu conditions development but does not dictate it, and she even mocked the idea that "cabalistical arrangements of color and form and sound . . . shall mysteriously force the young intelligence to flower" (*Women and Economics,* 287). Instead, she approached domestic interiors as spaces that condition the growth of their inhabitants by constraining some movements and facilitating others. She argued that the mechanism of development was not a passive reception of environmental effects but, rather, the active exertions that a milieu encourages or disallows. If life is a series of transactions between organism and environment, neither can remain static. As she wrote in *Women and Economics:*

> An absolutely uniform environment, one shape, one size, one color, one sound, would render life, if any life there be, one helpless, changeless thing. As the environment increases and varies, the development of the creature must increase and vary with it; for he acquires knowledge and power, as the material for knowledge and the need for power appear. (64)

For Gilman, environments did not so much determine growth as provide the sensory conditions that shaped it. The creature had to decide which capacities or activities, within those allowed, would be realized. "A living organism is modified far less through the action of external circumstances upon it and its reactions hitherto than through the effect of its own exertions," Gilman argued. As such, even though "to be surrounded by beautiful things has much influence upon the human creature," "to *make* beautiful things has more," since "what we do modifies us more than what is done to us" (66).

Gilman's Lamarckian approach prompted her to depict the relation between color and character in "The Yellow Wall-Paper" differently than did Howells and Frederic. Where the latter two began from an already-established personality that was revealed through passive responses to a room, and so confined their scenes to a single visit, Gilman adopted the conceit of the journal entry to dramatize the long process whereby an organism pushes with and against an environment to gain a particular sort of character. And whereas Howells and Frederic emphasized the designing hands of Silas and Celia, the better to situate the responses of Bromfield and Theron within the stratified social worlds of the novels, Gilman placed her narrator in a once-grand but since-neglected home, a "colonial mansion" whose design points not to any single individual but to a "hereditary estate," a common "ancestral" inheritance (3). Her goal was to draw attention to the effects of a diffuse and deeply entrenched arrangement that shaped the mental habits and emotional lives of middle-class white women restricted to the nineteenth-century home, and particularly to the "absolutely uniform environment" prescribed by the rest cure.[56]

In this way design reform discourse provided Gilman with a model for combining her sociological work with her artistic interests; it taught her to see aesthetics not as the lofty affair of "literature" that she derided in her letter to Howells but as a practical intervention into the conditions of sensory experience, a technique for reconstructing the organism–environment transactions that define the historical conditions of social and individual life. In particular, late-nineteenth-century treatments of color as an atmospheric agent that acted on inhabitants without their noticing gave Gilman a model of all that is consequential yet unseen in domestic arrangements. Color experience had long stood for the kinds of phenomena that require both a sensory stimulus and a perceptual mechanism: subtract either, and you lose the color experience. Design discourse redoubled this relational account by insisting that all color effects are the product of arrangements and that the task of the decorator is not simply to avoid certain hues and to use others but to cultivate a facility with chromatic harmonies. As Wheeler remarked, the trick is to improve one's color sense, and this meant learning both to respond to relational arrangements and to reflect on their effects (5).

Color thus crystallized what art historian E. H. Gombrich, echoing Ross, designated the distinctive type of perception involved in design, the "sense of order." This perceptual mode "orient[s] us in space and time to find our way in relation to the thing we seek or we avoid"; it often occurs without our noticing and in fact conditions what it is that we *can* notice (in "the perception of things").[57] What Gilman took from design discourse was an ability to make perceptible, to *sense,* the unnoticed social orders that shape our perceptions. "We are used to what we do not notice," she wrote; in fact, "it is perfectly possible for an individual," or even "a race, a nation, a class," "to become accustomed to the most disadvantageous conditions, and fail to notice them" (*Women and Economics,* 76–77).

In "The Yellow Wall-Paper," Gilman stages the aesthetic work of giving color—and all the unregistered conditions it indexes—a noticeable figure. She starts with the narrator herself, with her pathologically acute attention to the usually unnoticed impact of design elements: "It only interests me," the narrator says of the wallpaper, "but I feel sure John and Jennie are secretly affected by it" (142). Gilman then adds cross-modal descriptions of a "yellow smell" that pervades the house and images of a yellow smooch that spreads its color onto clothes and people—each ways that ephemeral color is given physical weight. But it is only when the narrator discerns a female form in the back pattern of the wallpaper that the task of giving shape to color takes center stage. Indeed, though critics have yet to notice it, the famous passage in which the narrator begins to perceive a figure hidden in the walls pulls its key images from the rhetoric of color in design.

> This wallpaper has a kind of subpattern *in a different shade,* a particularly irritating one, for you can only see it in certain *lights,* and not clearly then.
>
> But in places where it isn't faded and where the sun is just so—I can

see a strange, provoking, *formless* sort of figure, that seems to skulk about
behind that silly and conspicuous front design. (135; emphasis added)

The figure is explicitly "formless," intimately connected to the light, dis-
tinguishable only as a "different shade," and noticeably "provoking": in
other words, it's color. And as the yellow woman gains definition in the
narrator's mind, as she begins to creep behind the pattern, she never
loses this connection to chromatic designs and the relational effects they
index.

The function of this figure becomes clearer when we recall an early
comment about the husband John's "intense horror of superstition." As
the narrator notes, "[John] scoffs openly at any talk of things not to be
felt and seen and put down in figures" (3). Here "figures" refers to numbers and charts, the abstract tools of transcription through which scientific phenomena are stabilized and communicated. But as we have already seen, the narrator creates a figure of her own, one that, like John's,
gives a particular state of affairs a visible and physical body: when the
"faint figure" in the wallpaper "seem[s] to shake the pattern," the narrator gets out of bed and "[goes] to feel and see if the paper *did* move"
(138). Whereas John's figures translate physical forces, the narrator's
communicate psychological states, which, as we have already seen, were
understood as uniquely connected to the effects of pure color. We can
thus recognize the discovery of the yellow figure in the wallpaper as an
attempt to grasp and reflect on the environmental forces under which the
narrator suffers, forces that "shake" and intensify—but also promise to
unmoor—the patterns that guide what we notice and discuss. Elsewhere
in the story, atmospheric color is narrated as having precisely this effect
on interpretation: "It is the strangest yellow, that wall-paper! It makes
me think of all the yellow things I ever saw—not beautiful ones like
buttercups, but old foul, bad yellow things" (140). What begins as an
all-inclusive embrace turns instead into a sorting mechanism, a way of
making certain things visible and pertinent ("foul, bad yellow things")
and rendering others invisible or irrelevant. It acts as a *figure* by communicating an abstract and slippery force, and it specifies the importance
of finding such figures by dramatizing their influence on what can be
thought.

Reading "The Yellow Wall-Paper" in light of the colors of design helps
us understand the role of literary writing within Gilman's larger political

project. The goal, in almost all her stories, is to chart the unreflective habits of thinking and feeling that hamper the reform objectives proposed in her sociological work; their proto-stream-of-consciousness techniques (especially evident in "Through This" and "The Yellow Wall-Paper") dramatize the movements of individual minds suffering within well-worn social grooves and attempting, usually after a moment of complete despair, to jump them. This attempt to capture the atmospheric qualities produced through sensory arrangements has led some critics, even Gilman herself, to align her fiction with that of Edgar Allan Poe, another writer concerned with the superadded effects produced by sounds, colors, or the stones of an ancestral home in combination. But though Gilman may be said to share Poe's interest in manufacturing what Sianne Ngai calls "tone," understood as "a materially created semblance of feeling," she does so with a different sense of the stakes, since the source of her narrator's mental state lies first and foremost with the working conditions that allow an artificially produced sexual difference to parade as natural.[58] In putting the atmospheric setting into the literary foreground with her color-obsessed characters, Gilman moves beyond the sensory effects of color schemes to the social orders that sustain them. In her most famous story, this entailed dramatizing "degenerate" color perceptions to portray a particular problem facing late-nineteenth-century middle-class white women. But in the narratives of the 1910s, shortly after her encounter with Scriabin's color concert, Gilman elaborated the therapeutic potential of color hinted at in "Through This" to imagine utopian renovations of sensory life.

The Art of Mobile Color

In 1915, soon after she published her excited notice about color music, Gilman returned to the scene of nervous women staring at creeping colors with more energy, more *purpose,* than ever. She found in the "art of mobile color" a nimbler counterpart to design discourse, an aesthetic practice capable of bringing the subtle chromatic effects of domestic interiors under the controlling hand of a performer. The two arts were related: color music built on long-standing analogies between color and sound that permeated late-nineteenth-century design manuals; Gilman claimed that her own youthful speculations about this art were based on the idea that the "red, orange, yellow, green, blue, indigo, violet, of the rainbow, correspond to the 'do, re, me, fa, sol, la, si' of the octave."[59] But where decoration and painting could only present a single chromatic arrangement, color music extended these compositions in time, enabling audiences and performers alike to reflect on their sensory responses as they occurred. In two short stories published shortly after her notice about Scriabin, Gilman embraced the added dynamism of the color concert to resume her investigation of color perception and the aesthetic construction of sensory experience. Design discourse attuned her to color as an atmospheric assembly of felt relations variously perceived according to mental organization; color music suggested a technique for bringing these relations more sharply into conscious thought. The excitement of avant-garde color concerts, for Gilman and other progressives, lay in their potential for civilizing the color sense.

Gilman's interest in color music points to a forgotten framework for understanding the cultural meanings and aesthetic uses of abstract color in the early twentieth century. Most art historians cast Scriabin's color concert and similar experiments in mobile color as footnotes in the history of abstract painting, either as the logical development of Whistler's chromatic "symphonies" or as examples of the mystical elements of early modernism. But to Gilman's eyes, color music had as much Wheeler in it as Whistler, and color organs promised to nuance one's receptiveness to the sensory world rather than to unlock perceptions of a spiritual realm. She approached this new art as an extension of the same mix of color and character, of aesthetic techniques and social reform, that in the 1890s she had found in design discourse. She wasn't alone. Though color music did get aligned with occultist figures like Scriabin and Kandinsky, it was also defended on social-evolutionary grounds. In an article from *Littell's Living Age* in 1895, for instance, William Schooling based his call for "a new art that shall appeal to the emotions through color alone" not on Pater or painting but on Spencer. After explaining Spencer's idea that evolutionary progress "comes about by the differentiation of parts," he reasoned that the emphasis on color in modern art was destined to lead to "an art of color-music" in which mobile hues broke with static form and figuration to develop on their own terms. But he added that because abstract color required an advanced level of cognitive cultivation, its pleasures would elude those either not far enough advanced ("Orientals") or too far degenerated (Catholics) to muster the mental energy to attend to color for color's sake.[60] At the turn of the twentieth century, color music stood both as a sign of artistic progress and as a technique for cultivating the perceptual faculties said to mark the white, Protestant—"civilized"—body.[61]

Rimington, whose treatise *Colour-Music: The Art of Mobile Colour* (1912) Gilman singled out in her notice, pitched the art of luminous color as an intervention into the pitiful state of the color sense in the United States and Europe. "It can scarcely be disputed that at the present day large numbers of people are almost entirely insensible to colour," Rimington explained (77). He argued that the persistent "neglect of the cultivation of the color faculty" had resulted in "an evident decay of it in most Western nations," such that "amongst large sections of the populations in many nations"—including the working classes and the peasantry—"it is no exaggeration to say that any real feeling for colour has died out" (9, 10). This insensitivity posed a challenge to Rimington, who performed his own chromatic compositions on a color organ that he built himself, since the ailing public did not show the requisite mental energy to tolerate the cure: "The insufficient training of the colour sense" prevented people "from enjoying colour for its own sake" (72). Similar to design reformers, Rimington emphasized "the urgent need for the cultivation of the colour sense" to vitalize the flagging sensorium run down by industrial labor and discordant chromatic arrangements (78).

Rimington proposed an array of benefits that would follow from greater color sensitivity and that situate his art closer to Gilman's progressivism than to the spiritualism of the European avant-garde (Figures 12 and 13). The introductory note to *Colour-Music,* which presents the personal testimony of a satisfied color-organ user, praises the medicinal effects of the art: "To sit at this instrument and improvise for half an hour whilst watching the ever-varying combination of colour on the screen produced by the playing is not only an unspeakable delight, but of real health-giving effect on the sense of colour" (xiii). In addition to touting this mix of aesthetic delight and "health-giving" value, Rimington insisted that his art would improve a range of observational practices, including biology, chemistry, and spectroscopy; painting and design; and the art of poetry, since "our intellectual and even our literary capacity is injured if we do not possess a keen sense of color" (81). More generally, he suggested that because color "is everywhere in nature" and because "it enters so much into our surroundings," "we cannot safely afford to know nothing about it, or to neglect to study it intelligently and cultivate our feeling for it" (79). Color organs and the art of color music promised to help viewers grasp the subtle workings of this most pervasive force; they made it possible "to study the influence of colour upon our senses and upon our minds, and, through them, upon our lives" (11). The art of pure color joined the ranks

FIGURE 12. Color organ designed by Alexander Wallace Rimington to perform "colour-music" by projecting variously hued lights on a gauze curtain. Alexander Wallace Rimington, *Colour-Music: The Art of Mobile Colour* (London: Hutchinson, 1912), 44. RB 706032, Huntington Library, San Marino, California.

of Progressive-Era strategies for bringing the sensory and material forces shaping human consciousness under conscious control.

Gilman too promoted heightened sensitivity as a mark of social advancement, one that should be helped along by reform in dress, labor, and the built environment. "Is there any real reason," she once asked, "why blackboards must be black? A deep dull red or somber green would be restful and pleasant to the eye, and show chalk just as well."[62] Such hues, she felt, are worth bothering about because they contribute to the general sensory conditions that shape mental life and foster either progress or its opposite. In *Women and Economics* Gilman characterized the "process of development" in humans as involving "the increase of sensation in the socialized individuals with its enormous possibilities of joy and healthful sensitiveness to pain" (103). And her utopian fictions usually involve a depiction of heightened sensations, of human beings made fully awake and fit for the future by a well-arranged environment. The eugenic female utopia in *Herland* (1915), for instance, first reveals itself to Van and his fellow ethnographers in the form of synthetic dyes.

FIGURE 13. Screen on which color music was projected. Rimington, *Colour-Music,* 66. RB 706032, Huntington Library, San Marino, California.

When they see a green-tinted river with red and blue deposits on the bank, Terry identifies the deposits as "chemicals of some sort," and then as "dyestuffs"—an indication that the society they are seeking is not "savage" as they had supposed.[63] Once inside Herland, the team finds these dyes deployed as one of the many means of fostering a heightened sensorium in "socialized individuals," further evidence that Gilman, like Rimington, felt that "the possession of a refined colour sense" is of great "importance to a nation" (*Colour-Music,* 78).

In "Dr. Clair's Place," a story published in the *Forerunner* the month after the notice about Rimington and Scriabin, Gilman used the imagery of the color organ and its "health-giving effect" to envision a flexible solution for the sensory problems plaguing her earlier color-conscious narrators. The narrative follows a worn-out woman named Octavia (note the play on "octave") as she agrees to offer her case to Willy Clair, a female doctor who treats nervous disorders in a mountainside sanitarium. She arrives with "dull[ed]" eyes marked by a "heavy gloom," but soon undergoes a restorative regimen of sleep, nutrition, exercise, and social interaction, and prominent among her therapies is something Dr. Clair calls "the color treatment."[64] Octavia recalls the procedure as follows:

> [Dr. Clair] put in my hand a little card of buttons, as it were, with wire attachments. I pressed one; the room was darkened, save for the tiny glow by which I saw the color list. Then, playing on the others, I could fill the room with any lovely hue I chose, and see them driving, mingling, changing as I played. (183)

Once again Gilman casts her colors as lights dancing on a wall and filling a room with a potent hue, but this time the observer controls the play of lights, and her specific charge is to reflect on the psychological effects of various tints and shades. Indeed, the color treatment constitutes part of a three-pronged plan to foster greater awareness of sensory stimuli. Dr. Clair instructs Octavia, "When you feel the worst, will you be so good as to try either of these three things and note the result"; she then shows her patient how to experiment with music, color, and tastes. For each adjustment, Octavia is to "make a study of the effects and note it for Dr. Clair" (183). The healing process, as the story imagines it, involves examining the impact of our environment and submitting the felt but usually unnoticed influences—the same ones that design reformers said could cause such trouble—to empirical study. This reflective grasp on sensory life distinguishes Gilman's utopian visions from her chilling tales of modern domesticity; it separates the color treatment from the rest cure and, more broadly, it drives Gilman's sociological project of denaturalizing the environmental and historical forces that produced turn-of-the-century gender inequality. That is, whereas the narrators of "The Yellow Wall-Paper" and "Through This" have only the regular but always changing colors of the sun, which they either passively observe or actively engage but without being able to effect any meaningful change, Octavia controls the luminous colors that "creep" along her wall. Dr. Clair's contraptions give her an opportunity to immerse herself within a shifting environment and adjust it in real time, coming to know herself in and through her responses.

In "The Master of the Sunset" (1915), published four months after "Dr. Clair's Place," Gilman imagined the color treatment for individuals being scaled up in the form of a concert capable of training the color feelings of an entire audience. For the problem she wished to resolve was not just that some people's nerves get exhausted but also that a variety of social conditions embedded in habits of dress, the gendered division of labor, and the arrangement of physical space conspired to stunt sensory development, especially in the white women who were Gilman's primary concern. Drawing from Rimington, Gilman singled out industrial production as a key factor in the deadening of Western sensitivity, a deadening that color music could overcome. The story begins in a dismal town drained of vivid hues by local factories: "The country round about was dull and uninteresting, and the dark smear from the belching chimneys toned all its green to an aging gray. The dust of the road was gray, iron gray, blackening heavily as it neared the mills." Even "the pink feet of barefoot children grew gray as they played."[65] To this gray land, a child is born—Vizek, a child who longs for the stray sunbeam or the odd ribbon, a child thrilled by color. One day Vizek wanders over the hill that borders the town and also acts as a barrier for the soot of the factory, and he witnesses for the first time the spectacular hues of the setting sun. Gilman conjures the scene with nuanced tones that at once recall and outstrip the more basic palette of "Through This":

> Where the sun died the gold light blazed along the world's rim, and up
> across the ruffled hosts of cloudlets. . . . Cool stretches of jade green
> lay clear behind the crowding bars of crimson; a level sea of palest gold
> seemed to lie far and still among the long purple islands; the vivid yel-

low turned to glowing red, the red to rose, the rose to softest pink, the
pink to peach, the peach to mauve, the mauve to heliotrope, dove-gray
and pearl— (254)

Vizek nearly "burst[s]" with "ecstasy" at the scene, vowing to translate nature's transient hues into the stuff of art: "I'll catch you some day!" he
shouts at the sky, "I'll make you stay!" (255). The section that follows
offers a montage-like sequence detailing Vizek's restless quest to "catch"
luminous color. He moves from a dye shop to a paint factory, from a sign-
painter's shop to art school—where he becomes "a great colorist"—then
from making stained glass to studying chemistry, electrical engineer-
ing, cinema projection, and, before disappearing for a few years, music.
"Indeed, for awhile he went continually to hear great music; sitting with
his eyes shut, *hearing music and feeling color*" (255; emphasis added).
This apprenticeship culminates in an art of pure color, Vizek's grand attempt to "master" the sun.

Gilman's depiction of the winding route that Vizek takes to color
music reminds us that every component of this new art, from the color
organs that.projected it to the notation systems that scripted it, had to
be built from the ground up, including the very capacity to experience
"pure color" as a meaningful aesthetic medium. Against the medical
applications of colored light, or spiritualist beliefs about the correspon-
dences between colors and auras found in Scriabin or Kandinsky, Gilman
joined Rimington in insisting that the experience of "feeling color" resulted from *training,* not from a natural power inhering in blue, red, or
yellow. This perspective clarifies how and why advocates of pure color
aligned their art with music. While most accounts of this affiliation follow
Whistler in emphasizing music's power of expressing emotions without
figuration, just as important was the process of cultivation and training
that endowed pure sound with its aesthetic force. When color-musicians
invoked music, they often spoke of it as an aesthetic system that had been
built up through centuries of experimentation and calibration, such that
its position as an abstract stimulus of emotional experience testified to
the hard-won training of the musical sense through the construction of
a harmonic system and the perfection of musical instruments. It's this
training, as much as the emotional address itself, that concerned color-
musicians.[66] Vizek's education in an array of technical and aesthetic practices invites us to see his art as a means of instituting the instruments
and procedures for enabling audiences to feel color.

The elaborate description of Vizek's color concert in the second half of the story follows the process of sensory training as it takes hold in an audience. Before the curtain rises, we meet two unnamed characters whose reactions we follow throughout the performance: a "woman sculptor from Vermont" and her male friend. The sculptor worries that an art of color alone would be frivolous, perhaps even dangerous: "It seems to me so sensuous!" Her friend then teases her, "You precious combination of New England conscience, chastity and limestone! Why shouldn't it be! What do we have senses *for*? Don't the curves and lines you love give pleasure, too?" (255). Though as a woman with a creative vocation the sculptor is happily beyond the marred perceptions of those suffering either the restrictions of the rest cure or the chaos of domestic labor, she nonetheless resembles the characters of Gilman's other stories in that some intangible social agency—manifested in her Puritan conscience—prevents her from making full and proper use of her sensory faculties. When the show begins with simple pairings of color projections with piano and organ music (along the lines Gilman laid out in her "Color Music" notice), the friend explains that such warm-ups were necessary precisely because the sculptor is not alone in her insensitivity. "You see he had to begin that way. People have *no* color sense—he had to educate them" (256).

Gilman's understanding of what was achieved through such training remained consistent from her earlier stories: as in "The Yellow Wall-Paper," the role of pure color in Vizek's concert is to sensitize viewers to unnoticed aspects of their social environment. Gilman embraced Rimington's proposal that "the more the eye is trained to notice very slight differences of tint in color, the more sensitive does it become to these differences" (*Colour-Music,* 85), but she extended his relational presentation of self and world to encompass a reflection on the very processes by which perceiver and perceived get entwined in color. Her first step was to specify the abstraction involved in abstract colors not as an abstraction from "purpose" or politics but as the extraction of the *feeling* of an experience. As "pure," Vizek's colors do not abandon reference so much as create a new means for indicating an elusive quality of an organism's entanglement with its environment. Witness the audience banter after a performance called "Spring":

> "Wasn't it wonderful when that first little flicker of gold and purple made you *think* crocuses!" said a girl softly.
> "It's all wonderful," her companion answered. "It doesn't *look* like

anything in particular—it just makes it in your mind, a thousand times stronger somehow. I've seen apple orchards for thirty years, and never felt like this!" (257)

The shifting colors present the emotional quality of experiencing cro-cuses and apple blossoms without the mimetic figure. They not only delight viewers with intense sensations (the companion "never felt like this!") but also attune them to unnoticed features of their encounters with the world.

Vizek's next piece demonstrates how this capacity of color music can be harnessed to motivate social reform. Titled "Moods," the segment is said to have "no physical analogue to assist in interpretation, but only the sheer power of color . . . on the soul" (257). Yet it is precisely this composi-tion in which Vizek engages the drab industrial conditions that led him to his color-cultivation crusade. After a description of a "hard cold slate and black" arrangement broken occasionally with "soiled pinks" and "a touch of sullen red," a viewer exclaims, "Ugh! It's like Birmingham!" (257). As in Garland's "Homestead and Its Perilous Trades," the scene envisions the role of art as giving a perceptual image to the vague and often suppressed psychological effects produced by deleterious atmo-spheres, alongside the structures of power that sustain them. In aes-thetic constructions, Gilman suggests, such "moods" can be taken on, experienced, and, in reflection, addressed.

Vizek's finale clarifies the way that color music offered Gilman a tech-nique for installing within her realist project the techniques of abstrac-tion that would come to characterize artistic modernism but that at the turn of the century still bore the marks of social-evolutionary thought.[67] "The After-Glow," the fruit of Vizek's lifelong effort to hold down the hues of the sunset, fills the concert hall with radiant colors, which Gilman conveys with linguistic precision:

> As through a window wide as half the sky [the audience] saw that rose-fire gather and burn to living crimson, glow in coral, ruby, garnet and carnelian; play wide in waves of faint, soft carmine that melted into sea-shell shades, fruit tints, and delicate, clear yellow; then blue, blue like blue velvet and blue fire, deepened and paled before them. (258)

Once these images fade, Vizek concludes by assembling the components of his aesthetic performance, like a general addressing his troops: "With a slow marshaling of tints, as of a marching company of rainbows, the colors were gathered and dismissed. Shade by shade they fell into line together in exquisite harmonies, and faded softly from sight" (258). The juxtaposition of these two scenes—one of a richly felt invocation of the sunset, the other of an orderly display of abstract aesthetic tools—gives the reader a glimpse into the procedures involved in the aesthetic intensification of experience through the training of the color sense. "Mastering" the sunset involves contriving projection mechanisms capable of isolating and ordering its component parts, which can then be redeployed in increasingly complex aesthetic constructions that lead viewers to attune themselves to the sensory world. The result is twofold. As audience members grow more sensitive, they feel the world differently, and this new sensitivity manifests in new possibilities for action that promise to change the world that is felt. At stake here is the coconstitution of self and environment, rooted in a theory that links sensation and activity, which for Gilman guided the course of social change.

When approached through Gilman and Rimington rather than Scriabin and mystical modernism, color music provides an account of mediation central to the era of aniline dyes and the color sense. Just as synthetic indigo scrambled the division between "natural" and "artificial" colorants, so too did the Lamarckian thrust of color-sense training insist that technical manipulation and intellectual mediations are not opposed to nature; rather, they are intricate parts of its workings. In this regard, the constructions of color musicians aimed not simply to mimic the sunset but to produce artifices capable of shaping the perceptual processes that define the ongoing, relational creation of seer and seen, where new presentations of color, however artificial, constitute new possibilities for seeing and feeling the world. Gilman's Lamarckianism had prepared her to see color music in this light. And the vocabulary she musters for "The After-Glow," precise almost to the point of being technical, shows how far she thought her own linguistic medium could contribute to the educational dynamic that enhanced the feeling for color. She hoped that when seen through "carmine" and "carnelian," "beryl green" and "chrysoprase," the sunset's hues would appear all the more vivid to her readers. It is in this regard that her approach to pure color differs from the modernist attitude she rejected in her response to Howells. For her, artistic mediation and intellectual construction are not ways of getting outside or beyond nature, nor do they tragically divorce us from more immediate modes of experience. Instead, they are the very means by which we build the world we want to live in, as well as the "we" that will inhabit it.

By specifying a social program for aesthetics based in her Lamarckian thought and bordering on modernist abstraction, Gilman's handling of color both elaborates the political significance of pure hues hinted at in Garland's stories and clarifies two conceptual threads that will run throughout the subsequent chapters. The first is that efforts to stimulate the color sense appealed to a racialized understanding of the feeling body, in which greater responsiveness to stimulation meant greater capacity for evolution. The second is that artistic and even linguistic constructions could intervene in the continuous transactions between organisms and environments that constitute experience. The final image of "The Master of the Sunset" offers a frightening image of how these might relate in the person of Vizek, described as "pale, straight, proud, a conqueror" (258). This pairing of chromatic intensification with an increasingly pallid whiteness reminds us that, as Seitler and Schuller each argue, Gilman's Lamarckianism led to her eugenic feminism, whereby women's roles as reproducers of the race demanded that their sensory and intellectual health be secured through social reform. And indeed, Gilman's portraits of sensory reconstruction present white women as the sole target for perceptual training. Yet what is so clearly entwined in stories such as "The Master of the Sunset" and "Dr. Clair's Place" often appeared as separate phenomena in the hands of other writers, such as Stephen Crane, or within other domains, such as modernist art. Nowhere is this split more sharply defined than in the dual treatments of children and color at the turn of the twentieth century, which on the one hand, codified a set of principles for teaching children how to feel color, and on the other, celebrated an aesthetic ideal of the child's unique experience of bright hues, unbound by convention or even concepts. From the walls of domestic interiors and the art of projected lights, then, let us turn to the crayons and construction paper of primary schools and the luminous displays of colorful goods beckoning to consumers behind department-store windows—all components of the crisscrossing histories of a child's view of color.

3   The Production and Consumption of a Child's View of Color

In April 1912, right after a landmark exhibition of Matisse's sculptures, Alfred Stieglitz's art gallery at 291 Fifth Avenue mounted another provocatively modern show: an exhibit of works on paper by children, ages two through eleven (Figure 14). The children showcased were not especially precocious; their drawings and watercolors demonstrated little in the way of technique. Rather, these little painters were exhibited precisely because they had *not* adopted the conventions of Western art, because as children they enjoyed an unspoiled apprehension of the world and expressed it in a style free of routine. They possessed what Sadakichi Hartmann, an art critic, poet, and denizen of New York bohemian circles, praised in his review of *Exhibition of Drawings, Water-Colors, and Pastels by Children* as "purity and alertness" of vision, an ability to "see things vividly," manifested in their fondness for "startling contrast and glaring colors." Before Stieglitz's show, the only public venues for children's work had been classrooms and educational conferences, where the point was to demonstrate what children *had* learned about color, form, and design—but now the point was to celebrate what they *hadn't*.[1]

By promoting the work of children, Stieglitz's exhibition literalized Ruskin's trope of the "innocent eye" and reconfigured it in the process. In *The Elements of Drawing* (1857), Ruskin proposed "a sort of childish perception" of color as an idealized figure for painterly vision, while emphasizing that the "recovery" of "infantine sight" required technical training. (After all, the passage appears in a footnote to an instructional exercise.) In contrast, Hartmann, in praising Stieglitz's show, set the child's natural love of vibrant color in opposition to the "pedantic advice of the drawing teacher" and linked it instead to the work of African sculptors, Mexican potters, and other so-called primitive artists (45–46). Once routed through the supposed affinities between white children and nonwhite primitives,

FIGURE 14. Alfred Stieglitz posing in front of one of the Children's Art Exhibitions held at his gallery, 291, in New York City, circa 1914. Yale Collection of American Literature, Beinecke Rare Book and Manuscript Library, Yale University, New Haven, Connecticut.

the figure of "childish perception" underwrote a modernist art practice that veered away from the aesthetic empiricism Ruskin admired in Turner. Even Whistler's forays into abstract color exasperated Ruskin; one can only imagine how he would have reacted to Matisse. But the bohemian Hartmann, a follower of Mallarmé and a color-music enthusiast in the mystical tradition of Scriabin, welcomed the bold hues entering modern art under the aegis of the child.[2] He joined Stieglitz in equating "innocence" with the "primitive" and in connecting both to bright colors, set against the "darkening" influences of convention, systematic training, and conceptual mediation (45–46).

Stieglitz's exhibition and Hartmann's review helped solidify an affiliation between children and color that began in the nineteenth century and that persists in every preschool and toy store in the United States. These days, kids and colors go hand in hand. Children seem more childlike when absorbed in bright hues, and we imagine that colors are more colorful when seen by a child. Yet though this partnership is so familiar as to appear natural, it acquired many of its most familiar characteristics through the technical innovations, cultural discourses, and aesthetic practices that developed in the years between *The Elements of Drawing* and Stieglitz's 291 show. Before children could be so closely associated with their own colorful productions, construction paper, crayons, and colored chalk had to be mass-produced; before they could be enticed by the saturated hues of picture books and board games, the inks and dyes for such products had to be rendered durable and inexpensive; and before their instinctual delight in bright colors could be celebrated by artists, a whole network of psychological methods and equipment had to be installed in university laboratories and directed at the juvenile mind. The figure of the color-loving child was the beneficiary of a whole host of modern phenomena, and its history encompasses not only the modern art gallery but also the kindergarten classroom, the advertising studio, and the psychology lab.

The passionate and widespread attention paid to children's experiences of color at the turn of the twentieth century made the figure of the color-absorbed child a key site for investigating how concepts and sensations interact in the service of aesthetic training. Like Gilman, who embraced Rimington's color music as a model showing how a body could become more responsive to its environment by adopting more nuanced descriptive and conceptual categories, the educators who made color

instruction a standard part of the public-school curriculum insisted that
with greater *knowledge* came greater *sensitivity*. They followed psychologists in treating a childish attraction to bright hues as one stage in the
development of the color sense, which they aimed to raise from a "primitive" to "civilized" state. At around the same time, however, illustrators
and authors, and later advertisers and painters, embraced an aesthetic
style grounded in the sensory and affective appeal that bright hues were
thought to have with young perceivers, without the imperative to educate
it. Hartmann wanted to guard child artists from schoolmasters, to use
their naive sensations to stimulate a state of pure, primitive perceptual
power. But his antipedagogical stance, though hostile to formal education, nonetheless aimed at sensory training. He just cast it as restoration
rather than addition, an act of stripping away concepts rather than adding
them. As Walter Benjamin put it in a loving variation on this theme, the
"child's view of color" is defined by "pure receptivity," an openness that
at once makes it "the highest artistic development of the sense of sight"
and a component of the "phantasmagoria" of commodity spectacle.[3] In
all these domains, from art and advertising to illustration and education,
saturated hues and fixated children provided the content and style of a
perceptual absorption meant both to quicken the feeling of perceptual
immediacy and to use that feeling to fasten the viewer to the visual world.

Children's picture books embed within their very format the mix of
language and sensation, literary narrative and actual color, at the heart
of modern formulations of the child's view of color. As such they provide
a unique vantage on the process whereby an idea about childish perception, born in psychology and raised in the kindergarten, came to inform
an aesthetic of bright and wonderful colors. In particular, they reveal
how this process entailed reconfiguring the relation between vibrant
hues and dark-skinned bodies that, as discussed in chapter 2, informed
Gilman's depictions of nervous women and pale conquerors. "Primitive
color vision" had to be sanitized for white children and modern consumers, and this procedure coincided with the modernist move of instituting
a stark separation between (linguistic) mediations and (colorful) immediacy, the separation that was on exhibition in Stieglitz's gallery in 1912.

The first edition of *The Wonderful Wizard of Oz* (1900), written by
L. Frank Baum and illustrated by W. W. Denslow, crystallized this understanding of the color-absorbed child in the way it wove together Baum's
story and Denslow's printed hues. And when read alongside Baum's work

in commercial window trimming, it clarifies the relation of this perceptual mode to modern consumer spectacle. Indeed, in important yet un-
acknowledged ways, the original *Oz* is precisely *about* its hybrid, colorful
format, presented as part of the broader array of colorful goods beckoning to modern consumers. Yet while the continued popularity of the *Oz*
narrative depends in part on its accentuation of the wonderful at the expense of the primitive, other books by Baum, including *Father Goose, His
Book* (1899, with Denslow) and *The Woggle-Bug Book* (1905, illustrated by
Ike Morgan), demonstrate that an embrace of childish perception at the
level of style required a simultaneous disavowal of racial and ethnic others at the level of content. The task of the stories in these books is to instruct readers young and old in how to see the saturated hues decorating
the page, to teach them to balance the thrill of color with the restrained
postures of white civilization.

Psychological experiments, kindergarten activities, color-print technologies, the flashing signs along Broadway—these are the materials from
which the modern trope of the child's unique experience of radiant and
powerful hues was assembled, the practices that shaped it and that were
shaped by it in turn. The primitivist force of the child's instinctual response to color, invoked not only by Benjamin and Hartmann but also by
Matisse, Pablo Picasso, Paul Klee, Virginia Woolf, Aldous Huxley, and
any number of other twentieth-century artists and writers, carries in
its avant-garde promise to refresh perception a direct tie to the systems
contrived in the 1890s and the first decade of the twentieth century to
train color sensitivity.[4] To understand why modernists revered the color-
absorbed child, we must look to all the fascinating, wonderful, brightly
colored objects and activities presented to their generation when they
were just kids.

Child Study and the Naturalization of the Child's View of Color

Charles Darwin feared that his son was color-blind. Though a "bright-
coloured tassel" had captured his firstborn's attention at only seven
weeks old, as the child grew older he appeared "to be entirely incapable
of giving the right names to the colors of a color etching," even after
learning the words for "all the ordinary things." This consistent flubbing
of color names led Darwin to question the boy's sensitivity to color. But
like the ethnographers who interviewed Native Americans and Papua

New Guineans to find out whether the remarkable gaps in the color vocabularies of non-Western peoples really did express a "primitive" color sense, Darwin eventually realized that language could not provide a reliable index of perception. And soon enough his son started using "red" and "blue" just fine. Darwin recorded these observations in a private journal in the 1840s, and he then published them in 1877, when Gladstone's Lamarckian repackaging of his color-sense theory prompted evolutionary thinkers of all stripes to weigh in on the historical development of color perception, and just as psychologists turned their attention to the mental lives of infants.[5] These lines of inquiry were in fact entwined, and Darwin directed his discussion at them both. His description of an infantile vision responsive to brightly colored things and untouched by language stands as an early entry in late-nineteenth-century scientific formulations of the child's distinctive color experiences, formulations steeped in the Gladstone debate. Child psychologists, no less than Ruskin, gave the "innocent eye" its modern meanings.

Scientific interest in the cognitive experience of infants and children emerged at the end of the nineteenth century as a consequence of psychology's integration of evolutionary thought. Once researchers began to conceive of the mind as a process of growth rather than as a static substance, the early stages of mental development, previously dismissed as too rudimentary or crude to be of use, were regarded as essential windows into the formation of human cognition.[6] Child psychologists such as G. Stanley Hall, James Mark Baldwin, Oscar Chrisman, and James Sully argued that an empirical understanding of how children engage the world could correct gross mistakes made in the training, education, and upbringing of the young—mistakes attributable to the faulty assumption that children were just little adults. Under the broad banner of "child study," then, psychologists established the child as a subject of scientific scrutiny, and in so doing they naturalized the constituents of childhood celebrated by Friedrich Fröbel and other Romantic pedagogues: play, spontaneity, sensory receptiveness, and, importantly, a delight in vivid colors.[7] A youthful attraction to bright hues had been noted by previous generations, but in the 1890s such predilections were understood not as markers of a magical or innocent realm of childhood but as expressions of a particular phase of mental development, an index of an infant's fledgling cognitive powers.

Child study emerged amid the international debate over the Gladstone thesis, and its practitioners claimed to have discovered a way to resolve that controversy without either speculating about ancient texts or traveling to faraway lands. Better just to walk to the nursery. Like Gladstone, who in 1877 had borrowed Magnus's Lamarckian account of color sensitivity to claim that humanity had undergone an "education of the eye" equivalent to that of painters, late-nineteenth-century psychologists held that the development of the individual repeated that of the species— or, in Ernst Haeckel's influential terms, that "ontogeny recapitulates phylogeny." As Sully explained in "The New Study of Children" (1895), "[The] evolutional point of view enables the psychologist to connect the unfolding of an infant's mind with something that has gone before, with the mental history of the race."[8] One of child study's foundational texts, William T. Preyer's *Die Seele des Kindes* (1882, translated as *The Mind of the Child* in 1890), even recommended measuring the unfolding of the baby's color sensitivity using color patches devised by Magnus himself.[9] When Darwin read Gladstone's Magnus-inflected essay, he sent Gladstone a copy of his article on his infant son, advising him not to jump so quickly from word to sensation.[10] But Darwin's demurral didn't stop Gladstone, or the bulk of child psychologists, from adhering to the recapitulation thesis, with its affinities to the Lamarckian account of color sensitivity. And when Rivers made his case for "primitive color vision" in 1901, he cited Preyer and other figures from child study to support the idea that chromatic perception had evolved within historical time.[11] Throughout the heyday of child psychology, investigations into an infant's color responses doubled as investigations into the history of perception, a kind of archeology of the senses.

Infused with international scientific importance by the color-sense debates, children's experience of color attracted widespread psychological attention and served as a locus for methodological disputes within child study. The early investigations by Darwin, Preyer, and Milicent Washburn Shinn all noted infants' responses to brightly colored objects, observing that they appeared after the response to bright lights but before the recognition of form.[12] Having established the approximate point at which the color sense appears (three to four weeks), Preyer and Shinn then tested its development: Did the child see blue or red first? At what point would she see green? As Darwin's article illustrates, the initial investigations of these questions relied on the child's verbal reporting to establish perceptual salience. However, later studies noted that the mistaken conflation of linguistic and sensory development à la Gladstone skewed the results. Alfred Binet, who included assessments of color perception in his infamous intelligence tests, attempted to correct the problem by asking his child subjects to point to colors rather than name them.[13] But it was James Mark Baldwin, in the essay "A New Method of Child Study" (1893), who argued that once children learned the names for colors, their responses to chromatic stimuli were forever tinged. He therefore proposed that the development of color perception be confined to studies of infants, where the color sense could be observed through hand movements alone.[14] Yet how was one to tell whether the child's reach indicated the range of hues perceived or only the specific colors that tickled his fancy? By raising this question, Sully and Harry K. Wolfe provided one last methodological tweak that turned the seemingly simple "problem of the order of development of the color-sense in children" into a bona fide scientific enterprise best left to experts.[15] They also ensured that investigations of juvenile color perception followed the contemporaneous repackaging of Magnus's color-sense argument in the 1880s from a strictly physiological claim to a more ambiguous assertion about "preference," in which the subject's chromatic likes and dislikes indicated a "general mental proficiency."[16] Just as the Gladstone debate gave added impetus to child study, so too did the empirical methods of psychology hone the understanding of how language and color interacted in the color sense.

Researchers reached opposing conclusions about which color captures the child eye first—Baldwin said blue, others yellow or red. But in the course of refining their methods they crystallized an image of the child's experience of color as prelinguistic, free of conceptual taint, prior to form, and attracted to the most saturated strains of basic hues. They created a naturalized version of the innocent eye, one tied to actual children and conceived within an intellectual framework that equated the nursery years with primitivism, white children with noncivilized others. But while such studies gave an empirical imprimatur to Goethe's assertion that "savage nations, uneducated people, and children have a great predilection for vivid colours," they also raised a problem: how was one to separate the proclivities of children from those of savages?[17] How, in short, was one to *educate* young eyes?

Primitives and Primaries: How Color Entered the Classroom

In 1914, Henry Turner Bailey, editor of the *School Arts Magazine,* cast the adoption of colored materials as part of "the great transition in art-education [that] occurred between 1885 and 1895." "The modern teacher can hardly imagine the dreary gray desert stretches of a drawing exhibit in the early 80s," he surmised, so bold and plentiful had the colors become.[18] Early art instruction had focused on drawing and had elevated "form" as the "language of nature," at the expense of the "transient circumstance" of color.[19] But as Bailey explained, the insights of child study and the new prominence of color in manufacturing had made chromatic education a pressing concern. Invoking the authority of Preyer, Hall, and Stanford University education professor Earl Barnes, he summarized the "consensus of opinion among psychologists" that the "brain responds first to brilliancy, rather than to any particular hue of color; then to the most brilliant hues, yellow, orange, red; next, to intense blue, then to green, and lastly to purple."[20] Not all educators agreed on how to respond to this consensus—in fact, Bailey wrote his editorial to take a side in what he called "the war over Color"—but they all maintained that the primitive color impressions of young children had to be met with systematic color instruction.[21] Without it, children would be relegated to the condition of color insensitivity that Rimington decried in *Colour-Music*. At the end of the nineteenth century, color entered the classroom under the same banner that Rimington waved for abstract art: civilization.

But to the pedagogues responsible for brightening those "gray desert stretches," civilization meant different things, ranging from sensory refinement to technological progress. The three educators who led the charge for color—chromolithographer Louis Prang, color theorist Albert Munsell, and manufacturer Milton Bradley—offered a variety of explanations for why and how children should learn color. These explanations, in turn, exemplify the values that attached to the classroom use of child study's naturalized model of juvenile perception. Even more than child psychology, color education established the key concerns that clustered around children and color at the turn of the century and that the subsequent generation of artists would rework: concerns about progress and degeneration, about industrial production and mass consumption. As John Dewey wrote of "sense-training" in *The School and Society* (1900), a book that brought his psychological training to bear on educational reform, "The bare physical stimulus of light is not the entire reality; the interpretation given to it through social activities and thinking confers upon it its wealth of meaning."[22] Progressive educators devised exercises and systems aimed at giving the "bare stimulus" of color a "wealth of meaning," and their efforts placed the color-absorbed child within the "social activities and thinking" of the United States at the turn of the twentieth century.

Almost all color educators cited child study in pitching their approach, but Prang's *Color Instruction* (1893), cowritten with Mary Dana Hicks and John S. Clark, offered the most enthusiastic endorsement of the idea that education should begin with brilliant colors because schoolchildren have the eyes of primitives. The authors touted their program as the first to ground instruction in "the color perception of the child," leading students "to a knowledge of color through the development of the color sense."[23] Hicks—the real voice behind *Color Instruction,* despite the fact that Prang gets all the credit—conducted her own experiments on "the child's power of color perception" in 1891, and her results provide the basis for the Prang system. She concluded that children detect light hues better than dark ones and that they have a decided preference for yellow; as such, she and Prang told educators to start with that hue and proceed through orange, red, violet, and blue to green. But they followed this advice with the important caveat that instructors should test students early to tailor the course to their abilities, taking care—as Baldwin and Sully had warned—that "the impression or sensation of a color precede its name" (Figure 15).[24] Hicks believed that "the color sense varies greatly in different individuals, because of heredity and because of . . . degree of cultivation," and she cited not only Magnus but also data collected from the Carlisle Industrial Indian School, the Hampton Normal and Agricultural Institute, and the "Chinese children of Oakland" to argue that color sensitivity varied from race to race. She reported that whites liked yellow, but that Native American and black students preferred blue and Chinese kids favored red-orange and yellow-green.[25] *Color Instruction* aimed to train up each student's racially inflected manner of feeling color to the level of a civilized (white) adult.

In Prang's system, becoming a "civilized" perceiver meant something similar to what it signified for Gilman and Rimington: bringing the observer into a more intimate and responsive relation with the sensory world. In "Color in Public Schools," Hicks defined color not as merely an objective property or subjective quality but rather as "the result of the action of the color-sense" and thus as the site at which the permeable boundary between self and world was most evident and up for grabs.[26] Learning about color was a way to acquire a more impressible sensorium, and the more responsive to sensory differences the children were at graduation, the more able they would be to adapt and evolve in the modern workforce that awaited them. To facilitate this training, teachers used an "ideal color unit" made up of twelve different chromatic steps stretching from red to violet (Plate 3). Exercises led students to make finer and finer distinctions—in terms first of hue, then of tone and complementarity, and finally of the history of design—so that they would become better "acquainted with [their] environment" and more attuned to their entanglement with it. Through this dynamic process of color-sense cultivation, the authors explained, the world revealed by the senses would become "more and more real," and the students, properly sensitized, would shed the relative insensitivity associated with primitive vision to become civilized seers.[27]

Albert Munsell granted that children thrilled to bright hues—but he didn't see this as a reason to indulge crude tastes. "It is true," he wrote in *Color and an Eye to Discern It* (1907),

> that [the child] dearly loves to play Indian in the back yard, to scalp his sister, shoot the cat, paint horrid hieroglyphs upon the stable door and make the cook shudder with his yells, but I have yet to visit a school

FIGURE 15. A teacher tests the color sensitivity and preferences of students. Louis Prang, Mary Dana Hicks, and John S. Clark, *Color Instruction: Suggestions for a Course of Instruction in Color for Public Schools* (New York: Prang Educational Company, 1893), 28. Huntington Library, San Marino, California.

where such exercises form the introduction to singing or dancing. Only in color does such savagery exist.[28]

Just because children *like* bright colors, Munsell reasoned, does not mean that they should be offered them. After all, they also "crave candy, matches, the bass drum and the carving knife," but parents keep these out of reach. While Munsell agreed with child psychologists that the primitive behaviors of children recalled "our first parents" who liked "to run wild, to leap and shriek," he saw this as a tendency to be curbed, not quickened. He felt his task all the more pressing because the same chromatic indulgences suffered in the kindergarten were being promoted in mass culture, epitomized by the "crudities of the flaming tomato can and gaudy theatrical poster." "The gaudiest colors are found in the cheapest stores," he wrote, but "homes of cultivation and refinement prefer tempered color." To Munsell's genteel eye, billboards and chromos threatened to turn Americans into perpetual children, and color instruction that catered to the students' primitive impulses only hastened the decline.[29]

Munsell's pedagogical system, which he termed "a measured training of the color sense," tried to nip this problem in the bud. Based on the idea that "education aims at control of the body and the mind," it instilled in children a feel for tasteful color harmonies that calibrated their responses to the chromatic environment.[30] At the center of this effort was a set of five "middle hues," which Munsell derived through two key modifications to existing color systems. First, he demoted orange from a basic color to an intermediate between red and yellow, correcting what he perceived as an imbalance in favor of fiery hues. Second, he mapped color space not only in terms of *hue* (green, blue, red) and *value* (lightness and darkness)—the two axes of other systems—but also in terms of *chroma,* the measure of a color's saturation or its distance from gray. To illustrate, he presented color as a tree, where the trunk represented the scale from black to white (value) and the branches were the distinct hues, each gaining in purity or chroma as it distanced itself from the grayscale base (Figure 16). Some colors extended further than others: red, for instance, had nearly twice the units of chroma as green. The problem with systems like Prang's, Munsell argued, was that the colors they presented as equal in all but hue were in fact wildly divergent in terms of chroma, resulting in a bias toward highly saturated yellows and reds (of the sort that flamed on tomato cans). To arrive at a "measured" color unit, Munsell determined the midpoint between neutral gray and the farthest tip of red, the hue with the most units of chroma, and used this middle position to carve a balanced color sphere from the uneven color tree (Plate 4). The five hues that make up the equator of this sphere, equidistant from both black and white, in one direction, and gray and extreme chroma, in the other, served as Munsell's standards, the colors of the crayons, water-colors, and other materials used by beginners in the Munsell system. These "middle hues" provided the proper "starting-points for training the eye," and "only with such trained judgment," Munsell concluded, "is it safe to undertake the use of strong colors" (Plate 5).[31] Armored with a measured color sense, the graduates of Munsell's courses were meant to shed their taste for garish colors and turn their backs on consumerism's gaudy thrills.

Anyone who has been in a toy store or has been given a child's artwork from day care knows that Munsell's middle hues did not win the day. In

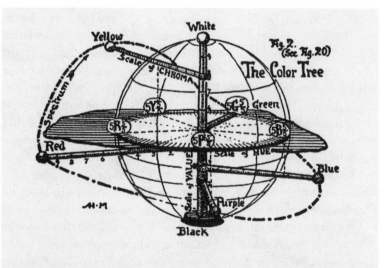

A COLOR SYSTEM WITH COURSE OF STUDY BASED ON THE COLOR SOLID AND ITS CHARTS.

FIGURE 16. The Munsell Color Tree, which illustrates color space in three dimensions. The trunk represents value (lightness or darkness), the branches represent hue, and the extension of the branches represents chroma (saturation). A. H. Munsell, *A Color Notation,* second edition (Boston: George H. Ellis, 1907), 23.

fact, Bailey was targeting Munsell in the aforementioned editorial when he cited child study to argue that the proper colors for early education were bright hues in their utmost "purity." He accused the "measured" approach of "banishing the brilliant colors from the face of the earth" and disregarding nature's most vivid chromatic displays, from "glorious golden mountain peaks" to "emerald hills" and "high-lying lakes of purest blue."[32] Munsell's legacy in fact resides not in the impulse-checking color sphere but in the three-dimensional mapping of color space illustrated by his color tree, which provided the foundation for nearly all color nomenclatures used in color manufacturing throughout the twentieth century. Ironically, the man who set out to stymie the rise of consumer culture generated the very tools that fueled its acceleration.[33] In the end, Munsell's measured training of the color sense stands as a disapproving acknowledgment of the links between white children, mass culture, and racial primitives that drove the explosion of bright, modern colors at the turn of the twentieth century.

Milton Bradley, the man Bailey hailed as "the god-father of color instruction in elementary schools," delivered a more positive articulation of these ties in several books on color pedagogy published in the 1890s. Like Prang and Hicks, Bradley appealed to the unique qualities of juvenile perception, reminding his readers that "bright color is the first thing to attract the infant's eye."[34] But unlike the authors of Color Instruction, and far from the advertisement-hating Munsell, Bradley embedded within the nomenclature and exercises of his educational program the perceptual habits of a modern manufacturer. Indeed, it was as a manufacturer that Bradley first came to color education. In the late 1860s, after making his name with the Checkered Game of Life (introduced in 1860), he attended a lecture by Elizabeth Peabody on the education theories of Fröbel, inventor of the kindergarten. Fröbel's curriculum involved a series of "gifts" and "occupations," beginning with six worsted balls of selected colors and including activities such as weaving, paper folding, and clay modeling. At the time, the materials Fröbel specified were only available as imports from his native Germany, but Peabody explained that if the kindergarten movement were to take hold in the United States, they would have to be manufactured domestically. Bradley jumped at the opportunity. Once he started production, however, he immediately ran into trouble: many of the occupations called for colored paper, but Bradley's suppliers could not agree on what any particular hue should look like. Even worse, the hues of the papers were unreliable, even across batches from the same paper mill, so that Bradley "found it impossible to . . . insure his customers that any color he had furnished them could be duplicated."[35]

In the process of solving this problem for business, Bradley formulated his educational program. He established a system of color standards designed to communicate colors between the warehouse and the factory and then used this system to shape students' engagements with the chromatic world. The first step was to institute his own set of standards. In consultation with artists and scientists, Bradley decided that the six distinct colors of the solar spectrum—red, orange, yellow, green, blue, and violet—provided the only solid touchstone for color (Plate 1). (Six rather than seven, because who sees indigo in the rainbow anyway? Newton snuck it in to get enough colors to match the seven notes of the musical scale.) The central conceit of the Bradley method is that these colors, as the fundamental colors of light, are somehow the world's realest colors and that the secret to developing the color sense is to create a "mental image" of them that would be as vividly present to the student "as that of the cube after it has been handled and modeled."[36] Whereas Prang's ideal color unit aimed to cultivate children's openness to their environment and Munsell's middle hues sought to protect students from the commercial environment's brash appeals, Bradley's solar spectrum encouraged children to approach the visible world as an assortment of decomposable colors able to be reconstructed and mass-produced on demand. To this end, students began their course by moving hue by hue through the standards, then studying the increments between them, then their mixtures with white, black, and gray, before finally—finally!—turning to the colors of the landscape, household objects, and flowers.

But even once they had reentered the realm of everyday color experience, their task was to treat it as a conglomeration of the abstract standards. The characteristic assignment in the Bradley system, detailed in Bradley's own books and in those of his followers, was the *color analysis,* in which children broke down the component parts of natural objects, often with the aid of a Milton Bradley Company Color Wheel (for demonstrations to the entire class) or a Color Top (for individual exercises) (Figures 1, 3, and 4). Students were asked to "scale the color in a stalk of celery" or to explain "how . . . the color of a pepper or a tomato differ[s] from standard green," and eventually they learned to do away with the conventional belief that celery is simply "green" and instead think of it as a mixture of standard hues.[37] These assignments aimed to "lead the pupil to closer observation, to see color where he has never thought of looking for it, to discover harmonies where he never knew before they could be found" (*Color in the Kindergarten,* 32). Yet we must ask what sorts of color experiences Bradley led the student to have. What did a child see when he noticed color where he had "never thought of looking for it"? From this perspective, color analysis transformed Fröbel's emphasis on the discovery of "inner unity" into an exercise in apprehending the world's hues as so many stacks of colored materials waiting to be called up from the warehouse and arranged in ever more spectacular chromatic goods. What the child learned to see using the spectrum standards was a sensory environment waiting to be harnessed and configured through modern technology. As Bradley boasted, "The graduate from a two year's course in the kindergarten may have a better color sense than is at present enjoyed by the average business or professional man."[38]

Instrumental in facilitating this improved color sense was the nomenclature that Bradley derived from his spectrum standards. Throughout his career in education, Bradley set out not only to educate the eyes of America's next generation of workers but also to facilitate the flow of commerce by constructing an objective way of communicating color and thus of ironing out the confusion that had launched him into education. He wanted to replace the loose and "contradictory" ways in which "artists, naturalists, manufacturers, tradesmen, milliners and the members of our household" speak about color with a precise nomenclature that would allow a businessman in Springfield to order the exact tint he needed from a supplier in Boston without ever boarding a train or mailing a sample (*Color in the Kindergarten,* 27, 23). He thus recommended that all colors be denominated as ratios of the mixtures of the spectrum standards (R, O, Y, G, B, V), along with black (N) and white (W). To illustrate, he translated some of the fanciful color names popular in the 1890s into his own vocabulary. "Ashes of roses," a shade of violet-red, became "R.8¼, V.2¼, W.15½, N.74"; "Oasis," a shade of yellowish-green, was written "Y.7, G.10½, W.8½, N.74"; and "Empire" green appeared as "G.18½, B.11, W.16½, N.53" (23).[39] Bradley bragged that his own company had already benefited from "telephoning colors" from the office to the mill, and in his educational books he encouraged teachers to introduce students to these exact ways of speaking (18). As an example of the benefits to be gained when "the days of 'baby talk'" about colors had passed, he told an anecdote about a "little child who had become somewhat familiar with the color wheel." One day, she asked her teacher the color of a dress "of the so-called 'mahogany color.'"

> Wishing to test the judgment of the child the reply was, "What do you think it is?" The child replied, "Well, I rather think it is a shade of red orange," which was a very close description of the color. And why is it not better to say a dark red orange than "mahogany color," if any definite expression is required? (40)

The child in this story has traded an understanding of color predicated on real-world referents ("mahogany") for one tied to a relational system designed with the needs of business in mind. Bradley's system of "definite expression" makes the very abstract idea that colors are entities unto themselves—separate from the objects and events they qualify—as elementary as *A, B, C.*

Bradley cast color education as a means of endowing students with the linguistic and perceptual faculties to participate in an advanced capitalist society, his version of "civilization." He pressed the case for color-sense training by noting that color, a quickly developing field of industrial production, was one of the West's weak spots: there had been "little or no advance in color perception . . . in modern times," he complained, and even "semi-civilized nations," whose drawings are "the least artistic," "greatly surpass us in natural color perceptions." "If color is the one thing in which we are deficient and in which we are making no advance," he challenged, "is it not necessary that we adopt a new line of operations for our color instruction in the primary grades?"[40] Bradley's system devised materials, lessons, and language for improving the "natural color perceptions" of American children, ultimately by treating colors as discrete sensory stimuli available for inclusion within a commodity in order to amplify its visual appeal. To be sure, all systems of color education at the turn of the twentieth century emphasized the commercial benefits of color-sense training, but Bradley's program built the manufacturer's mode of perception into its exercises most vividly, weaving them into the frameworks he inherited from Fröbel and child study.

Despite their differences, Prang, Munsell, and Bradley agreed that the unique chromatic proclivities of schoolchildren had to be met with systematic training and that such instruction—administered through elaborate nomenclatures, chromatic standards, coordinated materials, and classroom exercises—enriched rather than stifled students' experiences of color. They wanted to bolster children's inarticulate color perceptions with specialized languages for denoting thousands of tones and tints, in the hope that with greater conceptual nuance would come greater sensitivity. Prang and his coauthors even included poetic descriptions of chromatic experience, drawn from Tennyson, Henry Wadsworth Longfellow, Christina Rossetti, and several lesser-known writers, to model cultivated color feelings to upper-level students. Across these programs, education entailed infusing bare sensation with meaning, and in the specific features of their systems pedagogues at the turn of the twentieth century articulated the social significance that attached to color perception in the culture at large. Prang's students were treated as primitive perceivers working their way toward civilization; Munsell's embodied the conservative reaction to consumer culture; Bradley's came to see the world as manufacturers. Together these approaches reveal the way color education integrated the naturalized understanding of innocent vision codified in psychology into the economic objectives and racial frameworks of the United States as it moved into the twentieth century.

By the 1920s, however, when the rage for color in business was at its peak, the commitment to *system* had given way to a celebration of *expression,* with the result that language and perception became opposed in figurations of child vision. Finger painting replaced color analysis as the representative activity, and the celebration of children's uneducated and instinctual color experiences captured in Stieglitz's exhibition of children's drawings supplanted the emphasis on training and balance in Munsell's booklets of "children's studies in measured colors."[41] Hartmann decried the teacher's "pedantic advice," and Benjamin insisted that "color as perceived by children . . . can be related to no higher concept of color (through development)."[42] The revised image of the color-absorbed child also proved helpful for modern advertising, with its persistent truck in primitivism. As the color consultant Louis Weinberg wrote in *Color in Everyday Life* (1918), voicing sentiments that Hartmann would have seconded, "The Puritanic character of our education tends to make people feel that the color sense of children should be refined away from that of savages to the grays and color anaemia of civilized life"; however, "the child's love of colors will hurt neither its eyes nor its taste," and in fact must be "indulge[d]" if it is to be "conserved into adult years."[43] Indulgence rather than refinement: the ever-growing consumer economy needed spectators able to be color-struck more than it needed teenagers capable of dissecting complex tints. This imperative accorded well with the modernist vision of the child's view of color, in which education equaled convention and language was the enemy of immediacy. But the colors of art and commerce entailed their own pedagogies, and the 1920s configuration of childish perception did not so much abolish systematic color knowledge as sequester it as a matter for experts like Weinberg. In ways that would have made Munsell shiver, billboards and city streets continued to teach Americans to delight in bright hues. What links these two versions of color education? How did the color-absorbed child move from the classroom to the show window? Between the linguistically enhanced sensations of the pedagogues and the language-free wonders of commercial spectacle lay the mixtures of bright inks and verbal narratives that fill the pages of children's picture books, multimedia objects that continued the task of instructing kids in how to see consumerism's gaudy hues.

Bright Colors to Please a Child:
Picture Books and the Racially Innocent Eye

In 1903, with the lessons of child study foremost in his mind, art critic J. M. Bowles complained, "In no other field has the real fitness of things to their uses been so flagrantly disregarded as in the making of books for children."[44] Despite the "many special endeavors . . . to put forth works of art for the delectation of the child mind," the majority of illustrators, according to Bowles, miss the "most important point in educational method": "that the art must be reduced to the child's understanding to be of any real value or enjoyment to him" (377, 378). He condemned the "old monstrosities of picture-books" for their haphazard designs that "outrage[d] the color sense," and he then went further by dismissing the accomplished works of Bernard Boutet de Monvel and Kate Greenaway for requiring an "educated eye," "a developed sense for exquisite form and refined color" unavailable to young readers (380, 378). Artists who draw for children, Bowles insisted, must learn to "be truly simple for a child's mind and eye." The first rule: adopt "a palette limited to strong colors" because children "love color," especially "vivid and striking" ones (380, 379).

Bowles's call for "children's books for children" demonstrates that by the early twentieth century the creation and reception of picture books had incorporated the naturalized version of childlike vision theorized by child psychology and addressed in color pedagogy. Within this matrix, as Walter Field noted in "The Illustrating of Children's Books," the color illustrations made more prevalent by innovations in color printing administered a "powerful educative influence" important in "forming taste and influencing character," and parents were advised to choose their children's reading matter wisely. In particular, reviewers encouraged those buying books for children to acknowledge that a love of "pure bright color" is "the natural heritage of the child," but also to take care that this heritage not sink into the ribaldry of the Sunday comics.[45]

Tastemakers aside, however, children's books were not reducible to exercises in systematic color instruction. In fact, the upshot of the invocation of pedagogical theories to justify the new emphasis on bright, saturated hues was to create a visual style predicated on the unique color proclivities of children but detached from a strict developmental program. Illustrators and authors creating works for children at the turn of the twentieth century embraced the opportunity to visualize the chromatic experience of children without feeling saddled by an imperative to train it. They thus took up a particular task: enlisting the wide-eyed perception of vivid colors codified in psychology and education without thereby invoking images of racial primitives and the low-class thrills of mass culture. They sought, as Field put it, to create images that were "bright without being lurid," childish without being savage.[46] In the process, they remade the child's view of color into an aesthetic ideal, a technique for inciting wonder and stirring interest equally available to illustrators, artists, advertisers, and consumers.

For Bowles, the simplified forms and bold color patches that characterize W. W. Denslow's work for children exemplified the lineaments of an artistic style fashioned especially for kids. As a newspaper illustrator and art-poster designer, Denslow had abandoned the cross-hatching and detail of his contemporaries in favor of the strong lines and flat backgrounds he admired in Japanese woodcuts.[47] Such techniques proved perfect for capturing the "child's own method of expressing his ideas," and they informed Denslow's most characteristic and child-friendly trait: the abstract blocks of pure hue that float on his pages, bearing no relation to the objects or characters of the narrative.[48] Speaking of these "cleverly disposed spots and masses of color scattered throughout the Denslow books," Bowles reported that he "[had] seen a baby of twelve months beam with delight as some of these pages were turned, and fairly jump at color deliberately placed by the crafty Mr. Denslow" (382) (Figures 17 and 18). These patches proved that Denslow recognized the unique perceptual profile of his audience. He appreciated that "the baby goes for vivid color, effectively used, if for no other reason than he sees it first," and he pitched his palette to "arouse these little emotions" (380, 382). In short, Bowles proclaimed, "Denslow knows the baby mind" (384).

By praising Denslow's bold hues as appeals to infantine sight, Bowles marked an affinity between the newly naturalized child's view of color and the techniques of painterly abstraction emerging in the early twentieth century. He saw the floating masses of vivid color that dotted Denslow's pages not only as visualizations of an untutored color sense but also as applications of modern aesthetic principles, shaped to the child eye. He speculated:

> Were the baby or young child to analyze and explain to us the causes of his delight in color, it might reason as follows: "Den's panels, circles, and spots, and his solid pages of gorgeous hues with perhaps one tiny figure or object in a lower corner are simply baits to catch my attention through my eye, which as yet gets only general impressions. In other words, my friend Mr. Denslow is an impressionist for babies. He omits all but fundamentals and essentials. He leaves out of his books everything except things that exist in our own little world of fact." (382–83)

When Bowles penned this remarkable passage, he was not long out of his post as the editor of *Modern Art,* a "key site for the elaboration and circulation of an emerging modernist aesthetics" in the 1890s.[49] The magazine featured cover art by Arthur Dow, a doyen of modern American painting, and published such essays as "Mr. Prang's New Theory."[50] In fact, Prang's company printed *Modern Art.* When Bowles praised Denslow as an "impressionist for babies," then, he situated the child's view of color within the distinctive mix of avant-garde and popular styles characteristic of American modernism in the 1890s.

Yet note how the theory and practice of the innocent eye change once passed through the alembics of child psychology and color pedagogy. Ruskin proposed adopting a "childish" perception of "flat stains of color" as an ideal to help artists shirk conceptual habit and see the world as it is. The result was supposed to be something like Turner's fiery depictions of the sky or Monet's blue-tinged shadows: aesthetic manifestations

"And I should never get back to Kansas," said Dorothy.

"We must certainly get to the Emerald City if we can," the Scarecrow continued, and he pushed so hard on his long pole that it stuck fast in the mud at the bottom of the river, and before he could pull it out again, or let go, the raft was swept away and the poor Scarecrow left clinging to the pole in the middle of the river.

"Good bye!" he called after them, and they were very sorry to leave him; indeed, the Tin Woodman began to cry, but fortunately remembered that he might rust, and so dried his tears on Dorothy's apron.

Of course this was a bad thing for the Scarecrow.

"I am now worse off than when I first met Dorothy," he thought. "Then, I was stuck on a pole in a cornfield, where I could make believe scare the crows, at any rate; but surely there is no use for a Scarecrow stuck on a pole in the middle of a river. I am afraid I shall never have any brains, after all!"

Down the stream the raft floated, and the poor Scarecrow was left far behind. Then the Lion said:

"Something must be done to save us. I think I can swim to the shore and pull the raft after

FIGURE 17. An example of Denslow's "cleverly disposed spots and masses of color," as described by J. M. Bowles, here in the form of a red rectangle. L. Frank Baum, *The Wonderful Wizard of Oz,* illustrations by W. W. Denslow (Chicago: George M. Hill, 1900), 89; J. M. Bowles, "Children's Books for Children," *Brush and Pencil* 12, no. 6 (September 1903): 382. Kislak Center for Special Collections, Rare Books and Manuscripts, University of Pennsylvania, Philadelphia, Pennsylvania.

over her shoulder at the clumsy strangers, holding her
nicked elbow close to her side.

Dorothy was quite grieved at this mishap.

"We must be very careful here," said the
kind-hearted Woodman, "or we may hurt these
pretty little people so they will never get
over it."

A little farther on Dorothy met a most
beautiful dressed young princess, who stopped
short as she saw the strangers and started to
run away.

Dorothy wanted to see more of the
Princess, so she ran after her; but the china girl
cried out,

"Don't chase me! don't chase me!"

She had such a frightened little voice that
Dorothy stopped and said,

"Why not?"

"Because," answered the princess, also stop-
ping, a safe distance away, "if I run I may fall
down and break myself."

"But couldn't you be mended?" asked
the girl.

"Oh, yes; but one is never so pretty
after being mended, you know," replied the
princess.

"I suppose not," said Dorothy.

FIGURE 18. This brown spot is another color patch that Denslow uses to catch the
child's attention. Baum, *The Wonderful Wizard of Oz,* illustrations by Denslow, 231.
Kislak Center for Special Collections, Rare Books and Manuscripts, University of
Pennsylvania, Philadelphia, Pennsylvania.

of a superior empiricism. In literature, it motivated Garland's strained attempts to capture the shifting hues of light as they played on perception. The abstractions of "pure color," in these cases, were always folded back into a realist project. But in the years around Bowles's essay on Denslow, postimpressionist painters such as Matisse in France and Dow in America transformed the "simplified" presentation of chromatic patches into a staple of modernist art. The general principle remained unchanged from Ruskin: the child, like the primitive with whom it was associated, provided a fresh perspective that escaped the nets of convention. But since the understanding of what children saw had been altered by psychologists such as Baldwin and educators like Hicks, the visual results of adopting a child's perspective were different. By becoming an impressionist for babies, Denslow forged a style resonant with the postimpressionism of adults.[51]

As an illustrator for children, Denslow toed a line that the painters were happy to flout: his colorful style had to invoke the wondrous perceptions of childhood without advocating a primitivism that parents would not accept. He had to be "bright without being lurid." Doing so meant taking up the task of the educators and training children and parents alike to revel in the bright hues that custom would have them shun. Neither Denslow nor any other illustrator could do this alone; rather, the instruction occurred in the way picture books paired vivid illustrations with verbal stories, modeling for young readers how the colors on the page could and should be felt. The most common strategy involved pairing the *form* of the child's view of color (bright hues, vividly presented) with *content* that invited white readers to distinguish themselves from the ethnic and racial groups associated with bright hues. Rather than collapsing the thrill of color with the unsophisticated shenanigans of the slums, as with R. F. Outcault's sensational comic *Hogan's Alley,* Denslow's collaborations with Baum pried apart the rapturous wonder sparked by color from the uncontrolled sensitivity attributed to those whose color sense remained "primitive." They presented less "civilized" figures through chromatic printing techniques designed both to exaggerate racial difference and to dazzle the child reader, fostering a perceptual experience that harnessed the childish delight in color to the solidification of racial hierarchies. Drawing on Robin Bernstein's analysis in *Racial Innocence* (2011) of how racist ideology is perpetuated in the supposedly innocent space of childhood, we might say that children's books at the turn of the twentieth century transformed the innocent eye into the racially innocent eye: a figure for absorbed perception that carried within it the model of white superiority inherited from child study.[52]

Take Denslow's first collaboration with Baum, *Father Goose, His Book,* a book of nursery rhymes hand-lettered to resemble miniature art posters. In his introduction to the book, Baum noted that it aimed to excite the "fascination in the combination of jingling verse and bright pictures that always appeals strongly to children." The rhymes that follow, in addition to presenting a variety of animals and silly situations, direct that fascination toward a run of racial types, including an "Ab-o-rig-i-ne" doll, a "funny little Chinaman," a "little nigger boy," a freckled "Yankee boy," and a "bright Irish lad" (Figures 19–22). The Chinaman's pigtail is extended in one of Denslow's serpentine lines; the poem about the "nigger boy" dips into dialect and pokes fun at his poverty; the Irish lad lazes around and eventually joins the police force; the "funny" "Injun" doll, painted with bright red stripes, stands opposite its delicately shaded white owner. In each case the "fun" of the rhymes depends on the perpetuation of racist libel aimed at inflating the white reader's sense of privilege while delighting the youthful hunger for vivid hues. Baum specifies the cultural necessity of these "colorful" figures in "What Can a Civilized Boy Do Now," a rhyme that bemoans the loss of dragons and adventure in the wake of scientific modernity and insists on the need for a new imaginative landscape, one closely linked to the imperial adventures described in the poems "Rough Riders" and "Her Country's Enemies." What the civilized boy needs now, Baum and Denslow suggested, is an imagined engagement with other lands and other people, rendered in bright colors.

The chromatic coincidence of modern printing methods and primitive racial types occurs throughout juvenile print culture at the turn of the twentieth century, from the Jungle Imp in Winsor McCay's *Little Nemo in Slumberland* to the minstrel characters in Denslow's solo work and the catalog of racist images filling the funny papers. As Kyla Wazana Tompkins writes of advertising trade cards at the end of the nineteenth century, new color printing presses "provided a base for aesthetic experiments" involving the "detailed portrayal of ethnic and phenotypic difference—for instance, the ability to mark a character as Irish by making her hair bright orange."[53] A variety of such experiments fill the pages of *Kids of Many Colors* (1901), written by Grace Duffie Boylan and illustrated with saturated patches of color by Ike Morgan, Denslow's friend

Uncle Dick gave me a dolly,
  Funny doll, as you can see;
'Twas an Injun, so he called my
  Dolly "Ab~o~rig~i~ne."

Dolly's made of rags and
              patches,
Can't be broke by girls
              like me;
So I think he'll last
              forever—
Funny "Ab~o~rig~i~ne."

FIGURE 19. Example of the "racially innocent eye" in Denslow's collaborations with Baum. L. Frank Baum and W. W. Denslow, *Father Goose, His Book* (Chicago: George M. Hill, 1899), unpaginated. Baldwin Library of Historical Children's Literature, Special and Area Studies Collections, George A. Smathers Libraries, University of Florida, Gainesville, Florida.

Lee-Hi-Lung-Whan
Was a little Chinaman.
Wooden shoes with pointed
toes,
Almond eyes and tiny nose,

Pig-tail long and slick and black,
Clothes the same both front and back,
Funny little Chinaman,
Le-Hi-Lung-Whan.

FIGURE 20. Denslow's characteristic serpentine line is here applied to the pigtail of the "Chinaman." Baum and Denslow, *Father Goose, His Book,* unpaginated. Baldwin Library of Historical Children's Literature, Special and Area Studies Collections, George A. Smathers Libraries, University of Florida, Gainesville, Florida.

FIGURE 21. One of Denslow's characteristic spots of color, here applied to a racist caricature to accompany a racist rhyme. Baum and Denslow, *Father Goose, His Book*, unpaginated. Baldwin Library of Historical Children's Literature, Special and Area Studies Collections, George A. Smathers Libraries, University of Florida, Gainesville, Florida.

John Harrison Hoy
Was a cute Yankee boy,
With a face that was freckled and red;
"Each American boy
Is a King," said young Hoy,
"For a crown always grows on his head."

FIGURE 22. Another Denslow color spot sets off a "Yankee Boy." Baum and Denslow, *Father Goose, His Book,* unpaginated. Baldwin Library of Historical Children's Literature, Special and Area Studies Collections, George A. Smathers Libraries, University of Florida, Gainesville, Florida.

and former roommate. The book followed hot on the heels of the duo's successful *Young Folks' Uncle Tom's Cabin* (1901) and joined *Father Goose* in playing to the "wonder" that, in Boylan's words, "our little boys and girls" have about "other lands, across some distant sea."[54] The cover visualizes the central strategy and dynamic of the book: a white child peeks over an abstract color patch to gaze on a parade of exotic racial types (Plate 6). The color patch simultaneously separates the children (the white child watches while the others march) and forms the visual thread that connects them, as the same qualities of saturation spill into the faces and costumes of all of the children. Morgan's cover image thus displays the process whereby the absorption in bright hues that child study claimed as a link between white children and nonwhite others was employed precisely to break that link, reconfiguring it as the (white) child's "wonder" at "kids of many colors."

The rest of Morgan's illustrations continue the work of the cover by bending Denslow's "impressionism for babies" to the ends of exaggerating racial difference. In one of the earliest images, Morgan presents a child artist facing the reader and holding an oversized palette loaded with yellow, red, blue, and black—a version of the printer's pigments. Behind the child are three racist caricatures: a big-lipped, bug-eyed black head; a squinty-eyed, pony-tailed yellow head; and a painted and feathered red one (Plate 7).[55] The illustration invites young readers to imagine themselves as the artist, ready to use the vivid colors all children love to picture their difference from the exotic others on display in the book. Moreover, the images that follow apply their thickest hues either to the Denslow-like floating spots that tickle the child mind or to the skin and faces of the children "of many colors," demonstrating once again the affinities between a visual aesthetic of abstract hues aimed at children and the invocation of all those ethnic and racial groups thought to have a more rudimentary color sensitivity. *Kids of Many Colors* demonstrates that the direct connections with racial primitives were scrambled in order to free up the child's view of color for general consumption.

Repackaged as wonderful rather than primitive, childish color perception delineated a mode of perceptual engagement prized by advertisers, marketers, and all those seeking to attract the pedestrian's eye. Literary critic Gillian Brown has argued that children's absorbed play offered nineteenth-century Americans "a tableau of how absorption works," one useful "for attaching persons to different objects and interests," and the bright colors that enrapture young viewers provided a key resource in these endeavors.[56] What is prized in the child's response is immediacy and intensity—an unreflective thrill. Yet by the 1890s, color research outside child study had revealed "a surprising love of contrasts of highly saturated colors" in all adults, and advertisers sought to exploit this receptivity even as they continued to cast it as property of children and exotics.[57] In an aside, Bowles described the way commercial artists conjured chromatic absorption using strategies similar to those he praised in Denslow's drawings: "In the designers' room of a certain large manufacturer of cards and posters," he revealed, "the color red has been nicknamed 'the secret'" for its ability to stimulate viewers without their noticing (380). Just as Munsell feared, the creators of billboards and tin-can labels assumed the role of clandestine educators of the public eye, wielding the secrets of color harmonies to excite the child eye latent in adults.

Many of the artists making stories and images for children had dual careers in commercial color—Denslow, for instance, designed trade cards and theater posters before illustrating *Father Goose*—but nobody captured the entanglement of childish perception and consumer attractions more vividly than Baum. In the years leading up to *The Wonderful Wizard of Oz*, he edited the *Show Window*, a professional journal that offered practical advice to merchants and window trimmers on how to increase the appeal of their goods through aesthetic display. Baum's window work epitomized what historian William Leach calls the "commercial aesthetic" rooted in manipulations of "color, glass, and light." By appropriating these "visual materials of desire," traditionally used by armies, states, and religions to "depict otherworldly paradises" worthy of "devotion, loyalty, and fear," advertisers and show-window decorators stimulated consumption by suggesting a "*this*-worldly paradise" of pleasure and comfort.[58] Advertising posters, display cases, and department-store interiors all used bold hues meant to attract attention and stir affective responses. Baum's journal not only promoted these trends by publishing essays on the psychological impact of color combinations but also tested them in its own pages: as Leach notes, the journal "was bedecked in colors—rose, pink, yellow, green, tan, blue, and brown."[59] In 1900, Baum collected the best bits from the *Show Window*, added up-to-date examples, and published them as *The Art of Decorating Dry Goods Windows and Interiors*. Among advice on the use of manikins and papier-mâché props, the manual included a guide for producing attractive color effects, complete with a diagram of possible combinations for those without "an eye for color."[60] "Color combinations are governed by set laws," Baum explained, and by arranging colors intelligently, window trimmers could capture the coveted attention of passers-by (24). Baum's trade writing gave advertisers a course in color education—yet the goal was not to train to the child eye, but to awaken childlike perception.

In particular, Baum instructed his readers to use the laws of color to incite in viewers a tingle of sensory immediacy, a feeling of presentness that could then be transferred to the commodities. To this end, he recommended the "bright and varied colorings" of cheesecloth for the backgrounds of window displays. Easily harmonized and arranged, these hues make a window

> attractive enough to stop pedestrians, who, glancing at the display, unconsciously note that the goods on exhibition are thrown prominently into the foreground, while the coloring that made them pause has modestly retired and serves only as a foil for the articles of merchandise. (27)

Though undetected, colors performed the most essential work of advertising and marketing in the emerging consumer culture: that of "arrest[ing] the eye of the passive throng and so direct[ing] attention to the goods themselves." Even items "desirable in themselves," Baum noted, still "need a color effect to throw them out properly"; for as one of the merchant John Wanamaker's decorators once quipped, "People do not buy the thing, they buy the effect" (35).[61] And the effects they want, Baum maintained, are those with the illicit thrill of the primitive. "Suggest possibilities of color and sumptuous displays that would delight the heart of an oriental," he advised—but he could have just as easily invoked the "bright" hues that "appeal strongly to children."[62] Baum's call to master the laws of color to the end of producing an unknowing encounter with chromatic arrangements modified the task of color instruction and the understanding of the child's view of color it assumed. Rather than civilizing childish perception through exercises in harmony and contrast, linking intelligence and sensation in the mind of the student, advertisers were to display only the products of color knowledge, not its principles, with the goal of quickening the childlike, "oriental" heart in white adults.

In *The Woggle-Bug Book*, a collaboration with Ike Morgan of *Kids of Many Colors*, Baum built an entire plot around the primitive delights offered by the chromatic arrangements of modern commodities. The

Woggle-Bug at the book's center is a variation on the Zip Coon figure familiar from the minstrel stage, and like all such figures he has a penchant for exuberant clothes and overblown phrases. The Woggle-Bug "took care to clothe himself like a man; only, instead of choosing sober colors for his garments, he delighted in the most gorgeous reds and yellows and blues and greens; so that if you looked at him long the brilliance of his clothing was liable to dazzle your eyes."[63] Far from being incidental, the Woggle-Bug's passion for strong color combinations drives the story, which turns on his attempts to acquire a "marvelous dress" that he sees in a show window. "The designer must have had a real woggly love for bright colors," we are told, "for the gown was made of cloth covered with big checks which were so loud the fashion books called them 'Wagnerian Plaids'" (4) (Plate 8). The ensuing chase after the marvelous plaids leads the child reader through a train of stereotypes, using the antics of ethnic others to distinguish childish color experience from a racially marked love of bright color contrasts. Baum and Morgan invite their reader simultaneously to share the Woggle-Bug's passion, so vividly illustrated across the book's pages, and to distinguish themselves from the characters he encounters.

The love-struck Woggle-Bug pursues the garish garment as it passes from one owner to another, each time sliding further down the social ladder. Already heavily discounted at the beginning of the narrative (and thus removed from elite consumption), the dress passes from a "haughty" woman to her Irish servant, then to a dialect-speaking Swedish widow, then to an African American washerwoman who, "being colored—that is, she had a deep mahogany complexion—was delighted with her gorgeous gown" (24). When the Woggle-Bug frightens the washerwoman with his aggressive courtship, she sells it to "a Chinaman who lived next door." "Its bright colors pleased the Chink," so he "ripped [the dress] up and made it over into a Chinese robe" (26). Undeterred, the Woggle-Bug wrestles the fabric from the "Chinaman," only to have his opponent pull a knife and chase him into a hot-air balloon which, once airborne, passes by a witch from Oz. Yet the balloon lands not in the Emerald City but in an Arab country, where a sheikh commandeers the beloved fabric for a waistcoat but spares a square for the Woggle-Bug's tie. The conclusion makes explicit the notion of a civilizational hierarchy stretching from savage to Anglo-Saxon that underwrites the whole story by giving the final punch line to the chimpanzee Miss Chim, who quips that "men, whether black or white, seem to me the lowest of all created beasts" (42). Like *Kids of Many Colors,* Baum's collaboration with Morgan enforces the separation between the civilized white readers and the ethnic minorities whose colorful capers provide "racially innocent" amusement, with the addition that Baum links this separation directly to the dynamics of consumer desire.

The simultaneous embrace and disavowal of color in *The Woggle-Bug Book,* leading child readers to laugh at the minstrel-like Woggle-Bug's pursuit of "Wagnerian plaids" while at the same time indulging their "woggly love" of the bright hues put on the page by modern print technology, brokered a compromise among the disparate pedagogical takes on the color-absorbed child. That is, Baum and Morgan answered Munsell's warnings against indulging "savage" tendencies at the same time that they honored Prang's insistence on the unique chromatic experience of children and Bradley's push for consumer-minded color instruction. Not that they responded to these theories directly—Baum's references to education were slight. Rather, *The Woggle-Bug Book,* along with *Father Goose, Kids of Many Colors,* and so many other picture books at the turn of the twentieth century, took up the links between racial primitives, children, and saturated colors that concerned teachers and psychologists and reformulated them to craft a visual aesthetic of childlike perception embraced as distinctly modern. They performed a sensory pedagogy of their own, training readers to feel the primitive tingle of vibrant color experience without relinquishing their whiteness, and they thus played a constitutive role in savage color perception's transition from a pejorative attribution to a perceptual quality prized in modernist aesthetics and modern advertising alike. Works like *The Woggle-Bug Book* capture these processes in action, but the best example of how the trope of the child's view of color operated once revamped comes in Baum and Denslow's most famous collaboration, *The Wonderful Wizard of Oz.*

Oz and the Upset Ink Bottle

In the months leading up to the publication of *The Wonderful Wizard of Oz,* Baum wrote to his brother Harry to express his excitement about the look of his upcoming book: "Denslow has made profuse illustrations for it," he boasted, "and it will glow with bright colors."[64] We tend to think of *Oz*'s signature color trick as belonging to the film. But when MGM wowed moviegoers with the sudden switch from sepia-toned Kansas to Technicolor Oz, they were only repackaging the move that Baum and Denslow had made thirty-nine years earlier, when they mustered modern print technologies and design techniques to stage a dazzling transition to color in the pages of their book. With twenty-four full-color plates interspersed among 130 monochrome drawings in grey, blue, green, yellow, red, and brown, *The Wonderful Wizard of Oz* outshone every other children's book on the market in 1900, and reviewers never failed to remark on the book's "uncommon" images and "wild riots of color."[65] Indeed, the very story of Oz, starting with the initial shift from the drab to the spectacular, is in many ways *about* modern color and its ability to excite viewers to a state of rapt wonder. More than any other children's book, the original *Oz* demonstrates the visual aesthetic of the child's view of color joining with techniques of mass color printing to effect a sensory education in consumer spectacle.

Understanding *Oz* requires approaching it as a truly collaborative, multimedia work. One of the wonders of *The Wonderful Wizard* is its interweaving of illustrations and text, its thorough intermingling of Denslow's drawings with the printed words of Baum's tale. To one reviewer, this mélange of word and image "suggest[ed] the upset ink-bottle," and surely some of the most saturated pages of *Oz* run the risk of occluding the words in favor of the colors (Figure 23).[66] But though they may jostle, the hues on the page are carefully coordinated with those of the narrative. Baum divided his fantasy land into color-coded regions—the blue land of the Munchkins, the green-spectacled views of the Emerald City, the yellow territory in the west, and the red domain of the Quadlings—and as his characters pass from one area to another, Denslow's illustrations change hue to match the setting. The opening illustrations of Kansas and the cyclone are grey, the drawings of Dorothy's fortuitous fall among the Munchkins are blue, the Great Wizard appears in green, and so on. These single-color geographies showcased the color print technology displayed on nearly every page of the book while avoiding multicolor illustrations, which would have been prohibitively expensive. In this light, Dorothy's trip to the southern kingdom of the Quadlings after the Wizard's departure—which is generally treated as the anticlimactic result of sloppy writing—offered an occasion to add a red section to the blue, yellow, green, and brown ones that preceded it. Though we often think of illustrations as following the text, *Oz* presents a case of an author

The next morning the soldier with the green whiskers led the Lion to the great Throne Room and bade him enter the presence of Oz.

The Lion at once passed through the door, and glancing around saw, to his surprise, that before the throne was a Ball of Fire, so fierce and glowing he could scarcely bear to gaze upon it. His first thought was that Oz had by accident caught on fire and was burning up; but, when he tried to go nearer, the heat was so intense that it singed his whiskers, and he crept back tremblingly to a spot nearer the door.

Then a low, quiet voice came from the Ball of Fire, and these were the words it spoke:

"I am Oz, the Great and Terrible. Who are you, and why do you seek me?" And the Lion answered,

"I am a Cowardly Lion, afraid of everything. I come to you to beg that you give me courage, so that in reality I may become the King of Beasts, as men call me."

"Why should I give you courage?" demanded Oz.

"Because of all Wizards you are the greatest, and alone have power to grant my request," answered the Lion.

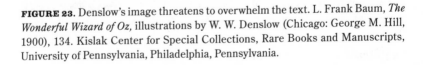

FIGURE 23. Denslow's image threatens to overwhelm the text. L. Frank Baum, *The Wonderful Wizard of Oz,* illustrations by W. W. Denslow (Chicago: George M. Hill, 1900), 134. Kislak Center for Special Collections, Rare Books and Manuscripts, University of Pennsylvania, Philadelphia, Pennsylvania.

composing a story with the medium of illustrations (though not the images themselves) fully in mind.[67]

This formal feature of Baum's narrative—the way it has the author's enthusiasm for Denslow's "bright colors" built into it—explains both the lasting appeal of *Oz* and its relevance for the history of color media. In short, in many ways the durability of Baum's tale results from its ability to showcase the visual technologies, and in particular the *color* technologies, through which it is told. This is why MGM turned to Oz to show off Technicolor in 1939; why NBC began its yearly airings of the movie in the 1950s, at the dawn of color television; and why a Blu-Ray version of the film accompanied its sixtieth anniversary in 2009.[68] For every new color technology, we get a new Oz. In all its iterations, Baum's story draws on the figure of the child protagonist immersed in bright hues to instruct viewers in how to respond to historical color technologies.

Nonetheless critics have been slow to recognize the imbrication of ink and tale so important for Oz's lasting importance, not least because Baum himself tried to hide it. The runaway success of *The Wonderful Wizard of Oz* led author and illustrator to bicker over who was most responsible for the book's sales. The partnership dissolved, and Baum's resentment—teamed with the expense of reprinting the book in its original splendor—ensured that subsequent editions of *Oz* appeared with different illustrations or with no drawings whatsoever. As a result, the collaborative component was effaced, the text was detached from its colors, and critics have approached Baum's hues as mere symbols or allegories. That is, Oz's colors have been read as analogues of populism, Gilded Age excess, the seasons, and Theosophy, but they have yet to be approached as what they actually are: bright, material inks, advertising the book's place within the modern history of color.[69]

The opening pages of *Oz* encourage readers to attend to the book's novel use of material color by figuring the flat, dreary plains of Kansas as the existing field of children's literature. Before the cyclone whisks her away, Dorothy lives with her aunt and uncle amid "the great gray prairie" of Kansas, where "the sun had baked the plowed land into a gray mass."[70] Everything in the first chapter is gray: the house, previously painted, has been "blistered" by the sun to be "as dull and gray as everything else"; the grass "was not green" but, rather, "the same gray color to be seen everywhere" (12). Gray, not brown. Actual sunbaked plains might be monochrome, but they are not *gray;* that is the color of printed text and images, a connection that Baum emphasizes by making the landscape "flat" like paper, with an "edge" which meets the sky in "all directions" (12).[71] Denslow's illustration for this opening chapter positions Dorothy with her back turned to us, peering out onto the gray expanse of the prairie like a child thumbing through a lackluster book (Figure 24). She is bored, and little Toto looks out at us with a sad face. Denslow sets Dorothy as a stand-in for the reader-viewer, just as he positions the Tin-Man and Scarecrow as perusing the front matter (Figure 25). Together with Baum's print-like characterization of Kansas, Denslow's drawings foreground the materiality of the book to maximize the impending shift to splendid color.

Baum draws on the tropes of the child's view of color to heighten the effect even further. The Kansas sun dulls not only the earth but also its inhabitants: Uncle Henry is gray "from his long beard to his rough boots," and Aunt Em, who had arrived in Kansas a "young, pretty wife," is now as dull as her husband. The sun and wind "had taken the sparkle from her eyes and left them a sober gray; they had taken the red from her cheeks and lips, and they were gray also" (13, 12). Denslow's second illustration for the first chapter pictures this relentless color drain by removing the black outlines around the dour family, leaving them only a pale grey tone that shows weakly against the more saturated text (Plate 9). Yet Dorothy and Toto retain their figurative "color" even in this bleak country. "Toto . . . made Dorothy laugh," the narrator explains, "and saved her from growing as gray as her other surroundings." Not that he was colorful—he was actually "a little black dog"—but he "played all day long, and Dorothy played with him" (13). Baum contrasts the laborious toil of adults with the spontaneous play of children, locating in the latter an insistent colorfulness that finds its match in the bright colors of Oz.

From the moment Dorothy opens the door onto the land of the Munchkins (and Denslow switches his ink from gray to blue), the narration never ceases to remark on the wide-eyed wonder with which the little girl meets the land of Oz. Her eyes grow "bigger and bigger" as she surveys her surroundings, and she "look[s] eagerly" at the "lovely patches of green sward," the "banks of gorgeous flowers," and the "birds with rare and brilliant plumage"—all the items that steal the attention of the subjects in early child study. When among the poppies, the color gets to her even before the "spicy scent": the "bright red flowers" were "so brilliant in color they almost dazzled Dorothy's eyes" (20, 93). Later, as they

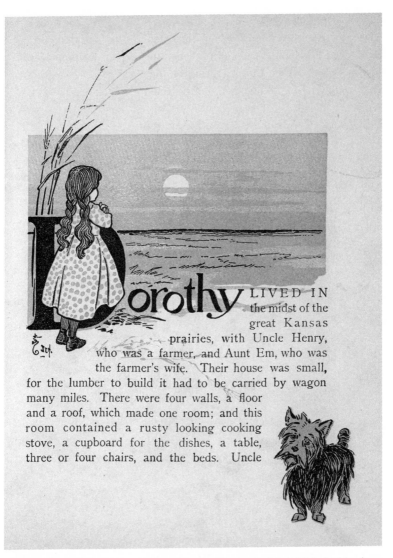

Dorothy LIVED IN the midst of the great Kansas prairies, with Uncle Henry, who was a farmer, and Aunt Em, who was the farmer's wife. Their house was small, for the lumber to build it had to be carried by wagon many miles. There were four walls, a floor and a roof, which made one room; and this room contained a rusty looking cooking stove, a cupboard for the dishes, a table, three or four chairs, and the beds. Uncle

FIGURE 24. Dorothy looks out over the gray Kansas prairie, which doubles here as an image of grayscale books. Baum, *The Wonderful Wizard of Oz,* illustrations by Denslow, 11. Kislak Center for Special Collections, Rare Books and Manuscripts, University of Pennsylvania, Philadelphia, Pennsylvania.

FIGURE 25. The Tin Woodman reads the copyright page, an example of the way characters often act as avatars for the child reader. Baum, *The Wonderful Wizard of Oz,* illustrations by Denslow, unpaginated front matter. Kislak Center for Special Collections, Rare Books and Manuscripts, University of Pennsylvania, Philadelphia, Pennsylvania.

enter the Emerald City, "Dorothy and her friends were at first dazzled by [its] brilliancy"; "even the painted eyes of the Scarecrow were dazzled" by the sparkling emeralds that lined the city's gate (121, 115). In Oz—and in *The Wonderful Wizard of Oz* after the Kansas chapter—all colors are bright and every gaze is bedazzled. The residents dress themselves in their "favorite" hues, and to justify their garish preferences, Baum sets his wonder tale in a "primitive" place: as the Witch of the North tells Dorothy, "The Land of Oz has never been civilized" (24). The ethnic and racial caricatures of *Father Goose* and *The Woggle-Bug Book* may be absent, but the logic of recapitulation that links bright colors with children and non-Anglo-Saxons persists. Baum used Munchkins and Scarecrows rather than Irish boys and "Chinamen" to model the excited reaction to vivid colors that he attributed to his child protagonist and that he hoped his book would spark in young readers.[72]

Denslow wielded his characteristic chromatic blocks, those hallmarks of "impressionism for babies," to reinforce Baum's presentation of the journey to Oz as a childlike immersion in color. Once in the land of the Munchkins, he trades the details of the Kansas landscape for a patch of pure blue, which Dorothy now sits *inside*, resting her hand on the color's edge (Figure 26). The subsequent chapter headings all repeat this motif, showing Dorothy and her friends playing with and within Denslow's color blocks. Sometimes the patches appear as mere color, an atmosphere that surrounds the characters without being directly perceived; at other times they form walls or gates, barriers and passageways in the protagonists' deepening voyage through the child's view of color. Only when Dorothy returns to Kansas at the end of the book does Denslow abandon the color blocks, though he does not return to the original gray. Rather, he washes the prairie scene in the red of Quadling territory: a bit of color that Dorothy brings back from her travels (Plate 10).

If Oz is a primitive country of childlike perception, then the Emerald City is the place where its chromatic effects are both intensified and examined. In the elaborately rendered page that begins chapter 10, Denslow transforms the color patch that replaced the Kansas prairie into the entrance of the Wizard's walled metropolis, complete with sparkling turrets and a door (Plate 11). Baum heightens the effect by heaping green upon green: in addition to the usual green houses and fences, the Emerald City itself emits a green glow, and its green walls are guarded by a gatekeeper who wears green clothing, stands on a green box, and

She WAS AWAKENED by a shock, so sudden and severe that if Dorothy had not been lying on the soft bed she might have been hurt. As it was, the jar made her catch her breath and wonder what had happened; and Toto put his cold little nose into her face and whined dismally. Dorothy sat up and noticed that the house was not moving; nor was it dark, for the bright sunshine came in at the window, flooding the little room. She sprang from her bed and with Toto at her heels ran and opened the door.

The little girl gave a cry of amazement and looked

FIGURE 26. Dorothy transported to the land of the Munchkins, where everything is blue. Baum, *The Wonderful Wizard of Oz,* illustrations by Denslow, 19. Kislak Center for Special Collections, Rare Books and Manuscripts, University of Pennsylvania, Philadelphia, Pennsylvania.

has greenish skin (111, 115, 116). The luminescence of the emerald-studded gate "dazzle[s]" the eyes of the onlookers, and the illustrations that accompany these descriptions glisten with green gems. To add to this general amplification of color, the gatekeeper issues green glasses to all the characters, explaining that such eyewear is necessary to protect inhabitants from "the brightness and glory" of the city (117). With these tinted spectacles strapped to their heads, the Wizard-seekers move through the Emerald City in a wash of green, unaware that the vivid color results from the glasses rather than the objects. They wonder at the "green clothes" and "greenish skin" of the inhabitants, the "window panes . . . of green glass," and the way that "even the sky above the City had a green tint, and the rays of the sun were green" (122, 121). When Dorothy peeks inside the shops, she sees an entire stock of green goods: "Green candy and green pop-corn were offered for sale, as well as green shoes, green hats and green clothes of all sorts. At one place a man was selling green lemonade, and when the children bought it Dorothy could see that they paid for it with green pennies" (122). Baum continues at this pace throughout the scenes in the Emerald City; during the two visits to the Wizard the word "green" appears almost one hundred times.[73]

In these scenes, the *greens* attract more attention than the objects themselves, and this repetition, combined with the narrative device of the green glasses, signals the Emerald City as a laboratory for exploring color effects. In particular, Baum isolates color to reflect on the aesthetic stimulation of perceptual states, the same effects he recommended to window trimmers. But whereas the colors of the show window were meant to retire "modestly" after throwing the goods "prominently into the foreground," the colors of the Emerald City occupy the spotlight and override the goods on which they appear. As Stuart Culver argues, the scenes of economic exchange Dorothy glimpses in the Emerald City depict an economy in which the theatrical effects used to stir consumer desire have eclipsed the more traditional emphasis on the use value of goods. Speaking of the green spectacles, Culver writes that they "project the supplemental feature, the desirable color, onto the items offered for sale"; they endow the whole city "with the magical value of greenness." As such, they function analogously to the plate-glass windows of storefronts, which "invest commodities with a certain supplemental value that, like greenness, can't be purchased or consumed."[74] In this topsy-turvy world, the aesthetic tricks of the window trimmer are staged on a grand scale, detached from any particular object (other than Oz himself). Even the relation between stable form and fluctuating color is reversed. In the Emerald City, shapes shift and colors remain the same: the Great Oz "can take on any form he wishes" to his various petitioners—a giant head, a ball of fire, a terrible beast, a lovely lady—but he's always green. Baum brings the supplementary and evanescent qualities of color into the foreground, stabilizing them and signaling the importance of bright color effects and the childish modes of perception they induce in the aesthetics of commodity culture.

Culver's analysis rightly foregrounds *Oz*'s function as a narrative parallel to Baum's work in advertising, but here too we must remain attentive to the colors on the page. For in addition to reflecting on how "color gave a buzz to product," as Michael Taussig puts it, the scenes in the Emerald City show Baum advertising the actual colors of his book.[75] "Greenness" might not be available for purchase, but the greens of *The Wonderful Wizard of Oz* were absolutely for sale. Indeed, whereas most writers use color terms to prompt their readers to *imagine* the hues of a described scene, Baum enlisted his language to press the reader's eye toward an actual encounter with variously colored inks. The words and the colors are as thoroughly entangled in *Oz* as they are in the wider visual culture from which it emerged, so that the book's material look is as important for its engagement with consumer display as the particulars of its fantasy. As Benjamin noted in 1928, advertisements, signage, and film had "pitilessly dragged" written language "out into the street," pulling it from its safe haven on the printed page and throwing it onto walls and placards. "Before a contemporary finds his way clear to opening a book," he wrote, "his eyes have been exposed to such a blizzard of changing, colorful, conflicting letters that the chances of his penetrating the archaic stillness of the book are slight."[76] The "upset ink-bottle" quality of Oz brought this blizzard of color into the supposedly still book. Reviewers complained that Denslow had "strewn many colored effects over the text in a way to tempt a child to 'skipping.'"[77] Such comments, though meant as insults, capture the way *Oz*'s format harnessed the energy of visual displays and in so doing demonstrated the extent to which the child's delight in bright hues had been awakened and mobilized within the wider spheres of mass culture.

In other words, *The Wonderful Wizard of Oz* is a distinctly Bradley-ish book. It trains its reader to see colors from a perspective imbued with the interests and insights of the modern chromatic economy; it downplays psychology's emphasis on the "primitive" perception of children and foregrounds the wonder and delight awaiting kids who learn to see color where they never thought to look for it before: above in electrical signs, below in tiles and carpets, around in posters and show windows, and inside children's books. And it does all this by using language to bend perception toward a more vivid encounter with modern color. Baum's narrative, like Bradley's nomenclature, provides the scaffolding through which the vision of reader-viewers is focused and intensified, readied for the wide-eyed enjoyment modeled by the characters and stimulated by the images. Far from recoiling at the flashing blizzard of colorful words that add to the phantasmagoria of capitalist culture, *Oz* embraced it, a reminder that writing at the turn of the twentieth century sought as much to capture the affective power of color as to bemoan it.

When the Wizard explains why he demanded that residents of Oz don green spectacles, his account captures the imbrication of language and color that characterizes not only modern visual culture but also the educational logic of the color sense and the abstracting strategies of the aniline aesthetic. Upon arriving in Oz, the Wizard ordered the people to build a city; "then I thought, as the country was so green and beautiful, I would call it the Emerald City. And to make the name fit better I put green spectacles on all the people, so that everything they saw was green" (187). The green of the Emerald City—for all its associations with the superimposed tints of the glasses—originated in the lush landscape of Oz, and in this way the process whereby the Wizard (and Baum and Denslow) intensified the city's greens parallels the operations of modern synthetic dyes: they extract a color from the natural world, amplify it, and then deploy it in fantastic combinations that would "delight the heart of an oriental." And the extraction hinges on the agency of a color *name;* language facilitates the translation of the initial green to its intensified counterpart, endowing the bare sensory stimulus with a social meaning in the process. In this way the colors of the Emerald City encapsulate a technique at the heart of Baum's work in both storytelling and window decorating: the use of "positive knowledge" about chromatic combinations to foster an unthinking encounter of aesthetic intensity.

Baum delighted in revealing the tricks that produced his modern magic, and this willingness to celebrate how the feeling of childlike wonder is stimulated situates him between the pedagogues such as Bradley and Prang and the modernists such as Hartmann and Stieglitz. When Toto tips over the screen that hides the Wizard, the Lion and the Tin-Man don't attack the charlatan or refuse his deceits. They don't even take the green glasses off. The explanation of the effects just adds to the fun. Baum imagines an ongoing loop between knowledge and sensation in the production and enjoyment of aesthetic effects, something similar to the trust of the educators that greater linguistic precision would bring finer color sensitivity, even if skewed more toward enchantment than refinement. The same dynamic plays out on the pages of *Oz*. But just as color instruction tilted away from systematic training and toward free expression after World War I, so too did the emphasis on the mediations involved in producing a childish color experience give way to the modernist trope of the child innocent of all knowledge and convention, apprehending the world in a primal wash of saturated colors that learning, language, or concepts could only dull. Even Benjamin, that acute observer of capitalist culture, kept his paeans to "color as perceived by children" separate from his analyses of chromatic commodities. He treated the stance of "pure receptivity" epitomized by the child's view of color as a philosophical figure rather than a historical phenomenon. Like the presentation of children's drawings at 291, then, Benjamin's statements about kids and color, fascinating as they are, obscure the social history that shaped the link between bright colors and childish receptivity, along with the interest in a dynamic relation between language and sensation located in the color sense.

The difference here may be largely rhetorical—the modernist trope of the innocent eye stresses the moment of sensory receptiveness necessary to loosen cultural habits, while the pedagogical approach emphasizes the subsequent stage of constructing new modes of perception. But it's a difference that has nonetheless structured historical accounts of modern cultural production in the United States and Europe. Without it, Gilman doesn't seem so far from Pater, and Denslow's proximity to Matisse comes into view. The wider history of the child's view of color reveals the modernist embrace of primitive immediacy as an inheritance of illustrations, picture books, storefront displays, and posters that muffled the explicit ties to the racialized sensorium of Lamarckianism while simultaneously drawing on those ties to infuse perception with savage intensity. The chromatic aesthetic of modernist primitivism employed the same extractive processes that made the Emerald City greener (and New

York and Chicago brighter): they pulled the *feeling* of sensory receptiveness from the dark-skinned bodies to which it supposedly belonged and resituated it within bold applications of saturated colors.

Baum's humbug Wizard points us toward a modern aesthetic tradition built on the abstractive power of aniline and the entanglement of language and color in the color sense, one even more operative in literature than in the visual arts. For just as the amplification of the Emerald City's green turned on a word, so too, as we will see in the next chapter, did writers such as Stephen Crane and Gertrude Stein concentrate on the peculiar ways language impinged on perception. Rather than capturing the evolving nuances of the natural world, like Garland's local colors or Gilman's creeping light, they used language to isolate the feeling of color and to manipulate that feeling within an aesthetic encounter. But unlike Baum, who relied on Denslow or Morgan or his other collaborators to provide the material referent for his hues, Crane and Stein experimented with the effect of color terms detached from their visual analogues. They anilinized their words to conjure scenes stranger and more splendid even than those of Oz.

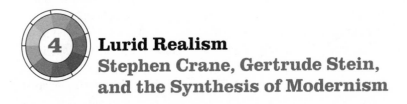

4 Lurid Realism
Stephen Crane, Gertrude Stein, and the Synthesis of Modernism

"Is literature becoming a mere scheme of color?"[1] When Charles Dudley Warner posed this question to the readers of *Harper's,* he had Stephen Crane's *The Red Badge of Courage* (1895) still lingering, like an afterimage, in his mind. The book had gripped him like "a most exciting and melodramatic dream, which [he] could not shake off when waking," and he associated "this effect" with the novel's chromatic intensity, its ambition "to make every page blaze with color, in order to affect the mind through the eye" (56). Yet even though Warner drew on Crane for his primary examples—citing "'red rage,' a 'black procession' of oaths, the 'red sickness of battle,' and so on, and so on"—his article mentions neither the author nor the novel by name. Instead, it presents the descriptive techniques of *Red Badge* as exemplary of a wider literary trend, one driven by "a belief that you can somehow dye the language and make it more expressive to the reading eye" (55). He hazarded a name for the new style: "lurid realism" (56).[2]

As a set of "experiments" in making "suggestions of real colors in words," Warner's notion of lurid realism positioned Crane within an aesthetic sensibility that, in 1890s America, was readily identified by its colors. Symbolism—with its Parisian chic and gnomic images—reached U.S. readers not only through color-music concerts, Loïe Fuller's multihued dance, and the bright chromatic patches in art posters and ephemeral bibelots, but also through volumes such as Stuart Merrill's *Pastels in Prose* (1890), a translation of prose poems by Charles Baudelaire, Stéphane Mallarmé, Joris-Karl Huÿsmans, and other fellow travelers—and a book whose very title announced its aspirations to render color in words. The English poet and *Yellow Book* contributor Richard Le Gallienne affirmed the importance of color for this avant-garde movement when he proclaimed in 1910, "Modern poets aim, as far as possible, at writing, so to say, in color"; their goal "[is] spiritual suggestion through the mysterious medium of color," and particularly through "colored words."[3] Warner registered something of this symbolist attempt to infuse language with chromatic quality when he read *Red Badge:* "It is almost a poem," he wrote, "except in form," and its cultivation of "the quality that has come to be called 'intensity' in literature" placed it outside the standard domain of realist writing. "It is real, in a way," Warner equivocated (56, 55).

But it was still realism. What's interesting about Warner's designation is its attempt to capture the surprising eruption of symbolist techniques within a conventional narrative and to locate this intersection within a more diffuse cultural interest in color. He wanted to pinpoint the exact "way" Crane's colorful phrases were real. To begin, he explained, lurid realism was not local color. Nor, we might add, did it resemble painterly efforts at chromatic description. Unlike the elaborate phrases penned by Garland or Gilman, Crane's curious chromatic expressions thwart literal visualization. What is red about a "red sickness"? Such phrases aim not at describing how the world looks but at capturing what words can make a reader see and feel. In this respect they have more in common with the haunting color of Mallarmé's "L'Azur" and the chromatic letters of Rimbaud's "Voyelles" than with the colored shadows in *Main-Travelled Roads.*[4] Yet even in its disregard for the standard uses of language, Crane's writing avoids the esoteric character of much symbolist verse. Despite feeling like a poem, *The Red Badge of Courage* spins its tale in prose, and its intensified colors recall the heightened greens of the Emerald City as much as anything from literary bohemia. Like the grand spectacles of greenness that Dorothy and her friends encounter in Oz, Crane's constructions of basic, bold hues override their objects to infuse his scenes with chromatic quality. And they do so explicitly through the medium of language; the prose precedes the perception, just as the Wizard first called his city "Emerald" and then built a place to fit the name.

In other words, the colors of lurid realism were those of the aniline era, and as such they traversed both high and low, avant-garde and commercial. They were intense, artificial, abstracted, and organized. Warner recognized as much when he proposed dyes rather than paints as the appropriate metaphor for Crane's writing: the reds "saturate" the page (56). By the 1890s organic chemists and industrial manufacturers had remade the world of commercial color, deriving from the sticky, black refuse of coal refinement a synthetic palette unrivaled in saturation and brilliance. Traditional pigments were made from roots, minerals, and other natural materials, but the new synthetic dyes—which boasted well over a thousand varieties by the time of Warner's editorial—resulted from a technical procedure of extraction and intensification. From the messy mix of organic matter found in crushed cochineal carcasses or steeped and beaten indigo plants, chemists abstracted the specific molecular compounds responsible for the colors and reconstructed them in the lab. The products were then marketed as "pure," as close to mere color as an object could get. Advertisers and artists alike embraced these brilliant hues to construct Oz-like chromatic spectacles, which in their very vibrancy bespoke not only the sensuous jolt of modernity but also a technical enterprise that promised to reengineer the natural world molecule by molecule, brightening it in the process.

For Crane, writing amid the proliferation of aniline dyes, being a realist in one's colors meant harnessing the affective thrill of abstract hues to quicken the reader's feeling of reality and then adding that feeling to the overall effect of the narrative. It meant exaggerating the difference between colors perceived and colors imagined to offer linguistic compositions that stretched what chromatic experience could be. Throughout his fiction, but especially in *The Red Badge of Courage,* Crane works like a chemist, extracting colors from objects, intensifying them, and recomposing them in new affective and perceptual compounds. He lifts the *feeling* of color from its visual appearances and spreads it across his words and scenes, saturating the page. This procedure aims at isolating what philosophers call color qualia, the feelings of what it is like to have particular chromatic sensations considered apart from any colored objects. In particular, it seeks to bring language into contact with the qualitative force of abstracted color and, in an extension of Garland's "blue-shadow idea," to create textual spaces that enable new perceptual encounters. Although Crane's experiments unfolded far from the classrooms and drawing rooms discussed in previous chapters, they shared with these sites a model of aesthetic training: as one newspaper reported, "Mr. Crane's 'black anger,' his 'crimson curses,' his 'livid fury,' his 'lurid altercations,' all appeal to the mind through the color sense."[5]

In the end, then, lurid realism names the dual attempt to bring language into the relational processes of color perception and to test the way words contribute to the fabrication of chromatic experience. Warner was right to put Crane at the center of these efforts and to connect the novelist's colors to the linguistic daring of the symbolists and the visual culture of the 1890s. Yet the purchase of lurid realism extended even wider. For in the decade of *Plessy v. Ferguson* (1896), in which the U.S. Supreme Court made a convoluted appeal to color to justify racial segregation, writers such as Charles Chesnutt pointed out that calling a man "black," especially a man visibly "white," was no different from calling a procession "black" or an altercation "lurid." In each case a color term supplied a perceptual charge to an otherwise invisible quality. Chesnutt and Crane each pored over the transformative effects of linguistic frameworks in these domains. And by foregrounding the affinities between the avant-garde's most startling chromatic constructions and the thoroughly naturalized color usages in racial discourse, their work illuminates the turn that lurid realism took in the work of Gertrude Stein. While her *Tender Buttons* (1914) was immediately greeted as a child of symbolism, and thus an early instance of modernist literature, Stein herself dated the beginning of her attunement to how words push and pull against one another to the composition of "Melanctha" (1909), in which she witnessed her color terms shift meaning when she transposed her story onto African American characters.

Literature may not have become the mere scheme of color that Warner predicted, but the attempt to saturate language with chromatic quality persisted in Ezra Pound's fascination with the poetic image and Stein's investigations of the perceptual experiences afforded through language alone. In the decades after *Red Badge,* the task of making language colorful came to designate an attempt to create verbal ensembles as densely relational and qualitatively alive as color sensations and to offer those ensembles to the reading eye where they might coax unprecedented configurations of consciousness. Warner offered the phrase "lurid realism" with hesitation, uncertain whether it fit; had he written twenty years later he might have just called it "modernism."

Crane's Four-Color Posters

Crane's colors provided great sport for his nineteenth-century readers. Unlike Warner, who took seriously the literary import of Crane's saturated phrases, most reviewers made light of what they saw as a peculiar amalgamation of the verbal and the visual. Their parodies offer vivid

glosses on Crane's style. Charles Battell Loomis mocked Crane's correspondence of the Greco-Turkish War by imagining the latter's response to
the news that he had missed the battle at Mati: "The fight must have been
between the Greeks and the Turks, and so it was full of my favorite color,
red—Turkey red." The caricature heaps on color words, reporting "huge
yellow oaths," "red and brown and green ants," and "a Turkish crash,
cream color with a selvage of red." In his most spirited exaggeration,
Loomis described a "short Greek" standing beside a youth who "looked
blue for a minute, and then at a remark from the youth . . . changed
color."[6] Frank Norris also lampooned Crane for his colors, weighing down
the first paragraph of "The Green Stones of Unrest" (1897) with "blue
stones," a "seal brown" day, a "vermillion valley," and a "mauve hilltop."
The protagonist of the parody, a Mere Boy, shines "a brilliant blue color"
and travels along a road of "raw umber" along which he sees pebbles,
"Naples yellow in color."[7] By shifting from Crane's limited range of basic
hues to a more nuanced spectrum, these parodies provide unwitting foils
for the force of Crane's colors at the same time that they demonstrate the
historical fascination with the way his prose keyed chroma to language.

Dozens of similar send-ups appeared in the wake of *Red Badge,* and
nearly all of them invoked contemporary chromatic technologies to convey the vivid colors seeming to bloom on Crane's sentences. In August
1898, *Life* magazine announced a new edition of Crane's war novel in
which the "descriptive color words" would be replaced by "a thick line
printed in ink of the adjectival hue."[8] The joke must have gone over well,
because the very next month *Life* followed up with a report that Crane
was so busy with his journalism that he had outsourced the coloring of
his newest novel to a team of house painters at "a well-known decorating concern on Union Square."[9] The most telling of these playful visualizations came from Norris, whose parody imagines "the blue Mere Boy
transport[ing] himself diagonally athwart the larger landscape, printed
in four colors, like a poster."[10] What Crane's writing looks like, Norris
suggested, is an advertising poster printed boldly in a limited range of flat
hues, something in the style of Denslow's illustrations for *Father Goose*
and *The Wonderful Wizard of Oz.* Other reviewers agreed. Jonathan Penn,
commenting in 1896 on Crane's "career in 'poster' literature" for the
little magazine the *Lotus,* described "the fondness Mr. Crane shows for
chromatic effects" as "a sort of poster commentary," and another writer
bemoaned Crane's "poster art" of laying on "gaudy chromo colors."[11] For

late-nineteenth-century readers, Crane's images invoked the techniques of print media, which in turn relied on the materials of organic chemistry, as models for the intensification of experience through color.

In this regard Crane's burlesquers have proven more perceptive than his recent critics, who for all their attention to both color and visual culture have said very little about the chromatic trends and technologies at the turn of the twentieth century. Even Bill Brown's extensive study of the "material unconscious" in Crane's work devotes only a few pages to the colors of mass amusement and never once mentions aniline dyes.[12] Moreover, the historical analogue most often invoked in Crane criticism—impressionist painting—is misleading, as it implies an authorial investment in the actualities of sensory perception that Crane's colors disrupt. Paul Sorrentino encapsulates this critical consensus when he claims that "like Impressionist painters, Crane recreated the sensory impressions that color and light have on the eye," focusing "on the individual's fleeting, subjective perception of reality rather than on an attempt to recreate reality objectively." But his own examples, which include "sorry blue" clouds and the "yellow light thrown upon the color of [Henry's] ambitions," demonstrate that Crane passed over the sorts of effects that might be captured by the eye to conjure chromatic possibilities peculiar to language.[13] Crane's colors are not Garland's—and as we saw in the first chapter, even Garland complicated the simple binary of subject and object that structures this account of impressionism. Far from relegating color to the "subjective perception of reality," as if this were separate from the workings of reality itself, the commercial aesthetic embraced bright hues to *build* a sense of reality, to contribute to its ongoing construction.

Indeed, when Crane's readers signaled an affinity between his fiction and the chromatic aesthetics of their day they indicated the way that, at the end of the nineteenth century, color itself had become a technology for intensifying experience, a primary constituent in a new, more lurid, realism. Take the blue of Crane's "The Blue Hotel" (1898). The opening compares the light-blue paint on the titular hotel to "a shade that is on the legs of a kind of heron, causing the bird to declare its position against any background." "The Palace Hotel then," the narration continues, "was always screaming and howling in a way that made the dazzling winter landscape of Nebraska seem only a gray swampish hush." These two sentences capture the procedures of the aniline aesthetic at work in commercial color: the brilliance of nature (the hue on the heron's legs) has been extracted, intensified, and deployed in a generalized, bold form that absorbs the attention of passers-by. No traveler could "pass the Palace Hotel without looking at it": everyone was "overcome at the sight" (799).[14]

The screaming blue of the hotel thus functions like the glowing greens of the Emerald City or the subtle color arrangements in Baum's show windows. And like the advertisers and designers who threw stylized colors onto billboards and posters in the 1890s, Crane exaggerated his hues on the assumption that colors themselves had direct, nonconscious effects on people. As graphic designer Joseph Binder explained, voicing a common sentiment among twentieth-century artists and marketing firms, "Everyone can experience . . . the various effects produced by different colours, quite apart from their importance for the subject of the picture." He therefore advised poster painters to use "normal colours in a pure and intensified manner"; if one is to paint a tree, he wrote, "paint [it] as powerfully and brilliantly green as possible," so that it might have the most stimulating effect.[15] This pursuit of color's ability to affect people in subtle ways went hand in hand with an understanding of the perceiving subject as open and responsive to environmental influence. Indeed, Crane's characters do more than encounter commercial colors; they also thrill to them in modern ways, from the visitors gawking at the Palace Hotel to Henry Fleming absorbing adrenaline-charged colors during an infantry charge. When the youth in "An Experiment in Luxury" (1894) visits the home of a rich family, for example, the "splendor of the interior fill[s] him with awe" as "color and form [swarm] upon him" (551, 553). The "marvelous hues" from the stained glass create a chromatic spectacle that "smothered certain of his comprehensions" (552). Such scenes of observers overwhelmed by magnified colors demonstrate Crane's abiding fascination with the aesthetic intensification of sense experience associated with the enticements of consumer display.

In addition to dramatizing the play of modern colors, Crane made explicit reference to a philosophical source that underwrote the chromatic character of the commercial aesthetic: Goethe's *Theory of Colours*. According to his fraternity brother Frank Noxon, Crane was impressed by Goethe's analysis of "the effect which the several colors have upon the human mind" and had used this "idea to produce his effects."[16] Goethe maintained that each hue has a unique physiological and psychological impact: "Every color produces a distinct impression on the mind, and thus addresses at once the eye and feelings."[17] He claimed that warm colors, "yellow, red-yellow (orange), yellow-red (minium, cinnabar)," provoke "quick, lively, aspiring" feelings, while cool colors, "blue, red-blue, and blue-red," "produce a restless, susceptible, anxious impression" (168, 170). Insisting on the agency of colors themselves, as well as on the relational character of color perception, he explained that individual and combined hues affect us "without relation to the nature or form of the object on whose surface they are apparent" (167). As such, they might be added to a perceptual scene to adjust its affective tone, like blue paint on a Western hotel or yellow and blue variations in an interior. Designers used *Theory of Colours* as a guide to produce pleasing chromatic arrangements, but Crane—who worked with language rather than wallpaper or textiles—found in Goethe an account of color feelings coextensive with yet separate from our relations to colored objects.

What sorts of literary hues did this understanding of colors and color sensitivity produce? As Norris and others noticed, Crane's chromatic compositions lay blocks of color side by side, poster-like. *The Red Badge of Courage* in particular arranges its colors in patches and sheets: "In the eastern sky there was a yellow patch like a rug laid for the feet of the coming sun; and against it, black and patternlike, loomed the gigantic figure of the colonel on a gigantic horse" (92–93). The dark silhouette cast in front of the bright background eschews shades and tints in favor of stark contrast. Likewise, the "sheets of orange light" that "illumine the shadowy distance," "the blue, enameled sky," and the notorious "red sun . . . *pasted* in the sky like a wafer" further the language of two-dimensionality in the novel (150, 176, 137; emphasis added). David Halliburton indicates the peculiarity of Crane's reliance on basic colors when discussing his description of a battle scene as "a smoke-wall penetrated by the flashing points of yellow and red" (201). "Although points of such color may well appear on a battlefield," he explains, "explosions from artillery are not typically in primary colors"; as such, the "yellow" in this passage "looks suspiciously like Goethe's paradigmatic yellow and the red looks equally pure."[18] What these images lack in depth or nuance, Halliburton suggests, they make up for with the brightness and intensity that accompanies pure colors. These hues come to the fore as Henry's regiment makes its final charge: "It was a blind and despairing rush by the collection of men in dusty and tattered blue, over a green sward and under a sapphire sky, toward a fence, dimly outlined in smoke, from behind which spluttered the fierce rifles of enemies" (204). The string of prepositional phrases in this sentence lays down the colors patch by patch, creating a scene in which the chromatic combinations overwhelm the actual action. Such passages show Crane's style at its most distinctive: unconcerned with the textured tones of the natural world and focused on saturated blocks of generalized color.

In the visual arts during the late nineteenth century, these flat colors and striking contrasts were popularized by art nouveau, a French import affiliated with symbolism that worked within the constrictions of color printing to create images that blurred the line between art and ads. Eugène Grasset's covers for *Harper's* in 1889, 1891, and 1892 popularized the style in North America, where it was taken up by Louis Rhead, Denslow, and Will Bradley. Rhead "embraced Grasset's willowy maidens, contour lines, and flat color," but "he rejected [the] pale colors" of early art nouveau "in favor of vibrantly unexpected combinations, such as red contour lines on bright blue hair before an intense green sky."[19] Peter C. Marzio's characterization of the modes favored by chromolithographic printing techniques suggests the constraints that these artists exploited. He explains that illustrator Virginia Granbery's style "was ideal for [Louis] Prang's chromos: the bright, hard colors, with little blending or graduating of tones, made the printing separations relatively easy and economical to produce."[20] Similarly, Denslow's "clean, sharp lines" were praised by newspaper men as "the delight of the zincographer."[21] Crane adopts this aesthetic when describing the "large pictures extravagant in color" that run through Henry's head, including "a blue desperate figure leading lurid charges with one knee forward and a broken blade high" and "a blue, determined figure standing before a crimson and steel assault" (83, 143). Even more, his second book of poetry, *War Is Kind* (1899), came adorned with art nouveau illustrations by Bradley (Figures 27, 28, and 29). And when the *Philistine* republished lines from Crane's *The Black Riders,* none other than Denslow provided the accompanying illustration (Plate 12). Inside his books and on their pages, Crane favored the flat blocks of color familiar from chromolithography and posters.

Crane playfully hinted at the commercial origins of his techniques in *The Third Violet* (1897) through a conversation between Miss Grace Fanhall and her suitor, the painter William Hawker. Miss Fanhall presses Hawker to tell her about life in the artist studios. He replies with talk of cigarettes and card playing and the occasional job and then tells her of

FIGURE 27. The cover of Stephen Crane's second book of poetry, *War Is Kind,* illustrated by Will Bradley (New York: F. A. Stokes, 1899). Kislak Center for Special Collections, Rare Books and Manuscripts, University of Pennsylvania, Philadelphia, Pennsylvania.

FIGURE 28. Art nouveau image by Bradley designed for Crane's *War Is Kind,* 8. Kislak Center for Special Collections, Rare Books and Manuscripts, University of Pennsylvania, Philadelphia, Pennsylvania.

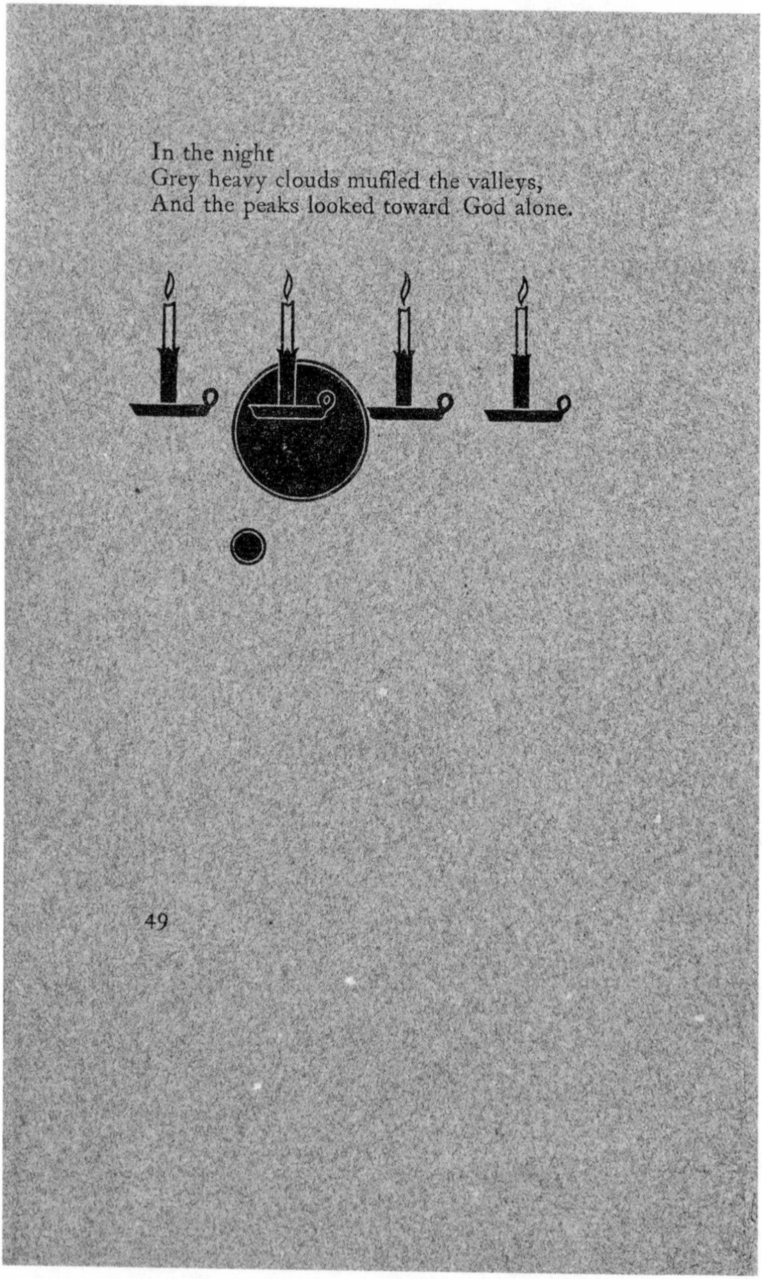

In the night
Grey heavy clouds muffled the valleys,
And the peaks looked toward God alone.

49

FIGURE 29. This illustration by Bradley for Crane's *War Is Kind,* 49, is especially reminiscent of the images by W. W. Denslow. Kislak Center for Special Collections, Rare Books and Manuscripts, University of Pennsylvania, Philadelphia, Pennsylvania.

his best-known work: the "beautiful red and green designs that surround the common tomato can." "Later," he continues, "I got into green corn and asparagus" (302). If Crane's writing approximates any of the work produced by artists at the turn of the century, it's not the blurred "impressions" of landscapes that Hawker displays in exhibitions but, rather, the "bright, flat colors, elaborate lettering, and iconic images" used by chromolithographed packaging "to create an emblematic presence for the product."[22] His colors, like those on the logos and trademarks becoming common during his lifetime, contributed to the creation of his unmistakable and endlessly mockable style.

To be sure, Crane's colors do not always appear so flat. The introductory paragraphs of many of the city sketches foreground the lively play of light from shop windows and street lamps on rainy pavements and snow. Yet even these moments, which seem to show Crane's colors at their most "impressionistic," function according to the rule of intensification through abstraction that Crane found in commercial art. When Crane begins "An Experiment in Misery" (1894) by describing a "fine rain [that] was swirling softly down, causing the pavements to glisten with hue of steel and blue and yellow in the rays of innumerable lights," he emphasizes the moisture to spread and to deepen the colors of the scene (538). He uses the rain—as he uses snow elsewhere—to create conditions under which intense colors might be more vividly imagined by his readers.[23] Crane opens *George's Mother* (1896) with similar colors, adding an explicit reference to the "picture" quality of the scene: "In the swirling rain that came at dusk the broad avenue glistened with that deep bluish tint which is so widely condemned when it is put into pictures. . . . Here and there . . . from the red street-lamps . . . a flare of uncertain, wavering crimson was thrown upon the wet pavements" (215). Once again, rain appears in the scene merely to heighten the imagined effects of the color; after the first paragraphs, it is not mentioned in any consequential way and is ignored by characters who talk idly in the streets without seeming to mind the drizzle. The first sentences of *Red Badge* use fog to similar effect, and in later chapters Henry's tent acts as a screen to catch luminous hues: the "sunlight" makes the tent "glow a light yellow shade," and at night Henry "stare[s] at the red, shivering reflection of a fire on the white wall of his tent" (82, 98). Such devices enable the color to intensify, to disconnect from any particular body and spread across the scene.

By following the techniques of commercial design in the aniline era,

Crane extracts and intensifies the colors of phenomena to charge the reading experience with a vibrant feeling of reality. The early reviews of *The Red Badge of Courage,* which widely assume that its depictions of war could only have been crafted by a veteran, demonstrate the effect of this method and foreground the puzzling way in which Crane's unrealistic stylization of visual experience became the hallmark of his realism. In *The Third Violet* Crane offers a commentary on his attention to aspects of experience that exceed the ordinary empirical field when the writer George Hollanden scoffs at one of Hawker's canvases: "If what you fellows say in your paintings is true," Hollanden remarks, "the whole earth must be blazing and burning, and glowing and—." Crane's colors blaze and burn, and their intensity, though exaggerated beyond naturalistic verisimilitude, affords insights both into the nature of mental experience and into its manipulation within aesthetic constructions.

Crane's vivid appeals to the "reading eye" beg for the sorts of matching or influence games played above—but my point is not to impose a symmetry between Crane's vision and that of the designers and illustrators. Crane did not attempt to replicate the style of art posters in any literal way. Rather, he was energized by the surge of colors in modern culture, and the specific techniques of the aniline aesthetic led him to conceive of color itself as a generalized force with real effects on minds and bodies. He transferred the bold, abstracted, synthetic hues of ad posters into a literary method both attuned to the sensory power of pure color and attentive to how this power might be folded into literature. In so doing, he rendered realism lurid.

The Redness of *The Red Badge of Courage*

Goethe warned against thinking too hard about color. "'The ox becomes furious if a red cloth is shown to him,'" he explained, "'but the philosopher, who speaks of colour only in a general way, begins to rave'" (xxvii). Certainly a particular color (the color of *this* red cloth, here and now) defies the universalizing tendencies of abstract thought, but, as Goethe's anecdote demonstrates, even the "general way" in which philosophy approaches color raises vexing difficulties. The tradition of lurid realism emphasizes a particularly thorny aspect of the problem in its attention to the relation between colors and color words. For example, watch how Crane gives Goethe's example another turn of the screw. In *The Third*

Violet Hawker's father drives an ox named Red, and as Hawker and Miss Fanhall stroll through the woods, they hear him attempting to excite the lethargic animal. "Git over there, Red. Git over! Gee! Git-ap!," he yells; "Red, git over there now, will you? I'll trim the skin off'n you in a minute. Whoa!" (322). One of points that drives philosophers mad is that oxen respond differently to "red" than to red.

Crane adapted techniques from his commercial context to address these difficulties—or, more precisely, to experiment with the possibilities they afforded. In particular, he made language into a vector of abstraction, a way of unmooring colors from objects and reassembling them in new perceptual compounds. And in the process he both transferred the aniline aesthetic to fiction and arrived at a model of color best grasped through Charles S. Peirce's philosophy of qualia. Works such as "The Broken-Down Van" and *The Red Badge of Courage* attempt to detach the feeling of colors from their actual appearance in objects and to produce textual—not visual—effects. They illustrate Crane's interest in the perceptual experiences afforded by language alone and thus align him with the symbolist techniques percolating through American avant-garde circles in the 1890s, often between book covers adorned in bright, art nouveau hues.

In "The Broken-Down Van" (1892), the earliest of the New York sketches, Crane turns a traffic jam into an occasion for amassing reds, greens, and blues around people and vehicles until the shades eclipse their objects. After introducing two red furniture vans "with impossible landscapes on their sides," Crane describes the arrival of "a horse car with a red light": "The car was red, and the bullseye light was red, and the driver's hair was red," and when the driver has to slow down because of the lumbering vans he gets so angry that he "pound[s] on the red dash board with his car-hook till the red light tremble[s]." The ensemble—car, light, dash, driver—constitutes a block of red that is soon joined by analogous aggregates of green and blue. The first few sentences of the sketch chart the manner in which these three colors prod and provoke one another into a chaotic frenzy; the blue car's whistle causes the conductor of the green car to ring his bell, which in turn incites the red conductor to "lose the last vestige of control of himself and . . . bounce up and down on his bell strap," and so on for two of the longest sentences Crane ever published (521). The force of the repetition causes the words themselves to break, to produce what Mary Esteve calls "chromatic blockages" that arrest our ability to imagine the scene.[24] Crane emphasizes the implications of their collapse through the wreck of the sketch's titular van and its "impossible landscape" that occurs when the fury of the three colors reaches a fever pitch. Even after the breakdown, Crane presses on: "A car with a white light, a car with a white and red light, a car with a white light and a green bar across it, a car with a blue light and a white circle around it, another car with a red bullseye light and one with a red flat light had come up and stopped" (523). Here the repetition and stylized abstraction go too far to achieve the realism celebrated by Warner. But they mark the task that Crane pursued in his subsequent works: the intensification and composition of colors to form "impossible landscapes," using only a limited stock of general terms.

In *The Red Badge of Courage*, Crane hones this technique to intensify the blue of the soldiers' uniforms. The entire novel uses war as an occasion to explore color, from the martial setting that pits blue against gray to the significance of each regiment's flag, or "colors." In the rush of the charge, Henry becomes keenly sensitive to chromatic sensations: "Each blade of the green grass was bold and clear" (183). The youth's attunement to the vivid, changing hues of the battle scene provide a model for Crane's readers, who are presented with skirmishes as aesthetic tableaux, bright artillery fire playing upon the smoke and fog of the landscape: "[a] sketch in gray and red"; a line of soldiers described as "purple streaks"; "[a] dark battle line" on "a sunstruck clearing that gleamed orange color" (108, 99, 101). In this sense, the youth's initial theory that he had joined a "blue demonstration" rather than a fighting army proves correct, insofar as it refers to the aesthetic nature of the novel (86).[25]

By the final charges, the narrative's treatment of color exceeds photographic depiction and relies on a method of stylization in which colors overtake form. As in "The Broken-Down Van" (in which the word "red" appears fifteen times in the second paragraph), Crane piles on color terms in these chapters to an almost distracting degree. Twenty-eight of the fifty-four uses of "blue" in the novel appear in the final third of the book, and Crane crams seven of these instances in less than a page and a half describing the second charge: "the blue wave," the "blue whirl of men," "the men in blue" (twice), "they in blue," the "swirling body of blue men," and "the scampering blue men" (205–7). As Henry surveys the battle, the "parts of the opposing armies" become "two long waves," and at one point "a spray of light forms go[es] in houndlike leaps toward the

waving blue lines." At another, a blue wave "dash[es]" against "a gray ob-
struction" (200). Crane allows the colors to dominate the confused scene,
describing Henry's failure to follow the battle as an inability to read the
flags, to tell "which color of the cloth was winning" (201). Yet unlike in
the earlier sketch, Crane keeps a tight reign on the abstraction in order
to figure the fluidity of color unmoored. The blue of the uniform shifts
from describing a hue of clothing (the men "who had donned blue") to
constituting a field the soldiers inhabit (the "men *in* blue"), a feature that
characterizes them ("blue men"), and even that which, in the rush of
battle, blocks out their humanity ("bundles of blue") (86, 205–6, 202).
His language detaches the blue from its objects and magnifies it until it
becomes the governing feature of the scene, a quality that floats through
events unattached to any one body or material.

Such a blue—one that does not inhere in any particular object or
subject and that does not appear in perceptual experience as such—
receives philosophical treatment in nineteenth- and twentieth-century
debates about qualia. In brief, a *quale* refers to the feeling of a sensation,
the *what*ness that makes a particular feeling or experience what it is.
A quale of blue refers to the feeling of what it is like to see or to experience blue apart from the cones and rods or particles and waves that make
up its physical facts. Peirce calls qualia "Firsts" and describes them as
"certain qualities of feeling, such as the color of magenta, the odor of
attar, the sound of a railway whistle," as distinguished from their actual
instantiations in objects (1.304). Alongside "Firstness," Peirce offers the
category of "Secondness" for actual existents and "Thirdness" for mediating relations. He thus discriminates between the sorts of colors viewed
by the artist—those that deal with the immediate "presentness" of the actual world, like the blue shadows that impressionists saw on the snow—
and those that characterize Firstness. For Peirce, a pure color quale, as
a First, is "a mere may-be," a general entity that has real bearings on the
world without being actualized in experience. The blueness of blue has
a qualitative distinctness that coexists with the characteristics of blue
objects, and its virtual status enables it to be linked with other relations
or situations within experience.[26]

Peirce recognized a link between the qualitative Firstness of color
and the terms we use to designate particular shades. When red appears in
phenomenal experience, he explained, it is always confounded with texture, light, and perspective and thus does not exist as the sheer redness

of red. To illustrate this latter sort of color quality, Peirce turned not to actual objects but to language:

> The word *red* means something when I say that the precession of the equinoxes is no more red than it is blue, and . . . it means just what it means when I say that aniline red is red. That mere *quality,* or suchness, is not in itself an occurrence, as seeing a red object is; it is a mere may-be. (1.304)

Language acts as an agent of abstraction. The word "red" approximates the virtual quality of redness because Firsts, too, must be drawn out through a process of selection and concentration; they are not just "there" in raw perception waiting to be identified. Peirce insists on this point through his examples. Aniline red and magenta rather than cochineal or the red of a rose, the smell of attar rather than the fragrance of rosemary, the blast of a railway whistle instead of the song of a nightingale: they are all so artificial that it is impossible to read Peirce as claiming that qualia are the natural building blocks of sensation. Instead, a First must be extracted or "prescinded" from experience, and language constitutes a powerful tool for isolating such qualities.[27] Like Henry's "engaged senses," quickened by the rush of battle, color terms intensify the world's hues, making it possible not only to be "aware of every change in the thin, transparent vapor that floated idly in sheets" (183) during a charge but also to activate the "mere may-be[s]" that generate literature's perceptual effects.

Peirce's presentation of the relation between language and color offers a more promising framework for following what writers such as Crane do with color than the parallel tradition of analytic philosophy often invoked in analyses of British modernism. Bertrand Russell, for instance, understood colors and other "sense data" to be so particular, so intimately and ineffably *had,* that they remained forever outside the generalities of language. According to Ann Banfield, Virginia Woolf and other modernists aimed at overcoming this insuperable gap between private experience and public expression by bending language against itself.[28] They struggled to communicate in words what was felt by the body. But to approach modernism this way stacks the deck against the writers, focusing attention on what they could not do rather than on what they did. For Peirce and Crane, language does not pose a problem for the communication of color perception; rather, it enables a different sort of color experience, one separate from the effects of light on the eye. This distinction is all the more important because the term "quale" in contemporary analytic philosophy is more likely to be used in the way that Russell meant "sense data" than in the way that Peirce meant "First."[29] The term now invokes private, ineffable experience, hidden deep inside a subject, rather than a generalized "quality of feeling" that remains virtual at its heart. "When I say it is a quality," Peirce wrote, "I do not mean that it 'inheres' in [a] subject" (1.304; brackets in original). Nor does it attach to an object (7.530). It is a metaphysical construct arrived at through abstraction that gives us a descriptive purchase on experience, not the name for an epistemological problem.

Peirce's terms allow for a more precise account of Crane's colors. In the final chapters of *Red Badge,* Crane begins with a Second (the color of coats), extracts a First (the blueness of blue), and then resituates it within new kinds of perceptual and affective objects; he loosens the qualities of colors from physical entities and reattaches them to abstract nouns and events. By detaching the feeling of seeing blue from the actual presence of blue, he converts the power of pure hues assumed by Goethe and advertisers into material for literature. Language, rather than the synthesizing work of chemists or the bold layout of poster artists, serves as his abstracting mechanism. The descriptions of "black rage" and the "red sickness of battle" that caught Warner's attention, as well as the "yellow discontent" of Maggie's coworkers in *Maggie: A Girl of the Streets* (1893) and George Kelcey's "yellow crash," offer examples of these new combinations (150, 212, 24, 246). In each case, color is *felt* rather than *seen;* it permeates an action with a unifying affective quality without being localized in a specific subject or object. When Henry imagines the roaring guns behind him "shaking in black rage," the blackness of the rage does not simply appear on the metal of the guns or in the fancy of the youth; rather, it adheres as a felt quality in the mutual interaction of the elements of the situation. Henry doesn't see the black any more than readers do, yet he feels it as a quality shaking the entire scene.

Crane signals his investment in the links between color words and chromatic Firsts through phrases that attach qualitative color to explosive speech acts. The tall soldier's "black procession of curious oaths," the lieutenant's "blue haze of curses," the youth's "outburst of crimson oaths," and the "red letters of curious revenge" Henry imagines all offer occasions in which language assumes the quality or affect of color (113,

185, 211, 189). Just as Crane's readers picked up on the author's affinities with commercial colors, so too did they single out (even if only for extra ridicule) such combinations as central to Crane's project. A reviewer in *Godey's Lady's Book* complained that *Red Badge* contained "all shades of red oaths except crushed strawberry and peachblow." And Paul Paine's parody "The Blue Blotch of Cowardice" features a "chameleon curse" that turns "to a light yellow, owing to the proximity of a pot of Spanish mustard," and a lieutenant who "looked over his stock of oaths, but could find none of the precise shade that he wanted."[30] Even as they pitch such chromatic curses as nonsense, these readers testify to the strange power of Crane's lurid realism, in which color words activate the very "colored-ness" of colors apart from their actual appearances.

At his most characteristic, then, Crane deals with colors in their abstract potentialities, as Firsts. Indeed, his writing assumes that literature can only approach color as "a mere may-be," a capacity to be actualized through reading. His virtual hues form virtual landscapes—impossible only in the sense that they are unable to be localized in particular objects or subjects. Crane makes this impossibility a virtue: a separation from preexisting instantiations of visual qualia and thus a capacity to remain open to novel ways of perceiving and feeling colors. As such, Crane's most interesting colors are not those we "see" but those we read. Such a distinction avoids two traps into which previous Crane criticism has fallen: either naively treating color in literature as analogous to color in visual experience (taking Crane's color tactics too literally) or reducing his color terms to moments of breakage and thus rendering Crane's palette in black and white (the deconstructionist urge to emphasize the materiality of the scene of writing).[31] However much Crane might have been interested in the gaps and slippages in language or in the corporeality of black ink on a white page, he cultivated the habitual associations that link the words "red," "yellow," and "blue" with their respective qualia. This account explains Crane's preference for familiar hues over precise shades: the habits for these terms are stronger, our sense of their qualities more vivid. We may see the world in nuanced tones, but we speak of it in a limited range of color words. Crane's writing both stimulates and tests these habits as part of an exploration of our experiences of generalized colors and the chromatic encounters that literature affords.

Crane's sustained investigation of the kinds of colors indigenous to writing set him in league with the fin-de-siècle aesthetes who, as

Le Gallienne put it, sought to write "in color."[32] If lurid realism seemed like a budding movement to Warner, it was because the black curses in *Red Badge* recalled a host of European authors who also tested the limits and capacities of color terms. In the lead essay to his collection *In the Key of Blue* (1893), for instance, the English poet and critic John Addington Symonds treated the problem of chromatic description as paradigmatic of aestheticist writing. He reasoned that because color words are rough approximations of visual tints and tones, the task of communicating a color sensation forces authors to lean on suggestion and imagination: as Symonds explained, the "poverty of language" with regards to color is "not wholly disadvantageous to a stylist" because "it forces him to exercise both fancy and imagination in the effort to bring some special tint before the mental vision of the reader." That is, if verbal description "be sufficiently penetrated with emotion, it has by its very vagueness a power of suggestion which the more direct art of the painter often misses."[33] In his praise of indirection and ephemerality, Symonds followed the lead of Baudelaire, who in his "Salon of 1846" included "color" as one of the defining features of modern art, alongside "intimacy," "spirituality," and "aspiration towards the infinite."[34] For Baudelaire and his many descendants, including Le Gallienne and the poets he praises, color encapsulated the efforts at suggestion and creation that distinguished the symbolist revolt against the descriptive aspirations of realism.

In fact, as Françoise Meltzer argues in her study of the "prominence and peculiarity of color in French symbolist verse," color semantics provided writers such as Mallarmé and Rimbaud with the perfect vehicle for creating "pure poetry" detached from material reference and aimed at attaining the *Idéal*.[35] For as Peirce observed, color terms refer not to particular things but to abstract qualities. And when a color term is combined in an unexpected way, as in Crane's fiction or Rimbaud's verse, it produces what Meltzer calls "a sort of semantic boomerang effect": "instead of intensifying the object it should modify, the color returns to itself, and suddenly stands out in isolation" (256). Meltzer contends that this ability to shoot off from the world of concrete objects, to shed even the affiliation with "the cumbersome catalogues of *signifiés* to which common language is shackled," aided the symbolists in their attempt "to amputate the word from its crass concrete context and transform it into pure idea" (257, 273).

Though Meltzer focuses on poetry, her claims can be extended to

the visual artists who took inspiration from the likes of Mallarmé and
Maurice Maeterlinck in fashioning abstract techniques for painting.
Kandinsky, for instance, cited such poetry as evidence that words themselves produced affective and sensory effects, even going so far as to
turn to language rather than pigment when explaining the extreme limit
of abstract color. In visual perception, Kandinsky explained, "colour cannot stand alone" but must be bounded by some form, yet "when the word
red is heard, the colour is evoked without definite boundaries." "A never-
ending extent of red can only be seen in the mind," he continued, and
"such red, as seen by the mind and not by the eye, exercises at once a
definite and indefinite impression on the soul," definite because the spiritual effect is unmistakable, indefinite because—like a First—"in itself it
has no suggestion of warmth or cold"; it is pure color.[36] Whereas most
accounts of chromatic aesthetics at the end of the nineteenth century
have moved from painting to poetry, Kandinsky's comments encourage
us to give equal attention to period's fascination with how color appears
in language.

For the symbolists no less than for Crane, the material character of
artificial dyes underwrote the attempt to saturate language with color.
Once mauveine, magenta, and other synthetic colorants overtook visual culture, "colours ceased to be envisaged as natural," bolstering a
decadent enthusiasm for artifice and stimulating speculation about what
color could become. Literary scholar Marc Porée argues that "poets, in
particular, ever eager to grant colours to their words and sentences, felt
under the obligation to foster a new lingua," something "neither symbolic nor referential, but more in line with a private rhetorics."[37] Merrill's
translation of Émile Hennequin's prose poem "Words" in *Pastels in Prose*
makes this connection explicit. After rhapsodizing that "there is no wine
that realizes the intoxication imagined by the word Wine; . . . there is
no perfume that our deceived nostrils find equal to the word Perfume;
no blue, no red that figures the tints with which our imaginations are
colored," Hennequin's speaker turns his back on the world and embraces
the visions afforded by language. To capture the strange brilliance of
these imagined visions, he likens his perceptions to "aquarelles that we
have anilinized."[38] He figures the techniques of symbolist writing as
the chemical process of intensifying the colors of the world and arranging them in brighter and brighter compositions: color experience "anilinized" through language.

It should come as no surprise, then, that members of the wider symbolist circle embraced Crane as one of their own. Yet his lurid realism—as
a *realism*—refused the retreat into private rhetoric.[39] Elbert Hubbard,
who published several of Crane's poems and short stories in the *Philistine*
and hosted a dinner in his honor, praised the young writer's "intense
imagination" and his ability to create "words that symboled color." "All
is packed with color, and charged with feeling," Hubbard held, implying
that the added color brought the affective charge. But he also insisted
that, unlike many other writers of the imagination, Crane bent his colors
toward the telling of facts. Witness "The Open Boat" (1897), "the stern-
est, creepiest bit of realism ever penned."[40] Indeed, even though Crane's
less sympathetic reviewers looked on his red oaths and black curses as
recalcitrant nonsense—often linking them to the symbolist figure of
the synesthete—Crane crafted his hues not to invoke a private realm of
subjective experience (as in the tradition of Russell, impressionism, and
Mallarmé) but to attune us to the aesthetic construction of a common
sensory world (like Peirce).[41] He joined the symbolists in detaching colors from objects and reaffixing them to abstract nouns and events. But
his aim was to isolate the virtual character of color in order to then wield
it as a qualitative force, one that pervades his language and engenders
new perceptual configurations able to extend beyond his pages.

In "An Illusion in Red and White" (1900), Crane reflects on the power
wielded by these verbal configurations. The story takes a gruesome tale
of ax murder as a parable of the consequences of colors felt and imagined but not seen. In particular, it relates a narrator's account of how
Farmer Jones—a man with gray hair, brown teeth, and hands "the color
of black walnut"—murdered his wife in plain view of their children and
then convinced the young eyewitnesses that they had seen "a man with
red hair and big white teeth and real white hands" wielding the ax. The
narrator, "one of the brightening stars of New York journalism," supposes
that Jones directed his children's confused minds with leading questions
packed with vivid color imagery. He guesses that the farmer created a
narrative that carried the palpability of actual perceptions by repeatedly
asking if the murderer had "very red hair" and bright white teeth and by
claiming to have glimpsed such a man leaving the house after the crime.
The journalist stresses the amount of conjecture in his account: "This is
how I imagine it happened."[42] The narrative presents a writer's imagining of the powers of the imagination; the illusion holds interest for Crane

insofar as it demonstrates the ability of color words to foster imaginative experiences whose vividness outstrips—and subsequently shapes—that of physical reality.

The poet Anne Carson has coined a phrase that captures the metaphysical implications of linguistic assemblies such as Crane's. In *Autobiography of Red* (1998), amid a discussion of the ancient poet Stesichorus, Carson describes the writer's ability to fasten and unfasten the "latches of being." "What is an adjective?" she asks. Whereas "nouns name the world" and "verbs activate the names," adjectives are "in charge of attaching everything in the world to its place in particularity. They are the latches of being."[43] Crane's colors clasp the latches in unfamiliar ways, and his different way of writing facilitates a different way of assembling the world, of fitting part to whole, color to object. We started this section attuned to the way Crane detached colors from visual experience. But his "Illusion in Red and White" demonstrates that this operation always functions within a broader circuit between the visual and verbal. The writer pulls from perceptual experience to isolate qualities that are then bound together through linguistic latches, which in turn direct how perception proceeds. The art of the fin de siècle delighted in the resulting intensifications; they gave a thrill, distinguished art from the everyday. Yet as Crane showed in his account of how language can turn "black walnut" hands into "bright white ones," such techniques can also misdirect. Lurid realism brought the chromatic aesthetics of symbolism into relation with the visual politics of Jim Crow.

The Color Line Feeling

Despite the bemusement bordering on outrage generated by Crane's black curses and red oaths, such linguistic color constructions were in fact remarkably common in late-nineteenth-century U.S. racial discourse, and they remain so. Not just "black woman" and "red man" but also phrases denoting "black" behavior and speech were so naturalized that African American writers had to go out of their way to draw attention to them. In *The Marrow of Tradition* (1901), for example, Charles Chesnutt stops the action to flag the odd mix of sensations implied in the idea of a "black voice." When Dr. William Miller, recently returned to his home state of North Carolina, notices people ducking into the bushes at the approach of his buggy, he suspects that "there was some race trouble

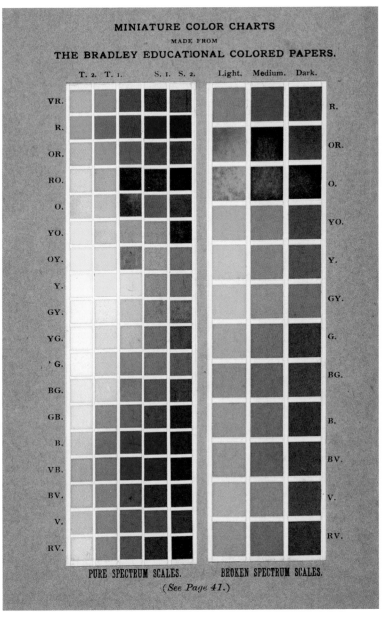

PLATE 1. Selection of Milton Bradley's Educational Colored Papers. Milton Bradley, *Elementary Color*, revised edition (Springfield, Mass.: Milton Bradley, 1895), unpaginated front matter. RB 603471, Huntington Library, San Marino, California.

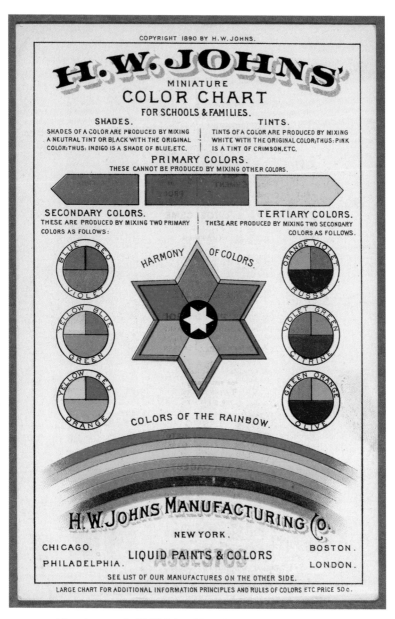

PLATE 2. Advertisement for H. W. Johns Manufacturing Company that explains the basic principles of color harmony and promises to reveal additional rules to customers who mail in fifty cents. "Textiles: Dyes and Dyers A–Z by Company," binder 1 of 9, Jay T. Last Collection, Huntington Library, San Marino, California.

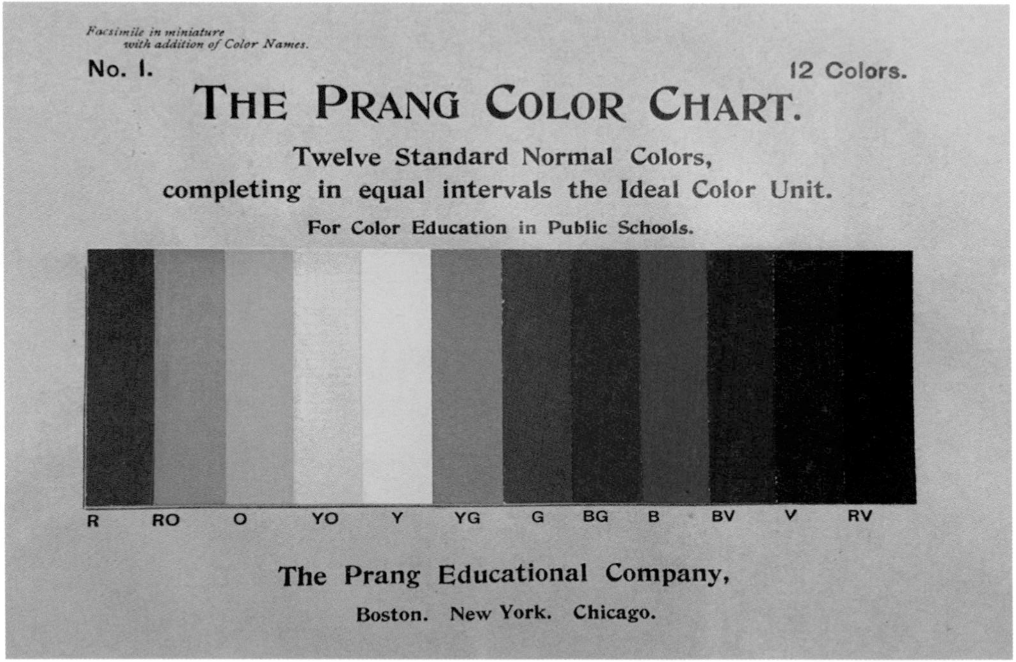

PLATE 3. The Ideal Color Unit used to train students' color perception in the course outlined by Prang, Hicks, and Clark. Louis Prang, Mary Dana Hicks, and John S. Clark, *Color Instruction: Suggestions for a Course of Instruction in Color for Public Schools* (New York: Prang Educational Company, 1893), 27.

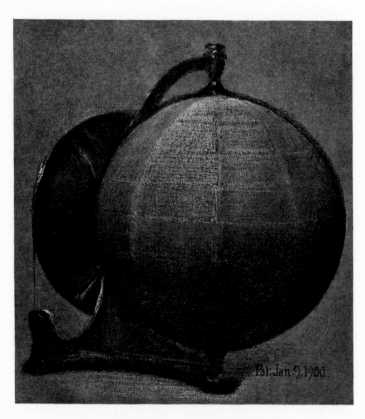

A BALANCED COLOR SPHERE

PASTEL SKETCH

PLATE 4. The Munsell Balanced Color Sphere, the basis of A. H. Munsell's "Measured Training of the Color Sense." A. Munsell, *A Color Notation,* second edition (Boston: George H. Ellis, 1907), unpaginated front matter.

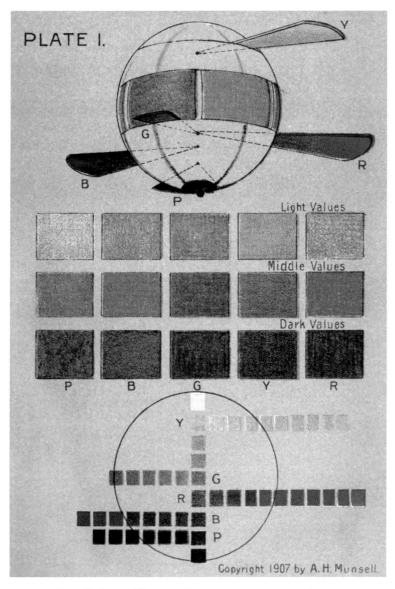

PLATE 5. Munsell's five middle hues. Munsell, *A Color Notation,* Plate 1.

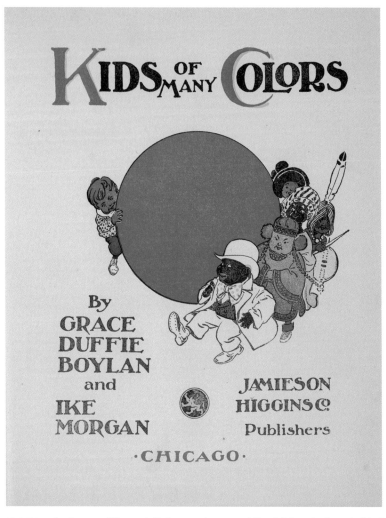

PLATE 6. An image of the racially innocent eye: a white child peeks from behind an abstract patch of red to see "exotic" racial types. Grace Duffie Boylan and Ike Morgan, *Kids of Many Colors* (1901) (New York: Hurst, 1909), unpaginated front matter. Reproduced courtesy of the Department of Rare Books and Special Collections, Princeton University Library.

PLATE 7. This image invites white child readers to imagine themselves as the artist, ready to use the vivid colors of children's picture books to mark their difference from the racist types depicted. Boylan and Morgan, *Kids of Many Colors*, 6. Reproduced courtesy of the Department of Rare Books and Special Collections, Princeton University Library.

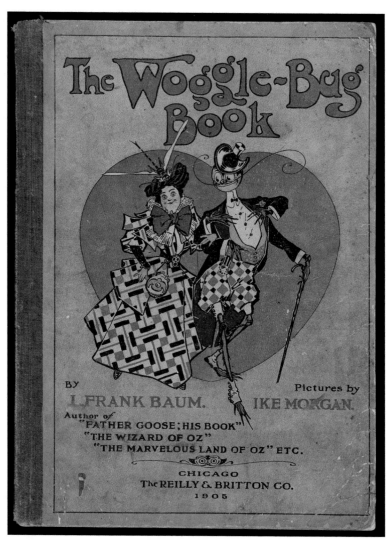

PLATE 8. Cover of L. Frank Baum's *The Woggle-Bug Book*, drawn by Ike Morgan. The Woggle Bug walks arm in arm with a mannequin wearing the "loud" cloth that catches his eye. L. Frank Baum, *The Woggle-Bug Book* (Chicago: Reilly and Britton, 1905). Reproduced courtesy of the Department of Rare Books and Special Collections, Princeton University Library.

by the child's laughter that she would scream and press her hand upon her heart whenever Dorothy's merry voice reached her ears; and she still looked at the little girl with wonder that she could find anything to laugh at.

Uncle Henry never laughed. He worked hard from morning till night and did not know what joy was. He was gray also, from his long beard to his rough boots, and he looked stern and solemn, and rarely spoke.

It was Toto that made Dorothy laugh, and saved her from growing as gray as her other surroundings. Toto was not gray; he was a little black dog, with long, silky hair and small black eyes that twinkled merrily on either side of his funny, wee nose. Toto played all day long, and Dorothy played with him, and loved him dearly.

To-day, however, they were not playing. Uncle Henry sat upon the door-step and looked anxiously at the sky, which was even grayer than usual. Dorothy stood in the door with Toto in her arms, and looked at the sky too. Aunt Em was washing the dishes.

From the far north they heard a

PLATE 9. Dorothy, Uncle Henry, Aunt Em, and Toto, all fading away in Kansas. L. Frank Baum, *The Wonderful Wizard of Oz,* illustrations by W. W. Denslow (Chicago: George M. Hill, 1900), 13. Kislak Center for Special Collections, Rare Books and Manuscripts, University of Pennsylvania, Philadelphia, Pennsylvania.

Chapter XXIV.
Home Again.

AUNT EM HAD JUST COME out of the house to water the cabbages when she looked up and saw Dorothy running toward her.

"My darling child!" she cried, folding the little girl in her arms and covering her face with kisses; "where in the world did you come from?"

"From the Land of Oz," said Dorothy, gravely. "And here is Toto, too. And oh, Aunt Em! I'm so glad to be at home again!"

PLATE 10. Dorothy returns to Kansas, bringing red color back with her from Oz. Baum, *The Wonderful Wizard of Oz,* illustrations by Denslow, 261. Kislak Center for Special Collections, Rare Books and Manuscripts, University of Pennsylvania, Philadelphia, Pennsylvania.

It WAS SOME TIME BEFORE THE Cowardly Lion awakened, for he had lain among the poppies a long while, breathing in their deadly fragrance; but when he did open his eyes and roll off the truck he was very glad to find himself still alive.

"I ran as fast as I could," he said, sitting down and yawning; "but the flowers were too strong for me. How did you get me out?"

Then they told him of the field-mice, and how they had generously saved him from death; and the Cowardly Lion laughed, and said,

"I have always thought myself very big and terrible; yet such small things as flowers came near to killing me,

PLATE 11. The gates of the Emerald City. Baum, *The Wonderful Wizard of Oz,* illustrations by Denslow, 109. Kislak Center for Special Collections, Rare Books and Manuscripts, University of Pennsylvania, Philadelphia, Pennsylvania.

I stood upon a High Place,
And saw, below, many Devils
Running, leaping,
And carousing in Sin.
One looked up, grinning,
And said, "Comrade! Brother!"
—Stephen Crane.

PLATE 12. W. W. Denslow's illustration of Stephen Crane's poem "I Stood upon a High Place," in Elbert Hubbard's magazine *Philistine* 8, no. 4 (March 1899): back cover. Kislak Center for Special Collections, Rare Books and Manuscripts, University of Pennsylvania, Philadelphia, Pennsylvania.

on foot," and he soon receives confirmation: "A black head was cautiously protruded from the shrubbery, and a black voice—if such a description be allowable—addressed him."[44] What appears as aesthetic boldness in Crane and Kandinsky requires a stylistic intervention even to be noticed once it has been transposed onto race, where such combinations parade as self-evident rather than peculiar. Yet the same operations are at work. Like Crane's chromatic curses, the color terms employed to denote racial groups simultaneously activate a feeling of visual difference and stretch that feeling across invisible realms.

Similar appeals to literal color are not hard to find in African American writing of this period, though they never did much good. The point was at once too obvious (of course race is not just color) and too obscure, since color metaphors do factor into the perception of race in complex and contradictory ways. Take Justice Henry Billings Brown's majority decision in *Plessy v. Ferguson,* the Supreme Court case that codified the doctrine of "separate but equal" treatment for whites and nonwhites. Brown argued that the "merely . . . legal distinction" between races imposed by segregation was "founded in the color of the two races" and that it "must always exist so long as white men are distinguished from the other race by color."[45] You would never know from this reasoning that Homer Plessy, the plaintiff, looked so "white" that he had to inform the train conductor that he belonged in the "colored" car. Plessy had trusted the self-evidence of his color to point up the absurdity of Jim Crow laws; instead, the Court appealed to the self-evidence of "the color of the two races" to support the idea that a person who looked white could be in fact black.[46]

Brown's decision and the racial logic it enshrined separated color from visual experience as decisively as any Crane story, with similar effects. As in "An Illusion in Red and White," words for color in late-nineteenth-century figurations of race functioned to infuse a perceptual scene with a qualitative feeling powerful enough to turn black hands "bright white." They aimed at refastening the "latches of being," determining which bodies would be deemed worthy of social recognition. In this way, racial discourse during Reconstruction—which leaned heavily on color in the absence of the old distinction between slave and citizen—hit upon a way of exploiting what had previously been a problematic relation between race (as essence) and color (as seen). Although eighteenth-century European race theorists appealed to skin color as a possible way to characterize human difference, and nineteenth-century anthropometric researchers devised elaborate systems for quantifying skin tone, visual color was never able to do the work that race was asked to do.[47] As color *words,* however, the chromatic metaphors of the *Plessy* era invoked the feeling of visual difference even in its absence, aiding in the perceptual education that produces the self-evidence of racial recognition.

Chesnutt included dramatizations of the linguistic influence on perception in his many stories of the color line. In *The House behind the Cedars* (1900), George Tyron learns that his beloved Rena has "African blood," and the narrator describes how form and color shift when he sees her in light of this new designation: "In all her fair young beauty she stood before him, and then by some hellish magic she was slowly transformed into a hideous black hag."[48] Chesnutt knew that such "hellish magic" was at work all the time in the United States, not just in dramatic moments of racial revelation but also in the habits of attention promoted by Jim Crow. He termed the mode of perception infused with such color classification "the American eye." In *The Marrow of Tradition,* the narrator remarks that although Dr. Miller and Dr. Burns had many features in common, "looking at these two men with the American eye, the differences would perhaps be more striking, or at least the more immediately apparent, for the first was white and the second black, or, more correctly speaking, brown."[49] The passage shows how a way of speaking about race through a loose or metaphorical use of color words trains the eye to fixate on particular differences, making them "immediately apparent." For Chesnutt, the techniques of "saturating language" do more than foster literary intensity; as a central component of racial discourse, they contribute to the production of race as a perceivable quality, something seen and felt like a color.

The American eye thus shows how color terms help make race visible, but it equally illustrates how race, no less than aniline, functions as a technology for intensifying color.[50] Viewed through the lenses of black and white, a whole array of sensations and qualities come to the fore, including a variety of colors. In "The Wife of His Youth" (1898), for instance, Chesnutt uses two blues to exhibit the heightened attention to skin prompted by racial seeing. While Sam Ryder is "white enough to show blue veins," Liza Jane is "so black that her toothless gums, revealed when she opened her mouth to speak, were not red, but blue."[51] The narrator, looking through the American eye, fixates on these blues and endows them with an outsized presence in the depiction of the scene.

Chesnutt uses this narrative perspective to dramatize what Frederick Douglass called "the color-line feeling," the complex way that white Americans perceived color through race. Writing in 1881 against the argument that "the color of the negro has something to do with the feeling entertained toward him," Douglass showed that black is no longer just black when it appears on a black man, just as blue is no longer just blue.[52] Instead, the color-line feeling sweeps up individual hues within a network of social differentials that intensifies color by making it stand for more than just itself. In its final scene, Chesnutt's story depicts the resulting imperative to dampen chroma to achieve whiteness: though Liza Jane arrives in "a blue calico gown of ancient cut, a little red shawl," and "a large bonnet profusely ornamented with faded red and yellow artificial flowers," when Ryder introduces her to the Blue Vein Society, she is "neatly dressed in gray" and wears "the white cap of an elderly woman."[53] In replacing her artificial flowers and multicolored clothing, Ryder attempts to reconfigure the relation that the wife of his youth holds to blackness by adjusting her relation to colors.

Chesnutt's investigations of the convoluted relations between color terms and the perception of race clarify why, according to the college friend who reported Crane's debt to Goethe, *The Monster* (1898) contains the most vivid display of Crane's chromatic effects. Set in the fictional town of Whilomville, the novella tells the story of Henry Johnson, an African American coachman whose face is disfigured by burning chemicals as he saves the son of his white employer from a burning house. As literary scholar Jacqueline Goldsby has shown, the scene of mutilation reimagines a lynching, of Robert Lewis, that occurred in Crane's former home of Port Jervis, New York, in 1892, and it does so with blindingly bright hues.[54] When Noxon illustrated Crane's Goethean color effects, this is the passage he chose: "Do you remember the colors of burning chemicals in 'The Monster'?" he asked; "there you had them all at once."[55]

Even before reaching the laboratory with its boiling chemicals, Henry exemplifies the intensification of color through race, primarily through his "lavender trousers" and "straw hat with its bright silk band" (395). The dandyish clothes mark him as a Zip Coon figure like the Woggle-Bug, and Crane suggests that, like all such minstrel characters, he is the creation of white spectators: when the men in the barber shop stare through the plate glass window at Henry, one comments, "didn't I give him those lavender trousers?" (397). Crane's narration during the rescue scene exaggerates these stock features, presenting Henry as even more of a minstrel type—"his legs gained a frightful faculty of bending sideways"—and repeatedly casting his actions in terms of his blackness. He "submits" before the flames "because of his fathers, bending his mind in a most perfect slavery to this conflagration"; and at the sight of the chemicals he lets out a "negro wail that had in it the sadness of the swamps" and "duck[s] in the manner of his race in fights" (404–6). As the colors intensify, so does the visibility of Henry's supposed racial character, culminating in the disfigurement that transforms him into the monstrous abstraction of blackness that haunts the residents of Whilomville.

The terms of that disfigurement invoke the brilliant colors of aniline dyes and the linguistic contortions of lurid realism. When Henry opens the doors to the laboratory, he "confront[s] a strange spectacle":

> The room was like a garden in the region where might be burning flowers. Flames of violet, crimson, green, blue, orange, and purple were blooming everywhere. There was one blaze that was precisely the hue of delicate coral. In another place was a mass that lay merely in phosphorescent inaction like a pile of emeralds. But all these marvels were to be seen dimly through clouds of heaving, turning, deadly smoke. (405–6)

The polychromatic "marvels" recall the spectacular commercial displays that marshaled the power of pure color and fostered the aniline aesthetic. Like the blue of "The Blue Hotel," the chemicals intensify the world's colors ("one blaze . . . was precisely the hue of delicate coral") and reconfigure them within a cultivated arrangement (the room resembles a "garden" rather than a wilderness, despite the kaleidoscopic appearance). Yet the passage also distances these vivid images from the scene they are meant to describe, foregrounding Crane's technique of pulling colors from objects. The convoluted syntax of the primary simile—"The room was like a garden in the region where might be burning flowers"— puts far more space between "garden" and "burning flowers" than one would expect. It's not just that the flowers are presented as a feature of the region rather than the garden, so that the emphasis falls on aesthetic composition; it's also that the flowers only "might" be there. Crane adds to this speculative dimension a few sentences later by introducing clouds of smoke that dim the glowing hues for Henry, putting their full brilliance in the purview of the narrator and reader alone: colors read and felt rather than seen.

The laboratory scene reaches its unique heights of chromatic exuberance because it brings the abstracting operations of Crane's style together with the analogous procedures of color in racial discourse, where they resonate in a kind of escalating feedback loop. They always overlapped—the same linguistic tricks that make a curse "black" make a man "black," and the power ascribed to aniline dyes drew on the long-standing affiliation of bright hues with exotic peoples. Yet in these passages their mutual imbrication takes center stage. The jewellike colors seem magnetically attracted to Henry's Zip Coon clothing ("an orange-colored flame leaped like a panther at the lavender trousers") (406). And the isolation of blackness from other racial signifiers that results from Henry's burns receives a linguistic analogue when Dr. Trescott shouts at Alek, "You old black chump! You old black!" (417). Crane did not offer incisive analyses of racial metaphors as Chesnutt did; as a white writer, he would not have felt their pressure in the same way. Yet in *The Monster* he testified to a strange correspondence between domains usually kept separate: the chromatic techniques of modern literature, with their visual parallels in commercial colors, and the linguistic habits that guide how race is perceived. His lurid realism flourished where the language of color met the language of race.

Stein's Mixtures: Color as Composition

The resonance between literary color and racial discourse probably caught Crane unawares; outside *The Monster,* he never pursued it. Yet if Crane's career provides only a fleeting glimpse of how lurid realism coincided with the metaphors of racial color, the early work of Gertrude Stein shows these affinities in full view, with colors blazing. The poems in *Tender Buttons* abound in color combinations more startling than anything found in Crane, and though they have long been understood as part of the symbolist legacy within modernism, they result as much from Stein's encounter with racial discourse in "Melanctha" as they do from her immersion in the Parisian avant-garde. In writing "Melanctha"—her "negro story," which she declared "the first definite step . . . into the twentieth century in literature"—Stein experienced the remarkable sensitivity that words have to their contexts.[56] This insight drove her subsequent experiments in portraiture, especially *Tender Buttons,* and pushed her to characterize that entire phase of her career as an attempt to translate color into writing, to make language colorful. With Stein, lurid realism bloomed into modernism.

That Stein translated the lesbian romance depicted in the conventionally written *Q.E.D.* into the middle story of *Three Lives* is by now well known, and critics have offered compelling accounts of how the "cover of blackness" facilitated the linguistic daring of "Melanctha."[57] Most have focused on Stein's imaginative engagement with racial others, arguing that, as Laura Doyle puts it, "the modernists' racializing of language, characters, and plots is of a piece with, rather than an unfortunate diversion from, their literary innovations."[58] What remains to be emphasized is that in setting her narrative in Baltimore's African American community, Stein adopted a linguistic domain in which the convoluted semantics of color terms accentuated the responsiveness of words to their contexts. She engaged not just with imagined racial others but also with the language of race, particularly its color metaphors, to experiment with the way linguistic assemblages stabilize or unsettle the latches of being. Indeed, Carson proposes as much by beginning her discussion of literature's latches with a quotation from Stein that captures the lesson she learned when writing *Three Lives:* "I like the feeling of words doing as they want to do and as they have to do when they live where they have to live that is where they have come to live."[59] The excitement in composition was in experiencing how that feeling shifts when words change where they live.

The stories that come before and after "Melanctha" in *Three Lives* exhibit a narrative fixation on color that must have preceded Stein's final revisions of the middle part. In "The Good Anna" and "The Gentle Lena," the color words are plentiful and carry their straightforward visual denotations: "blue dressings" and "a green parrot," "greenish colored paper" and "the white stone steps of the little red brick house," green paint and red fabric.[60] Even skin color refers to a visual property in these stories, one that can change over time. As Anna ages, her "skin stained itself pale yellow," turning "more pale yellow" over the course of the narrative (31, 80). Lena on the other hand was "a brown and pleasant creature," but not the brown of a "black" person. Rather, Lena's skin was "brown as blond races often have them brown, brown, not with the yellow or the red or the chocolate brown of the sun burned countries, but brown with the clear color laid flat on the light toned skin beneath" (240). Color terms in these stories aim at describing visual qualities so that they appear in the mind's eye.

In "Melanctha," however, none of the chromatic terms denote their visual referents, especially not those that purport to describe skin. Rose proclaims, "I'd never kill myself . . . just 'cause I was blue"—and this use of "blue" to mean melancholy recurs several times at the beginning and end of the story, when the color terms are most prominent (87). Likewise, on the same page where the narrator calls John "light brown," James Herbert refers to him as "yellow," meaning cowardly. These obviously conventional senses of "blue" and "yellow" point to the equally nonliteral uses of color words in racial discourse, which Stein repeats with distracting frequency. Rose Johnson is "real black," Melanctha is "pale yellow," Jefferson Campbell's parents are "brown," and Jane Harden is "so white" that "hardly anyone could guess" she was black (85, 86, 103). Of course Melanctha is no more "yellow" than she is "blue," except within the peculiar language of race. That is, she is not yellow like Anna is yellow. And unlike in the other sections of *Three Lives*, the narrative voice of the middle story displays little inclination to convey actual visual hues. When Jeff and Melanctha walk together "in the bright fields," specific color terms are noticeably absent; we read only that Jeff "loved all the colors in the trees and on the ground, and the little, new, bright colored bugs he found in the moist ground" (149). For a story obsessed with color, there's remarkably little interest in the hues that hit the eye.[61]

In "Melanctha" Stein became preoccupied with the fact that the meaning of her words transformed once she retold her narrative through African American characters. Not that this realization pushed Stein to join Chesnutt in denouncing the dangerous ways color terms condition racial sight; when she describes the scene of a razor fight as "filled full with strong black curses," she does not attend to the differences such casual designations enforce (113). Yet read within the context of *Three Lives*, Stein's nonvisual color terms show her exploiting the semantic complexity of color in the language of race—the way "black" and "yellow" mediate between what is said and what is seen—to begin the investigation of how words fit together and pull apart, how they react to and constitute a context, that she developed in *Tender Buttons*. As poet and critic Harryette Mullen has argued, both texts treat "color and race as different yet overlapping preoccupations," and both "splurge on adjectives," as in the epithets that repeat throughout "Melanctha." Rose, for instance, is not simply "black" but "a real black, tall, well built, sullen, stupid, childlike, good looking negress" (85).[62] These constructions show Stein fastening the latches of being with such insistence that the linguistic performance itself becomes the object of attention. They expand an insight condensed in the nonvisual colors of racial discourse into an investigation of how words fit together, which she soon pressed to create color constructions more outrageous than any of those that irritated Crane's reviewers.

If the descriptive catalogs in "Melanctha" show Stein assembling and reassembling character, linking arrangements of words with patterns of perception in ways recognizable from racial discourse, the colors of *Tender Buttons* push the relation between language and vision to its limit. The results are unlike any colors ever seen: "a not torn rose-wood color," "a pink cut pink," a "precocious . . . bit of blue," "a single hurt color."[63] Stein's colors do Crane's one better, as they not only modify nonvisual nouns but also appear as substances in their own right, capable of being cut up, torn apart, and sewn back together to create impossible combinations. Not "roses are red" but "the red is rose"; not individual colors with their self-evident qualities but, as the poem "A LONG DRESS" in *Tender Buttons* has it, a situation in which "only a yellow and green are blue, a pink is scarlet, and a bow is every color" (13, 17). The latches have been clasped in convoluted ways in these poems, yet Stein's strategies build on those of Crane and the symbolists. She exaggerates the processes of abstraction and reconstellation that Crane harnessed in his prose to investigate what happens when words like "red" and "white" combine and clash in the reading eye and what sorts of feelings, ranging from clarity to disruptive confusion, the arrangement of such words can generate. In the link between feeling and language captured in colors, she made an even bolder attempt to saturate her writing, claiming for literature color's combination of relational complexity and qualitative intensity.

That Stein carried forward the interest in color she sharpened in writing *Three Lives* is clear from the sheer preponderance of chromatic terms in *Tender Buttons:* more than two hundred in just over sixty pages. Even more, in *Lectures in America* (1935), Stein cast the entire project of that early book of poetry, and the period of portraiture it initiated, as an attempt to write color. She specified that this task involved evacuating the referential content of language in favor of creating a linguistic composition that, through the push and pull of the relations established, "made" the thing rather than "described" it. As Stein put it, "I became more and more excited about how words which were the words that made whatever I looked at look like itself were not the words that had in them any quality of description." Looking is paramount here, and so color takes priority. In fact, Stein reported that one of her preoccupations during this period "was the relation of color to the words that exactly meant that but had no element in it of description." She called the technique she developed to address the problem "this color thing."[64]

Stein's interest in modernist painting goes only so far in explaining her "color thing," for in the end she joined Crane in caring more for what color can do and become within writing than for how it functioned in art. To be sure, Stein learned much about composition from Picasso and Matisse, but she had already formed the understanding of color that she used in her writing before she set foot on the Left Bank. As I discussed in the introduction, Stein collaborated with Leon Solomons to research color perception at the Harvard Psychology Lab when she was an undergraduate at Radcliffe.[65] Using a color wheel of the sort Milton Bradley had recommended for use in the classroom, they tested the least perceptible difference of color saturation—in particular, they arranged white, black, and red discs in various proportions on the wheel to determine when red starts to look redder. They found—contrary to their initial hypothesis that more red on the wheel would mean more red in the perceiver—that the qualitative feeling of redness does not correspond to a particular objective stimulus; instead, it corresponds to a complex calculation of relations across the visual field. The "ratio of the color to the white" on the wheel, along with background illumination and the brightness of the viewing conditions, regulated the intensity of the red more than the actual amount of red material in the arrangement.[66] By this account, chromatic qualia were not stable entities registered in experience but, rather, experience's way of feeling the full set of relations that defines a visual environment. They "make" a color more than they "describe" it.

Stein weaves references to the particular tasks she performed with Solomons throughout the colors of *Tender Buttons*. Especially in "ROOMS," the section of the book most devoted to the conditions of perception, Stein invokes colors that lighten and darken, that appear and disappear, that are arranged and observed on a wall or a wheel. And unlike in the first two sections, she presents these hues as if in recollection. "Explaining darkening and expecting relating is all of a piece," she writes (64), and "red which is red is a dark color. An example of this is fifteen years and a separation of regret" (72–73). Other passages recall the color wheel and the protocols of experimentation. "The whole arrangement is established. The end of which is that there is a suggestion, a suggestion that there can be a different whiteness to a wall. This was thought" (64). The tone and diction recall that of a lab report, one that involves establishing arrangements to test a suggestion of a different whiteness. Likewise: "To begin the placing there is no wagon. [Only a wheel?] There is no change lighter. It was done. And then the spreading" (63). These passages imagine conditions of "change" and of the "spreading" differences that occur as early as the opening poem with its "single hurt color," situating them within the interplay between an attentive observer and a "whole arrangement" of blurring colors on the wheel.

At the end of the book, Stein connects the images of color research to her "color thing" through a series of "why" questions that functions both as a statement of research interests and as a set of protocols for *Tender Buttons:*

> Why is a pale white not paler than blue, why is a connection made by a stove, why is the example which is mentioned not shown to be the same, why is there no adjustment between the place and the separate attention. Why is there a choice in gamboling. Why is there not necessary dull stable, why is there a single piece of any color, why is there that sensible silence. Why is there the resistance in a mixture, why is there no poster, why is there that in the window, why is there no suggester, why is there no window, why is there no oyster closer. (69–70)

As in the section "FOOD," the process of cooking (the "connection made by a stove") here marks a qualitative transformation that nonetheless maintains continuity, a link in which "there is no resemblance" (66). A "single piece of any color"—when produced through the movement of the color wheel—constitutes a similar process and a similar link, one that does not have any necessary stability but instead offers "resistance" in its very nature as a "mixture," something that links not only the "place" to the "separate attention" but also the constituents of the various relations within the place. Bringing this sort of transformative connection to the work of writing means abandoning any transparent description or easy relation between inside and outside: there is no way to bring the two ends of the process together like the two halves of an oyster when the connection is made by a stove.

A paragraph in "BREAKFAST" links color directly to these processes of mixture and transformation, further illustrating the suppositions about perception and writing that favor making over description. "An ordinary color, a color is that strange mixture which makes, which does make which does not make a ripe juice, which does not make a mat" (43). Ordinary color proceeds from a "strange mixture," a productive linking of perceiver and perceived, and the way it "makes" is not that of a "ripe juice," ready to be ex-pressed, nor is it that of a mat, something that stands under, like a sub-stance. Instead, color is the quality of mixtures that characterize the transformations throughout *Tender Buttons*—the cooking, cleaning, looking, licking, and above all writing that seek to make by transforming rather than repeating or describing. A portrait that results from this technique might appear wrong, but as Stein insists in the final sentences of the book, it nevertheless shows *care:* "The care with which the rain is wrong and the green is wrong and the white is wrong, the care with which there is a chair and plenty of breathing. The care with which there is incredible justice and likeness, all this makes magnificent asparagus, and also a fountain" (78). An asparagus stem has a point, and in its own way a fountain does too. The mode of reference, of pointing, modeled by Stein's carefully wrong colors is one that generates "incredible justice" by carrying forward the calculations and transformations involved in giving qualitative unity to a complex assemblage.[67]

Reading Stein's portraits through her colors reconciles two ways of explaining them that are usually kept separate and, in the process, clarifies how she continues Crane's investigations into language and qualia. On the one hand, there's Stein's own insistence that her portraits sought to convey the feeling of what it's like to look at something, that they attempted to make the thing without relying on "words that had in them any quality of description."[68] On the other hand, there's the understanding of *Tender Buttons* as "studies of exchanges at word junctions and across word membranes, designed to show the ways in which words join together in functional multi-word units," as Steven Meyer has written (another way of getting at Stein's "feeling of words doing as they want to do and as they have to do when they live where they have to live").[69] When understood as both proceeding from a "strange mixture" and as having a single, qualitative unity, color perception offers a model for how a linguistic construction might use its own materials to capture the feeling that makes a thing look like itself. Just as color consists of a quale that accompanies a perceptual calculation of an entire complex of relations and ratios—a calculation that registers something that is "there" but not in any one-to-one mimetic sense—so too do Stein's portraits aim at creating the "intensity" of a thing by translating these relations into language, a medium as relational as they come. Crane saturated language by dousing it in impossible color terms that spread chromatic quality across his linguistic combinations; Stein drew on color psychology to do something similar, but her "color thing" looks beyond even color words to treat *all* literary constructions as colors.

For as Stein's other psychology teacher William James observed, relations have a qualitative unity that cannot be confined to either the experiencing subject or the experienced world. In a passage from *Principles of Psychology* (1890) that presages his radical empirical approach to knowledge, James wrote, "There is not a conjunction or a preposition, and hardly an adverbial phrase, syntactic form, or inflection of voice, in human speech, that does not express some shading or other of relation." We might speak of these relations either "objectively" or "subjectively," and thereby attune ourselves either to what appears as "the real relations" or to the way those relations are "matche[d] . . . by an inward coloring." Yet both ways of talking rely on the perceptual activity in which proto-subject and proto-object are entwined and that, as experienced, has its own qualitative unity. James concluded, "We ought to say a feeling of *and,* a feeling of *if,* a feeling of *but,* and a feeling of *by,* quite as readily as we say a feeling of *blue* or a feeling of *cold*"—and in its injunction to think of words and their relations as available for qualitative feeling we might think of this famous sentence as the slogan for Stein's colors.[70] She sought to make literature colorful by treating language as something felt in the same way as blue.

This refusal to posit an unbridgeable gap between sensory immediacy and linguistic mediations is what links Stein to Crane against the related efforts of the symbolists and their followers. Once again, Peirce provides useful terms to illustrate the difference. "Color is sometimes given as an example of an impression," he wrote, something simple and immediately had. But "it is a bad one; because the simplest color is almost as complicated as a piece of music. Color depends upon the *relations* between different parts of the impression." As such, Peirce asserted, "color is not an impression, but an inference."[71] Stein, whose research with Solomons gave empirical support to Peirce's account, thought of color inferentially, but many of her modernist contemporaries presented it as an impression. Pound, for instance, explained his concept of the *image* by invoking Kandinsky's theory of color as a force that acts directly on the soul. "The image is the poet's pigment," he explained; "with that in mind you can go ahead and apply Kandinsky, you can transpose his chapter on the language of form and color and apply it to the writing of verse." Pound's images, which he illustrated with his short poem "In a Station of the Metro" (1913), seek to give language the immediacy of color, to make it something that "is real because we know it directly," like a sense impression.[72] Here too language aims at becoming colorful, but only through a kind of poetic magic whereby what is inherently general and conventional (language) becomes individual and immediate (color), the same sort of straining to express subjective experience that Meltzer, referring to the symbolists, calls "an experiment against language," one that is "doomed" from the start (273).[73]

For Stein, as for Crane, writing does not so much repackage already-existing experiences as create new qualia. As Mabel Dodge wrote of *Tender Buttons,* Stein's portraits "[impel] language to induce new states of consciousness"; they use "familiar words to create perceptions, conditions, and states of being, never before quite consciously experienced."[74] Stein's words act as colors to create distinctive feelings of consciousness, new qualia that redo the latches. Two short paragraphs from "SUGAR" condense the acts of translation through which she moved from phenomenal color through qualia to the words that make a thing without describing it to induce new perceptual states:

> A white bird, a colored mine, a mixed orange, a dog.
> Cuddling comes in continuing a change. (46)

The first sentence moves from the colored object (a white bird) to a "colored mine," which suggests not only ownership (the color is mine, the self is colored) but also a source of colors—a dark hole from which they might be mined, or perhaps the mind that harvests them. The objective and subjective aspects of color are then explicitly "mixed" in the orange (a color term that readily connotes both a sensation and an object), before the sentence takes a sharp turn, leaving colors behind to land on "dog." Yet a dog is a companion; "I am I because my little dog knows me," Stein wrote elsewhere.[75] The next sentence of "SUGAR" figures this constitutive relation in terms appropriate to her companionate model: "cuddling"—

proximity, intimacy—"comes in continuing a change." It comes not by forming a likeness—since "a likeness has blisters"—but by carrying forward the transformations and calculations that are always involved in our experiences of color (45).

This is why Stein's color thing encompasses more than just her color words. Indeed, the example she gives in *Lectures in America* of her attempt to make color in language, her portrait of sculptor Jacques Lipchitz, does not contain a single term like "red," "pink," or "blue." Rather, it consists of permutations of a few key sentences and phrases— "Like and like likely and likely likely and likely like and like," "When I knew him then he was looking looking at the looking at the looking"— that establish a field of relations meant to be synthesized into a color-like quality of Stein's subject.[76] Continuity and fidelity in such portraits consist in situating writing within the flow of experience and dramatizing the operations by which feelings of immediacy emerge though the experience of mediations. Once apprehended in terms of process, color in perception and color in language are not so hard to reconcile; they each provide spurs and conditions for the other, intertwining in the ongoing mixture of experience. Even Pound, despite his rhetoric of immediacy, is perhaps best understood as advocating for a qualitative apprehension of the set of linguistic relations that make up the image, which may be felt like an impression but which in fact proceeds inferentially. Stein's cuddling colors promise to clarify the modernist practices obscured by the modernists' own critical accounts.[77]

The mixtures of *Tender Buttons* might appear so strange as to push them far beyond Crane's comparatively straightforward narratives, even when routed through the colors of *Three Lives*. Yet the comparison, especially when read against the shared background of symbolist aesthetics, reveals how a multifaceted attempt to make literature a scheme of color drove literary experimentalism from the 1890s to the 1910s, and it points up the entanglement of these experiments with both the commercial color revolution and chromatic metaphors of race. The difference between Crane and Stein is that Stein allowed the color to overtake and rewrite her realism; she embraced the perception *of* language as the extreme case of the perception *through* language that occupied Crane and, in a different register, Chesnutt. In each case, however, the aim was at an aesthetic education, something akin to Bradley's recommendation that children adopt his precise color nomenclature or Rimington's efforts to revive and train the color sense through color concerts. Like these other color enthusiasts, Crane, Chesnutt, and Stein trusted that new ways of speaking could, by directing attention and orienting responses, reshape visible reality. Yet in their intense focus on *literary* colors—which bracket the visible world even as they maintain transformative chains of reference to it—these writers provide a more elaborate account of the linguistic and conceptual aspects of color experience than we saw in children's books, with their actual colors, or even in Garland's and Gilman's works, with their investments in visual perception.

When the latches are fastened in writing, the effects spill into the world. Such is the hope of avant-garde literature, including Stein's, but also of literary realism such as Chesnutt's. Ten years after *Tender Buttons,* in one of the brightest and most colorful urban centers in the world, a group of authors combined these traditions to confront the long history of racism in the United States and its imbrication with commercial color. They remade lurid realism into a technology not only for intensifying the feeling of reality but also for fashioning modern performances of blackness filled full of rich colors and nuanced sensory perceptions. And they offered those performances to white and black audiences alike, hoping that the modes of being they had clasped would take hold. In the Harlem Renaissance, the strategies for capturing and conveying color discussed in the previous chapters attain a new urgency and focus. For our final investigation, then, we will turn our attention uptown, where modernist experimentation flourished amid cabaret lights to create intoxicating chromatic experiences.

5   On Feeling Colorful and Colored in the Harlem Renaissance

Few characters in literary history are as attuned to color as Helga Crane, the fashionable and mixed-race protagonist of Nella Larsen's *Quicksand* (1928). She begins the novel immersed in a colorful interior "furnished with rare and intensely personal taste." A reading lamp "dimmed by a great black and red shade" casts its soft glow over a "blue Chinese carpet," an "oriental silk," a "shining brass bowl crowded with many-colored nasturtiums," and Helga herself, dressed in a "vivid green and gold negligee" and sunk in a chair "against whose dark tapestry her sharply cut face, with skin like yellow satin, was distinctly outlined."[1] The narration displays the loving attention to the colors of fabrics, lights, and skin tones that Helga cultivates throughout the novel, signs of an exquisite color sense if ever there was one.

Yet almost as soon as this scene of aesthetic balance is set, Larsen tips it over, showing Helga's delight in colors sliding readily from personal expression to racial characteristic. At Naxos, the fictionalized version of the Tuskegee Institute where Helga keeps her room, vibrant hues are prohibited for the same reasons that Albert Munsell banished them from early education: they smack of so-called primitive taste. Helga objects, and in narrating her character's complaints against the "dull attire" of her female coworkers, Larsen contrasts two models of blackness, parsed according to their relation to color. The first comes through the remembered voice of the dean of women, a "great 'race' woman" whose speech about proper dress Helga recalls in fragments: "'Bright colors are vulgar'—'Black, gray, brown, and navy blue are the most becoming colors for colored people'—'Dark-complected people shouldn't wear yellow, or green or red'" (16). Such is the code of respectability that prevails at Naxos. But Helga looks on these "drab colors" with contempt and insists on an alternative, more colorful way of being black:

Something intuitive, some unanalyzed driving spirit of loyalty to the inherent racial need for gorgeousness told her that bright colors *were* fitting and that dark-complexioned people *should* wear yellow, green and
red. Black, brown, and gray were ruinous to them, actually destroyed
the luminous tones lurking in their dusky skins. One of the loveliest
sights Helga had ever seen had been a sooty black girl decked out in a
flaming orange dress, which a horrified matron had next day consigned
to the dyer. Why, she wondered, didn't someone write *A Plea for Color*?
(16–17)

Helga's appeal returns attention to the visible surface of color against
the matron's fixation on its social meanings. She wants to celebrate
"gorgeousness," the chromatic alchemy by which red and yellow make
"dusky" skin shine, but to do so she has to revise the long-standing libel
about the crude sensuousness of African Americans. She has to decouple
the primitivist lineage of the color sense from the perceptual pleasures
and aesthetic refinements that mark a modern delight in sumptuous hues.

In this plea for color, and in the gradual dimming of Helga's love of
gorgeousness over the course of the novel, Larsen pinpoints the tricky appeal color held for African American writers in the 1920s, a decade jam-
packed with paeans to chromatic brilliance. World War I had temporarily
interrupted the mass production of colorful items—in part because so
many synthetic dyes had come from Germany—but by the mid-1920s the
craze for color had returned in force, outstripping even the excitement of
the 1890s.[2] "Everybody uses color," proclaimed Louis Weinberg in *Color
in Everyday Life* (1918), and the "study of color moreover is a source of
great pleasure, opening up a whole world of sensations."[3] Art magazines
and industry trade journals joined Weinberg in heralding a "new age of
color" marked by an irruption of sensory energies. In their 1930 article
"Color in Industry," the editors of *Fortune* magazine announced that the
"Anglo-Saxon" had been "released from chromatic inhibitions" and that
America stood poised to "gratify its instinct for color by bathing itself in
a torrent of brilliant hues."[4] Four years later, Winold Reiss, the German
immigrant whose illustrations of Harlem luminaries and "types" adorned
the first edition of Alain Locke's *The New Negro* (1925), was quoted expressing the same sentiment in an *Art Digest* article titled, tellingly, "Plea
for Color." "The American public . . . wants color and demands it," he
asserted. Though "it was once considered vulgar or even sinful to use
too bright a red or blue," he rejoiced that those Puritan days had thank-

fully passed, freeing people "to express our feelings without restraint."[5] When Larsen penned Helga's plea, bright red and vivid blues were being praised more loudly than ever, as white Americans reveled in the chromatic sensations bursting into everyday life.

These related appeals reveal a fascination with "primitive" color perceptions that fueled the acceleration of visual and media technologies in the early twentieth century. Not only did the new colors produced for industrial design come with exotic-sounding names (*Fortune* listed "T'äng Red, Orchid of Vincennes, Royal Copenhagen Blue, Ivoire de Medici, . . . Ionian Black, . . . Ming Green, and Meissen White," among others), but their saturation and intensity invited a sensory immersion long associated in the West with "uncivilized" people ("Color in Industry," 85). For Michael Taussig, this connection between bright colors and "colored" bodies subtends the whole of chromatic experience in the United States and Europe. He argues that color's effects—such as the mix of enlivened delight and disgusted reproach excited by a "sooty black girl" in a "flaming orange dress"—owe much to the entwined histories of colonialism and capitalism that have shaped sensory experience, and he specifies color's force in its ability to "gather together all that is otherwise inarticulate and powerful in the bouquet of imagery and gamut of feelings brought to mind by the 'Orient.'"[6]

When Larsen described the "oriental silk" and "blue Chinese carpet" in Helga's room at Naxos—an anagram of "Saxon"—she was building on the intimate entanglement of the modern and barbaric located in commercial color. Indeed, not just Larsen but all the writers who turned their attention to Harlem in the late 1920s forged their ubiquitous, exuberant color descriptions within this framework. Exhibiting a facility with color, in this context, meant performing a relation to one's feeling body and its movements among the barrage of chromatic sensations that marked the modern city. Yet such chromatic ease could easily collapse back into racist stereotypes, especially if the body in question was not white. The Harlem Vogue and the industrial embrace of color emerged as mutually enabling phenomena: on the one hand, the marketing of modern hues exploited the excitement over exotic sensations that drove whites uptown; on the other, the urbane embrace of vibrant color created rhetorical spaces for new literary figurations of blackness. In their representations of black life, Larsen, Carl Van Vechten, Claude McKay, and Zora Neale Hurston all pulled directly from the colorful world of cabaret lights, multihued cars, and vivid clothing that thrived in cities like New York. The New Negro, too, was a product of the color revolution.

Moreover, because of their position within the racially striated space of American culture, the authors of the Harlem Renaissance grasped the complicated relation between color sensitivity and racial embodiment with unparalleled insight.[7] They confronted head-on the primitivist currents in color-sense discourse that made figurations of chromatic modernity—and by extension the signature styles of aesthetic modernism—volatile cargo for any black writer who wanted to take them on. Individual responses were varied, from Larsen's keen awareness of the pressures exerted by white audiences on public expressions of blackness to McKay's enthusiastic embrace of sensory abandon as a political challenge to "civilization." But shared strategies emerged that came to characterize the depiction of race in Harlem Renaissance writing and that directly confronted the perceptual techniques that coalesced around the color sense. First, against the habits of perception that tie racial visibility to a restricted, metaphorical language of color (black and white, red and yellow), novelists in the 1920s crafted a nuanced, vibrant palette that set skin alongside modern fabrics and synthetic colors to unsettle the supposedly self-evident signs of racial legibility. Helga's description of "skin like yellow satin," for instance, evokes texture and luminescence alongside hue while situating skin tone as one chromatic surface among many. Second, writers such as Hurston and McKay adopted the link between color sensitivity and racially marked feeling that had long been used to disqualify dark-skinned people from the ranks of the so-called civilized—from Goethe's remarks about the "predilection for vivid colours" among "savage nations" to W. H. R. Rivers's belief that Papua New Guineans did not feel blue as responsively as Europeans—to instead mount a challenge to the bodily practices and metaphysical categories of white Western life. In Hurston's phrase, they used the experience of colors to describe "how it feels to be colored."[8] Whereas the first strategy concerns the epistemology of race, the second deals with its phenomenology. Taken together, they reveal how writers in the Harlem Renaissance appropriated color-sense discourse for their own ends, reconfiguring its central tropes and articulating more forcefully than anyone before them the political promise of a relational, embodied model of chromatic perception.

Outdoing the Barbarians

Of the many colorful items that flooded the market in the 1920s—blue telephones, red drapes, yellow glassware, polychromatic cars—none seemed to capture the infiltration of modern hues into the private spaces of everyday life so well as the tinted bathtub. Magazines such as *Fortune* and *Nation's Business* hailed "the appearance of the bathroom as a show place" as "one of the most surprising results of the revolution" in commercial color, evidence of the "youthful supremacy" of America in the Jazz Age. They deemed "the modern bathroom in Venetian hues," fitted with a "green tub" or "azure lavatories," as the epitome of the sensory pleasures offered by a booming economy.[9] It's fitting, then, that when Larsen wrote to her friend Van Vechten at around the time she began work on *Quicksand,* she included "Nile green bath rooms, beautifully tiled," in her list of the many "things there are to write," alongside flappers, acrobats, businessmen, and "gay moods and shivering hesitations": all topics that the modern writer might present "in an intensely restrained and civilized manner," with the "ironic survival of a much more primitive mood" underneath.[10] Like Helga's plea for color, Larsen's invocation of green bathrooms captures the clash of "civilized" restraint and "primitive" energy that defined the rhetorical space of modern color and thereby marked out the context within which literary figurations of color experience were written and read.

As this tale of a green tub suggests, the colors of the Harlem Renaissance emerged within the renovation of the visual environment wrought by commercial hues and their attendant imagery. To assert as much is to restore the work of African American authors to the brightly colored urban environment that formed their material context. Though the significance of the city has long been recognized in studies of the New Negro movement, critics have stopped short at discussing the social function of Harlem—its role as "the laboratory of a great race-welding," as Alain Locke called it—and have overlooked the material aspects of New York that gave texture and cohesion to uptown society: the lights of the cabarets, the clothing along Lenox Avenue, the rouge and powder sold in beauty shops.[11] Understanding what writers like Larsen did with color requires digging into the marvelous hues that surrounded them in Harlem.

In the early decades of the twentieth century, the chromatic developments sparked by the nineteenth-century union of industry and organic chemistry expanded their colorful reach. Georges Claude's invention of neon lights in 1915 and the introduction of affordable spray-colored bulbs seven years later turned the night sky into a backdrop for dancing colors cast along Broadway billboards and towering skyscrapers.[12] The DuPont Company's development of Duco, a fast-drying nitrocellulose lacquer, brought the chromatic revolution to the automotive industry, and innovations in colored plastics enlivened the growing number of appliances that crowded the modern home, especially those in the kitchen and the bathroom.[13] "Today, color is the modern note everywhere," one commentator wrote in 1930; "we have special color effects in bathrooms, kitchens, cooking utensils, house furnishings, and even at night some of us climb into bed between colored sheets."[14] As a "modern" feature that added little to the utility of goods and much to their appeal, color also became a key element of the emerging fashion industry, and decorators and designers advised shoppers on how to coordinate their clothing and makeup and on which colors were in and out of season. The opportunities afforded by the newly vivified built environment were in fact so widespread—and at times so puzzling—that for the first time a person could make a living as a "color expert," helping others implement the slippery principles of chromatic harmony.[15]

As colors got more vibrant, the descriptions of them as both an invasion of savage energies and the apex of technological ingenuity became more strident. *Fortune* praised the "thoroughly painted home of 1928" as an illustration that "old traditions [were] being abandoned and old suppressions being released" (85–86). Its editors regarded the surge in color as progress, since it wielded the cutting edge of science and technology: "With spectrophotoelectric curves," they announced, "the Anglo-Saxon . . . prepares to outdo the barbarians" (85). Others, however, warned that the chromatic trends of American industry augured not the invigoration of "Anglo-Saxons" but their potential demise. Allen L. Billingsley, writing for the journal of the U.S. Chamber of Commerce, insisted that what was "happening in America today" was that the "invasion of the Czecho-Slovakians, Italians and other races from Southern Europe" was stimulating "interest in the primary colors." Drawing on Henry Turner Bailey, editor of the *School Arts Magazine,* he argued that "people go through certain stages of development in their color preferences" and that "after indulging their elemental cravings for reds and greens and yellows," they advance to "softer shades." Similarly, he reasoned that once the "newer races" were "absorbed in American civilization, the crude colors favored today will grow softer, more subtle."[16] Billingsley's blatantly nativist reading of the color revolution demonstrates that behind the pervasive excitement about the sensations unleashed by commerce there lurked a continued belief in a racially marked color sense, making modern wonders like a green tub or an orange fridge ambiguous emblems of both progress and degeneration.

Advertising and mass culture circulated such items and the sensory pleasures they promised to a wide range of audiences, so that white consumers could embrace the so-called primitive perceptions stirred by polychrome goods without thereby giving up the claims of whiteness. In other words, the absorptive thrills of modern color could both invoke and brush aside their reference to a hierarchy of civilization, depending on who was enjoying them. We have already seen this primitivist procedure at work in earlier decades—in the visual aesthetic of children's picture books, for instance, or in Stephen Crane's efforts to harness the intensity of commercial hues, or even in the way organic chemistry detached the color economy from its initial pathways through colonial trade routes. But in the 1920s the movement of these chromatic sensations through culture was more robust than ever. Nancy Bentley describes the broader context of this disjunction between racialized perceptions and racialized bodies: "Inside the dizzying spaces of mass culture," she explains, "an individual's specific social location no longer seemed to strictly dictate experience or perception, even as traits of specific bodies—the defiant postures of white men, the angular grace of cakewalk dancers, the prowess of the Indian warrior—were among the fragments of sensory subjectivity" in circulation.[17] McKay signaled these perceptual dislocations when he advised white audiences, who were disappointed at finding none of the "Congo wriggle" or "jungle whoop" they expected in the Broadway musical *Shuffle Along* (1921), to "visit Coney Island and the circuses to get acquainted with the stunts of Savagedom."[18] He might have mentioned the showroom at Macy's department store as well.

Billingsley's article about the "barbaric invasion" of color into American business includes an illustration that pictures the intimate relationship between the white consumer and the sensory allures associated with "colorful" people (Figure 30). In the image, several men from southern and eastern Europe offer textiles and design objects to a modishly clothed and coiffed white woman, who is set in the center and raised more than a head higher than the men. The caption relates Billingsley's thesis that modern "styles reflect an interest in primary colors . . . stimulated by the invasion" of these immigrants, but the picture goes further, showing that the modernity of the white consumer (generally coded as female) depends on her appropriation of the aesthetic qualities associated with people given as exotic. The woman drapes the proffered fabrics over her arms, turning herself into a denizen of the 1920s by adorning her body with the chromatic tastes of "barbaric" people, mediated through the manufacturing trends of a bull market. The love of bright color in this illustration is not a regression from modern sensibility but, rather, its very badge. It may invoke ethnic "foreigners," but it's tailor-made for white consumers.

As a modern trend that relied on the language and imagery of primitivism, the color revolution established the rhetorical space within which literary presentations of color in the 1920s acquired meaning. Think of F. Scott Fitzgerald's *The Great Gatsby* (1925). Jay Gatsby's spectacular parties, yellow roadster, and trove of many-colored shirts all contribute to his status as an upstart and racial outsider; as Tom Buchanan sneers,

FIGURE 30. This illustration portrays the intimacy between white consumers and the sensory power of "colorful" people during the color revolution of the late 1920s: a modish woman selects fabrics offered by immigrants from eastern and southern Europe. Allen L. Billingsley, "Color—A Real Business Problem," *Nation's Business* 16 (August 1928): 22. Kislak Center for Special Collections, Rare Books and Manuscripts, University of Pennsylvania, Philadelphia, Pennsylvania.

no "Oxford man" would wear a "pink suit." As such, the residents of East Egg, avatars of chromophobic respectability, stay "carefully on guard against" the "spectroscopic gaiety" of Gatsby and his "gaudy" guests.[19] Similarly, William Carlos Williams ends *Spring and All* (1923) with a vibrant outburst of color, praising the "Black eyed Susan"—"rich orange / round the purple core"—as "rich / in savagery— / Arab / Indian." Contrasted with the "white daisy," which is white like "farmers," the vivid hues energize the sexually charged feelings that swirl around modern color and suggest that even the earlier colors in the collection— including the red wheelbarrow beside the white chickens, or the "reddish / purplish, forked, upstanding twiggy / stuff" along the road at springtime—rely on these exotic affiliations for their potency.[20] In this regard, the colors of Williams's poems are not far from those of advertisements for automobiles, which achieved their modernity by borrowing "their hues from the waters of the Nile, the sands of Arabia, the plumage of birds and the fire of gems."[21]

These connotations of modern color gained special urgency in the literary depictions of Harlem, where they became focal points in controversies over the proper means of representing the behavior and feelings of African Americans. Nowhere was this clearer than in Van Vechten's *Nigger Heaven* (1926), the best-selling novel that polarized black writers and expanded the literary market for books about Harlem. As Miriam Thaggert has argued, Van Vechten divides his characters according to their relation to sensory experience, granting success "to those who know best how to use their bodies in navigating the black, urban and modern space."[22] I would only add that these divisions are most vividly articulated through color. For instance, the flamboyant hustler known as the Scarlet Creeper opens the novel in "a tight-fitting suit of shepherd's plaid" with a glistening stone in "his fuchsia cravat," and he promenades between brightly lit shops and "multi-hued taxicabs" on his way to the Black Venus, a cabaret whose entrance is "flanked by two revolving green lights."[23] Once inside, he and Ruby Silver join a party that outshines any spectroscopic gaiety on Gatsby's West Egg: "On all sides of the swaying couple, bodies in picturesque costumes rocked, black bodies, brown bodies, high yellows, a kaleidoscope of colour transfigured by the amber searchlight. Scarves of bottle green, cerise, amethyst, vermilion, lemon" (14). In this whirl of bright color, skin, scarves, and lights all blend together and partake of the sensory energies of the city, with the Creeper weaving his dexterous way among them.

As in Williams's "wildflower," color in *Nigger Heaven* aligns with a sexualized conception of the body, a prurient notion of the "instinctual" elements of black life to which characters can be more or less attuned. Soon after the "wild" scene of the cabaret, Van Vechten presents a contrast to the Creeper in Mary Love, one of the New Negro characters whose story makes up the bulk of the narrative. Mary has "sober" taste: "Her bedcover was plain white; her dressing-table austere and generally devoid of articles," and she has "an instinctive horror of promiscuity" (41, 54). As such she has only an intellectual relation to "the primitive birthright" that manifests as "this love of drums, of exciting rhythms, this naïve delight in glowing colour—the colour that exists only in cloudless, tropical climes—this warm, sexual emotion" (89–90). The juxtaposition of Mary with the Creeper signals the way color, as a figure of the "spontaneous" sensory enjoyment of the "low life" of Harlem, threatened to feed into existing stereotypes about the hypersexualized black body, even for well-meaning advocates of Negro writing like Van Vechten (107).

Larsen's *Quicksand* adopts this explosive configuration of race, sex, and bright hues to articulate the various relations that seeing colors could have to being "black," relations that prove especially vexing for its mixed-race protagonist. Beginning with Helga's plea for color and ending in her unadorned room in Alabama, the novel plots a zigzagging trajectory driven by Helga's shifting relation to sensuous color and the modes of racial affiliation that enlist or deny it. At Naxos her fashion sense gets her into trouble; she "loved clothes, elaborate ones," and her "queer" colors—"dark purples, royal blues, rich greens, deep reds"—distinguish her from the bleached-out versions of blackness at the school (17). This sensory delight in colorful outfits infuses the narrative voice, which regularly pauses to take pleasure in a neat arrangement of clothing: Anne Grey's "cool green tailored frock," Fru Dahl's "olive green" outfit with a "trailing purple scarf and correct black hat," Aubrey Denney's "simple apricot dress," and of course the series of ensembles worn by Helga (39, 60, 55). These moments display a loving attention to how hues are felt and arranged that echoes the emerging discourse of fashion, which encouraged consumers to flaunt distinctive chromatic preferences to individualize their wardrobe. (Larsen, for her part, once reported feeling "particularly moved by the color green.")[24] What matters to Helga is that her meticulous eye for fashionable harmonies be counted as a marker of her "intensely personal taste" (1). In the early chapters of *Quicksand,* color means self-expression.[25]

When Helga lands in Denmark, however, the possibilities of a personal color sense are met with a framework that links color's expressivity to a racialized identity. As soon as she arrives, Fru Dahl attempts to outfit her in vibrant clothing that distorts the grounds of Helga's love of color. "'You must have bright things to set off the color of your lovely brown skin,'" Fru Dahl reasons, "'striking things, exotic things'" (62). Helga feels "dubious" and "resentful" at the suggestion: "Certainly she loved color with a passion that perhaps only Negroes and Gypsies know. But she had a deep faith in the perfection of her own taste, and no mind to be bedecked in flaunting flashy things" (63). The scene recycles key elements of the plea for color, but in the process it reveals the way that any appeal to "inherent racial needs"—here understood as the passion particular to "Negroes and Gypsies"—remains open to appropriation and distortion by white audiences. As a result, the tone of Helga's Copenhagen wardrobe takes on a sinister character:

> There were batik dresses in which mingled indigo, orange, green, vermilion, and black; dresses of velvet and chiffon in screaming colors, blood-red, sulphur-yellow, sea-green; and one black and white thing in striking combination. There was a black Manila shawl strewn with great scarlet and lemon flowers, a leopard-skin coat, a glittering opera-cape. There were turban-like hats of metallic silks, feathers and furs, strange jewelry, enameled or set with odd semiprecious stones, a nauseous Eastern perfume, shoes with dangerously high heels. (67–68)

In place of the "rich" and "royal" colors of her previous clothing, Helga's new wardrobe presents a "screaming" jungle, full of "blood," "sulphur," exotic animals, vivid flowers, and "feathers and fur." In Denmark, that is, her perfect taste yields to "the fascinating business of being seen, gaped at" as the aesthetic surface is made to carry the depths of racial meaning (68).

Helga's love of color and its subsequent convolution into an exotic spectacle illustrate the dangers involved in crafting an identity from the colorful matter of mass culture. Larsen goes to great lengths to demonstrate the extent to which colors can bite back, either as elements of exoticism or as aspects of Helga's failed attempts to turn her attractiveness into power.[26] The perils of the former are made especially clear in Axel Olsen, the painter who makes indecent advances to Helga while composing a portrait that presents "some disgusting sensual creature with her features" rather than Helga herself (83). The scene suggests that Helga's initial embrace of color as a means of self-expression is doomed to fail, given that the task of expressing the self entails a parallel imperative to make visible one's race. Even Billingsley, who read the color revolution as a product of immigration, wrote that "color taste . . . is an individual matter" and that "the more daring one's color sense, the more he wants to indulge it."[27] Helga indulges her color taste for most of *Quicksand,* but the promise of distinguishing herself through modern colors eventually fades, and in the final scenes Larsen drains away all visual hues. Helga becomes "Mrs. Green"—and in so doing gives up her green-and-gold negligee. Indeed, once Helga decides that she is bound to the "dark hordes" in Harlem by ties deeper than "mere outline of features or color of skin"—that is, once she trades aesthetic color for racial color—the quality of chromatic descriptions changes remarkably (89). Earlier invocations of precious materials to describe the tone and luminescence of skin—ebony, bronze, copper, alabaster—give way to "conspicuous black, obvious brown, or indistinguishable white," phrases that express the interpretive gaze of a racialized perspective. As in Gertrude Stein's *Three Lives,* a book Larsen admired, the introduction of race as the defining perceptual category mutes or distorts the attention to literal hues.[28]

Other African American writers followed Helga's oscillations between sensory restraint and colorful exuberance.[29] Some, like Larsen's horrified matron, upheld the ideals of "civilized" respectability by toning colors down. They began where Helga ended, regarding color as too hazardous to overemphasize. Jessie Redmon Fauset's passing novel *Plum Bun* (1929), for instance, has little in the way of vibrant hues, even though its protagonist is a painter; it trades the sensory revelry associated with the Scarlet Creeper for a "nice feeling for colour" (with a *u*!) linked to cultural refinement.[30] In *The Blacker the Berry* (1929), Wallace Thurman joins Larsen in detailing how this avoidance of bright hues goes hand in hand with racial color prejudice. When Emma Lou meets Hazel, a schoolmate with a flare for color, she muses, "Negroes always bedecked themselves and their belongings in ridiculously unbecoming colors and ornaments." Hazel's "red roadster," "white hat," and "red-and-white-striped sport suit" all strike Emma Lou as relics of a "primitive heritage" better left behind.[31] Other writers, however, such as McKay and Hurston, tried to mine the possibilities fostered by modern enthusiasm for red roadsters and even "primitive heritage" to stretch the representative repertoire without falling into caricatures like the Creeper. They picked up Helga's early plea but pushed it in different directions, avoiding her colorless conclusion in Alabama. Modern color had its traps, to be sure, but it also held aesthetic potentials that outstripped the familiar narratives of modernist primitivism.

"Colored People"

Reflecting on a trip to Beale Street, Langston Hughes captured the integration of modern colors into the performance of race with a Harlemite's pride. "Portions of Fifth or Lenox Avenues in New York's Harlem were . . . ," he boasted, "equally tough, equally colorful, and quite as colored as the famous Memphis thoroughfare."[32] Equally colorful and quite as colored: like the narrator of *Quicksand,* who takes in the green of Helga's negligee and the yellow of her face with one sweeping and satisfied assessment, Hughes invites his readers to delight in chromatic arrangements of people and clothing, to conflate the "colorful" and the "colored" in a single aesthetic spectacle. As calls to linger over the surface of dark skin, these invitations would seem to court primitivist pleasures. But in the process they do something remarkable that in fact scrambles the conceptual categories upon which primitivism depends. They forge a chromatic lexicon for describing skin that routes the visibility of race through the materials of modern color and so disrupts the perceptual habits that make bodily surfaces markers of racial identity. By entwining the colorful and colored, the authors of these chromatically charged passages reconfigure the linguistic means by which skin, the most privileged sign of racial legibility, is apprehended.

The chromatic arrangements of clothing, lights, cosmetics, and skin that run throughout Harlem Renaissance novels make up one of the movement's most distinctive literary features and contrast sharply with earlier handlings of racial color. Like Charles Chesnutt, who as we saw in chapter 4 protested that the color terms of racial discourse had ceased to signify visual qualities, many black writers came to consider any appeal to color as dangerous to their political aims. Better to invoke music. But by the 1920s, the rhetorical spaces cleared by modern color had changed the situation entirely. The work of W. E. B. Du Bois nicely illustrates the shift. In *The Souls of Black Folk* (1903) he placed far more emphasis on sound than color, confining his few references to skin tone to the standard jargon of "white," "olive," "yellow," "brown," and "black." Several decades later, however, he asked his imagined white interlocutor in *Dusk of Dawn* (1940), "can there be any question but that *as colors,* bronze, mahogany, coffee, and gold are far lovelier than pink, gray, and marble?"[33] Whereas Du Bois had earlier asked readers to listen, here he encouraged them to look.

The writing of the Harlem Renaissance teems with similar catalogs of what Hughes called the "whole rainbow of life above 110th Street," and part of what those works ask readers to see is the sheer variety papered over by the catchall terms "Negro" or "black" (271). In *Quicksand* Helga "marvel[s]" at the gradations within this oppressed race of hers": "sooty black, shiny black, taupe, mahogany, bronze, copper, gold, orange, yellow, peach, ivory, pinky white, and pasty white" (54). Likewise, in *Home to Harlem* (1928) the Jamaican-born McKay savors the description of "all the various and varying pigments of the human race" assembled along Seventh Avenue: "dim brown, clear brown, rich brown, chesnut [*sic*], copper, yellow, near-white, mahogany, and gleaming anthracite."[34] These passages transfer the excited tone of modern industrial colors ("T'äng Red, Orchid of Vincennes, Royal Copenhagen Blue") to the realm of skin and race, where so much of the spectrum had been ignored or disparaged. In his review of *Shuffle Along,* McKay had complained about the lack of variety in representations of black life, chiding the producers of the show for using cosmetics to flatten the chromatic variety of the cast. "Instead of making up to achieve a uniform near-white complexion," he wrote, "the chorus might have made up to accentuate the diversity of shades among 'Afro Americans' and let the white audiences in on the secret of the color nomenclature of the Negro world": "chocolate, chocolate-to-the-bone, brown, low-brown, teasing-brown," and so on.[35] McKay called writers not to homogenize colors but, rather, to unlock a language that would accentuate variety without reproducing the color prejudices that elevated light skin over dark—"gleaming anthracite" alongside "dim brown" and "pinky white."[36]

Just as common as these lists of luscious hues were ensembles that set them in relation to the colors of clothing or cosmetics: "mahogany" next to shining silk blouses, or "a sooty black girl" in a "flaming orange dress." These combinations pull a basic principle from chromatic design—that no color exists on its own, that we always see colors in relation—and apply it to skin, working toward the end of reimagining the conditions under which the colors of bodies become visible. In *Home to Harlem,* for instance, skin almost never appears outside the array of colorful fabrics or lights that bring it out. One of the first people that the central character Jake meets on returning to Harlem after World War I is Felice, who "had tinted her leaf-like face to a ravishing chesnut" and clothed herself in "an orange scarf over a green frock" with "champagne-colored stockings" (11). Later, inside Madame Suarez's speakeasy, Jake mingles with "charmingly painted pansies" who "luxuriate . . . among the colored cushions and under the soft, shaded lights," "their arms and necks and breasts tinted to emphasize the peculiar richness of each skin" (104, 105). We might expect the application of makeup and other manufactured hues to obscure the color of skin, but instead it intensifies and clarifies it: "The girls' complexion was heightened by High-Brown talc powder and rouge" (193). Skin tone becomes yet another shining product of the color revolution.[37]

McKay's ensembles set the primitivism of Van Vechten's *Nigger Heaven* in a different light. That text too brims with descriptions that undo the division between the natural and the artificial that essentialist notions of "black blood" require. Think back to the opening cabaret scene, with its "kaleidoscope of colour transfigured by the amber searchlight," its colorful bodies decked in colorful scarves (14). Or the Charity Ball scene, in which the calcium lights provide an "unnatural illumination" of "constantly shifting hues" that play over the audience's sleek clothing and bared shoulders (152–53). Throughout the novel, Van Vechten introduces characters through similar arrangements of skin and modern colors. Of Mary he writes, "The rich golden-brown color of her skin was well set off by the simple frock of Pompeian-red crêpe which she wore" (25); Ruby's "golden-brown" skin" is "as soft as velvet" and "encased in coral silk" and "golden-brown stockings" (9); Adora Boniface has "almost black" skin and wears a "pansy chiffon robe which matched the pansy lights in her lustrous eyes" (27, 28). Though the color of clothing usually "sets off" the skin, it can also blend with it, reinforcing the constitutive relation between the visibility of bodies and the colors of clothing. One woman wears "a frock of ecru crêpe which exactly matched the colour of her superbly formed shoulders," and Lasca Sartoris, whose name invokes Van Vechten's fascination with the sartorial, wears a dressing gown of "soft, filmy *golden-brown* chiffon" that leaves "her *golden-brown* arms . . . bare" (96, 237–38; emphasis added).

These descriptions invite readers to see skin as akin to taffeta, chiffon, and crêpe, all fabrics made more popular by the rise in synthetic fibers and all able to be brightly colored thanks to synthetic dyes. What's important is not simply that they link skin and fashion but that they adopt the imagery and materiality of aniline dyes and the other products of modern chemistry that changed the stuff of color. They apply the aniline aesthetic to the manufacture of race. Just as multihued textiles involved a modern procedure of reconstructing natural materials at the molecular level, so too did the racial visibility of skin result from a complex process that relied not on a natural essence but on a kind of second nature, what Anne Anlin Cheng calls "a second skin."[38] Cheng argues that the trim look of modern fashion, which sought to reveal the body's shape rather than to embellish it, shared a philosophical problem—which became a *stylistic* problem—with the modernist rejection of ornamentation and the historical workings of racialization: namely, the problem of separating what's essential from what's superficial to create a "natural" surface. In this way, "the possibility of a modern, newly liberated, streamlined body, facilitated by innovations in synthetic textile fibers that act like a second skin on the flesh, is an *extension of,* not an antithesis to, the idea of the atavistic, unruly, mobile body born out of primitivized animality" (77). Both rely on the notion of a natural body that might be separated from artificial coverings. The ensembles of colorful fabrics and skin in *Home to Harlem* and *Nigger Heaven* give the lie to such assumptions, showing the body of race to be as much a fabrication as the dresses of "raspberry velvet" or "orange taffeta" at the Charity Ball (*Nigger Heaven,* 152). As Cheng writes of Josephine Baker's performances, what emerges in these moments is "not the affirmation or the denial of Modernist Primitivism but the failure of its terms to inscribe its own passions" (5).

In the second part of *Nigger Heaven,* devoted to an aspiring writer named Byron, the "unnatural illumination" of the dance floor produces the novel's most spectacular conflations of natural and artificial surfaces, resulting in its most peculiar figurations of racial legibility. At the Winter Palace, "parties of white people, parties of coloured people, mixed parties" fill the tables, but "the amber light which flooded the gold and black hall gave everybody present much the same complexion, save one brown girl who had put on too much powder and consequently looked dirty green" (242). Van Vechten returns to this image in the final chapter, when Byron, drugged and desperate, returns to the Black Venus. Sitting alone at his table, his appraisal of the scene mingles jungle imagery with the unnatural colors of modernity.

> Would that drummer never stop? Jungle! Savages! Amber moonlight! Why did that girl have a purple face? Rouge on chocolate. And that other girl was green as an olive. Powder on chocolate.
> . . . The music shivered and broke, cracked and smashed. Jungle land. Hottentots and Bantus swaying under the amber moon. Love, sex, passion . . . hate. . . . The dancers swayed from one side to the other like sailors heaving an anchor. Black, green, blue, purple, brown, tan, yellow, white: coloured people! (280, 281)

Byron's detached gaze would seem to model the anxious patrolling of "blood" mixtures demanded by the "one-drop rule," under which all those with any "Negro" ancestry were considered "black." But what he deciphers is not blood but skin, and not bare skin but skin perceived through a spectacular array of artificial hues. Whereas Mary's narrative makes "delight in glowing colors" a sign of a "primitive birthright," this scene uses those same burning hues to fix attention so tightly on the aesthetic surface that the racial significance of skin color—what Frantz Fanon called the "fact of blackness" produced by "epidermalization"— is eclipsed by an artificial display of chromatic transfigurations (*Nigger Heaven,* 89).[39] The Black Venus may be a "jungle," but it is produced by the magic of modern color.

The conflation of skin and synthetic colorants produced equally dazzling descriptions in the works of McKay and of Jean Toomer. When *Cane* (1923) shifts locations from the rural South to the urban North, Toomer's portrayals of skin swap images of flowers and sky ("skin like dusk on the eastern horizon") for the vibrant lights and combinations of the color revolution. A white character's face "is a healthy pink the blue of the evening tints a purple pallor"; others appear "orange" and "blue." And in the story "Box Seat," Muriel's orange dress "goes well" with the "pale purple shadows" on her cheeks and the "deep purple" of her hair."[40] McKay goes even further, allowing the language of race and the language of fashion to bleed into one another, as when in *Home to Harlem* Susy arrives at the cabaret in a "fur coat of rich shiny black, like her complexion," or when Zeddy wears an "elegant nigger-brown sports suit" (95, 90).[41] The effects are dizzying, and at one point McKay extends them to encompass the performance of gender alongside race. Though women wear most of the cosmetics in *Home to Harlem,* the book's most made-up character is the "straw-colored boy" who performs at the Congo Rose. He wears "high-brown powder, his eyebrows [are] elongated and blackened up, his lips streaked with the dark rouge so popular in Harlem, and his carefully-straightened hair lay[s] plastered and glossy under Madam Walker's absinthe-colored salve 'for milady of fashion and color'" (91). In this "striking advertisement of the Ambrozine Palace of Beauty," McKay intensifies bodily color to produce a queer spectacle that unravels the legibility of bodily surfaces.

But the clearest invocation of aniline and its scrambling of nature and artifice comes when McKay includes *mauve* in a list of the "strikingly ex- otic types" produced by "civilization": "Ancient black life rooted upon its base with all its fascinating new layers of brown, low-brown, high-brown, nut-brown, lemon, maroon, olive, mauve, gold" (57). Nowhere else have I found healthy skin described as mauve.[42] And given the passage's re- peated references to the material world (lemon, olive, gold), as well as the novel's several descriptions of mauve clothing—Madame Laura's mauve dress, the mauve dressing gown Susy gives Zeddy, the pianist "curiously made up in mauve"—McKay's use of the word directly situ- ates his chromatic catalogs of skin tones within the revolution effected by aniline dyes (232, 100, 107). Just as William Perkin's synthesis of mauveine created a new color, one that simultaneously added to the visual rich- ness of the modern environment and disposed of any natural connection between color and its referents to the material world, so too, for McKay, did the global contacts facilitated by "civilization" create beautiful new shades of skin that cannot be tied to an essentialized notion of black- ness. Seeing skin as mauve places it beyond the dichotomy of nature and culture that undergirds primitivist notions of "ancient black life" and situates it within the material processes that shaped the senses over the course of McKay's life.

The chromatic ensembles in Harlem Renaissance writing facilitate performances of blackness grounded in the mix of colorful and colored epitomized in mauve skin. They ask readers to look, even to take pleasure in looking, but what they show thwarts the perceptual techniques that accompanied earlier descriptions of skin as a marker of race. In this sense, books such as *Home to Harlem* model themselves on the dramas unfolding along Lenox Avenue. As historian Davarian L. Baldwin writes, city streets in this period offered a "public showcase for black 'expressive behavior,'" a "moving theater . . . where black people were staging new versions of blackness in the particular ways they looked and were looked at within the structured space of local exhibition."[43] The trick was to position the reader within the crowd. This is where Van Vechten falters, by allowing Byron to keep his distance. McKay, by contrast, jumps in. When the narrator of *Home to Harlem* details the wide cabaret windows where the "joy-loving ladies and gentlemen of the Belt collected to show their striking clothes and beautiful skin," he cannot help but join the fun: "Oh, it was some wonderful sight to watch them from the pavement!" (29). McKay's enthusiasm signals the unfamiliar perspective opened by the chromatic strategies of the Harlem Renaissance: a perspective based not on the alienating effects of the gaze but on the relational, immersive qualities of color perception.

How It Feels to Be Colored Me

Seeing the vibrant ensembles along the streets of Harlem, or reading the descriptive catalogs that conjure their appeal, calls for far more than just a pair of eyes; it demands a full-bodied effort. The chromatic revolution was a sensory revolution, and black writers brought the whole sweep of perceptual experience into their depictions of Harlem life. As such, the role of color in the Harlem Renaissance far exceeded the visual. "Harlem is not to be seen. Or heard," Thurman wrote in 1927; "it must be felt."[44] In presenting *how* the hues of Harlem are felt, especially within the lively space of the jazz cabaret, authors such as McKay and Hurston articulated a distinctive mode of racial being, a way of feeling "colored" figured through a way of feeling colors. This effort involved them in the rhetoric of primitivism, which as we have seen was the primary idiom used to describe the rush of sensations released by modern color. Whereas the descriptive leveling of skin, light, and clothing sought to reshape how race is seen, the invocations of "savage" feelings on the dance floor—one of the most recognizable features of the Harlem Vogue—aimed at appropriating the link between color sensitivity and racial identity that threads through the modern discourse of color to challenge the bodily practices constitutive of whiteness. Through scenes of rhythmic motion and collective exuberance, conveyed through the affective dimensions of color, Harlem writers fostered an active mode of sensory receptivity that they used to convey not just the colorful sights of the city but also a distinctive way of thrilling to them.

For black writers, depicting a cabaret was even riskier than lingering over skin. Images of jungles and painted savages abound in descriptions of jazz clubs in the 1920s, often to the point of presenting modern Harlem as a relic of the primitive past. Van Vechten, for his part, wastes no time getting Ruby and the Scarlet Creeper into a club where the couple "swayed and rocked to the tormented howling of the brass, the barbaric beating of the drum" (12). Subsequent dance scenes continue in this vein, reaching an absurd climax in the after-hours club the Black Mass. There, in a "circular hall entirely hung in vermillion velvet," with a "floor of translucent glass" through which "clouds of light flowed, now orange, now deep purple, now flaming like molten lava, now rolling seawaves of green," the earlier depictions of modern jazz as a "barbaric ceremony" are literalized in the "evil rites" performed by a nude girl "with savage African features" (212, 254–55). The scene paints a portrait of the cabaret worthy of *Quicksand*'s Axel Olsen, and even though other passages attempt to undercut the belief that the dances in these spaces are linked to African blood (Byron learns to dance the Charleston from "[a] couple of white fellows at college"), Van Vechten's grotesque and widely read depictions made the treatment of cabaret culture a vexed issue for Harlem writers (142).

The spectacle of the Black Mass, with its feverish combination of atavistic bodies with the luminous hues of color music, encapsulates the dialectic of modern primitivism that characterized both commercial color and its literary manifestations. As Taussig tells it, the history runs as follows: the entwined enterprises of colonialism and capitalism that brought Europeans into contact with non-Europeans depended on a peculiar idea of embodiment premised on locating the self *outside* the body, in an immaterial soul that governs and restrains the excitations of its fleshy vessel. But this model denies something essential: the "forms of sensateness, of bodily knowing, that exist below the radar of consciousness and are all the more powerful for so being," what Taussig terms the "bodily unconscious."[45] As compensation for what was lost, white Europeans did two things. First, they projected a distorted image of sensory life onto non-Westerners, producing the racist libel that dark-skinned bodies have an instinctual love of color that proceeds from a crude and overactive sensory responsiveness. Second, at the end of the nineteenth century they satisfied the urge for embodied activity by creating the wonderland of consumer capitalism, full of vibrant colors. In the color revolution, no less than in the technological illumination of a "savage" body at the Black Mass, we see what Taussig describes as "the surfacing of 'the primitive' within modernity as the direct result of modernity."[46] From this perspective, the intensity of modern color draws its power from the way it exercises the felt relation to the sensory environment denied by the "civilizing" mission in the West.

This tidy dialectic helps identify the delicate task that writers of the Harlem Renaissance set themselves when they turned to the cabaret. As a central site of modern primitivism, it simultaneously provided a space for fashioning bodily practices opposed to the strictures of whiteness and threatened to fold those practices back into the racialized division of civilized and savage. Larsen, ever sensitive to such ambiguities, dramatizes them in Helga. In a cabaret scene just prior to her move to Denmark, Helga tastes the sensory abandon of the dance floor, only to pull back. In the moment, she feels "drugged, lifted, sustained, by the extraordinary movement" and loses herself to "the color, the noise, the grand distorted childishness of it all" until "the essence of life seemed bodily motion." But when the song ends, she reproaches herself for this ecstatic release: "She wasn't, she told herself, a jungle creature" (54). As with her love of colorful fabrics, which is thrown back at her in the screaming hues of her Danish wardrobe, the sensuous abandon that promises an escape from the demand to claim a racial identity functions instead as yet another feature assigned to black bodies. As such, the ecstasies of color and movement lose their appeal for Helga, who from start to finish wants what the racially divided worlds of Europe and the United States can't give her: a social space that doesn't require her to tie her selfhood to a racial category.[47]

Hurston, on the other hand, mined the full potential of the cabaret's colorful energies to twist primitivism to her own ends—namely, by creating an oppositional performance of blackness aimed at breaking the very frameworks and historical processes that gave birth to the "primitive." This strategy informs a central passage of her essay "How It Feels to Be

Colored Me" (1928), published the same year as *Quicksand* and *Home to Harlem*. To illustrate an instance in which she is made to feel her race, Hurston describes a scene in the New World Cabaret, where she and a white person listen to a jazz orchestra. The "narcotic harmonies" and "rambunctious" sounds of the music assume the form of a wild animal that "rears on its hind legs" and "claws" through "the tonal veil" until it reaches "the jungle beyond." The orchestra sweeps Hurston into the primal scene, and she quickly finds herself "in the jungle and living in the jungle way": "My face is painted red and yellow and my body is painted blue. My pulse is throbbing like a war drum." The music stops, and Hurston "creep[s] back slowly to the veneer we call civilization" to find her white companion "sitting motionless in his seat, smoking calmly." When he remarks, "'Good music they have here,'" Hurston realizes the difference between them: "Music! The great blobs of purple and red emotion have not touched him. He has only heard what I have felt." At such moments, she continues, "he is so pale with his whiteness . . . and I am *so* colored."[48] Color for Hurston presses against its visual modality to encompass a way of feeling the sights and sounds of Harlem, to figure a mode of experience. She conveys the feeling of being colored through the experience of color feelings, including the "great blobs of purple and red emotion" that the pale white world of "civilization" fails to register.

As a student of Franz Boas and an author of ethnographic studies, Hurston was intimately familiar with the tropes of color and feeling in primitivism and with ways of thinking around them. Color, as we saw in the introduction and chapter 2, played a formative role in the early years of anthropology. W. H. R. Rivers joined his Cambridge colleagues in the discipline-defining Torres Strait Expedition to settled the Gladstone controversy over whether a limited color vocabulary implied a deficient perceptual sensitivity, and his conclusion that Papua New Guineans did indeed experience color differently from Europeans perpetuated the notion of "primitive color vision" into the twentieth century. Meanwhile, Boas launched a different branch of anthropology, one that would challenge the social hierarchy that ran from primitive to civilized, after getting frustrated with his doctoral project on measuring the colors of water. Boas found that people couldn't agree on what color they saw, even when they were looking at the same thing, and in investigating what caused people to have different qualitative experiences of the same stimulus (the color green, the "alternating sounds" of Native American languages), he eventually arrived at the culture concept.[49] Though later Boasians would come to interpret culture as something almost as stable and unifying as "race" had been for Rivers (including Melville J. Herskovits, who had Hurston measure the skin tones of Harlemites with a Milton Bradley Color Top for *The Anthropometry of the American Negro*), Boas himself emphasized cultural diffusion: the way styles, patterns of behavior, and ways of feeling traveled across social groups.[50] Chromatic sensitivity, in this case, was not tied to racial essence; rather, it formed a component of culture, considered as a mobile entity developing in relation to its material surroundings and intercultural contacts. When Hurston described a style of color feeling to communicate the historical experience of being black, she was using one branch of anthropology to combat the primitivism supported by another.

Moreover, by invoking the immersive experience of literal colors (the lights of the cabaret) to convey a particular way of feeling the sights and sounds of Harlem, Hurston drew on a third role that color played in early anthropology: as a tool in ethnographic writing. Ethnography involves taking up the practices and feelings distinct to a particular culture and translating their "tone" onto the page. And in this regard, according to Taussig, the methods of participant observation owe much to the kinds of connections between color perceptions and color feelings that Hurston established in her essay and that we earlier saw in the writing of Hamlin Garland. Taussig calls this the affinity between color and "color"—literal and local color—and he tracks the relation between the two realms by comparing the diaries kept by Bronislaw Malinowski during his field work in the Trobriand Islands and the convention-setting ethnographies he later produced from this research. Though most known for their lascivious passages about the Trobriand women—exemplars of primitivism in which Malinowski represses his own erotic feelings and at the same time insists that it's the indigenous people who are overly sexual—these diaries are marked by vivid descriptions of tropical colors: "Sariba a blazing magenta; fringe of palms with pink trunks rising out of the blue sea."[51] Taussig argues that these passages show Malinowski both facilitating and communicating the sensation of abandoning himself to the saturated environment that surrounded him. They show that "color in the tropics for the sensitive European can reorient the body as much as the mind" and thereby stimulate "the bodily unconscious."[52] Color encourages a bodily awareness that enables Malinowski to feel the "color" of New Guinea, much as the colorful lights and multihued "blobs of emotion" in the cabaret allow Hurston to feel and communicate the "color" of Harlem.

Home to Harlem brims with vibrant colors meant to activate a sensory receptivity necessary for feeling Harlem. When Jake and Felice enter a newly opened venue, the narrator describes the interior as a space tailor-made for those races who "love color": "The owner of the cabaret knew that Negro people . . . love the pageantry of life. . . . And so he had assembled his guests under an enchanting blue ceiling of brilliant chandeliers and a dome of artificial roses bowered among green leaves." The narrator figures the attunement to sensory life promoted by the cabaret as a whirl of hues:

> It was a scene of blazing color. Soft, barbaric, burning, savage, clashing, planless colors—all rioting together in wonderful harmony. There is no human sight so rich as an assembly of Negroes ranging from lacquer black through brown to cream, decked out in their ceremonial finery. Negroes are like trees. They wear all colors naturally. And Felice, rouged to a ravishing maroon, and wearing a close-fitting, chrome-orange frock and cork-brown slippers, just melted into the scene. (320)

To be a Negro here means to feel one's way into a riotous scene in order to experience its chaos of "planless colors" as a "wonderful harmony." It marks a collective identity more than an individual one; unlike Helga's, Felice's makeup and outfit cause her to "melt into the scene," not stand out. The colors themselves matter less than what they do, how they are felt. Though this relation to vibrant hues is given as "natural," the nature involved is hardly one of essences, nor is it opposed to artifice, as signaled by the "chrome-orange frock." Rather, it exhibits the "primitive drag" that Sam See theorized in relation to Langston Hughes: a strategy of deploying the rhetoric of primitivism to naturalize, and thereby depathologize, feelings classed as degenerate.[53] The intense chromatic feeling that for so long signaled a deficient color sense appears instead as a force that binds together the people it touches—observers included—into a beautiful, riotous harmony.

Like Hurston, McKay makes color into a figure for racial feeling by tying it to movement and music. Moreover, the speed of his chromatic catalogs, the way they link an array of hues in quick succession, isolates chromatic quality from objects in much the same way that Stephen

Crane's lurid realism works in the final pages of *The Red Badge of Courage,* when the repeated references to "blue" accumulate at such a rate that they facilitate a pervasive feeling of blueness. McKay repeats this process with a variety of hues, isolating not the qualia of particular colors so much as the energetic charge of color in general. At the end of reading "dim brown, clear brown, rich brown, chestnut, copper, yellow, near-white, mahogany, and gleaming anthracite," it's possible to lose sight of what has been described and focus solely on the feeling that infuses the telling. This effect does not so much cancel the techniques of rendering skin tone discussed above as identify a parallel function in McKay's writing, one that he makes explicit when he uses similar lists to describe the emotions stirred by the "blues" of a cabaret band: "Red moods, black moods, golden moods. Curious syncopated slipping-over into one mood, back-sliding back into the first mood. Humming in harmony, barbaric harmony, joy-drunk" (54). The "barbaric harmony" encompasses a spectrum of shifting, chromatic moods that separate color from the visual to attach it to a mode of feeling cultivated in black vernacular practice. The narrative shifts its attention from the individual dancers to the collective moods that bind them. The chromatic catalogs serve as ramps to propel the novel to these heights, often signaled by McKay's characteristic ellipses: "Dandies and pansies, chocolate, chestnut, coffee, ebony, cream, yellow, everybody was teased up to the high point of excitement . . ." (32; ellipses in the original). Literal color yields to local color, though here it's not just about feeling Harlem but about feeling *black* in Harlem.

For this reason, McKay's "savage" images differ from classic examples of primitivism. Whereas the latter separate viewer and viewed, and thus neutralize the immersive qualities of chromatic experience, McKay's colors tease everyone up in a collective practice of engaging the bodily unconscious. For instance, when Ray, Jake's educated and intellectual Haitian friend, almost overdoses on cocaine, he experiences the world as a "blue paradise" in which "everything was in gorgeous blue of heaven": "Woods and streams were blue, and men and women and animals, and beautiful to see and love. And he was a blue bird in flight and a blue lizard in love. And life was all blue happiness." Like the dancers in a cabaret, whom McKay describes as "gorgeous animals," Ray abandons himself to the wash of blue, and within this colorful medium all "taboos and terrors and penalties were transformed into new pagan delights, orgies of Orient-blue carnival" (108, 158). The passage provides a foil for the Black Mass scene in *Nigger Heaven*. Each literalizes the primitivist metaphors associated with jazz by intensifying its chromatic content, but where Van Vechten's description heightens the colors to increase the visibility of race—as made clear by the spectatorial structure of the scene and its fascination with the "savage African features" of the gazed-upon girl—McKay uses blue to push the perceiver into the perceived, foreclosing objectification by canceling the structural division between subject and object upon which it relies. As a result, his "new pagan delights" refer to a mode of feeling, not of seeing, and they strain against the rigid emotions McKay in *Home to Harlem* associated with the "magnificent monster of civilization" (155).

In McKay's work, the "primitive" marks the eruption of a "high point of excitement" conjured by colors and aimed against "civilization." Like Hurston's blue body paint and war drum, the jungle metaphors that weave throughout his jazz scenes—the "savage ecstatic dream" of a pianist," the "wild rhythm" of a dancer," or the people "abandon[ing] themselves to pure voluptuous jazzing"—attempt to appropriate the figures from primitivist discourse to describe an experience of affect and movement opposed to the "grand business of civilization" (94, 196, 108, 154). His primitivism appeals not to an ancestral racial identity but to a set of contingent feelings created through specific relations to the history of colonialism, nationalism, and capitalism—forces that McKay presents together as "the steam-roller of progress" (155).[54] As Brent Hayes Edwards argues of the "vagabond" characters in McKay's second novel *Banjo* (1929), the dancers in *Home to Harlem* reject the bodily exploitation that drives modern capitalism and offer the seed of an "ethical system . . . *exterior* to the crushing logic of 'civilization.'"[55] The colorful sights and sounds of "primitive" jazzing stand as forms of collective resistance that occur at the level of sensation, movement, and perception yet strike at some of the foundational concepts of Western society, including the individual self and the detached intellect. They produce a "mad riotous joy" that McKay sets against "the well-patterned, well-made emotions of the respectable world" (*Home to Harlem,* 337).

In *Banjo,* which follows Ray to Marseilles, where he joins an international group of dockworkers and drifters, McKay elaborates the image of color as a challenge to the forces of civilization. Ray resolves that "civilization would not take the love of color, joy, beauty, vitality, and nobility out of *his* life and make him like one of the poor mass of its pale creatures"; and the narrator celebrates other black characters for "retain[ing] their taste for bright color and ornaments that the Protestant missionaries were trying to destroy."[56] As in *Home to Harlem,* color here signals a way of feeling that has been pathologized by whites. And embracing it, for Ray, doubles as a refusal "to accept the idea of the Negro simply as a 'problem'" (272). "If the Negro had to be defined," Ray continues, "there was every reason to define him as a challenge rather than a 'problem' to Western civilization" (273). In *Banjo*'s final chapter, Ray gives this idea a remarkable image that turns on the trope of "primitive color":

> He [Ray] was a challenge of civilization itself. He was the red rag to the mighty-bellowing, all-trampling civilized bull.
>
> Looking down in a bull ring, you are fascinated by the gay rag. You may even forget the man watching the bull go after the elusive color that makes him mad. The rag seems more than the man. If the bull win it, he horns it, tramples it, sniffs it, paws it—baffled.
>
> As the rag is to the bull, so is the composite voice of the Negro— speech, song and laughter—to a bawdy world. More exasperating, indeed, than the Negro's being himself is his primitive color in a world where everything is being reduced to a familiar formula, this remains strange and elusive. (314)

Aside from the way McKay reverses the usual direction of dehumanization by making white civilization the instinct-driven bull and the Negro the matador, what stands out is the clever split between the red rag and the man that holds it. Whereas the bull sees only the rag, the man "watch[es] the bull go after the elusive color" and so has a privileged analytical position, one reflected in Ray's choice of preposition: "a challenge *of* civilization" rather than a challenge *to* civilization. The challenge emerges *within* civilization itself, part of the complicated process whereby the "primitive color" of the Negro stimulates a response that both demonizes it (makes it a "problem," seeks to trample it) and misses it altogether (even when it is caught, the bull is "baffled"). And the perceived threat comes not from any individual but from a "composite voice"—even more, a composite of rhythms and movements, pulling people together in a "barbaric harmony." For some writers of the 1920s, the stock scenes of frenetic dancing were a problem; for others, they posed a challenge.

Hurston and McKay adopted the links between racial identity and chromatic sensitivity forged in the discourses of primitivism to present oppositional figurations of blackness through and as feeling. They presented race itself as a feeling tone, an atmospheric quality grounded in material experience yet in no way reducible to it, something as relational as color perception itself: Hurston requires a "white background" to throw out her color; the red rag needs the civilized bull. The literal colors of Harlem nightlife, combined as they were with music and movement, provided occasions for approaching the rich "color" of the New Negro by activating the "primitive" qualities of sensory life that oppose the "world-conquering and leveling machine civilization" and its normalization of white modes of embodiment (*Banjo*, 66). In claiming these colors as their own, Harlem Renaissance writers reinvented the inherited discourse of what it means to be "colored."

Aesthetic Education as Harmonious Riot

Meeting the challenge of color involves undergoing an aesthetic education, a process of learning how to feel. Already, then, the chromatic strategies of Harlem Renaissance writers brought them into proximity with the projects of color-sense training that had flourished at the turn of the twentieth century. But just as the descriptions of colorful ensembles and voluptuous jazzing modified existing threads of color-sense discourse, so too did the presentations of artistic receptivity in black writers of the 1920s reimagine the hierarchies of sensation and intellect on which earlier models of artistic training, and the civilizing mission they supported, depended. Especially in his treatment of Ray's ambitions as a writer, McKay treats sensory reception as an active seeking-out rather than a passive taking-in; he presents reflection and feeling as mutually enhancing elements in the ongoing rhythm of experience. As such, *Home to Harlem* returns us to the relation between intellectual training and sensory vividness that sits at the heart of the color sense and allows us to register the way the aesthetic challenge of "primitive" feeling revises earlier efforts to improve color sensitivity. The aesthetic philosophy John Dewey developed in the 1920s and 1930s—which both influenced and drew inspiration from the artistic flourishing in Harlem—is illuminating here. Taken together, McKay and Dewey clarify the philosophical and political importance of aesthetic education conceived on the model of chromatic feeling.

Ray's presence in McKay's novels indicates that neither Jake's bohemian charm nor the outsider stance of the vagabonds in Marseilles can alone accomplish the aesthetic task of bringing the force of color into writing. In *Home to Harlem* in particular, the friendship between Jake and Ray unfolds as a meditation on a much-discussed issue in the Harlem Renaissance: how to incorporate the energies of black vernacular expression into modern literature. Yet rather than opposing literature to the sensory intensity of embodied practices like cabaret dancing or sidewalk strolling, McKay presents writing as a technique for forming a deeply felt impression capable of being conveyed to others, a technique that brings one closer to the scene rather than farther away from it. Indeed, Ray's sensitivity trumps Jake's. "Ray felt more," "his range was wider," and as a result "life burned in [him] perhaps more intensely than in Jake." To handle this rush of sensations, which were more than "he could distill into active animal living," Ray "felt he had to write" (265). Far from being a detached intellectual project, writing here emerges as the practice of integrating the chaotic overflow of experience into coherent and vivid events. As such, Ray's literary ambitions mirror the cabaret scene in which "barbaric, burning, savage, clashing, planless colors . . . all [riot] together in wonderful harmony": to write is to create a harmonious riot (320).

When Ray dreams of translating the "thoughts he felt" and the "impressions that reach him" into patterned words, he claims his ability to feel the "violent coloring of life" as at once a racial and an artistic asset (227, 228). Voicing a familiar sentiment from the interwar years, he claims that civilization had exhausted itself, that the wisdom of previous centuries had expired, and that he feels "alone, hurt, neglected, cheated, almost naked." "But he was a savage," the narration continues, "even though he was a sensitive one, and he did not mind nakedness" (226). Ray then surveys a number of experiments in modernist fiction—the portions of James Joyce's *Ulysses* published in the *Little Review,* Sherwood Anderson's *Winesburg, Ohio,* Henri Barbusse's war fiction—and finds an affinity with D. H. Lawrence, whose "reservoir of words too terrible and too terrifying for nice printing" had "fascinated" him (227). The image of a reservoir later returns to establish Ray as a writer who might out-Lawrence Lawrence: "[Ray] was a reservoir of that intense emotional energy peculiar to his race," and as such "life touched him emotionally in a thousand vivid ways" (265). McKay connects Ray's sensitivity to the feeling of being "colored" that he and Hurston dramatize through their cabaret scenes, and in this way their reconstructed primitivism grounds their claims for modern authorship.

Writers both black and white made similar claims about sensory receptivity in the 1920s—illustrations of yet another aspect of the rhetoric of color in modernist writing. Of course there is Lawrence, and the Williams of "The Wildflower" and "To Elsie"; indeed, most of the writers and artists who had any truck with primitivism (Picasso, Gauguin) had a sense that civilization had stunted sensory life and that artistic advance lay in the appropriation of nonwhite sensory modes. Even Toomer, who resisted the label "Negro writer," aligned his artistic abilities with racial feeling when he recounted his experience of writing *Cane*. He explained that his "growing need for artistic expression" pulled him "deeper and deeper into the Negro group," and that this embrace of African American culture nurtured his literary potential: "My powers of receptivity increased," he reported, and he felt his "creative talent" "stimulated and fertilized."[57] An immersion in black life, it seems, helped Toomer not just to write about African Americans but simply to write at all. In his depiction of Ray, McKay joined Toomer in drawing on the aesthetic elevation of sensory qualities historically opposed to "civilization" to position black writers at the vanguard of modernism.

But just as McKay's celebration of primitive color leveled a sweeping charge against the bull of civilization, so too did his alignment of Ray's sensitivity with modern aesthetics signal a radical change in the understanding of art, one given classic expression in Dewey's *Art as Experience* (1934). Dewey placed the paradoxical formulation of a refined primitivism, a harmonious riot, at the center of his aesthetic theory.[58] He rejected the notion that art signifies a lofty realm of sanctified objects and instead defined aesthetic experience in terms that recall the scenes of primitive color in Hurston and McKay—namely, as moments of quickened and intensified perception in which we feel ourselves alive to the perceptual world. As such, Dewey recognized that "art" happens in a number of unexpected places—he listed "the movie, jazzed music, [and] the comic strip" as the "arts which have the most vitality for the average person"— and, like McKay, he offered the sights and sounds of the modern city as occasions for aesthetic engagement.[59] To grasp the contours of the aesthetic, Dewey contended, we should note the scenes that capture our attention, such as "the fire-engine rushing by; the machines excavating enormous holes in the earth"; and the "tense grace of the ball-player" (5).

Dewey's catalog resonates with the colorful panoramas of McKay's novels, and though the two men's particular examples differ, they shared a belief that quotidian moments of intense absorption have something in common with the experiences we valorize as art.

For both, moreover, the fully alive moments of aesthetic engagement run contrary to the fate of the senses in modernity. Dewey faulted industrial labor conditions for altering "the habits of the eye as a medium of perception" and enforcing a false division between body and mind, between useful and fine arts (342). But with the challenge of primitive color in mind, we can recognize that the larger context for Dewey's critique is what McKay called the "magnificent monster of civilization." As such, when Dewey turns to the figure of the "savage," as he does in the first chapter of *Art as Experience,* we should see this move as of a piece with McKay's appropriation of racial feeling or Taussig's appeals to the bodily unconscious—that is, as an attack on the binaries of Western philosophy and their role in the history of colonialism. "When the savage is most alive," Dewey wrote, "he is most observant of the world about him and most taut with energy"; his attention causes him to vibrate with his environment, so that "as he watches what stirs about him, he, too, is stirred." For Dewey, this cohesion of thought and action pushes against the way that in modernity the senses had been twisted into "mere pathways along which material is gathered to be stored away for a delayed and remote possibility," the passive channels of traditional empiricism. In contrast, aesthetic experience reveals the senses as "sentinels of immediate thought and outposts of action" (19). In such passages, Dewey takes the qualities of movement and absorption that inflect the jungle imagery in writing about Harlem cabarets and applies them to the experience of seeing and hearing. Hurston, we will recall, danced her wild dance at the New World Cabaret without ever leaving the table. By this model, notes Dewey, the goal of art is to lead us into experiences characterized by "the union of sense, need, impulse and action" equally on display in the "savage" and the modern pedestrian transfixed by a construction site (25).

In art approached through the challenge of color, there is no opposition between sensation and the intellect and no inherent separation of things that are immediate and those which are mediated. In this regard, Dewey's aesthetic theory and McKay's fiction turn on the same basic revision of the terms of primitivist discourse: from the opposition between "lower" bodily faculties and "higher" mental processes deployed by anthropologists like Rivers and social theorists such as Gilman, to a distinction between bodily practices that accept this false division (civilized) and those that deny it (primitive). The harmonious riots that result from engaged absorption incorporate the fruits of intelligent inquiry to enrich the felt impression of an event. It's in this sense that Ray "respond[s] to sensations that were entirely beyond Jake's comprehension" (222). In Dewey's terms, he "carr[ies] to new and unprecedented heights that unity of sense and impulse, of brain and eye and ear, that is exemplified in animal life, saturating it with conscious meaning derived from communication and deliberate expression" (22–23). Ray's perceptions are imbued with the import of his wide range of experiences, from Haiti to Harlem and on to Marseilles.

It should come as no surprise, then, that when Dewey wrote the introduction to a 1953 collection of McKay's selected poems, he singled out the poet's ability to wed the sensory and the social in an act of artistic expression. In that piece, Dewey praised McKay for capturing with "startling vividness" the "immediately sensitive response to scenes of the world in which the physical and the human blend into an indivisible yet distinctive unity."[60] Dewey named these moments the "common" elements of life, the aspects of experience shared by all those who engage the world with the organs of the body. Ostensibly, he took this term from one of McKay's lines: "And wonder to life's commonplaces clings." But in *Art as Experience,* Dewey had already presented the work of art as that which "keeps alive the power to experience the common world in its fullness" (133). In any case, the sentiment was shared by both philosopher and poet, and it occurs yet again in *Home to Harlem*'s third section, when Ray has exited the narrative proper but lingers in the voice of the narration. Jake takes a walk in the Bronx, at this point a green getaway from the city. He sits on a "mount thick-covered with dandelions" and takes in the natural scene: "Oh the common little things were glorious there under the sun in the tender spring grass," the narrator remarks, and then he muses on the ways such "physical" scenes gain new significance when blended with "human" experiences.

> There are hours, there are days, and nights whose sheer beauty overwhelms us with happiness, that we seek to make even more beautiful by comparing them with rare human contacts. . . . It was a day like this we romped in the grass . . . a night as soft and intimate as this on which we

forgot the world and ourselves. . . . Hours of pagan abandon, celebrating ourselves. (280)

The passage adds the enjoyments of human contacts to the beauty of the natural world in order to achieve an ecstasy of "pagan abandon" that resonates with what Dewey valued in art: the way it "quickens us from the slackness of routine and enables us to forget ourselves by finding ourselves in the delight of experiencing the world about us in its varied qualities and forms" (*Art as Experience,* 104). The common world, in these passages, marks the mixture of perceptual experience and social meaning that elsewhere in McKay's work finds ready expression in vibrant color.

Dewey and McKay locate the political promise of art in its ability to orient audiences to the common world in different ways, not through intellectual argument but through a qualitative engagement with other forms of attunement. As Dewey wrote, "All art is a process of making the world a different place in which to live," and it accomplishes this grand-sounding goal through small-scale adjustments of perceptual habits—in short, through aesthetic education.[61] Herein lies the political goal of the cultural project articulated in Locke's *The New Negro* and carried out through so many paintings, plays, novels, and poems in the 1920s: our encounters with artworks adjust our impulses and affective habits; they help us feel the social world differently. Dewey is rather sanguine on this point. "When we enter into the spirit of Negro or Polynesian art," he contends, "barriers are dissolved and limiting prejudices melt away"; like Felice's merging with the colorful crowd, this "insensible melting" occurs at the level of sensory and affective life and thus "enters directly into attitude" (*Art as Experience,* 334). Recent theorists have made similar claims for the aesthetic in more contemporary idioms—Cheng's analysis of "visual pleasure in the zone of contamination" or Jacques Rancière's account of how art recomposes the "distribution of the sensible." But the idea is the same.[62] "Works of art," as Dewey puts it, "are the means by which we enter, through the imagination and the emotions they evoke, into other forms of relationship and participation than our own" (333). They are tools for altering styles of feeling.

As elements in perceptual education, the hues of Harlem Renaissance writing extend earlier initiatives in color-sense training, but with an important difference that Dewey's aesthetics help highlight. At the turn of the twentieth century, attempts to improve color sensitivity proceeded

on the assumption that the products of intellectual reflection could enhance chromatic experience, bringing it into more intimate and responsive touch with the world. Some version of this belief motivates Garland's
local color writing, Gilman's interest in color music, all the color pedagogies discussed in chapter 3, and the experiments with purely literary
hues in Crane and Stein. But very often the full challenge of this idea—
the way it strikes at the divisions of mind and body, abstraction and sensation, that run throughout traditional empiricism—is muffled by the
simultaneous embrace of a "civilized" body whose superiority to "primitive color vision" inheres in its ability to keep its distance from color's unruly energies. Against barbarism, color pedagogues taught refinement;
against the chromatic riots of commercial spectacles, they encouraged
harmonies. McKay, on the other hand, nominates as the goal of aesthetic
training something impossible by the standards of these educators: a
harmonious riot, a barbaric harmony. These formulations appear paradoxical only from the vantage of a lingering opposition between feeling
and thinking. Within the charged moment of aesthetic experience, they
name the techniques by which writing modifies sensory attunement and
so adjusts how a person feels and responds to the sensory world. Both
McKay's colors and Dewey's aesthetics detach the mechanism of color-
sense training from the teleological framework that marked its founding.

Coda: A Night at the Savoy

The feeling of being colorful and colored in the Harlem Renaissance
assembled elements from mass culture, ethnography, and pragmatist
aesthetics. Writers such as Larsen, Hurston, McKay, and Van Vechten
engaged the bright hues of the urban landscape to stage performances of
blackness grounded in the perceptual disruptions of material culture and
resonant with the portrayals of sensory life and affective experience that
occupied anthropologists and philosophers alike. How fortuitous, then,
and how tantalizingly suggestive, is the record of a spring night in 1926
when Nella Larsen accompanied Bronislaw Malinowski to the newly
opened Savoy Ballroom, with John Dewey tagging along as chaperone.
No detailed account of their evening remains—just a brief mention in the
society pages.[63] But I like to think that between foxtrots, as they watched
the multihued spotlights speckle the crowd, the trio remarked on the
brilliance of the Savoy's colors. Not only remarked on but *felt* them, and

in feeling experienced the active, full-bodied absorption that they explored in their writing.

What did Malinowski feel as he bent his European ballroom steps to match the rhythms of the Charleston? In Trobriand, he had recorded the sensation of sailing in a shallow canoe over the breaking waves as an immersion into the tropical colors of the landscape. The movement over the "intense blue of the sea," Taussig tells us, allowed Malinowski to "escape—into color—and thereby into another world of the senses" in which the body opens onto the unfolding of the environment.[64] Movement and color: add music and you have all the ingredients of the cabaret, all the sensory qualities that pulsed around the anthropologist as the Savoy's spotlights dazzled his ethnographer's eye. Yet with an urban sophisticate like Larsen as his dancing partner, Malinowski would never have been in danger of thinking himself back in the field. I wonder what she thought of the Polish tourist, how she answered his probing questions about life in Harlem. Perhaps she kept her distance, taking pride in the beautiful lives strutting outside on Lenox Avenue even as she worried about the portraits this Olsen-like figure might paint of her—a cautious stance honed through her friendship with Van Vechten. Did she, like Hurston, feel her color when she danced with Malinowski? Did she press the anthropologist into faster dance steps and more frenzied jazzing as the night wore on, as if to pit her ease with the local scene against his outsider awkwardness? And what of the wallflower philosopher? In 1926 Dewey was in the thick of developing his aesthetic theory, and with the right ears we can hear his night at the Savoy echoing in the "jazzed music" he lists as one of the modern era's most vital arts. And with the right eyes we might see the paint appear on Dewey's face as he watches the colorful spectacles of the Harlem club scene, an image of the attentive observation he illustrates with the stalking savage.

McKay could not have been present that night; he spent much of the 1920s and early 1930s in Europe. But we can imagine the zest with which he would have written the scene. The lights would be bright, the band loud, and the drinks strong; it would be a "scene of blazing color." Dewey, by all accounts a spry sixty-seven-year-old, would get up to join the dancing, and he and Malinowski would come back to Harlem the next night decked out in clothes so vivid they would make their wives blush. It makes a lovely snapshot of the cultural and intellectual climate of the Harlem Renaissance: a novelist, an anthropologist, and a pragmatist philosopher, all melting together in a wonderful riot of color.

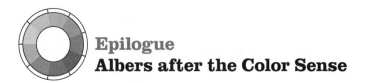

Epilogue
Albers after the Color Sense

In the 1930s, the once-widespread invocations of a trainable color sense began to dwindle. Not that color ceased to stir interest—though the stock-market crash of 1929 curtailed the accumulating force of the commercial color revolution, chromatic innovations in film, animation, lighting, and clothing persisted throughout the Great Depression. Joseph Urban's polychromatic designs for the 1933 Century of Progress International Exhibition in Chicago; *The Wizard of Oz* (1939), MGM's Technicolor adaptation of Baum's story; Walt Disney's color-music animation *Fantasia* (1940); and, in a different register, Wallace Stevens's "The Man with the Blue Guitar" (1937) all testify to the continued pursuit of chromatic effects.[1] But in the discussions around these and related endeavors, the phrase "color sense" and its variants appear far less frequently than in previous decades. Why is this so?

The discourse of the color sense between 1880 and 1930 held together two things that have been pulled apart in the nearly hundred years since: a fascination with color's immediate sensory power and a commitment to the systematic training of perception. The underlying premise of color-sense training was that greater sensitivity to chromatic effects could be achieved through a rationalized, rule-based instruction, and that an individual's responsiveness to color indicated where he or she fell within a similarly rationalized racial schema, stretching from "savage" to "civilized." The era of the color sense, the era of aniline, was defined by the tensions produced by the links between chromatic immediacy and pedagogical mediations, tensions that eventually led to the dissolution of the turn-of-the-century version of chromatic sensitivity. We have already seen signs of the mounting pressure in the rejection of the precise color exercises devised by Albert Munsell and Milton Bradley in favor of finger painting, or in L. Frank Baum's advice to window dressers on how to deploy surreptitiously the principles of color harmony in window displays. Baum in particular demonstrates the fate of color systems in the age of consumer culture: what had once been presented as a tool for managing one's own relation to the built environment (as in Charlotte Perkins Gilman's works) became instead the tricks of the trade in advertising, the specialized knowledge of the "color experts" who appeared on the professional scene. Rules and systems for the experts, intense color experiences for the shoppers. As the marvels of commercial color became more common, and more thoroughly managed, the two strands of color-sense discourse became increasingly separate.

Indeed, what had been joined in the color sense came to be not just decoupled but opposed. A chasm opened between color, sensation, and quality, on the one hand, and language, mediation, and measure on the other, so much so that color came to stand for an *escape* from linguistic systems and the power structures they support. As David Batchelor notes, "The idea that colour is beyond, beneath or in some other way at the limit of language" constitutes one of modern color's primary appeals, even for writers.[2] Something of this idea drives Jacques Derrida's insistence that "color has not yet been named" and Bruce R. Smith's call for literary and cultural critics to turn to color as a way to move "from language to the body."[3] Systems of color instruction and color harmonies— attempts to articulate a "language of color" in the nineteenth and early twentieth centuries—came to be seen as a block to intensive color experience rather than a bridge. And to be sure, the systems were always breaking down, leaking exceptions like a rusty paint box.

But there were two distinct ways to abandon systems in the twentieth century, corresponding to two different legacies of the color sense, and their diverging trajectories bring this study of modern color to its close. Aldous Huxley illustrates the first in his high-keyed descriptions of visionary experiences, such as those he enjoyed after taking mescaline. In *The Doors of Perception* (1954), Huxley relates that with the help of psychedelic drugs he came to see an ordinary garden chair as bursting with perceptual intensity and inherent meaning. And like Hamlin Garland and the impressionists before him, he signaled his immersion in the scene with a description of blue shadows: "Where the shadows fell on the canvas upholstery, stripes of a deep but glowing indigo alternated with stripes of an incandescence so intensely bright that it was hard to believe that they could be made of anything but blue fire." "At any other time I would have

seen a chair barred with alternate light and shade," Huxley writes; but
at that moment "the percept had swallowed up the concept," revealing
a world entirely different from the one given in traditional empiricism.
Immersed in what Huxley calls the "Mind at Large" rather than the individual self, "the so-called secondary characters of things are primary."[4]
From this vantage, John Locke got it backwards; it's color that "turns out
to be a kind of touchstone of reality" (58).

Seeing the world at this pitch of intensity requires an educated eye.
Mescaline acts as the teacher: it "raises all colours to a higher power
and makes the percipient aware of innumerable fine shades of difference,
to which, at ordinary times, he is completely blind." To prove his point,
Huxley references William Gladstone's thesis about the color sensitivity
of the ancient Greeks. "To judge by the adjectives which Homer puts into
their mouths," he explains, "the heroes of the Trojan War hardly excelled
the bees in their capacity to distinguish colours." But in the intervening
millennia, "mankind's advance has been prodigious," with psychedelics
promising to push the progress further. The trajectory seems familiar;
Huxley even discusses "man's highly developed colour sense" (13–14).
Yet the course of this perceptual education runs in reverse from that proposed by Gladstone and Hugo Magnus, away from rather than toward
the concepts or the language used to sharpen attention. For Huxley, it's
the colors that are real and the words that are "secondary," reactionary
abstractions from concrete experience that mar one's ability to perceive
the inherent value of things (as opposed to their commercial or utilitar-
ian value). "At the antipodes of the mind," as Huxley terms the regions of
visionary experience, "we are more or less completely free of language,
outside the system of conceptual thought."[5] In these untamed regions,
color flourishes.

Huxley's plea for the cultivation of visionary experiences that transport one to the "antipodes" by dispensing with concepts and language
demonstrates the survival of the primitivist aspects of modern color into
the psychedelic era, when *The Doors of Perception* became a kind of guidebook for the counterculture. Just as color jumps to mind when someone
says "modern art," so too is it impossible to imagine the Summer of Love
without images of Day-Glo colors and psychedelic light shows. Color's
"primitive" energy proved useful once again in the 1960s, this time as a
way of figuring the authentic reality hidden behind inherited habits, both
social and perceptual.

The color instruction of Bauhaus veteran Josef Albers, made famous through his *Interaction of Color* (1963), presents a very different way of resisting systems in the name of experience. Where the mystic/drugged model requires one to relax thought, to let go and drop out, the Albers model demands a more rigorous concentration, a more exacting attention to the constituents of color perception as they take shape in everyday experience. Starting in 1933, when he moved from Germany to Black Mountain College in North Carolina to escape the Nazis, Albers cultivated an approach to color education in the United States that embraced the relational activity of colors as a model for "thinking in situations."[6] Rather than deriding the abstracting functions of thought and inquiry, he situated them. As he explains in *Interaction of Color*, "No color system can develop one's sensitivity for color," so his method dispenses with totalizing rulebooks for chromatic practice and immerses students in the experience of color (2). In these ways, Albers's pedagogy exemplifies a tendency that runs throughout color-sense discourse and to which *Chromographia* has given special attention: the way working with colors fosters a radical empirical attitude, an attunement to experience as a relational process. This is why Garland sounds like William James, why Stephen Crane and Gertrude Stein echo Charles S. Peirce, why Claude McKay and John Dewey recognized themselves in one another, and why Goethe's *Theory of Colours* sometimes reads like a predecessor to Brian Massumi's expanded empiricism or Isabelle Stengers's cosmopolitics. Thinking about color entails thinking about experience, and those who also thought *with* color started to think like pragmatists.

This affinity between color practice and pragmatist philosophy was made explicit at Black Mountain College (BMC) in the 1930s and 1940s, when Albers headed the faculty and Dewey sat on its advisory council. Even more, as one of the most significant hubs in the network of twentieth-century art, Black Mountain spread a concern for process, relations, and experience—the fundamentals of chromatic pragmatism— throughout the American avant-garde. The storied record of the college's brief existence (1933–57) includes an almost improbable list of significant figures from the history of twentieth-century art: John Cage, Merce Cunningham, Walter Gropius, Willem de Kooning, Charles Olsen, Buckminster Fuller—to name some of the most prominent. These illustrious alumni all assembled in Buncombe County, North Carolina, to participate in an educational experiment modeled on Dewey's pedagogical principles and exemplified in Albers's demanding courses in color, drawing, and materials. "Experience" was the watchword, and color provided a vivid means of engaging it.

Dewey never taught at Black Mountain, but he was nonetheless a shaping influence on the college, making multiple visits and donating hundreds of books to its library. John Rice, BMC's first rector, knew Dewey and positioned himself within the progressive education movement that took its cues from Dewey's *Democracy and Education* (1916) (a book that Albers encountered in German translation).[7] A 1936 report on the college in *Harper's* captured the thrust of this movement. "In BMC there is no head-cramming," the author explained. "There education is *experience* that involves in action the whole person," and its procedures "[are] predicated upon the concept that both the world and the individual who is to be prepared for it are changing, moving, dynamic."[8] "Learning by doing," a Deweyan phrase worn thin by overuse, here retains its original metaphysical grounding in a relational, process-based account of experience. Progressive education unfolds at the dynamic site of interaction between self and surroundings, where students and teachers alike develop in relation to and in preparation for a changing world.

To meet this modern maelstrom, both Black Mountain and Dewey privileged art. When the college enrolled its first students, Dewey had just delivered the lectures that would be published as *Art as Experience* (1934), and manifestations of Dewey's experience-based aesthetic flourished at Black Mountain. The arts courses exemplified the college's mission and were taken by all students, not in the hopes of producing a graduating class of Cages and de Koonings but on the idea that practices of making and perceiving fostered habits essential for democratic living. In particular, the arts shaped patterns of seeing and feeling. Rice elaborated the point to the reporter from *Harper's* in terms that evoke the long history of color-sense training as it bled into modernism: "There are subtle means of communication that have been lost to mankind, as our nerve ends have been cauterized by schooling"; if we are to "*feel* . . . our way into the future," he continued, "these nerves must be re-sensitized."[9] The sentiment also appears in the college catalog for the 1933–34 school year:

> Through some kind of art experience, which is not necessarily the same as self-expression, the student can come to the realization of order in the world; and, by being sensitized to movement, form, sound,

and the other media of the arts, gets a firmer control of himself and his environment than is possible through purely intellectual effort.[10]

As Ruth Erickson argues, "Pedagogy at Black Mountain began with art to end with democracy."[11] The same holds for Dewey, who as we saw in chapter 5 turned to aesthetics in order to combat the separation of feeling and intellect that had yielded both a paltry empiricism and the stultifying conditions of industrial labor.

Albers's color pedagogy put experience first, elevating it above system and self-expression alike. In 1941, Albers greeted the incoming class by explaining that "experimentation means learning by experience"— and that at Black Mountain they would be invited to experiment.[12] In particular, his own classes immersed students in the activities of arranging and testing the fundamental elements of painting and design and then asked them to reflect on the results. The goal, no less than for Bradley or Rimington, was the cultivation of an educated eye—a rare thing. As John Ruskin wrote in a passage Albers was fond of quoting, "Hundreds of people can talk, for one who can think. But thousands of people can think, for one who can see."[13] Albers doubted that any established color system could promote such seeing, but he was equally suspicious—at times disdainful—of the opposite push to encourage color practice as self-expression. In *Interaction of Color* he professed a "disbelief in self-expression, either as a way of study or as its aim, in schools." And as Eva Díaz argues, this emphasis on experimental process "sidestepped the growing tendency to define the project of art as untrammeled, self-revelatory immediacy."[14] Instead, his classes encouraged discipline, even rationalism—an attitude far removed from Huxley's ecstatic visions. In this way Albers extended the belief that reflection can enhance sensation, the belief that motivated color-sense training at the turn of the twentieth century, but he detached it from the search for system and the primitivist desire for authentic experience.

In *Interaction of Color,* the fruit of decades of teaching at Black Mountain and at Yale University, Albers gave a brilliant and influential formulation to these aspects of color-sense discourse. At once a pedagogical guide for color instruction and a meditation on how to think without absolutes, the book illustrates how an experimental approach to color goes hand in hand with a pragmatist model of experience. Invoking Dewey's famous Lab School at the University of Chicago, Albers pitches his approach as a "laboratory" course, an "experimental way of studying color and of teaching color" that engages students in the work of experiencing chromatic relations (9, 1). "The aim of such study," he continues, "is to develop—through experience—by trial and error—an eye for color." This involves more than vision, more than the ability to discriminate orangish red from reddish orange; indeed, Albers often describes perception as an act of "reading colors," an act that involves not just a visual stimulus but what a person does with it (5). Developing a sensitive or trained eye, he explains, means "seeing color action as well as feeling color relatedness" (1, 53, 14). Process and feeling, activity and relation: Albers installs these pillars of radical empiricism at the center of his project and gives them a concise formulation in his title. The study of color is a study of *inter-actions,* of relations and processes, of learning to see "what happens between colors" (5).

Albers's distinctive approach emerges from his topic. The mantra of *Interaction of Color* is that "color is the most relative medium in art," and one of the consequences of this principle is that systems of color harmony reveal more about the personalities and desires of the system builders than about the behavior of actual colors (8).[15] For much of the book, Albers describes exercises designed to bring students to this realization, to show that "any color 'goes' or 'works' with any other color" if arranged in the right way, so that no final rules about harmony can be generalized beyond a limited set of cases (44). Similarly, and most famously, he leads his readers through a process of experiencing the changeable, relational character of color by making one color look like two, or making two different colors appear the same, by varying the context within which the colors appear. For example, one illustration taken from the students' coursework makes the same strip of ochre appear both yellowish (against a light-blue background) and nearly brown (when surrounded by orange) (plate IV-1). Albers recommends using colored papers rather than paints to ensure consistency in these exercises, though he advises teachers to avoid "tuned" sets like the ones produced by Munsell (6). (The Milton Bradley Company had stopped manufacturing its papers at this point.) After students have worked out their own solutions to these perceptual challenges and have also shared their results with the class—after, that is, they have felt and perceived these chromatic effects in action—they will have developed a "taste" for color. "Good painting, good coloring, is comparable to good cooking," Albers writes; following a recipe is not enough, for even a good one "demands tasting and repeated tasting when it is being followed" (42).

Acquiring a taste for the relational activity of color promotes a set of cognitive habits that Albers terms "thinking in situations." Colors always appear in context. Though we can "hear a single tone . . . we almost never . . . see a single color unconnected and unrelated to other colors." Working with colors thus entails thinking relationally, since they "present themselves in continuous flux, constantly related to changing neighbors and changing conditions" (5). Moreover, since one of the relations involved is the one between perceiver and perceived—the relation that produces "a discrepancy between physical fact and psychic effect" so that, for example, three colors can look like two—working with colors also involves learning to situate oneself within this flux (9). From this perspective, "thinking in situations" looks a lot like Donna Haraway's "situated knowledges": it entails rejecting the disembodied, totalizing, and of course entirely imaginary stance of the Knower who stands apart from the Known in order to know it, and embracing the partiality, process, and bodily involvement of the perceiver to formulate revised notions of objectivity and reality. Situating knowledge means refusing to generalize it beyond the sphere of its activity; it means putting the work of knowing within the processes of experience, so that it acts with and through its "changing neighbors and changing conditions." It rejects the "god trick" of standing above, surveying all.[16] Albers's color studies encourage this stance by asking students to move back and forth between a chromatic arrangement and its perceptual effect, testing out slight variations and conducting "continued comparison" until they achieve "a thorough visual training" (31). An eye for color requires a mind for process.

Thinking in situations is a way of reading relativity without falling into mere relativism. This is a hard task—sometimes I think it is *the* hard task, the one that postmodernism got wrong and pragmatism gets right. When James criticized the spectator theory of knowledge, for instance, he did so by grounding the knower in the processes of the world and recasting truth as a matter of connections formed within experience, what Stengers calls an "art of consequences."[17] *Interaction of Color* clarifies what this looks like. From the opening pages, Albers insists that "color deceives continually," but this observation does not lead him into Locke's position that chromatic sensations can't be trusted to yield true knowledge (1). "Deceit" and "illusion" are not dirty words for Albers, nor do they imply the need for a quest to find the real truth hiding behind appearances. Rather, Albers takes the relativity and changeability of color as an invitation to pay closer attention to how chromatic effects are produced; he asks students to join in the illusion, not to dispel it but to craft it. By quickening student interest in the practical work of fabricating color experience and by providing techniques and language for assessing the relation between action and effect, Albers's educational approach cultivates an art of consequences honed through color but transportable to the intellectual situation that still confronts us. It remains difficult to abandon system and foundations without sliding into the individualism of "self-expression." Color provides a training ground for situating thought between these two extremes in the relational activity of experience.

Albers believed that this way of thinking through color held profound social promise. "As in life so with color" he used to say, and this analogy captures what Díaz calls his "ethics of perception," a way of connecting "visual to social habits" rooted in the principles of Dewey's pragmatist pedagogy.[18] By instilling a taste for situated thinking, *Interaction of Color* teaches readers to hold their prejudices lightly. Albers recommends that students work with colors they dislike so that they can experience their preferences changing as they put themselves in continual relation to what they once tried to avoid (48). Likewise, because colors have no inherent properties, only relational ones, any one hue is bound to change its character when situated differently. Albers describes an exercise in which students are asked to find an arrangement of four colors in which all are "equally important" and "none of the colors dominates" (49). The possible arrangements are infinite, Albers writes, and "the more they vary, the more they invite one to follow and to alter" the "constant change" the colors undergo. He extrapolates a moral from this lesson: "We may consider such calculated juxtaposition as a symbol of community spirit, of 'live and let live,' of 'equal rights for all,' of mutual respect" (50). Or as Albers put it on a different occasion, "In art we have to present an example in which we might live together, and not shoot each other."[19] Such is the spirit of the aesthetic education offered at Black Mountain and embedded in *Interaction of Color.* The interactivity of color—of experience, of life—also means "interdependence" (71). Once this principle comes to be felt as well as known, then students arrive at what Albers (using what was for him, a man who had fled Germany with his Jewish wife in 1933, a loaded phrase) called "the healthy belief that there is no final solution in form." Rather, "form demands unending performance and invites constant reconsideration—visually as well as verbally" (73).

Albers's pedagogy offers a model for how to situate various experiences of color within the common world without hierarchizing them. Colors come to us with the shine of self-evidence—what else can you say about red other than that it is red?—and so when others profess to parse perception differently than we do, the tendency is to defend one's own experience at all costs. At the turn of the twentieth century, as we have seen throughout *Chromographia,* certain kinds of color perceptions were deemed "primitive" and "degenerate," signs of the compromised or undeveloped nervous sensitivity of the perceivers. These days it would take a true science skeptic to claim that different races see colors differently; nonetheless, popular articles about the supposed color blindness of the ancient Greeks have recently enjoyed a vogue, showing that the notion of an evolving color sense continues to fascinate. It's just more palatable to entertain this fascination in the realm of historical rather than racial difference.[20]

Similar and perhaps more familiar appeals are pitched at the level of the individual. Who among us hasn't been captivated for a time by the suggestion that one person's red might be another person's green? The ground beneath our feet seems to fall away at the prospect. If we can't assume a shared experience of basic things like colors, what can we trust? We're intrigued by the possibility that color experience is radically subjective because such a possibility threatens a deep-seated need to believe that action and perception address a reality held in common. Remember the dress that broke the Internet? Some people saw it as white and gold, others as black and blue.[21] As the image bounced around social media, the shared sensory fabric seemed to rip in two, revealing a division all the more unsettling because nobody had suspected it existed. A trivial instance, to be sure, but the upshot aligns with the more serious lesson of *Interaction of Color:* that the metaphysical expansion required to bring colors back into reality entails an ethical obligation as well, a demand to include not only color but also the varieties of chromatic experience in the continued production of a common world.

To be sure, colors don't always lead people to advocate Albers's call for unending performance. The tendency to use color instead to solidify or encode human difference remains strong. Baby-boy blue, little-girl pink; bright hipster hues and the drab outfits of working stiffs; red states, blue states. Because colors are visually salient but have very little if any inherent meaning, they are easily enlisted to take on whatever significance people want them to, especially when considered as individual hues. They will continue to be used in this way.[22] But Albers reminds us that for all the social codes that colors support, the relational essence of color itself prompts us to approach such meanings not as fixed systems but as mobile configurations of relationships that remain tied to context and subject to change. He shows that the cultivation of a "sensitive and critical eye for color relatedness" has implications beyond the historical meanings of the color sense (53). Color, in all its situated interactions, still has much to teach us.

Acknowledgments

As the writers in this study never tired of pointing out, no color stands alone; each one takes its particular tone and quality from those that surround it. That's equally true of this book, which would not be what it is without the brilliant, generous people I've been lucky to have around me.

The project began as a dissertation at the University of North Carolina at Chapel Hill, under the inspiring directorship of Jane Thrailkill. Her guidance is deep in the DNA of this book, and I continue to learn from her work and benefit from her advice and friendship. I also had the good fortune to work with two other paragons of intellectual energy, Robert Cantwell and Priscilla Wald. Both pushed this project in more interesting and important directions than I could have found on my own. John McGowan and Gregory Flaxman sat on my committee and have continued to serve as mentors—and now friends—after the defense. I thank Eliza Richards, Tim Marr, and Tyler Curtain, as well as all my graduate-student colleagues (especially Meredith Farmer, Joe Fletcher, Ben Rogerson, Kelly Ross, Ben Sammons, Aaron Shackelford, Joel Winkelman, and Elissa Zellinger) for helping me hammer out the initial version of this manuscript. It's bittersweet to put the final period on a piece of work that has kept me tied to this terrific group of people and those happy years.

A postdoc in the Society of Fellows at the University of Chicago gave me my first opportunities to revise the dissertation, and I was lucky to have a fascinating and brilliant group of colleagues and friends to help me do so. For their insightful comments and challenging questions, and for pub nights and general camaraderie, I would like to thank Katie Chenoweth, Andrew Dilts, Erin Fehskens, Michael Gallope, Markus Hardtmann, Rafeeq Hasan, Julia Klein, Leigh Claire LeBerge, Robert Lehman, Benjamin Lytal, Jordan Martins, Benjamin McKean, Timothy

Michael, Lauren Silvers, Emily Steinlight, Bettina Stoetzer, Neil Verma, Audrey Wasser, and Angela Watkins. I also thank my former colleagues in the English department, especially Adrienne Brown, Bill Brown, James Chandler, Hilary Chute, Patrick Jagoda, Benjamin Morgan, Lisa Ruddick, Richard So, and Kenneth Warren. Gwendolen Muren brought enthusiasm and care to her work as my research assistant during this time; I'm thankful for the sources she dug up.

The final version of this book came together while I was at Rutgers University. I had amazing colleagues there, and their unflagging energy and insight provided an invigorating environment in which to revise. I am especially grateful to Brad Evans, who generously read the entire manuscript—multiple times, in various versions—and who always saw what was best about the project, and helped me see it, too. Meredith McGill has been a careful and patient reader and offered valuable advice at crucial stages. I have been lucky to have Kyla Schuller as a friend and colleague; our conversations helped me get over several obstacles in the manuscript (and through many long commutes on NJ Transit). John Belton, Elin Diamond, Billy Galperin, Andrew Goldstone, Chris Iannini, Colin Jager, David Kurnick, Jeff Lawrence, Mukti Mangharam, Carter Mathes, Michael McKeon, Sarah Novacich, Stéphane Robolin, Margaret Ronda (for a time at Rutgers—too short!—and then from a distance), Louis Sass, Evie Shockley, Susan Sidlauskas, Jonah Siegel, Henry Turner, Rebecca Walkowitz, Cheryl Wall, and Abigail Zitin all helped me improve this book, either through direct feedback or, more often, by making me think harder about my methods and claims. Or just by being excellent colleagues who made Murray Hall a bright place to work, despite the shortage of windows. I also thank my students, especially those in my graduate course "Literature and Visual Culture" and in my undergraduate courses on color in literature; our conversations helped me clarify what I wanted to say in this book. Thanks to Carolyn Williams and Michelle Stephens, who, in addition to being insightful interlocutors, offered support and guidance in their role as chair. The School of Arts and Sciences and the English department provided course releases and a sabbatical that gave me the time I needed to finish, as well as subvention money. The Research Council provided a subvention grant to help defray the cost of color illustrations.

In 2014–15, I was a fellow at the Penn Humanities Forum for the seminar on color, led by Chi-ming Yang. I am very thankful to the Penn Humanities Forum and the Andrew W. Mellon Foundation for the time to write, and to Chi-ming for assembling such a fascinating group of scholars whose work on color helped me realize, finally, what this book was about. I would like to thank Jennifer Conway, Jim English, Sarah Varney, and all the participants in the seminar, especially my fellow postdocs Dhanveer Brar, Kevin Connolly, Gina Rivera, and Ruth Toulson, as well as Meredith Bak, Louise Daoust, Gary Hatfield, Antje Pfannkuchen, and Leonard Primiano and, outside the seminar, Nancy Bentley.

Many people generously read parts of the manuscript and offered essential encouragement and advice: David Alworth, Erik Bachman, Robin Bernstein, Annie Bourneuf, Todd Carmody, Natalia Cecire, Brad Evans, Brian Hochman, Laura Kalba, Jeff Lawrence, Benjamin Morgan, Sina Najafi, Rachel Nichols, Charlotte Ribeyrol, Michael Rossi, Jonathan Schroeder, Kyla Schuller, Susan Sidlauskus, Kate Stanley, Rachel Teukolsky, Cheryl Wall, Audrey Wasser, Autumn Womack, Chi-ming Yang, and Dora Zhang. Extra thanks go to Erica Fretwell, Katherine Hunt, and Lindsay Reckson, who read so many chapters and so many drafts over so many years. Even bigger thanks to Jennifer Fleissner, Emily Ogden, and the anonymous reader for the University of Minnesota Press, who read the entirety of a much longer version of the book and gave me the focus and confidence I needed to make final changes. I am grateful to these many friends and colleagues for their time and expertise. The book is much better because of their feedback.

I would also like to acknowledge all the institutions and working groups that invited me to present my research: the Americanist Speaker Series at Duke University and the University of North Carolina at Chapel Hill, the Birkbeck Forum for Nineteenth-Century Studies, Haverford College, King's College London, the London Modernism Seminar, the Centre for Modernist Studies at Sussex University, the American Research Seminar at the University of Cambridge, the American Studies Seminar at the University of Manchester, and the Oxford Americanist Seminar. As this list suggests, I spent a good deal of time working on this project in the United Kingdom, and I would like to thank Rebecca Beasley, Josephine McDonagh, Lloyd Pratt, and Ed Sugden for helping me find an intellectual home away from the States.

Color is a topic that crosses fields and disciplines, and one of the pleasures of working on this book has been meeting people who approach our shared interest from different vantages. For their insights into the history and philosophy of color, I am grateful to Zed Adams, Regina Lee Blaszczyk, Natasha Eaton, Laura Kalba, Charlotte Ribeyrol, Michael Rossi, Vanessa Schwartz, Sarah Street, and Joshua Yumibe. I have also learned how to approach color through conversations on more general topics with Michelle Coghlan, Paul Grimstad, Tobias Menely, Steven Meyer, Adam Nocek, Joan Richardson, Melanie Sehgal, and Matthew Taylor.

My research was supported by a two-month fellowship at the Huntington Library, and I thank the librarians there, especially Dan Lewis, David Mihaly, and Krystle Satrum, for their help in navigating the collections. Even more, I thank those in charge of awarding fellowships for also giving one to Katherine Hunt, who helped me navigate my Altima from Pasadena to Chicago and who has been my guiding light ever since we fell in love among the palm trees and desert gardens. The librarians at the Baldwin Library of Historical Children's Literature at the University of Florida, the Beinecke Rare Book and Manuscript Library at Yale University, the Cambridge Museum of Archeology and Anthropology, Cornell University, the Huntington Library, the New York Public Library, and Princeton University all helped me acquire reproductions of the images printed in the book. Danielle Kasprzak has been an enthusiastic and careful editor; I am thankful to her and the entire team at the University of Minnesota Press for their support and their work on the book. Gabrielle Everett cleaned up the manuscript, created the bibliography, and checked the sources, all with admirable care and precision. Kathy Delfosse did a superb job copyediting the book. Thank you to the editors of the journals *Configurations, Cabinet,* and *American Literature* for granting permission to reprint previously published material.

My deepest thanks goes to my family, who has been a constant source of strength throughout the long haul from dissertation to book, and well before that. Thank you to my parents, Wayne and Marsha Gaskill, for their unerring love and steady encouragement. I am grateful to my sisters, Lauren and Becca, and their beautiful families, for their warmth and laughter. My extended family, too, helped keep me on track, always showing interest in what I seemed continually to be working on and celebrating each milestone in ways that gave me energy to keep going. In London, Annie and Tim Hunt welcomed me into their home and offered much-needed assistance to make time for me to write. Finally, and most important, I thank my partner, Katherine Hunt, whose impeccable insights have made this a sharper and more interesting book, and without whose love and support this would not be a finished book at all. And thank you to our son, Leo, who liked yellow first, but then confounded all nineteenth-century expectations by loving purple second. He is the brightest spot in our lives. Whatever sparkles in this book is dedicated, with love, to him and Katherine.

Notes

Introduction

1. For the color names, see Bradley, *Color in the Kindergarten,* 23. For Bradley's early appreciation of color, see Shea, *It's All in the Game,* 49.

2. Bradley, "The Color Question Again," 176.

3. The articles that discuss Bradley's standards are too numerous to list here. For representative examples, see Bradley, "The Color Question Again"; and Pillsbury, "A Scheme of Colour Standards," with replies from Spencer and Louis Prang. J. H. Pillsbury collaborated with Bradley on determining the standard hues.

4. Rivers, "Primitive Color Vision"; Rivers, "Color Vision," 75; Eaton, *Colour, Art and Empire,* 188.

5. Herskovits, *The Anthropometry of the American Negro,* 5.

6. Wittgenstein, *Culture and Value,* 66.

7. Solomons, "The Saturation of Colors," 51.

8. Chevreul, *The Principles of Harmony and Contrast of Colors, and Their Application to the Arts.* See also Phillips, "Relative Color"; and Kalba, *Color in the Age of Impressionism,* chap. 1. For the shift to physiology and psychology in the scientific study of color, see Crary, *Techniques of the Observer,* chap. 3; Turner, *In the Eye's Mind;* and Rossi, *The Republic of Color.* For the role of color in physiological aesthetics, see Morgan, *The Outward Mind,* chap. 1.

9. Peirce, "[On a Method of Searching for the Categories]," 515–16.

10. For a description of many of these experiments, see Nichols, "The Psychological Laboratory at Harvard"; and Münsterberg, *Psychological Laboratory of Harvard University.*

11. Melville, *Moby-Dick,* 160.

12. Wilson, "The Relation of Color to the Emotions," 823.

13. For more on the study of color in nineteenth-century psychology, see Gage, *Color and Meaning.* For more general studies, see Boring, *A History of Experimental Psychology;* and Meyer, *Irresistible Dictation.*

14. Daston and Galison, *Objectivity,* chap. 5, especially the section "The Color of Subjectivity." See also R. Steven Turner, *In the Eye's Mind.*

15. Melville, *Moby-Dick,* 165.

16. Chirimuuta, *Outside Color,* 36.

17. John Locke, *An Essay Concerning Human Understanding,* bk. 2, chap. 8, secs. 9–10, pp. 134, 135, and bk. 2, chap. 8, sec. 15, p. 137.

18. Goethe, *Theory of Colours,* 1. Subsequent citations will appear parenthetically.

19. Whitehead, *Science and the Modern World,* 91. Kenneth Burke explains how this reorganization would look when he uses color to describe the "new realism" that followed in James's wake: "We must not speak of green as an 'illusion,' a mere phenomenal restating of certain vibrations affecting nervous tissues"; rather, we should treat the entire "arc" of perception, including all its elements, as "the real experience," such that green is embraced as "an actual part of the universe." Burke, *Permanence and Change,* 260. Many thanks to Erik Bachman for drawing my attention to this passage. For a twenty-first-century staging of how our experience of color demands an "expanded" empiricism, see Massumi, "Too-Blue: Color-Patch for an Expanded Empiricism," in *Parables for the Virtual,* 208–56.

20. For accounts of the long history of treating color's relation to the sensuous body as a liability rather than an asset, see Lichtenstein, *The Eloquence of Color;* Batchelor, *Chromophobia;* and Taussig, *What Color Is the Sacred?*

21. Indeed, most philosophical writing about color has missed the full metaphysical challenge posed by its topic. Analytic philosophy, where the majority of philosophical work on color has been done, has until recently been stuck in the same framework that caused Locke and Frege to banish colors from the real world. Eliminativists argue that colors are epiphenomenal and therefore reducible to physical properties in the brain (and so not real); realists counter by locating color in properties of objects, such as Surface Spectral Reflectance. Yet each assumes that for something to be real it has to be physical, as opposed to mental. See Byrne and Hilbert, *Readings on Color,* vol. 1, *The Philosophy of Color.*

More promising are Evan Thompson's ecological view, which treats colors as inseparable from the perceptual activities of specific organisms and their environments (Thompson, *Color Vision*), and M. Chirimuuta's adverbial approach, which draws on vision science to insist that "color perception relates perceiver to perceived in a particular way." Chirimuuta, *Outside Color,* 17. These views aim to overhaul the back-and-forth between realists and eliminativists using ideas dear to radical empiricism (though without discussing that tradition at any length). For a handy overview of the complex terrain of the philosophy of color, see Maund, "Color."

22. Masury, *How Shall We Paint Our Houses?,* 75.

23. Finck, "The Development of the Color-Sense," 19.

24. "Textiles: Dyes and Dyers A–Z by Company."

25. Stewart, "Color in Science and Poetry," 78. Subsequent citations will appear parenthetically.

26. Leslie, *Synthetic Worlds,* esp. chap. 2.

27. There are several histories of mauve and other synthetic dyes. See Philip Ball, *Bright Earth,* chap. 9; Blaszczyk, *The Color Revolution,* chap. 1; Taussig, *What Color Is the Sacred?,* chap. 28; Garfield, *Mauve;* Travis, *The Rainbow Makers.*

28. McKay, *Home to Harlem,* 107.

29. Beer, *The Mauve Decade.*

30. Blaszczyk, *The Color Revolution.*

31. Quoted in Eskilson, "Color and Consumption," 27.

32. Batchelor, *The Luminous and the Grey*, 48.

33. *New York Journal*, 17 October 1896, quoted in Hayward, *Consuming Fictions*, 90.

34. See Blackbeard, *R. F. Outcault's the Yellow Kid*.

35. Howells, *A Hazard of New Fortunes*, 259.

36. Gilman, "Then This."

37. See Pickering, "Decentering Sociology."

38. Delamare and Guineau, *Colors*, 102.

39. For a discussion of this shift focused on the appropriation of color and light by merchants and advertisers, see Leach, *Land of Desire*.

40. Godkin, "Chromo-Civilization." Originally published in the 24 September 1874 issue of the *Nation*.

41. Howells, *The Rise of Silas Lapham*, 59. Subsequent citations will appear parenthetically.

42. Batchelor, *Chromophobia*. See also Taussig, *What Color Is the Sacred?*

43. "Color in Industry," 88–90.

44. See Ribeyrol's introduction to her edited volume *The Colours of the Past in Victorian England*.

45. Le Rider, *Les couleurs et les mots;* see also Porée, "'Popularity' in Blue."

46. Pynchon, *Gravity's Rainbow*, 168, 169. The historical Rathenau spelled his given name "Walther," not "Walter."

47. For an extended treatment of these links in relation to German literature and philosophy, see Leslie's *Synthetic Worlds*.

48. Dewey, *Art as Experience*, 46, 11.

49. Williams, *Spring and All*, in *Imaginations*, 89, 134.

50. Rivers, "Primitive Color Vision," 49.

51. Gladstone, *Studies on Homer and the Homeric Age*, 3: 457. Subsequent citations will appear parenthetically.

52. For a discussion of the social and intellectual contexts of Gladstone's work, see Hickerson, "Gladstone's Ethnolinguistics."

53. Geiger, "On Colour-Sense in Primitive Times and Its Development," 51.

54. Magnus, *Die Entwickelung des Farbensinnes*, as translated by Deutscher in *Through the Language Glass*, 48. As Deutscher points out, this work is nearly identical to *Die geschichtliche Entwickelung des Farbensinnes*, which was published the same year.

55. See Hofstadter's *Social Darwinism in American Thought*, and Stocking, *Race, Culture, and Evolution*, for classic accounts of Larmarckianism in late-nineteenth-century thought. For "impressibility," see Schuller, *The Biopolitics of Feeling*.

56. Gladstone, "The Colour-Sense," 366. Subsequent citations will appear parenthetically.

57. Haeckel, "Ursprung und Entwickelung der Sinneswerkzeuge," as cited in Deutscher, *Through the Language Glass*, 49.

58. Bellmer, "The Statesman and the Ophthalmologist," 34.

59. Wallace, "On the Origin of the Colour-Sense," in *Tropical Nature, and Other Essays,* 247.

60. The same researchers worked on both aspects of "abnormal" color perception. For instance, the leading U.S. authority on color blindness, the ophthalmologist Benjamin Joy Jeffries, collaborated with Magnus to produce Jeffries, *Color-Names, Color-Blindness, and the Education of the Color-Sense in Our Schools.* See also Deutscher, *Through the Language Glass,* chap. 2; Musselman, *Nervous Conditions,* chap. 3; and Rossi, *The Republic of Color,* chaps. 3 and 4.

61. McLaughlin, *Painting in Oil,* 25, 22.

62. Church, *Colour,* 112. Church's book went through several U.S. and U.K. editions, including in 1887, 1891, 1897, 1905, and 1911—which explains why this quotation, originally printed before the color-sense debate hit its peak, came to be so widely cited.

63. Even color theories that were explicitly Darwinian rather than Lamarckian were folded back into arguments about the progressive stages of human color sensitivity. For instance, Christine Ladd-Franklin's "evolutionary" theory of color vision, by some accounts the most substantial American contribution to nineteenth-century color science, proposed that chromatic perception had developed over deep evolutionary time as the consequence of chemical changes undergone by a color-sensitive molecule located somewhere in the visual system of animals. Ladd-Franklin didn't think that different races saw colors differently; rather, she believed that color vision across species had evolved and that the mechanisms of that evolution explained certain incongruities between the physical and psychological explanations of color. Nonetheless, her work was cited alongside Magnus's and used to bolster a belief in a hierarchy of chromatic sensitivity in humans. See the way Ladd-Franklin is cited in Hicks, "Color in Public Schools," or discussed in Sloane, *The Visual Nature of Color,* chap. 22. For an excellent account of Ladd-Franklin's contribution to American color science, see Rossi, *The Republic of Color,* chap. 5.

64. Crofts, "Colour-Music," 257. See also Finck, "The Development of the Color-Sense," 26.

65. See Bellmer, "The Statesman and the Ophthalmologist," 41–42; Deutscher, *Through the Language Glass,* 63; and Magnus, "A Research Study of Primitive Peoples' Awareness and Perception of Colour," in Saunders, *The Debate about Color Naming,* 133–82.

66. Another prominent belief about racial color sensitivity held that the "lower" races had superior visual acuity because they devoted more of their mental "energy" to these baser faculties, while Europeans invested their powers in higher cognitive functions such as reasoning. The idea, which originated in early reports of non-Western peoples by Western observers and was associated with Spencer, provides another reason that the color sense proved so useful: it allowed Europeans to assert their dominance in an arena in which they supposedly came up short by shifting the field so that the keenness of sensory impressions depended on a cultivated nervous system. For an account of this Spencerian view, see Richards, "Getting a Result," 137.

67. Allen, *The Colour-Sense,* 35.

68. See my "The Articulate Eye."

69. Buck-Morss, "Aesthetics and Anaesthetics," 6.

70. I have adopted this formulation from Charlotte Ribeyrol, whose work explores "the inscription of chromatic materiality in nineteenth century art and literature," as she wrote in the description for "The Changing Colours of 19th Century Art and Literature," a conference held at the Ashmolean Museum, Oxford University, 2 June 2017.

71. Ellis, "The Colour-Sense in Literature," 714.

72. Ellis, "The Colour-Sense in Literature," 729. For examples of those who extended Ellis's work, see Pratt, *The Use of Color in the Verse of English Romantic Poets;* and Mead, "Color in Old English Poetry."

73. Cole, *Franz Boas,* 52–54.

74. Skard, "The Use of Color in Literature," 174.

75. For representative examples, see Eco, "How Culture Conditions the Colours We See"; and Sahlins, "Colors and Cultures."

76. Most prominently, Berlin and Kay's *Basic Color Terms* postulated a fixed set of basic and universal color terms that held across all cultures. There were of course objections. For an overview of the extensive literature on this topic, see Sloane, *The Visual Nature of Color;* and Deutscher, *Through the Language Glass.*

77. Woodworth, "The Puzzle of Color Vocabularies," 331.

78. For a nineteenth-century discussion of how the advent of synthetic dyes related to poetic descriptions of color and to Gladstone's thesis about the color sense, see Symonds, "In the Key of Blue," in *In the Key of Blue, and Other Prose Essays;* and Symonds, "Colour-Sense and Language," in *Essays Speculative and Suggestive.*

79. For an overview of this trope, see Batchelor, *Chromophobia,* chap. 4. See also Benjamin, "The Rainbow"; Barthes, "Cy Twombly," 166; Derrida, *The Truth in Painting,* 169; and Taussig, *What Color Is the Sacred?*

80. Huxley, *Heaven and Hell,* 59.

81. Kristeva, "Giotto's Joy," in *Desire and Language,* 221.

82. Bruce Smith's *The Key of Green,* by far the most ambitious and insightful consideration of color by a literary scholar in decades, illustrates how the opposition between language and color can motivate even literary analyses of sensory experience. For Smith, color offers an antidote to the habits and limitations of the linguistic turn, a way of turning "from language to the body" and of attuning literary scholars to the historical configurations of sensory experience. Smith, *The Key of Green,* 5.

83. Dewey, *Art as Experience,* 119. For more on how Whitehead reconstructs the relation between the abstract and the concrete, see Gaskill and Nocek, "Introduction" in *The Lure of Whitehead.*

84. For an indispensable survey of studies of literary color from Gladstone through the 1930s, see Skard, "The Use of Color in Literature."

85. Cézanne, quoted in Merleau-Ponty, "Eye and Mind," 180.

1. The Place of Perception

1. For readings of local color fiction that stress its insider/outsider dichotomy, even as they complicate it by interpreting it through the historical frameworks of imperialism, economic expansion, globalization, and aesthetic internationalism,

see Kaplan, "Nation, Region, Empire"; Foote, *Regional Fiction;* Fetterley and Pryse, *Writing Out of Place;* Lutz, *Cosmopolitan Vistas;* and Evans, *Before Cultures.*

2. Garland, quoted in Gerdts, *American Impressionism,* 147.

3. See, for instance, Garland, *Crumbling Idols,* 103–4. Subsequent citations are in parentheses in the text and refer to this edition.

4. In the terms of his day, de Piles was a *Rubeniste,* an advocate of Peter Paul Rubens and the colorist tradition that stretched back to the Venetians, against the *Poussinistes,* proponents of the classicism of Nicolas Poussin and its extension of the Florentine emphasis on drawing. For a landmark study of the philosophical implications of the "designo vs. colore" debate, see Lichtenstein, *The Eloquence of Color.*

5. De Piles, *The Principles of Painting,* 185; de Piles, *Cours de peinture par principes,* 304–5.

6. Gilpin, *Three Essays,* 3; emphasis in original.

7. Gilpin, *Remarks on Forest Scenery, and Other Woodland Views,* 2: 233. For an extensive treatment of black convex mirrors both before and after their use in picturesque landscape painting, see Maillet's *The Claude Glass.*

8. Maillet argues for the importance of the black mirror in de Piles's work in *The Claude Glass,* 108–11, 162.

9. Maillet, *The Claude Glass,* 32.

10. Plumptre, quoted in Maillet, *The Claude Glass,* 153.

11. Ruskin, *The Elements of Drawing,* 210.

12. Ruskin, *Modern Painters, Vol. 1,* vol. 3 of *The Works of John Ruskin,* library edition, 3: 614, 3: 140. Parenthetical citations to *The Works of John Ruskin* will follow the conventional method of volume number followed by page number.

13. Ruskin, *Elements of Drawing,* 22; emphasis in original.

14. Nicholson, "Of the Local Colour," 13.

15. Gullick and Timbs, *Painting Properly Explained,* 8, quoted in Oxford English Dictionary entry on "Local Colour."

16. McLaughlin, *Painting in Oil,* 38–39.

17. Parkhurst, "Sketching from Nature," 30.

18. Véron, *Æsthetics,* 228. Subsequent citations in parentheses in the text.

19. Peirce, *Collected Papers,* 5.42. Parenthetical citations for Peirce's *Collected Papers* will follow the conventional method of volume number followed by paragraph number.

20. Cross, *Color Study,* 17.

21. See Véron, *Æsthetics,* 231.

22. Sorensen discusses the importance of colored shadows for Goethe's color theory in *Seeing Dark Things.* Empiricists like Helmholtz held that such chromatic illusions were the product of mental judgments, while nativists like Hering explained them through the theory of opponent colors and thus grounded them in the mechanisms of color perception itself. For an overview of these debates, see Kargon, "The Logic of Color." And for specific examples, see Bezold, *The Theory of Color in Its Relation to Art and Art-Industry,* 152–53, and Rood, *Modern Chromatics,* 256, both of which summarize and support Helmholtz's view; also Hall, *American Journal of Psychology,* 198.

23. The shining exception here is Schroeder's "The Painting of Modern Light." I am grateful to the author of that essay for encouraging me, through both his work and our conversations, to sharpen the historical argument of this chapter.

24. Kapor, *Local Colour.* See also Kapor, "Couleur locale—a Pictorial Term Gone Astray?"

25. Howells, *Criticism and Fiction, and Other Essays,* 12–13.

26. "The Study of Local Color," 865.

27. Austin, *The Land of Little Rain,* 27.

28. Rewald, *The History of Impressionism,* quoted in Pizer, *Hamlin Garland's Early Work and Career,* 133. Also see Pizer for an account of Garland's involvement in the visual arts (133–40).

29. Garland, *Main-Travelled Roads,* 89, 90. Subsequent citations in parentheses in the text.

30. Garland, *A Son of the Middle Border,* 251. For more on Garland's interest in evolutionary theory, see Pizer, *Hamlin Garland's Early Work and Career,* 8–11; and Newlin, *Hamlin Garland,* 64–73.

31. See Pizer, *Realism and Naturalism in Nineteenth-Century American Literature;* Pizer, *Hamlin Garland's Early Work and Career;* and Evans, *Before Cultures,* introduction and chap. 3.

32. James Lane Allen, "Local Color," 13.

33. Austin, *The Land of Journey's Ending,* 437.

34. Garland, quoted in Pizer, *Hamlin Garland's Early Work and Career,* 21.

35. Garland, "Sanity in Fiction," 346.

36. Garland, quoted in Newlin, *Hamlin Garland,* 180; emphasis in original.

37. Grant Allen, *The Colour-Sense.*

38. Spencer, "The Valuation of Evidence," 162, 165, 166–67.

39. Wright, "Color-Shadows," 563.

40. Garland, quoted in Harkins, "Famous Authors," 44.

41. *Main-Travelled Roads,* 196; "Western Landscapes," 805; *Wayside Courtships,* 85.

42. For similar attempts to out-color the colorists, see Ruskin's description of a moment when "nature herself takes a colouring fit" (3: 285–86) and Goethe's description in *Theory of Colours* of his descent from the Brocken at twilight (19–20).

43. Garland, "Productive Conditions of American Literature," 695.

44. Garland, "Productive Conditions of American Literature," 690, 692.

45. Garland included this explanation in response to an inquiry from Eldon Hill, a PhD student writing about Garland in the late 1930s. Garland, "Garland on Veritism." The scholar Keith Newlin has posted a copy of the letter on his website.

46. Donald Pizer too recognizes an affinity between pragmatism and veritism on the grounds of their commitment to evolutionary theory, yet his characterization of James flattens out the complexities of verification into a philosophy bordering on relativism. Pizer, *Hamlin Garland's Early Work and Career,* 127.

47. James, *Pragmatism,* 574.

48. James, "Remarks on Spencer's Definition of Mind as Correspondence," 908.

49. Jane F. Thrailkill offers a similar revision of realism: "Works of literary realism . . . are not photographic representations of a real world elsewhere; they are condensations and expansions of human thought, sentience, and experience." Thrailkill, *Affecting Fictions,* 26.

50. In *A Natural History of Pragmatism* Joan Richardson offers a brilliant account of literary and philosophical efforts to assimilate the Darwinian information.

51. Garland, quoted in Harkins, "Famous Authors," 44.

52. For the definitive analysis of how in the 1890s representations of the local circulated in an international market of modern aesthetic styles, see Evans, *Before Cultures.*

53. See Wells, "Hamlin Garland's 1887 Travel Notebook." See also Pizer, *Hamlin Garland's Early Work and Career,* 140–41.

54. Garland, quoted in Pizer, *Hamlin Garland's Early Work and Career,* 140.

55. The first two appear in the posthumous "Chicago Studies" (c. 1890), published in Stronks, "A Realist Experiments with Impressionism," 49. For the others, see Garland, *Crumbling Idols,* 98, 99; *Main-Travelled Roads,* 8, 200, 202; quoted in Pizer, *Hamlin Garland's Early Work and Career,* 141; "Western Landscapes," 808; and *Main-Travelled Roads,* 201, 16, 25, 100.

56. Garland, "Western Landscapes," 808.

57. Garland, quoted in Pizer, *Hamlin Garland's Early Work and Career,* 140–41; Garland, *A Spoil of Office,* 40.

58. Respectively, see Kaplan, "Nation, Region, Empire"; Lutz, *Cosmopolitan Vistas;* and Foote, *Regional Fictions.* My account is closest to Lutz's.

59. Garland, "Salt Water Day," 394.

60. Garland, "Homestead and Its Perilous Trades," 4, 20.

61. Garland, "Salt Water Day," 392.

62. Garland, quoted in Pizer, *Hamlin Garland's Early Work and Career,* 141; Garland, *Rose of Dutcher's Coolly,* 69.

63. Elizabeth Mills Stetson, "The Management of Details," 18.

64. Austin, "The American Form of the Novel," 86.

65. Williams, *Spring and All,* in *Imaginations,* 112, 89. See Steiner's *The Colors of Rhetoric* for an account of how the relation between painting and writing plays out in modernism.

2. Charlotte Perkins Gilman and the Uses of Abstraction

1. Gilman, *The Living of Charlotte Perkins Gilman,* 121.

2. Baker, "*Prometheus* and the Quest for Color-Music."

3. Gilman, "Color Music," 140.

4. Pater, *The Renaissance,* 140; original in italics. Important studies of color music include Zilczer, "'Color Music'"; Zilczer, "Music for the Eyes"; Gage, *Color and Culture,* chap. 13; Gage, *Color and Meaning;* and Elder, *Harmony + Dissent.*

5. Gilman, *The Living of Charlotte Perkins Gilman,* 31.

6. Wilde, "The Critic as Artist" (1891), 398.

7. Rimington, *Colour-Music,* 7, 78. Subsequent citations in parentheses in the text.

8. Wilde, "The Critic as Artist," 406.

9. Gilman, *The Man-Made World.*

10. Gilman, "The Yellow Wall-Paper," 139. Subsequent citations in parentheses in the text.

11. Edelstein, "Charlotte Perkins Gilman and the Yellow Newspaper," 74; Lanser, "Feminist Criticism, 'The Yellow Wallpaper,' and the Politics of Color in America," 425; Heather Kirk Thomas, "'[A] Kind of "Debased Romanesque" with *Delirium Tremens,'"* 189; Heilman, "Overwriting Decadence," 177; "urine" quotation in Veeder, "Who Is Jane?," 65; "feces" quotation in Lane, *To Herland and Beyond,* 129; and Golden, *The Yellow Wall-Paper,* 77. See also Doran, *The Culture of Yellow,* chap. 3.

12. Lanser, "Feminist Criticism, 'The Yellow Wallpaper,' and the Politics of Color in America," 425.

13. Golden and Zangrando, *The Mixed Legacy of Charlotte Perkins Gilman;* Seitler, *Atavistic Tendencies,* 178.

14. The question Why yellow?, will no doubt continue to nag at some readers. Barbara Hochman has offered the most convincing answer in her short note about Gilman's use of Harriet Beecher Stowe's *House and Home Papers,* an 1864 series of articles on home decorating and domesticity. Hochman argues that many of the details of Stowe's text—which like Gilman's tale includes characters named John and Jennie, as well as a recommendation for yellow wallpaper—suggest that it "inspired Gilman to make a grotesque parody of domestic values by recasting Stowe's material." Barbara Hochman, "Stowe's *House and Home Papers,*" 84.

15. See Daston and Galison, *Objectivity,* chap. 5; and Crary, *Techniques of the Observer.*

16. Schuller, *The Biopolitics of Feeling.*

17. Eaton, *Colour, Art, and Empire,* 152–53.

18. Quoted in Gage, *Color and Meaning,* 192. For the discourse of nervousness in the United States, see Lutz, *American Nervousness, 1903.* And for a related account of the different ways that Rivers, Magnus, and Franz Boas linked color and civilization, see Rossi, *The Republic of Color,* chap. 4.

19. Silverman, *Art Nouveau in Fin-de-Siècle France,* 84, 85.

20. References to Ponza's theory abound in the periodicals of the late 1870s. Some representative takes include "Blue Glass Science," 121; "The Blue Glass Excitement"; and "A Pane of Blue Glass."

21. Babbitt, *The Principles of Light and Color,* 21, 80, 62.

22. The quotation comes from an advertisement for Berger's Matone lead paint from 1918, which pictures such a ward "for shell-shock and nerve cases" done up in "Firmament Blue" and "Sunlight Yellow." Reprinted in Gage, *Color and Meaning,* 208.

23. Garland, *Crumbling Idols,* 101.

24. Nordau, *Degeneration,* 27, 142, 24.

25. Ruskin, *The Elements of Drawing,* 161–62.

26. Charles Walter Stetson, *Charles Walter Stetson,* 128.

27. Pater, *The Renaissance,* 250; Seitler, *Atavistic Tendencies,* 185.

28. Charlotte Perkins [Gilman] Stetson, *Women and Economics,* 81–82. Subsequent citations in parentheses in the text.

29. Reed, *W. E. B. Du Bois and American Political Thought*. For an influential example, see Spencer, "The Comparative Psychology of Man."

30. Allen, *The Colour-Sense,* 254. Subsequent citations appear in parentheses in the text.

31. Gatschet, "Adjectives of Color in Indian Languages," 477.

32. Rivers, "Primitive Color Vision," 46. For more on the debates about color vision in anthropology, see Deutscher, *Through the Language Glass.*

33. Gilman, *The Home,* 153.

34. Seitler, *Atavistic Tendencies,* chap. 5. For a major statement of the argument, see Bederman, *Manliness and Civilization.* For a challenge to this critical consensus, see Judith A. Allen, *The Feminism of Charlotte Perkins Gilman.*

35. Gilman, *The Home,* 151.

36. For a brief introduction to "Through This," see Golden's comments in *The Yellow Wall-Paper,* 34; Gilman, "Through This," 34–37. Subsequent citations in parentheses in the text.

37. Wilde, *Decorative Art in America,* 11.

38. See Jones, *The Grammar of Ornament.* For discussions of historical ornament and the debate about how to understand the development of design motifs, see Frank, *Denman Ross and American Design Theory,* 8, 78–80; and Gombrich, *The Sense of Order.*

39. Gilman, *The Living of Charlotte Perkins Gilman,* 45–47, 112.

40. Ross, quoted in Frank, *Denman Ross and American Design Theory,* 82, 83.

41. Loos, "Ornament and Crime," 167; emphasis in original. Subsequent citations in parentheses in the text.

42. Loos, "Ladies' Fashion," quoted in Cheng, *Second Skin,* 78; Gilman, *The Dress of Women;* Gilman, *Herland,* 23.

43. Howells, *The Rise of Silas Lapham,* 189–90. Subsequent citations in parentheses in the text.

44. Cook, *The House Beautiful,* 48–49.

45. Frederic, *The Damnation of Theron Ware,* 323. Subsequent citations in parentheses in the text.

46. This phrase comes from the introductory note to an excerpt of the novel published in *Current Literature* 20, no. 1 (July–December 1896), 2–5.

47. De Kay, "Colors and the Mind."

48. Young, "Household Decoration," 46.

49. Wheeler, "The Philosophy of Beauty Applied to House Interiors," 7–8. Subsequent citations in parentheses in the text.

50. Mao, *Fateful Beauty,* 5.

51. Quoted in Kalba, "Fireworks and Other Profane Illuminations," 671.

52. Mao, *Fateful Beauty,* 103, 5.

53. Mao, *Fateful Beauty,* 107.

54. See Stocking, *Race, Culture, and Evolution,* esp. chap. 10, for a classic account of Larmarckianism in late-nineteenth-century thought. See also Hofstadter, *Social Darwinism in American Thought;* and Judith A. Allen, *The Feminism of Charlotte Perkins Gilman.*

55. Gilman, quoted in Knight, "'I Could Paint Still Life as Well as Any One on Earth,'" 490. Knight's article provides a useful and thoroughgoing account of Gilman's early artistic activities.

56. Another way to state this difference is to note that while Howells considered "this thing we call civilisation" to be "an affair of individuals" (*The Rise of Silas Lapham,* 103), Gilman approached it as a matter of populations.

57. Gombrich, *The Sense of Order,* 151.

58. Ngai, *Ugly Feelings,* 81.

59. Gilman, "Color Music," 140.

60. Schooling, "Color-Music," 349–56.

61. For a more detailed account of how the belief in an evolved and racially marked color sense contributed to the development of abstract color as an artistic medium, see my "The Articulate Eye."

62. Gilman, "Parlor-Mindedness," 8.

63. Gilman, *Herland,* 4. Subsequent citations in parentheses in the text.

64. Gilman, "Dr. Clair's Place," 178. Subsequent citations in parentheses in the text.

65. Gilman, "The Master of the Sunset," 253. Subsequent citations in parentheses in the text.

66. See Gaskill, "The Articulate Eye," 489–91.

67. See DeKoven's *Rich and Strange* for a related account of how Gilman's engagement with feminist reform efforts led her to forge a modernist style.

3. The Production and Consumption of a Child's View of Color

1. Hartmann, "Exhibition of Children's Drawings," 45. Subsequent citations in parentheses in the text. The 291 gallery exhibited three other shows of children's art in 1914, 1915, and 1916. See Greenough's *Modern Art and America,* 47–49, 543–47. Thanks to Sarah Blythe for leading me to Hartmann's review.

2. Hartmann's *Buddha: A Drama in Twelve Scenes* (1897) ends with an elaborate ekphrasis of a "concert of self-radiant colors" that rivals Gilman's "The Master of the Sunset" in its enthusiasm but sets the art of abstract color firmly within the spiritualist line that leads to Kandinsky rather than the alternative exemplified in Rimington.

3. Benjamin, "A Child's View of Color," 50, 51.

4. A full inventory of modernist invocations of the child's view of color would be too long to list here, but for representative instances see the discussions of Klee and Picasso in Gombrich, *The Preference for the Primitive;* Matisse, "Looking at Life with the Eyes of a Child"; Woolf, "Walter Sickert," 234; and Huxley, *The Doors of Perception.* For an instructive discussion of this trope, see Fineberg, *The Innocent Eye.*

5. Darwin, [A Biographical Sketch of a Young Infant], 376. I have used the translation provided by Marc Bornstein in "On the Development of Color Naming in Young Children." The anecdote about the colored tassel appears in the English version, Darwin, "A Biographical Sketch of a Young Child," 286, published in *Mind.*

6. James Mark Baldwin, *The Mental Development of the Child and the Race,* 1–2; Hall, "Child Study and Its Relation to Education," 695–96.

7. For an overview of child study and its relation to British literature, see Shuttleworth, *The Mind of the Child*. See also Sully, "Child Study and Education"; Chrisman, "Child-Study," 728; and Barus, "Methods and Difficulties of Child-Study," 113.

8. Sully, "The New Study of Children," 582. See also Levander, *Cradle of Liberty*.

9. Preyer, *The Mind of the Child*, 6–22.

10. Bellmer, "The Statesman and the Ophthalmologist," 34.

11. Rivers, "Primitive Color Vision," 55–56, 58.

12. Shinn, *Notes on the Development of a Child*, 25–56.

13. Binet and Simon, "The Development of Intelligence in the Child."

14. James Mark Baldwin, "A New Method of Child Study," 213–14. A revised version of this essay became chapter two of Baldwin's *The Mental Development of the Child and the Race*.

15. Sully, "The New Study of Children," 587.

16. Winch, "Colour Preferences of School Children," 65. For more on these studies, see Bornstein, "On the Development of Color Naming in Young Children," 88.

17. Goethe, *Theory of Colours*, 30.

18. Bailey, "The Editorial Point of View," 1.

19. Walter Smith, *Art Education, Scholastic and Industrial*, 63.

20. Bailey, "The World of Color," 107.

21. Bailey, "The Editorial Point of View," 1.

22. Dewey, *The School and Society*, 99.

23. Prang, Hicks, and Clark, *Color Instruction*, iii–iv.

24. Prang, Hicks, and Clark, *Color Instruction*, 7.

25. Hicks, "Color in Public Schools," 914. Hicks credits Barnes for the data on the Chinese children—and one imagines that to her contemporaries the liminal nature of their preferences (red-orange rather than red or orange) counted as evidence of the supposedly inassimilable character of Chinese immigrants. For more on Hicks's experiments, see Stankiewicz, *Roots of Art Educational Practice*, 99–100; and Blaszczyk, *The Color Revolution*, 49–50.

26. Hicks, "Color in Public Schools," 910.

27. Prang, Hicks, and Clark, *Color Instruction*, 13.

28. Munsell, *Color and an Eye to Discern It*, 14.

29. Munsell, "A Measured Training of the Color Sense," 363, 369, 378.

30. Munsell, *Color and an Eye to Discern It*, 14.

31. Munsell, *The Munsell Color System*.

32. Bailey, "The World of Color," 114.

33. See Landa and Fairchild, "Charting Color from the Eye of the Beholder," 442–43; Blaszczyk, *The Color Revolution*, chap. 2; and Rossi, *The Republic of Color*.

34. Bradley, *Color in the School-Room*, 14.

35. Bradley, *Color in the Kindergarten*, 4. Subsequent citations in parentheses in the text.

36. Bradley, *Elementary Color*, 79. For a detailed account of how Bradley arrived at his standards, see my "Learning to See with Milton Bradley."

37. These exercises come from Helden, *A Note on Color for Teachers of Elementary Schools*, published by the Milton Bradley Company and in many ways a direct exten-

sion of Bradley's system (45–46). Bradley describes similar exercises in *Color in the Kindergarten,* 40, and *Elementary Color,* 88–89, 96–97.

38. Bradley, *Elementary Color,* 6.

39. See also Bradley, *Elementary Color,* 43.

40. Bradley, *Elementary Color,* 6.

41. Munsell, *The Munsell Color System.*

42. Benjamin, "The Rainbow, or The Art of Paradise," 226–27.

43. Weinberg, *Color in Everyday Life,* 114.

44. Bowles, "Children's Books for Children," 377. Subsequent citations in parentheses in the text.

45. Field, "The Illustrating of Children's Books," 460, 458; reprinted as chapter 9 of Field's *Fingerposts to Children's Reading.*

46. Field, "The Illustrating of Children's Books," 459.

47. Greene and Hearn, *W. W. Denslow,* 24–28.

48. Field, "The Illustrating of Children's Books," 458. Field is referring to Denslow here.

49. Mancini, *Pre-Modernism,* 20.

50. Ball, "Mr. Prang's New Theory," no pagination.

51. The discourse around postimpressionism is full of references to the perceptions and artistic productions of children. As one example, see McCarthy's catalog essay "The Post-Impressionists," for the exhibition *Manet and the Post-Impressionists,* 7–13, as discussed by Rebecca Beasley in *Ezra Pound and the Visual Culture of Modernism.*

52. Bernstein, *Racial Innocence.* I owe this formulation to Erica Fretwell.

53. Tompkins, *Racial Indigestion,* 157.

54. Boylan and Morgan, *Kids of Many Colors,* 5.

55. Boylan and Morgan, *Kids of Many Colors,* 6.

56. Brown, "Child's Play," 20.

57. Gage, *Color and Meaning,* 192.

58. Leach, *Land of Desire,* 9. Blaszczyk's *The Color Revolution* tells the history of this commercial aesthetic through the color experts who produced and directed it.

59. Leach, *Land of Desire,* 60. In the September and October 1898 issues of the *Show Window,* Baum published William M. Couran's article on "The Scientific Arrangement of Color." Hearn, *The Annotated Wizard of Oz,* 61.

60. Baum, *The Art of Decorating Dry Goods Windows and Interiors,* 23. Subsequent citations in parentheses in the text.

61. Also quoted in Leach, *Land of Desire,* 83.

62. Baum, quoted in Leach, *Land of Desire,* 60–61.

63. Baum, *The Woggle-Bug Book,* 4. Subsequent citations in parentheses in the text.

64. Baum, quoted in Hearn, *The Annotated Wizard of Oz,* xl.

65. Hearn, *The Annotated Wizard of Oz,* xliii; quoted in Greene and Hearn, *W. W. Denslow,* 94.

66. Quoted in Hearn, *The Annotated Wizard of Oz,* xliii.

67. This perspective on *Oz* addresses a quibble among Baum's fans about why he

expanded the reach of the colors of each region in the first Oz sequel, *The Marvelous Land of Oz*. For example, whereas in *The Wonderful Wizard* the blues of Munchkin Country are confined to Munchkin-made products such as houses, fences, clothing, and rugs, in *The Marvelous Land* even the hues of the grass and the dirt change according to location. In the land of the Gillikins, "the grass is purple, the trees are purple, and the houses and fences are purple. . . . Even the mud in the roads is purple. But in the Emerald City everything is green that is purple here." Readers have attributed this expansion of the color scheme to Baum's poor memory of his own imaginary land, but if we consider that the author reflected on the *look* of the first book when preparing the sequel, the shift reflects Baum's appropriation of Denslow's Oz, the monochrome pages of illustrations that embellished the text.

68. For a broader account of color's role in modern media, see Neil Harris, *Cultural Excursions,* chap. 15.

69. Littlefield, "The Wizard of Oz"; Leach, *Land of Desire,* 252; Algeo, "The Wizard of Oz"; Hearn, *The Annotated Wizard of Oz,* 61.

70. Baum, *The Wonderful Wizard of Oz,* 12. Subsequent citations refer to this edition and will appear parenthetically.

71. I owe this point about brown being the more likely color of Kansas to Brad Evans.

72. Other critics have rightly drawn attention to the continued reliance on racist images and assumptions in *Oz*—from the pickaninny braids on the Wicked Witch to the Moorish architecture of the Emerald City—but what is striking, relative to Baum's other books, is how indirect these references are. See Ritter, "Silver Slippers and a Golden Cap," 186; St. John, "Lyman Frank Baum"; and Swartz, *Oz before the Rainbow,* 68.

73. For comparison, *The Marvelous Land of Oz* has only forty-eight total mentions of "green," even though much of its action takes place in and around the Emerald City, and the third and fourth books in the series have fewer than twenty-five apiece.

74. Culver, "What Manikins Want," 102, 107.

75. Taussig, *What Color Is the Sacred?,* 234.

76. Benjamin, "Attested Auditor of Books," 171, 172.

77. "The Book-Buyer's Guide," 574.

4. Lurid Realism

1. Warner, "Editor's Study," 55. Subsequent citations in parentheses in the text.

2. "Lurid," as a chromatic term, was in flux at the end of the nineteenth century. Though its original use signified a pale or wan color, it also denoted a "red glow," as in "flame mingled with smoke" in the eighteenth and nineteenth centuries. By the early twentieth century, the word had accomplished an almost complete reversal, meaning not "pale" but "bright," "gaudy," or "loud" in color. Warner certainly has the "red" definition in mind; he probably intends the "bright" one as well. *Oxford English Dictionary,* definitions 1, 2a, and draft additions September 2007.

3. Le Gallienne, "Miss Irwin's 'Color Poems,'" 8. Le Gallienne penned this letter to the editor to defend Beatrice Irwin's performance of *Color-Poem Afternoon,* a recital of her symbolist verses set to variously colored lights.

4. For readings of how color functions in these and other symbolist verses, see Meltzer, "Color as Cognition in Symbolist Verse," and Meltzer, "Rimbaud's 'Voyelles.'"

5. "Stephen Crane's Slum Story," *Chicago Daily Tribune*, 6 June 1896, reprinted in Monteiro, *Stephen Crane*, 104.

6. Loomis, quoted in appendix 8 in Stallman, *Stephen Crane*, 552–53.

7. Norris, "The Green Stones of Unrest," 87.

8. *Life* 32 (25 August 1898), reprinted in Weatherford, *Stephen Crane*, 154.

9. *Life* 32 (8 September 1898), reprinted in Weatherford, *Stephen Crane*, 154.

10. Norris, "The Green Stones of Unrest," 87.

11. Penn, "A Little Study of Stephen Crane," reprinted in Monteiro, *Stephen Crane*, 117, 119; Morrow, "Stories of the Slums," reprinted in Monteiro, *Stephen Crane*, 113.

12. Bill Brown, *The Material Unconscious*, 166, 241. Katherine Biers draws on an earlier version of the present chapter, published as "Red Cars with Red Lights and Red Drivers: Color, Crane, and Qualia," to establish a link between Crane's colors and the sensory excesses of mass culture, which she sees as threatening writing's "relationship to transcendence." Biers, *Virtual Modernism*, 56.

13. Sorrentino, *Stephen Crane*, 170–71. For an account of the critical tradition that classes Crane as an impressionist, see Nagel, *Stephen Crane and Literary Impressionism*.

14. This and all subsequent citations of Crane's primary works, unless noted otherwise, are from *Stephen Crane: Prose and Poetry* and will be cited parenthetically.

15. Binder, *Colour in Advertising*, 17.

16. Crane, *Letters*, 336.

17. Goethe, *Theory of Colours*, 192. Subsequent citations in parentheses in the text.

18. Halliburton, *The Color of the Sky*, 113.

19. Meggs and Purvis, *Meggs' History of Graphic Design*, 207. For an example, see J. H. Twachtman's chromolithograph poster for Harold Frederic's *The Damnation of Theron Ware*, which sets Celia Madden's bright red hair against a background of blue sky and green leaves. Library of Congress Prints and Photographs Division, http://www.loc.gov/pictures/item/2002720164/.

20. Marzio, *The Democratic Art, Chromolithography, 1840–1900*, 119.

21. Quoted in Greene and Hearn, *W. W. Denslow*, 28.

22. Meggs and Purvis, *Meggs' History of Graphic Design*, 158. See also Last, *The Color Explosion*, 243–63.

23. Crane introduces colors in contexts that magnify their vibrancy and scope to prime readers to envision later uses of chromatic imagery with similar intensity, and in doing so he fits Elaine Scarry's account of authors including "the material antecedents of the perception to be produced" to aid in the construction of realistic mental pictures. Scarry, *Dreaming by the Book*, 16. Though Scarry places too much explanatory emphasis on speculative claims that the techniques of successful writers "compl[y] with the structure of the human mind," her study lists many general methods for the rendering of vivid images that Crane directs toward colors (145).

24. Esteve, "A 'Gorgeous Neutrality,'" 678.

25. For an account of the "aesthetic" nature of Crane's battle scenes, especially in the final "competition over who has control over the colors," see Thrailkill, *Affecting Fictions,* 150.

26. Halliburton offers a related way to link Crane and Peirce in *The Color of the Sky,* 113. Peirce worked extensively on color—from his first and only monograph, *Photometric Researches* (1878), which offered a new theory of the relation between color and brightness in perception, to his entries for color words in the *Century* dictionary in the 1880s and on through his metaphysical work on qualia. Michael Rossi discusses these endeavors and ties them to Peirce's pragmatist semiotic in *The Republic of Color,* chap. 2.

27. Peirce, "On a New List of Categories," 287–98. Elsewhere Peirce describes "*quale*-consciousness" as "that kind of consciousness which is intensified by attention." Peirce, *Collected Papers,* 6.222.

28. Banfield, *The Phantom Table.* Dora Zhang builds on Banfield's argument, bringing it more directly into analytic notions of qualia. Zhang, "Naming the Indescribable." Critics such as Sorrentino who call Crane an impressionist follow a similar approach. One important exception to this tendency is Jesse Matz, in his *Literary Impressionism and Modernist Aesthetics.*

29. For a history of qualia that distinguishes Peirce's view from the one that dominates current debates, see Tim Crane, "The Origins of Qualia."

30. Chelifer, "The Rise of Stephen Crane," reprinted in Monteiro, *Stephen Crane,* 91; Paul M. Paine, "The Blue Blotch of Cowardice," reprinted in Weatherford, *Stephen Crane,* 152–53.

31. For a reading of Crane's work in terms of black marks on white surfaces, see Fried, *Realism, Writing, Disfiguration.*

32. Le Gallienne, "Miss Irwin's 'Color Poems.'"

33. Symonds, "In the Key of Blue," in *In the Key of Blue, and Other Prose Essays,* 3, 16.

34. Baudelaire, "The Salon of 1846," 53.

35. Meltzer, "Color as Cognition in Symbolist Verse," 253. Subsequent citations in parentheses in the text.

36. Kandinsky, *Concerning the Spiritual in Art,* 28.

37. Porée, "'Popularity' in Blue," 185. The second part of this quotation translates a passage from Jacques Le Rider's *Les couleurs et les mots.*

38. Merrill, *Pastels in Prose,* 203, 204.

39. For a description of this circle, including an account of Crane's place in it, see Evans, "What Travels?"

40. Hubbard, untitled, 123.

41. For examples of reviewers accusing Crane of "despotically us[ing] words out of their proper relevance and significance" and of invoking both symbolist poets and synesthesia as analogies, see Monteiro, *Stephen Crane,* 119, 91, 109–10, 136, 167.

42. Crane, "An Illusion in Red and White," 155, 154, 156.

43. Carson, *Autobiography of Red,* 4.

44. Chesnutt, *The Marrow of Tradition,* 277.

45. Brook Thomas, *Plessy v. Ferguson*, 43.

46. This "black and white" view of racial politics is, of course, too narrow. For a broader perspective, see Shoemaker, "How Indians Got to Be Red"; and Keevak, *Becoming Yellow*.

47. Blumenbach, "On the Natural Variety of Mankind," 201–2. See Gossett's *Race* and Rossi's *Republic of Color* for discussions of anthropological attempts to correlate race and color.

48. Chesnutt, *The House behind the Cedars*, 102.

49. Chesnutt, *The Marrow of Tradition*, 49.

50. For an account of the imbrication of race and media, with attention to color, see Brian Hochman, *Savage Preservation*, esp. chaps. 4 and 5.

51. Chesnutt, *The Wife of His Youth, and Other Stories of the Color Line*, 1, 10.

52. Douglass, "The Color Line," 575, 574.

53. Chesnutt, *The Wife of His Youth, and Other Stories of the Color Line*, 10, 24.

54. Goldsby, *A Spectacular Secret*, chap. 3.

55. Crane, *Letters*, 336.

56. Stein, *The Autobiography of Alice B. Toklas*, 66.

57. Stein, *The Autobiography of Alice B. Toklas*, 66; Mackey, "Other," 65. See Nielsen, *Reading Race*; DeKoven, *Rich and Strange;* North, *The Dialect of Modernism;* as well as the critical excerpts collected in DeKoven's Norton Critical Edition of Stein, *"Three Lives" and "Q.E.D."*

58. Doyle, "The Flat, the Round, and Gertrude Stein," 256. The bibliography of such work is too long to list here. In Stein's case, important interventions include Saldívar-Hull, "Wrestling Your Ally"; and English, *Unnatural Selections*.

59. Stein, *Narration*, 15. Carson quotes the first half of this passage.

60. Stein, *Three Lives*, 26, 30, 59, 17, 241. Subsequent citations in parentheses in the text.

61. I would like to thank Natalia Cecire and Yaron Aronowicz for drawing my attention to the conventional uses of color in "Melanctha."

62. Mullen, *The Cracks between What We Are and What We Are Supposed to Be*, 20.

63. Stein, *Tender Buttons*, 12, 24, 14, 9. Subsequent citations in parentheses in the text.

64. Stein, *Lectures in America*, 192, 191, 192.

65. There is a long history of explaining Stein's writing through her psychological research (both for praise and condemnation), but, surprisingly, her work on color perception has hardly been mentioned. Key examples include the reviews by Edith Sitwell, B. F. Skinner, and Michael Gold collected in Hoffman, *Critical Essays on Gertrude Stein;* Meyer, *Irresistible Dictation;* and Chodat, *Worldly Acts and Sentient Things*.

66. Solomons, "The Saturation of Colors," 51.

67. Stein, *Lectures in America*, 191. See Gass, "Gertrude Stein and the Geography of the Sentence," 63–123, for another reading of pointing in *Tender Buttons*, with reference to asparagus.

68. See Stein, "Transatlantic Interview—1946," where she glosses several passages from *Tender Buttons* in these terms.

69. Meyer, *Irresistible Dictation*, 80; original in italics.

70. James, *The Principles of Psychology*, 245–46. For a brief but insightful reading of how this passage relates to Stein's use of color, see Hejinian, "Two Stein Talks," 101–3.

71. Peirce, "[On a Method of Searching for the Categories]," 515–16.

72. Pound, *Gaudier-Brzeska*, 100.

73. For more on how the figure of color works across literature and the arts in modernism, see Gaskill, Street, and Yumibe, "Literature and the Performing Arts."

74. Dodge, "Speculations, or Post-Impressionism in Prose," 27–28.

75. Stein, *Geographical History of America*, 99.

76. Stein, "Lipchitz," 491, 492.

77. More than any other of Stein's readers, William H. Gass picks up on her links between color, qualia, and modernist writing in his work *On Being Blue*, which for all of its bawdy swagger culminates in a Steinian plea for the feelings words can create.

5. On Feeling Colorful and Colored in the Harlem Renaissance

1. Larsen, *Quicksand*, 1, 2. Subsequent citations in parentheses in the text.

2. For a discussion of the nationalist overtones of the American color industry during the war, see Blaszczyk, *The Color Revolution*, chap. 3.

3. Weinberg, *Color in Everyday Life*, xii, xi.

4. "Color in Industry," 85, 90. Subsequent citations in parentheses in the text. See also "The New Age of Color," 28.

5. "A Plea for Color," 24.

6. Taussig, *What Color Is the Sacred?*, 245, 155.

7. George Hutchinson has outlined the misunderstandings fostered by the collapse of the literary, political, and historical movements centered on the New Negro and Harlem in the 1920s into the catchall term "Harlem Renaissance." Surely the three major trends of the Negro Renaissance (the flowering of literary and artistic production by African Americans), the New Negro movement (the political and social advocacy for equal rights), and the Harlem Vogue (white America's brief fascination with Harlem and its nightlife) had distinct trajectories even as they overlapped. Though my analysis focuses on what might more properly be called the Negro Renaissance and the Harlem Vogue, I retain the moniker of the Harlem Renaissance for the sake of convention and for its virtue—which is also its scholarly weakness—of capturing the interrelated energies of the discourses and practices affiliated with the New Negro in the 1920s. Hutchinson, "Introduction."

8. Goethe, *Theory of Colours*, 30; Rivers, "Primitive Color Vision."

9. "Color in Industry," 86; Hornbeck, "Industry Courts the Rainbow," 114.

10. Larsen, quoted in Wall, *Women of the Harlem Renaissance*, 94.

11. Alain Locke, "The New Negro," 7. Historians have been better attuned to the material aspects of black urban life than have been literary critics; see, for instance, Davarian L. Baldwin, *Chicago's New Negroes*.

12. For neon, see Leach, *Land of Desire*, 342; for the introduction of floodlights

into the American cityscape, see Eskilson, "Color and Consumption," 23–24; and Blaszczyk, *The Color Revolution,* chap. 5.

13. Eskilson, "Color and Consumption," 24–25.

14. Quoted in Eskilson, "Color and Consumption," 27.

15. For color's role in the fashion industry, see Blaszczyk, *The Color Revolution,* chap. 7; and Leach, *Land of Desire,* 94, 313–17.

16. Billingsley, "Color—A Real Business Problem," 76.

17. Bentley, *Frantic Panoramas,* 15.

18. McKay, "A Negro Extravaganza," 63–64.

19. Fitzgerald, *The Great Gatsby,* 129, 49, 44. Walter Benn Michaels argues that Gatsby figures as a racial outsider within the structure of Fitzgerald's novel and its instantiation of the nativist imagination of modernist fiction. Michaels, *Our America.*

20. Williams, *Spring and All,* in *Imaginations,* 151, 95.

21. Eskilson, "Color and Consumption," 17.

22. Thaggert, *Images of Black Modernism,* 124.

23. Van Vechten, *Nigger Heaven,* 3, 6, 12. Subsequent citations in parentheses in the text.

24. Larsen, quoted in Wall, *Women of the Harlem Renaissance,* 120. Wall quotes from Larsen's application to the Harmon Foundation, a philanthropic organization that supported work by black writers and artists (and that awarded prizes to both Larsen and McKay). For more on Larsen's sartorial style, see Thadious M. Davis, *Nella Larsen, Novelist of the Harlem Renaissance,* 6, 223; and Hutchinson, *In Search of Nella Larsen,* 6.

25. For an analysis of the ways in which Helga's search for a viable identity proceeds according to images of desire and individuality defined by fashion discourse in the 1920s, see Simone Weil Davis, *Living Up to the Ads,* chap. 4.

26. Anne Hostetler tracks the ways in which "the fascination with clothing and color that marks [Helga's] character is an attempt to construct a female identity, to use her attractiveness as power." Hostetler, "The Aesthetics of Race and Gender in Nella Larsen's *Quicksand,*" 35.

27. Billingsley, "Color—A Real Business Problem," 22.

28. Hutchinson, *In Search of Nella Larsen,* 248.

29. For a similar account of the "ambivalence surrounding primitivist representation," see Judith Brown, *Glamour in Six Dimensions,* 125.

30. Fauset, *Plum Bun,* 13.

31. Thurman, *The Blacker the Berry,* 18.

32. Hughes, *The Big Sea,* 217. Subsequent citations in parentheses in the text.

33. Du Bois, *Writings,* 657; emphasis added.

34. McKay, *Home to Harlem,* 289. Subsequent citations in parentheses in the text.

35. McKay, "A Negro Extravaganza," 64.

36. An enabling condition of McKay's appeal for a greater color nomenclature that could bring attention to the variety of tones within the blanket category "Negro" is, of course, that the people in question are already marked as all belonging to one

race. As a result, the visual strategies described in this section are notably absent from passing novels.

37. Cosmetics played an ambiguous role in the history of the New Negro, providing venues for race pride and economic advancement on the one hand and enforcing white models of beauty on the other. See Peiss, *Hope in a Jar,* chap. 7; and Davarian L. Baldwin, *Chicago's New Negroes,* chap. 2.

38. Cheng, *Second Skin,* 78.

39. Fanon, *Black Skin, White Masks.* Paul Gilroy glosses epidermalization as a "historically specific system for making bodies meaningful by endowing them with qualities of 'color.'" Gilroy, *Against Race,* 46. Several recent critics, including Anne Cheng, have called for a closer look at the meaning and function of skin color in racial performance as a way to expand the analytic frame beyond the colonial context as presented by Fanon. For instance, Michelle Ann Stephens analyzes performances of blackness "that take us closer to the fleshy materiality of the black body, in all its tactile color and texture" to "offer pathways through and away from the skin of race as a product of colonial and biopolitical discourse." Stephens, *Skin Acts,* xii. See also Brooks, *Bodies in Dissent.*

40. Toomer, *Cane,* 3, 75, 52, 63, 64.

41. McKay uses "nigger-brown" as a color designation several times in *Home to Harlem* and *Banjo,* and in fact the term was in official circulation at least through the 1950s, when it appeared in the British Colour Council's *Dictionary of Colour Standards.* See Nead, "'Red Taffeta under Tweed.'"

42. The only other example of mauve skin that I've found occurs in the final pages of Larsen's *Passing:* as the party walks down the stairs after Clare has plummeted from the window, the narrator notices how "the golden brown" of a character's "handsome face changed to a queer mauve color" (213–14).

43. Davarian L. Baldwin, *Chicago's New Negroes,* 45.

44. Thurman, *The Collected Writings of Wallace Thurman,* 33.

45. Taussig, *What Color Is the Sacred?,* 15. See also Richard Dyer's argument that the distinctive feature of white embodiment is its relation to the spirit-made-flesh in the figure of Christ. Dyer, *White,* 24–25.

46. Taussig, *Mimesis and Alterity,* 20. Taussig presents this as Walter Benjamin's "enduring theme." For important accounts of the history of modern primitivism, see Torgovnick, *Gone Primitive;* and Torgovnick, *Primitive Passions.* For a deeper history, see Boas and Lovejoy, *Primitivism and Related Ideas in Antiquity.*

47. My reading here leans on Sianne Ngai's treatment of "irritation" as the defining trope of *Quicksand,* especially the way she reads the cabaret scene as an instance of Larsen's "subtle parody of the thematization of color in Harlem Renaissance fiction." Ngai, *Ugly Feelings,* 204. For studies that treat Helga's moments of abandon as pathways out of identitarian thinking, see Posnock, *Color and Culture;* and Esteve, *The Aesthetics and Politics of the Crowd in American Literature.*

48. Hurston, "How It Feels to Be Colored Me," 154.

49. Boas, "On Alternating Sounds," 50.

50. Evans, "Where Was Boas during the Renaissance in Harlem?," esp. 84, 86. For other accounts of the role the cultural concept played in the Harlem Renais-

sance, see Hutchinson, *The Harlem Renaissance in Black and White;* and Hegeman, *Patterns for America.* For Hurston and the Bradley top, see Herskovits, *The Anthropometry of the American Negro,* 5.

51. Quoted in Taussig, *What Color Is the Sacred?,* 83. For more on Malinowski's diaries, see Torgovnick, *Gone Primitive.*

52. Taussig, *What Color Is the Sacred?,* 94.

53. See, "'Spectacles in Color.'"

54. For a similar account of McKay's primitivism, see Stephens, *Black Empire,* chaps. 5 and 6.

55. Edwards, *The Practice of Diaspora,* 223.

56. McKay, *Banjo,* 164, 30. Subsequent citations in parentheses in the text.

57. Toomer, quoted in Darwin T. Turner, introduction to the 1975 edition of *Cane,* 128.

58. For more thorough accounts of Dewey's relation to the Harlem Renaissance, see Hutchinson, *The Harlem Renaissance in Black and White,* chaps. 1 and 6; and Posnock, *Color and Culture.*

59. Dewey, *Art as Experience,* 5–6. Subsequent citations in parentheses in the text.

60. Dewey, "Introduction to *Selected Poems of Claude McKay,*" 59. McKay asked Dewey to write the introduction, though the collection did not appear until five year's after McKay's death.

61. Dewey, *Experience and Nature,* 363.

62. Cheng, *Second Skin,* 167; Rancière, *The Politics of Aesthetics.*

63. Hutchinson, *In Search of Nella Larsen,* 202. Hutchinson found a reference to this encounter in an undated clipping from *Courier Magazine Section* titled "Those Were the Fabulous Days!" (544n13).

64. Taussig, *What Color Is the Sacred?,* 98.

Epilogue

1. For a discussion of Urban's designs, and of polychromy in modern architecture more generally, see Blaszczyk, *The Color Revolution,* chap. 8.

2. Batchelor, *Chromophobia,* 81.

3. Derrida, *The Truth in Painting,* 169; Bruce Smith, *The Key of Green,* 5.

4. Huxley, *The Doors of Perception,* 32, 14. Subsequent citations in parentheses in the text.

5. Huxley, *Heaven and Hell,* 59. Huxley published this book in 1956 as a sequel to *The Doors of Perception.*

6. Albers, *Interaction of Color,* 9. Subsequent citations in parentheses in the text.

7. Erickson, "A Progressive Education," 79; Molesworth, "Imaginary Landscape," 33.

8. Adamic, "Education on a Mountain," 520.

9. Rice, quoted in Adamic, "Education on a Mountain," 519, emphasis original.

10. BMC 1933–34 college catalog, quoted in Erickson, "A Progressive Education," 80.

11. Erickson, "A Progressive Education," 80. See also Mary Emma Harris, *The Arts at Black Mountain College,* esp. the section "Art as Experience" (16–46).

12. Albers, quoted in Díaz, *The Experimenters,* 15.

13. Ruskin, quoted in Weber, "Foreword," x.

14. So much for abstract expressionism. Albers, *Interaction of Color,* 68; Díaz, *The Experimenters,* 10.

15. For more on how the "discovery" that color was relative prompted Albers to drop established color systems from his course, see Albers, *Interaction of Color,* 60, 65.

16. Haraway, "Situated Knowledges," 582.

17. Stengers, *Thinking with Whitehead,* 113.

18. Albers, *Interaction of Color,* 48; Díaz, *The Experimenters,* 19, 26.

19. Albers, quoted in Díaz, *The Experimenters,* 43.

20. These articles rarely support Gladstone's thesis, but they raise it as an intriguing possibility. See, for instance, the "Colors" episode of NPR's *Radiolab* (season 20, episode 13); or Sassi, "The Sea Was Never Blue." For a recent novelistic use of the basic idea behind the color sense, see Jasper Fforde's *Shades of Grey* (2009), which takes place in Chromatacia, a society hierarchized according to the number and quality of colors its members are capable of seeing. Amusingly, Fforde casts Albert Munsell as an authoritarian figure involved in formulating Chromatacia's draconian laws.

21. Google it. Or see Wikipedia's entry "The Dress": https://en.wikipedia.org/wiki/The_dress.

22. Thanks to Mohan Matthen, who made this point at "Values of Color," Graduate Humanities Forum Symposium at the University of Pennsylvania, 20 February 2015.

Bibliography

Adamic, Louis. "Education on a Mountain: The Story of Black Mountain College." *Harper's,* April 1936, 516–29.

Albers, Josef. *Interaction of Color.* 50th anniversary edition. New Haven: Yale University Press, 2013.

Algeo, John. "The Wizard of Oz: The Perilous Journey." *Quest* 6, no. 2 (Summer 1993): 48–55.

Allen, Grant. *The Colour-Sense: Its Origin and Development: An Essay in Comparative Psychology.* London: Trübner, 1879.

Allen, James Lane. "Local Color." *Critic* 8 (9 January 1886): 13–14.

Allen, Judith A. *The Feminism of Charlotte Perkins Gilman.* Chicago: University of Chicago Press, 2009.

Austin, Mary. "The American Form of the Novel" (1922). In *Beyond Borders: The Selected Essays of Mary Austin,* edited by Reuben J. Ellis, 83–88. Carbondale: Southern Illinois University Press, 1996.

——. *The Land of Journey's Ending.* Facsimile of original 1924 edition. Santa Fe, N.M.: Sunstone Press, 2007.

——. *The Land of Little Rain* (1903). New York: Modern Library Classics, 2003.

Babbitt, Edwin D. *The Principles of Light and Color: The Classic Study of the Healing Power of Color.* Edited and annotated by Faber Birren (1878). New Hyde Park, N.Y.: University Books, 1967.

Bailey, Henry Turner. "The Editorial Point of View." *School Arts Magazine* 14, no. 1 (September 1914): 1–6.

——. "The World of Color." *School Arts Books* 10, no. 2 (October 1910): 107–21.

Baker, James M. "*Prometheus* and the Quest for Color-Music: The World Premiere of Scriabin's *Poem of Fire* with Lights, New York, March 20, 1915." In *Music and Modern Art,* edited by James Leggio, 61–96. New York: Routledge, 2001.

Baldwin, Davarian L. *Chicago's New Negroes: Modernity, the Great Migration, and Black Urban Life.* Chapel Hill: University of North Carolina Press, 2007.

Baldwin, James Mark. *The Mental Development of the Child and the Race.* New York: Macmillan, 1895.

——. "A New Method of Child Study." *Science* 21, no. 533 (14 April 1893): 213–14.

Ball, Katherine M. "Mr. Prang's New Theory." *Modern Art* 1, no. 2 (Spring 1893): no pagination.

Ball, Philip. *Bright Earth: Art and the Invention of Color*. Chicago: University of Chicago Press, 2001.

Banfield, Ann. *The Phantom Table: Woolf, Fry, Russell, and the Epistemology of Modernism*. Cambridge: Cambridge University Press, 2000.

Barthes, Roland. "Cy Twombly: Works on Paper." In *The Responsibility of Forms: Critical Essays on Music, Art, and Representation*, translated by Richard Howard, 157–76. Berkeley: University of California Press, 1985.

Barus, Annie Howes. "Methods and Difficulties of Child-Study." *Forum* 20 (September 1895): 113–19.

Batchelor, David. *Chromophobia*. London: Reaktion Books, 2000.

———. *The Luminous and the Grey*. London: Reaktion Books, 2014.

Baudelaire, Charles. "The Salon of 1846." In *Selected Writings on Art and Artists*. Translated by P. E. Charvet, 47–107. Cambridge: Cambridge University Press, 1981.

Baum, L. Frank. *The Art of Decorating Dry Goods Windows and Interiors: A Complete Manual of Window Trimming, Designed as an Educator in All the Details of the Art, According to the Best Accepted Methods, and Treating Fully Every Important Subject*. Chicago: Show Window Publishing, 1900.

———. *The Marvelous Land of Oz*. Chicago: Reilly and Britton, 1904.

———. *The Woggle-Bug Book*. Illustrated by Ike Morgan. Chicago: Reilly and Britton, 1905.

———. *The Woggle-Bug Book: A Facsimile Reproduction*. Illustrated by Ike Morgan. Introduction by Douglas G. Greene. Delmar, N.Y.: Scholars' Facsimiles and Reprints, 1978.

———. *The Wonderful Wizard of Oz*. Illustrations by W. W. Denslow. Chicago: George M. Hill, 1900.

Baum, L. Frank, and W. W. Denslow. *Father Goose, His Book*. Chicago: George M. Hill, 1899.

Beasley, Rebecca. *Ezra Pound and the Visual Culture of Modernism*. Cambridge: Cambridge University Press, 2007.

Bederman, Gail. *Manliness and Civilization: A Cultural History of Gender and Race in the United States, 1880–1917*. Chicago: University of Chicago Press, 1995.

Beer, Thomas. *The Mauve Decade: American Life at the End of the Nineteenth Century*. New York: Alfred A. Knopf, 1926.

Bellmer, Elizabeth Henry. "The Statesman and the Ophthalmologist: Gladstone and Magnus on the Evolution of Human Colour Vision; One Small Episode of the Nineteenth-Century Darwinian Debate." *Annals of Science* 56, no. 1 (1999): 25–45.

Benjamin, Walter. "Attested Auditor of Books" (from *One-Way Street*, 1928). In *The Work of Art in the Age of Its Mechanical Reproducibility, and Other Writings on Media*. Edited by Michael W. Jennings, Brigid Doherty, and Thomas Y. Levin, 171–72. Cambridge, Mass.: Harvard University Press, 2008.

———. "A Child's View of Color" (1914–15). In *Selected Writings*, vol. 1, *1913–1926*, edited by Marcus Bullock and Michael W. Jennings. Cambridge, Mass.: Belknap Press of Harvard University Press, 1996.

———. "The Rainbow: A Conversation about Imagination." In *Early Writings:*

1910–1917, edited and translated by Howard Eiland, 214–23. Cambridge, Mass.: Belknap Press of Harvard University Press, 2011.

———. "The Rainbow, or The Art of Paradise." In *Early Writings: 1910–1917,* edited and translated by Howard Eiland, 224–27. Cambridge, Mass.: Belknap Press of Harvard University Press, 2011.

Bentley, Nancy. *Frantic Panoramas: American Literature and Mass Culture, 1870–1920.* Philadelphia: University of Pennsylvania Press, 2009.

Berlin, Brent, and Paul Kay. *Basic Color Terms: Their Universality and Evolution* (1969). Chicago: University of Chicago Press, 1991.

Bernstein, Robin. *Racial Innocence: Performing American Childhood from Slavery to Civil Rights.* New York: New York University Press, 2011.

Bezold, Wilhelm von. *The Theory of Color in Its Relation to Art and Art-Industry.* Translated by S. R. Koehler. Boston: Louis Prang, 1876.

Biers, Katherine. *Virtual Modernism: Writing and Technology in the Progressive Era.* Minneapolis: University of Minnesota Press, 2013.

Billingsley, Allen L. "Color—A Real Business Problem." *Nation's Business* 16 (August 1928): 21–22, 73–76.

Binder, Joseph. *Colour in Advertising.* London: Studio Publications, 1934.

Binet, Alfred, and Théodore Simon. "The Development of Intelligence in the Child." Translated by E. S. Kiffe. In *The Development of Intelligence in Children,* edited by H. H. Goddard, 182–273. Baltimore: Williams and Wilkins, 1908.

Blackbeard, Bill. *R. F. Outcault's the Yellow Kid: A Centennial Celebration of the Kid Who Started the Comics.* Northampton, Mass.: Kitchen Sink Press, 1995.

Blaszczyk, Regina Lee. *The Color Revolution.* Cambridge: MIT Press, 2012.

"The Blue Glass Excitement." *Forest and Stream* 8, no. 4 (1 March 1877): 52.

"Blue Glass Science." *Scientific American* 36, no. 8 (24 February 1877): 121.

Blumenbach, Johan Friedrich. "On the Natural Variety of Mankind" (1775). Translated by Thomas Bendyshe. In *Slavery, Abolition, and Emancipation: Writings from the British Romantic Period,* vol. 8, *Theories of Race,* edited by Peter J. Kitson, 141–211. London: Pickering and Chatto, 1999.

Boas, Franz. "On Alternating Sounds." *American Anthropologist* 2, no. 1 (January 1889): 47–54.

Boas, George, and Arthur O. Lovejoy. *Primitivism and Related Ideas in Antiquity.* Baltimore: Johns Hopkins University Press, 1935.

"The Book-Buyer's Guide." *Critic* 37, no. 6 (December 1900): 566–78.

Boring, Edwin G. *A History of Experimental Psychology.* New York: Century, 1929.

Bornstein, Marc H. "On the Development of Color Naming in Young Children: Data and Theory." *Brain and Language* 26 (1985): 72–93.

Bowles, J. M. "Children's Books for Children." *Brush and Pencil* 12, no. 6 (September 1903): 377–87.

Boylan, Grace Duffie, and Ike Morgan. *Kids of Many Colors* (1901). New York: Hurst, 1909.

Bradley, Milton. *Color in the Kindergarten: A Manual of the Theory of Color and the Practical Use of Color Material in the Kindergarten.* Springfield, Mass.: Milton Bradley, 1893.

———. *Color in the School-Room: A Manual for Teachers.* Springfield, Mass.: Milton Bradley, 1890.

———. "The Color Question Again." *Science* 19, no. 477 (25 March 1892): 175–76.

———. *Elementary Color.* Introduction by Henry Lefavour. Springfield, Mass.: Milton Bradley, 1895.

British Colour Council. *The British Colour Council Dictionary of Colour Standards: A List of Colour Names Referring to the Colours Shown in the Companion Volume.* Vol. 1. 2nd ed. London: British Colour Council, 1951.

Brooks, Daphne. *Bodies in Dissent: Spectacular Performances of Race and Freedom, 1850–1910.* Durham, N.C.: Duke University Press, 2006.

Brown, Bill. *The Material Unconscious: American Amusement, Stephen Crane, and the Economics of Play.* Cambridge, Mass.: Harvard University Press, 1996.

Brown, Gillian. "Child's Play." In *The American Child: A Cultural Studies Reader,* edited by Caroline Levander and Carol J. Singley, 13–39. New Brunswick, N.J.: Rutgers University Press, 2003.

Brown, Judith. *Glamour in Six Dimensions: Modernism and the Radiance of Form.* Ithaca, N.Y.: Cornell University Press, 2009.

Buck-Morss, Susan. "Aesthetics and Anaesthetics: Walter Benjamin's Artwork Essay Reconsidered." *October* 62 (Autumn 1992): 3–41.

Burke, Kenneth. *Permanence and Change: An Anatomy of Purpose* (1935). Third edition. Berkeley: University of California Press, 1984.

Byrne, Alex, and David R. Hilbert. *Readings on Color.* Vol. 1, *The Philosophy of Color.* Cambridge: MIT Press, 1997.

Carson, Anne. *Autobiography of Red: A Novel in Verse.* New York: Vintage Books, 1998.

Cheng, Anne Anlin. *Second Skin: Josephine Baker and the Modern Surface.* New York: Oxford University Press, 2011.

Chesnutt, Charles. *The House behind the Cedars* (1900). New York: Modern Library, 2003.

———. *The Marrow of Tradition.* Boston: Houghton, Mifflin, 1901.

———. *The Wife of His Youth, and Other Stories of the Color Line.* Boston: Houghton, Mifflin, 1899.

Chevreul, Michel Eugène. *The Principles of Harmony and Contrast of Colors, and Their Application to the Arts* (1854). 2nd ed. London: Longman, Brown, Green, and Longmans, 1855.

Chirimuuta, M. *Outside Color: Perceptual Science and the Puzzle of Color in Philosophy.* Cambridge: MIT Press, 2015.

Chodat, Robert. *Worldly Acts and Sentient Things: The Persistence of Agency from Stein to DeLillo.* Ithaca, N.Y.: Cornell University Press, 2008.

Chrisman, Oscar. "Child-Study: A New Department of Education." *Forum* 16 (February 1894): 728–36.

Church, A. H. *Colour: An Elementary Manual for Students.* London: Cassell, Petter, and Galpin, 1872.

Cole, Douglas. *Franz Boas: The Early Years, 1858–1906.* Seattle: University of Washington Press, 1999.

"Color in Industry." *Fortune* 1 (February 1930): 85–94.

Cook, Clarence. *The House Beautiful* (1881). New York: Dover, 1995.

Crane, Stephen. *Stephen Crane: Prose and Poetry.* Edited by J. C. Levenson. New York: Library of America, 1984.

———. "An Illusion in Red and White." In *The University of Virginia Edition of "The Works of Stephen Crane,"* vol. 8, edited by Fredson Bowers, 154–59. Charlottesville: University of Virginia Press, 1969.

———. *Stephen Crane: Letters.* Edited by R. W. Stallman and Lillian Gilkes. New York: New York University Press, 1960.

———. *War Is Kind.* New York: F. A. Stokes, 1899.

Crane, Stephen, and University of Virginia. *The University of Virginia Edition of "The Works of Stephen Crane."* Vol. 8. Charlottesville: University of Virginia Press, 1969.

Crane, Tim. "The Origins of Qualia." In *History of the Mind-Body Problem,* edited by Tim Crane and Sarah Patterson, 169–94. London: Routledge, 2000.

Crary, Jonathan. *Techniques of the Observer: On Vision and Modernity in the Nineteenth Century.* Cambridge: MIT Press, 1990.

———. *Suspensions of Perception: Attention, Spectacle, and Modern Culture.* Cambridge: MIT Press, 1999.

Crofts, J. "Colour-Music." *Gentleman's Magazine* 259, no. 1857 (September 1885): 251–71.

Cross, Anson K. *Color Study: A Manual for Teachers and Students.* Boston: Ginn, 1896.

Culver, Stuart. "What Manikins Want: *The Wonderful Wizard of Oz* and *The Art of Decorating Dry Goods Windows." Representations* 21 (Winter 1988): 97–116.

Current Literature. Introductory note to Harold Frederic, *The Damnation of Theron Ware* (1896). *Current Literature* 20, no. 1 (July–December 1896): 2–5.

Darwin, Charles. "A Biographical Sketch of a Young Child." *Mind* 2, no. 7 (June 1877): 285–94.

———. [A Biographical Sketch of a Young Infant]. In German. *Kosmos* 1 (1877): 367–76.

Daston, Lorraine, and Peter Galison, *Objectivity* (2007). Cambridge, Mass.: Zone Books, 2010.

Davis, Simone Weil. *Living Up to the Ads: Gender Fictions of the 1920s.* Durham, N.C.: Duke University Press, 2000.

Davis, Thadious M. *Nella Larsen, Novelist of the Harlem Renaissance: A Woman's Life Unveiled.* Baton Rouge: Louisiana State University Press, 1994.

DeKoven, Marianne. *Rich and Strange: Gender, History, Modernism.* Princeton: Princeton University Press, 1991.

Delamare, François, and Bernard Guineau. *Colors: The Story of Dyes and Pigments.* New York: Harry N. Abrams, 2000.

Denslow, W. W. Illustration of Stephen Crane's poem "I Stood upon a High Place." *Philistine* 8, no. 4 (March 1899): back cover.

Derrida, Jacques. *The Truth in Painting.* Translated by Geoff Bennington and Ian McLeod. Chicago: University of Chicago Press, 1987.

Deutscher, Guy. *Through the Language Glass: Why the World Looks Different in Other Languages.* New York: Metropolitan Books, Henry Holt, 2010.

Dewey, John. *Art as Experience* (1934). New York: Perigee Books, 1980.

——. *Experience and Nature* (1925). Mineola, N.Y.: Dover, 1958.

——. "Introduction to *Selected Poems of Claude McKay*" (1953). In *The Later Works, 1925–1953,* vol. 17, *1885–1953, Miscellaneous Writings,* edited by Jo Ann Boydston, 58–60. Carbondale: Southern Illinois University Press, 1990.

——. *The School and Society* (1900). Chicago: University of Chicago Press, 1990.

Díaz, Eva. *The Experimenters: Chance and Design at Black Mountain College.* Chicago: University of Chicago Press, 2015.

Dodge, Mable. "Speculations, or Post-Impressionism in Prose." In *Critical Essays on Gertrude Stein,* edited by Michael J. Hoffman, 27–31. Boston: G. K. Hall, 1986.

Doran, Sabine. *The Culture of Yellow, or The Visual Politics of Late Modernity.* London: Bloomsbury, 2013.

Douglass, Frederick. "The Color Line." *North American Review* 132 (June 1881): 567–77.

Doyle, Laura. "The Flat, the Round, and Gertrude Stein: Race and the Shape of Modern(ist) History." *Modernism/Modernity* 7, no. 2 (April 2000): 249–71.

Du Bois, W. E. B. *Writings.* New York: Library of America, 1987.

Dyer, Richard. *White.* London: Routledge, 1997.

Eaton, Natasha. *Colour, Art, and Empire: Visual Culture and the Nomadism of Representation.* London: I. B. Tauris, 2013.

Eco, Umberto. "How Culture Conditions the Colours We See." In *On Signs,* edited by Marshall Blonsky, 157–75. Baltimore: The Johns Hopkins University Press, 1985.

Edelstein, Sari. "Charlotte Perkins Gilman and the Yellow Newspaper," *Legacy* 24, no. 1 (2007): 72–92.

Edwards, Brent Hayes. *The Practice of Diaspora: Literature, Translation, and the Rise of Black Internationalism.* Cambridge, Mass.: Harvard University Press, 2003.

Elder, Bruce R. *Harmony + Dissent: Film and Avant-Garde Art Movements in the Early Twentieth Century.* Waterloo, Ontario: Wilfrid Laurier University Press, 2008.

Ellis, Havelock. "The Colour-Sense in Literature." *Contemporary Review* 69 (1896): 714–29.

English, Daylanne K. *Unnatural Selections: Eugenics in American Modernism and the Harlem Renaissance.* Chapel Hill: University of North Carolina Press, 2004.

Erickson, Ruth. "A Progressive Education." In *Leap before You Look: Black Mountain College, 1933–1957,* by Helen Molesworth, with Ruth Erickson, 76–85. New Haven: Yale University Press, 2015.

Eskilson, Stephen. "Color and Consumption." *Design Issues* 18, no. 2 (Spring 2002): 17–29.

Esteve, Mary. *The Aesthetics and Politics of the Crowd in American Literature.* Cambridge: Cambridge University Press, 2007.

——. "A 'Gorgeous Neutrality': Stephen Crane's Documentary Anaesthetics." *ELH* 62, no. 3 (Autumn 1995): 663–89.

Evans, Brad. *Before Cultures: The Ethnographic Imagination in American Literature, 1865–1920.* Chicago: University of Chicago Press, 2005.

——. "What Travels? The Movement of Movements, or Ephemeral Bibelots from Paris to Lansing, with Love." In *Print Culture Histories beyond the Metropolis,* edited by James J. Connolly, Patrick Collier, Frank Felsenstein, Kenneth R. Hall, and Robert G. Hall, 181–214. Toronto: University of Toronto Press, 2016.

———. "Where Was Boas during the Renaissance in Harlem? Diffusion, Race, and the Cultural Paradigm in the History of Anthropology." In *Central Sites, Peripheral Visions,* edited by Richard Handler, 69–98. Madison: University of Wisconsin Press, 2006.

Fanon, Frantz. *Black Skin, White Masks.* Translated by Charles Lam Markmann. New York: Grove, 1967.

Fauset, Jessie Redmon. *Plum Bun: A Novel without a Moral.* New York: Frederick A. Stokes, 1929.

Fetterley, Judith, and Marjorie Pryse. *Writing Out of Place: Regionalism, Women, and American Literary Culture.* Urbana: University of Illinois Press, 2003.

Fforde, Jasper. *Shades of Grey: The Road to High Saffron.* New York: Penguin, 2009.

Field, Walter Taylor. *Fingerposts to Children's Reading.* Chicago: A. C. McClurg, 1907.

———. "The Illustrating of Children's Books." *Dial* 35 (16 December 1903): 457–60.

Finck, Henry T. "The Development of the Color-Sense." *Littell's Living Age* 144, no. 1855 (3 January 1880): 19–28.

Fineberg, Jonathan. *The Innocent Eye: Children's Art and the Modernist Artist.* Princeton: Princeton University Press, 1997.

Fitzgerald, F. Scott. *The Great Gatsby* (1925). New York: Scribner, 2004.

Foote, Stephanie. *Regional Fictions: Culture and Identity in Nineteenth-Century American Literature.* Madison: University of Wisconsin Press, 2001.

Frank, Marie. *Denman Ross and American Design Theory.* Hanover, N.H.: University of New England Press, 2011.

Frederic, Harold. *The Damnation of Theron Ware, or Illumination* (1896). New York: Penguin, 1986.

Fried, Michael. *Realism, Writing, Disfiguration: On Thomas Eakins and Stephen Crane.* Chicago: University of Chicago Press, 1987.

Gage, John. *Color and Culture: Practice and Meaning from Antiquity to Abstraction.* Berkeley: University of California Press, 1993.

———. *Color and Meaning: Art, Science, and Symbolism.* Berkeley: University of California Press, 2000.

Garfield, Simon. *Mauve: How One Man Invented a Color That Changed the World.* New York: W. W. Norton, 2001.

Garland, Hamlin. *Crumbling Idols: Twelve Essays on Art Dealing Chiefly with Literature, Painting, and the Drama* (1894). Edited by Jane Johnson. Cambridge, Mass.: Belknap Press of Harvard University Press, 1960.

———. "Garland on Veritism." Accessed November 26, 2016. http://people.uncw.edu/newlink/garland/veritism.htm.

———. "Homestead and Its Perilous Trades: Impressions of a Visit." *McClure's Magazine* 3, no. 1 (June 1894): 3–20.

———. *Main-Travelled Roads* (1891). Lincoln: Bison Books of Nebraska University Press, 1995.

———. "Productive Conditions of American Literature." *Forum* 17 (August 1894): 690–98.

———. *Rose of Dutcher's Coolly.* Chicago: Stone and Kimball, 1895.

———. "Salt Water Day." *Cosmopolitan* 13, no. 4 (August 1892): 387–94.

———. "Sanity in Fiction." *North American* 176, no. 556 (March 1903): 336–48.

———. *A Son of the Middle Border* (1917). St. Paul, Minn.: Borealis Books, 2007.

———. *A Spoil of Office: A Story of the Modern West.* New York: D. Appleton, 1897.

———. *Wayside Courtships.* New York: D. Appleton, 1897.

———. "Western Landscapes." *Atlantic Monthly* 72, no. 434 (December 1893): 809–14.

Gaskill, Nicholas. "The Articulate Eye: Color-Music, the Color Sense, and the Language of Abstraction." *Configurations* 25, no. 4 (2017): 475–505.

———. "Learning to See with Milton Bradley." In *Bright Modernity,* edited by Regina Lee Blaszczyk and Uwe Spiekermann, 55–73. Basingstoke, U.K.: Palgrave, 2017.

———. "Red Cars with Red Lights and Red Drivers: Color, Crane, and Qualia." *American Literature* 81, no. 4 (2009): 719–45.

Gaskill, Nicholas, and A. J. Nocek. "Introduction: An Adventure of Thought." In *The Lure of Whitehead,* edited by Nicholas Gaskill and A. J. Nocek, 1–40. Minneapolis: University of Minnesota Press, 2014.

Gaskill, Nicholas, Sarah Street, and Joshua Yumibe. "Literature and the Performing Arts." In *A Cultural History of Colour in the Modern Age,* edited by Anders Steinvall and Sarah Street. London: Bloomsbury, forthcoming 2019.

Gass, William H. "Gertrude Stein and the Geography of the Sentence." In *The World within the Word,* 63–123. New York: Basic, 1976.

———. *On Being Blue: A Philosophical Inquiry* (1976). New York: NYRB Classics, 2014.

Gatschet, A. S. "Adjectives of Color in Indian Languages." *American Naturalist* 13, no. 8 (1879): 475–81.

Geiger, Lazarus. "On Colour-Sense in Primitive Times and Its Development." In *Contributions to the History of the Development of the Human Race: Lectures and Dissertations,* translated by David Asher, 48–63. London: Trübner, 1880.

Gerdts, William H. *American Impressionism.* New York: Abbeville Press, 1984.

Gilman, Charlotte Perkins. *Art Gems for the Home and Fireside.* Providence, R.I.: J. A. and R. A. Reid, 1888.

———. "Color Music." *Forerunner* 6, no. 6 (May 1915): 140.

———. "Dr. Clair's Place." In *"The Yellow Wall-Paper" and Selected Stories of Charlotte Perkins Gilman,* edited and introduced by Denise K. Knight, 177–84. Newark: University of Delaware Press, 1994.

———. *The Dress of Women: A Critical Introduction to the Symbolism and Sociology of Clothing.* Edited and introduced by Michael R. Hill and Mary Jo Deegan. Westport, Conn.: Greenwood Press, 2002.

———. *Herland* (1915). New York: Dover, 1998.

———. *The Home: Its Work and Influence* (1903). Urbana: University of Illinois Press, 1972.

———. *The Living of Charlotte Perkins Gilman.* New York: Appleton-Century, 1935.

———. *The Man-Made World, or Our Androcentric Culture.* New York: Charlton, 1911.

————. "The Master of the Sunset." *Forerunner* 6, no. 10 (October 1915): 253–58.

————. "Parlor-Mindedness." *Forerunner* 6, no. 5 (March 1910): 6–10.

————. "Then This." *Forerunner* 1, no. 1 (November 1909): 1.

————. "Through This." In *The Yellow Wall-Paper: A Sourcebook and Critical Edition*, edited by Catherine J. Golden, 34–37. New York: Routledge, 2004.

————. "The Yellow Wall-Paper." In *The Yellow Wall-Paper: A Sourcebook and Critical Edition*, edited by Catherine J. Golden, 131–44. New York: Routledge, 2004.

Gilpin, William. *Remarks on Forest Scenery, and Other Woodland Views*. Vol. 2. Edited by Sir Thomas Dick Lauder. Edinburgh: Fraser, 1834.

————. *Three Essays: "On Picturesque Beauty"; "On Picturesque Travel"; and "On Sketching Landscape"; To Which Is Added a Poem, on Landscape Painting*. London: R. Blamire, 1792.

Gilroy, Paul. *Against Race: Imagining Political Culture beyond the Color Line*. Cambridge, Mass.: Harvard University Press, 2002.

Gladstone, William. "The Colour-Sense." *Nineteenth Century* 2 (October 1877): 366–88.

————. *Studies on Homer and the Homeric Age*. Vol. 3. Oxford: Oxford University Press, 1858.

Godkin, E. L. "Chromo-Civilization" (1874). In *Reflections and Comments, 1865–1895*, 192–205. New York: Charles Scribner and Sons, 1895.

Goethe, Johann Wolfgang von. *Theory of Colours* (1810). Translated by Charles Lock Eastlake. Mineola, N.Y.: Dover, 2006.

Golden, Catherine J. *The Yellow Wall-Paper: A Sourcebook and Critical Edition*. New York: Routledge, 2004.

Golden, Catherine J., and Joanna Schneider Zangrando, eds. *The Mixed Legacy of Charlotte Perkins Gilman*. Newark: University of Delaware Press, 2000.

Goldsby, Jacqueline. *A Spectacular Secret: Lynching in American Life and Literature*. Chicago: University of Chicago Press, 2006.

Gombrich, E. H. *The Preference for the Primitive: Episodes in the History of Western Taste and Art*. New York: Phaidon, 2002.

————. *The Sense of Order: A Study in the Psychology of Decorative Art*. Ithaca, N.Y.: Cornell University Press, 1984.

Gossett, Thomas F. *Race: The History of an Idea in America*. Oxford: Oxford University Press, 1997.

Greene, Douglas G., and Michael Patrick Hearn, *W. W. Denslow*. Introduction by Patricia Denslow Eykyn. [Mount Pleasant]: Clarke Historical Library, Central Michigan University, 1976.

Greenough, Sarah. *Modern Art and America: Alfred Stieglitz and His New York Galleries*. Washington, D.C.: National Gallery of Art, 2000.

Gullick, Thomas J., and John Timbs. *Painting Properly Explained*. London: Kent, 1859.

Haeckel, Ernst. "Ursprung und Entwickelung der Sinneswerkzeuge." *Kosmos* 2, no. 4 (1878): 20–114.

Hall, G. Stanley, ed. *American Journal of Psychology*. Worchester, Mass.: E. C. Sanford, 1891.

———. "Child Study and Its Relation to Education." *Forum* 29 (August 1900): 688–702.

Halliburton, David. *The Color of the Sky: A Study of Stephen Crane.* Cambridge: Cambridge University Press, 1989.

Haraway, Donna. "Situated Knowledges: The Science Question in Feminism and the Privilege of Partial Perspective." *Feminist Studies* 14, no. 3 (Autumn 1988): 575–99.

Harkins, E. F. "Famous Authors: Hamlin Garland" (1901). In *The Critical Reception of Hamlin Garland, 1891–1978,* edited by Charles L. P. Silet, Robert E. Welch, and Robert Bourdreau, 37–46. Troy, N.Y.: Whitson, 1985.

Harris, Mary Emma. *The Arts at Black Mountain College.* Cambridge: MIT Press, 1987.

Harris, Neil. *Cultural Excursions: Marketing Appetites and Cultural Tastes in Modern America.* Chicago: University of Chicago Press, 1990.

Hartmann, Sadakichi. *Buddha: A Drama in Twelve Scenes.* New York: Author's edition, 1897.

———. "Exhibition of Children's Drawings." *Camera Work* 39 (1912): 45–46.

Hayward, Jennifer. *Consuming Fictions: Active Audiences and Serial Fictions from Dickens to Soap Opera.* Louisville: University of Kentucky Press, 1997.

Hearn, Michael Patrick. *The Annotated Wizard of Oz: The Wonderful Wizard of Oz.* New York: W. W. Norton, 2000.

Hegeman, Susan. *Patterns for America: Modernism and the Concept of Culture.* Princeton: Princeton University Press, 1999.

Heilman, Ann. "Overwriting Decadence: Charlotte Perkins Gilman, Oscar Wilde, and the Feminization of Art in 'The Yellow Wall-Paper.'" In *The Mixed Legacy of Charlotte Perkins Gilman,* edited by Catherine J. Golden and Joanna Schneider Zangrando, 175–88. Newark: University of Delaware Press, 2000.

Hejinian, Lyn. "Two Stein Talks." In *The Language of Inquiry,* 83–130. Berkeley: University of California Press, 2000.

Helden, Caroline West van. *A Note on Color for Teachers of Elementary Schools.* Springfield, Mass.: Milton Bradley, 1912.

Helmholtz, Hermann von. *Treatise on Physiological Optics.* 3 vols. Edited by James P. C. Southall. New York: Optical Society of America, 1924–25.

Herskovits, Melville J. *The Anthropometry of the American Negro.* New York: Columbia University Press, 1930.

Hickerson, Nancy Parrott. "Gladstone's Ethnolinguistics: The Language of Experience in the Nineteenth Century." *Journal of Anthropological Research* 39, no. 1 (Spring 1983): 26–41.

Hicks, Mary Dana. "Color in Public Schools." In *National Educational Association: Journal of Proceedings and Addresses; Session of the Year 1894, Held at Asbury Park, New Jersey,* 906–15. St. Paul, Minn.: National Educational Association, 1895.

Hochman, Barbara. "Stowe's *House and Home Papers:* A Neglected Source for Gilman's 'The Yellow Wall-Paper.'" *American Literary Realism* 37, no. 1 (2004): 83–86.

Hochman, Brian. *Savage Preservation: The Ethnographic Origins of Modern Media Technology.* Minneapolis: University of Minnesota Press, 2014.

Hoffman, Michael J. *Critical Essays on Gertrude Stein.* Boston: G. K. Hall, 1986.

Hofstadter, Richard. *Social Darwinism in American Thought* (1944). Boston: Beacon Press, 1955.

Hornbeck, Nan. "Industry Courts the Rainbow." *Nation's Business,* January 1929, 114–17.

Hostetler, Ann E. "The Aesthetics of Race and Gender in Nella Larsen's *Quicksand.*" In "African and African American Literature," special topic, *PMLA* 105, no. 1 (January 1990): 35–46.

Howells, William Dean. *Criticism and Fiction, and Other Essays.* Edited by Clara Marburg Kirk and Rudolf Kirk. New York: New York University Press, 1965.

———. *A Hazard of New Fortunes.* New York: Harper and Brothers, 1890.

———. *The Rise of Silas Lapham* (1885). Reprint ed. Edited by Don L. Cook. New York: W. W. Norton, 1982.

Hubbard, Elbert. Untitled. *Philistine* 11, no. 4 (September 1900): 123–28.

Hughes, Langston. *The Big Sea* (1940). Vol. 13 of *The Collected Works of Langston Hughes,* edited by Joseph McLaren. Columbia: University of Missouri Press, 2002.

Hurston, Zora Neale. "How It Feels to Be Colored Me" (1928). In *I Love Myself When I Am Laughing . . . and Then Again When I Am Looking Mean and Impressive: A Zora Neale Hurston Reader,* edited by Alice Walker, introduced by Mary Helen Washington, 152–55. New York: Feminist Press, 1979.

Hutchinson, George. *The Harlem Renaissance in Black and White.* Cambridge, Mass.: Belknap Press of Harvard University Press, 1995.

———. *In Search of Nella Larsen: A Biography of the Color Line.* Cambridge, Mass.: Harvard University Press, 2006.

———. "Introduction." In *The Cambridge Companion to the Harlem Renaissance,* edited by George Hutchinson, 1–10. Cambridge: Cambridge University Press, 2007.

Huxley, Aldous. *The Doors of Perception.* New York: Harper and Brothers, 1954.

———. *Heaven and Hell* (1956), printed with *The Doors of Perception* (1954). London: Vintage Books, 2004.

James, William. *Pragmatism.* In *Writings, 1902–1910,* 479–624. New York: Library of America, 1987.

———. *The Principles of Psychology.* Vol. 1. New York: Henry Holt, 1890.

———. "Remarks on Spencer's Definition of Mind as Correspondence" (1878). In *Writings, 1878–1899,* 893–909. New York: Library of America, 1992.

Jeffries, Benjamin Joy. *Color-Names, Color-Blindness, and the Education of the Color-Sense in Our Schools.* Boston: Louis Prang, 1882.

Jones, Owen. *The Grammar of Ornament.* London: Day and Son, 1856.

Kalba, Laura Anne. *Color in the Age of Impressionism: Commerce, Technology, and Art.* University Park: Pennsylvania State University Press, 2017.

———. "Fireworks and Other Profane Illuminations: Color and the Experience of Wonder in Modern Visual Culture." *Modernism/Modernity* 19, no. 4 (November 2012): 657–76.

Kandinsky, Wassily. *Concerning the Spiritual in Art.* Translated by M. T. H. Sadler. New York: Dover, 1977.

Kaplan, Amy. "Nation, Region, Empire." In *Columbia History of the American Novel,* edited by Emory Elliott, 240–66. New York: Columbia University Press, 1991.

Kapor, Vladimir. "Couleur locale—a Pictorial Term Gone Astray?" *Word and Image* 25, no. 1 (2009): 22–32.

———. *Local Colour: A Travelling Concept.* Romanticism and After in France 13. Oxford: Peter Lang, 2009.

Kargon, Jeremy. "The Logic of Color: Theory and Graphics in Christine Ladd-Franklin's Explanation of Color Vision." *Leonardo* 47, no. 2 (2014): 151–57.

Kay, Charles de. "Colors and the Mind." *New York Times,* 9 May 1901.

Keevak, Michael. *Becoming Yellow: A Short History of Racial Thinking.* Princeton: Princeton University Press, 2011.

Knight, Denise K. "'I Could Paint Still Life as Well as Any One on Earth': Charlotte Perkins Gilman and the World of Art." *Women's Studies* 35 (2006): 475–92.

Kristeva, Julia. *Desire and Language: A Semiotic Approach to Literature and Art.* Edited by Leon S. Roudiez and translated by Thomas Gora, Alice Jardine, and Leon S. Roudiez. New York: Columbia University Press, 1980.

Ladd-Franklin, Christine. "A New Theory of Light Sensation." *Science* 22, no. 545 (14 July 1893): 18–19.

Landa, Edward R., and Mark D. Fairchild. "Charting Color from the Eye of the Beholder." *American Scientist* 93 (September–October 2005): 436–43.

Lane, Ann J. *To Herland and Beyond: The Life and Work of Charlotte Perkins Gilman.* New York: Pantheon, 1990.

Lanser, Susan. "Feminist Criticism, 'The Yellow Wallpaper,' and the Politics of Color in America." In "Feminist Reinterpretations/Reinterpretations of Feminism," special issue, *Feminist Studies* 15, no. 3 (Autumn 1989): 415–41.

Larsen, Nella. *Passing.* New York: Alfred A. Knopf, 1929.

———. *Quicksand* (1928). Mineola, N.Y.: Dover, 2006.

Last, Jay T. *The Color Explosion: Nineteenth-Century American Lithography.* Santa Ana, Calif.: Hillcrest Press, 2005.

Leach, William. *Land of Desire: Merchants, Power, and the Rise of a New American Culture.* New York: Vintage Books, 1993.

Le Gallienne, Richard. "Miss Irwin's 'Color Poems.'" Letter to the editor. *New York Times,* 26 November 1910.

Le Rider, Jacques. *Les couleurs et les mots.* Paris: Presses Universitaires de France, 1997.

Leslie, Esther. *Synthetic Worlds: Nature, Art and the Chemical Industry.* London: Reaktion Books, 2005.

Levander, Caroline. *Cradle of Liberty: Race, the Child, and National Belonging from Thomas Jefferson to W. E. B. Du Bois.* Durham, N.C.: Duke University Press, 2006.

Lichtenstein, Jacqueline. *The Eloquence of Color: Rhetoric and Painting in the French Classical Age.* Translated by Emily McVarish. Berkeley: University of California Press, 1993.

Littlefield, Henry M. "The Wizard of Oz: Parable on Populism." *American Quarterly* 16, no. 1 (Spring 1964): 47–58.

Locke, Alain. "The New Negro." In *The New Negro* (1925), 1st Touchstone ed., edited by Alain Locke, 3–10. New York: Simon and Schuster, 1997.

Locke, John. *An Essay concerning Human Understanding.* Edited by Peter H. Nidditch. Oxford: Clarendon Press, 1975.

Loos, Adolf. "Ladies' Fashion." In *Spoken into the Void: Collected Essays, 1897–1900,* translated by Jane O. Newman and John H. Smith, 98–103. Cambridge: MIT Press, 1982.

———. "Ornament and Crime." In *Ornament and Crime: Selected Essays,* translated by Michael Mitchell, 167–76. Riverside, Calif.: Ariadne Press, 1998.

Lutz, Tom. *American Nervousness, 1903: An Anecdotal History.* Ithaca, N.Y.: Cornell University Press, 1991.

———. *Cosmopolitan Vistas: American Regionalism and Literary Value.* Ithaca, N.Y.: Cornell University Press, 2004.

Mackey, Nathanial. "Other: From Noun to Verb." *Representations* 29 (Summer 1992): 51–70.

Magnus, Hugo. *Die Entwickelung des Farbensinnes.* Jena, Germany: Hermann Dufft, 1877.

———. *Die geschichtliche Entwickelung des Farbensinnes.* Leipzig, Germany: Veit, 1877.

———. "A Research Study of Primitive Peoples' Awareness and Perception of Colour." In *The Debate about Colour Naming in 19th Century German Philology,* ed. Barbara Saunders, 133–82. Leuven, Belgium: Leuven University Press, 2007.

Maillet, Arnaud. *The Claude Glass: Use and Meaning of the Black Mirror in Western Art.* New York: Zone Books, 2004.

Mancini, J. M. *Pre-Modernism: Art-World Change and American Culture from the Civil War to the Amory Show.* Princeton: Princeton University Press, 2005.

Mao, Douglas. *Fateful Beauty: Aesthetic Environments, Juvenile Development, and Literature, 1860–1960.* Princeton: Princeton University Press, 2008.

Marzio, Peter C. *The Democratic Art, Chromolithography, 1840–1900: Pictures for a 19th-Century America.* Boston: D. R. Godine and Amon Carter Museum of Western Art, Fort Worth [Texas], 1979.

Massumi, Brian. *Parables for the Virtual: Movement, Affect, Sensation.* Durham, N.C.: Duke University Press, 2002.

Masury, John W. *How Shall We Paint Our Houses? A Popular Treatise on the Art of House-Painting; Plain and Decorative; Showing the Nature, Composition and Mode of Production of Paints and Painters' Colors, and Their Proper and Harmonious Combination and Arrangement.* New York: D. Appleton, 1868.

Matisse, Henri. "Looking at Life with the Eyes of a Child" (1953). In *Matisse on Art,* edited by Jack Flam, 217–18. Berkeley: University of California Press, 1995.

Matz, Jesse. *Literary Impressionism and Modernist Aesthetics.* Cambridge: Cambridge University Press, 2001.

Maund, Barry. "Color." In *Stanford Encyclopedia of Philosophy,* Winter 2012 ed., edited by Edward N. Zalta. http://plato.stanford.edu/entries/color/.

Mavor, Carol. *Blue Mythologies: Reflections on a Colour.* London: Reaktion Books, 2013.

McCarthy, Desmond. "The Post-Impressionists." In *Manet and the Post-Impressionists,* 7–13. London: Ballantyne, 1910.

McKay, Claude. *Banjo: A Story without a Plot* (1929). New York: Harvest, 1970.

———. *Home to Harlem* (1928). Foreword by Wayne F. Cooper. Boston: Northeastern University Press, 1987.

———. "A Negro Extravaganza" (1921). In *The Passion of Claude McKay: Selected Poetry and Prose, 1912–1948,* edited by Wayne F. Cooper, 63–64. New York: Schocken Books, 1973.

McLaughlin, M. Louise. *Painting in Oil: A Manual for the Use of Students.* Cincinnati, Ohio: Robert Clarke, 1888.

Mead, William E. "Color in Old English Poetry." *PMLA* 14, no. 2 (n.s., 7, no. 2) (1899): 169–206.

Meggs, Philip B., and Alston W. Purvis. *Meggs' History of Graphic Design.* 4th ed. Hoboken, N.J.: John Wiley and Sons, 2006.

Meltzer, Françoise. "Color as Cognition in Symbolist Verse." *Critical Inquiry* 5, no. 2 (Winter 1978): 253–73.

———. "Rimbaud's 'Voyelles.'" *Modern Philology* 76, no. 4 (May 1979): 344–54.

Melville, Herman. *Moby-Dick.* 2nd ed. Edited by Hershel Parker and Harrison Hayford. New York: W. W. Norton, 2001.

Merleau-Ponty, Maurice. "Eye and Mind" (1960). In *The Primacy of Perception, and Other Essays on Phenomenological Psychology, the Philosophy of Art, History and Politics.* Edited by James M. Edie, 159–90. Evanston, Ill.: Northwestern University Press, 1964.

Merrill, Stuart, trans. and ed. *Pastels in Prose.* New York: Harper and Brothers, 1890.

Meyer, Steven. *Irresistible Dictation: Gertrude Stein and the Correlations of Writing and Science.* Stanford: Stanford University Press, 2001.

Michaels, Walter Benn. *Our America: Nativism, Modernism, and Pluralism.* Durham, N.C.: Duke University Press, 1995.

Molesworth, Helen. "Imaginary Landscapes." In *Leap before You Look: Black Mountain College, 1933–1957,* with Ruth Erickson, 25–75. New Haven: Yale University Press, 2015.

———. *Leap before You Look: Black Mountain College, 1933–1957.* With Ruth Erickson. New Haven: Yale University Press, 2015.

Monteiro, George. *Stephen Crane: The Contemporary Reviews.* Cambridge: Cambridge University Press, 2009.

Morgan, Benjamin. *The Outward Mind: Materialist Aesthetics in Victorian Science and Literature.* Chicago: University of Chicago Press, 2017.

Morrow, Marco. "Stories of the Slums." *Womankind,* August 1896.

Mullen, Harryette. *The Cracks between What We Are and What We Are Supposed to Be: Essays and Interviews.* Tuscaloosa: University of Alabama Press, 2012.

Munsell, Albert. *Color and an Eye to Discern It.* Boston: Author, 1907.

———. *A Color Notation.* 2nd ed. Boston: George H. Ellis, 1907.

———. "A Measured Training of the Color Sense." *Education* 29, no. 6 (February 1909): 360–80.

———. *The Munsell Color System: Children's Studies in Measured Colors.* Boston: Wadsworth, Howland. Box 44, env. 04. Print Ephemera. Huntington Library, San Marino, Calif.

Münsterberg, Hugo. *Psychological Laboratory of Harvard University.* Cambridge, Mass.: Harvard University Press, 1893.

Murphy, Murray G. *The Development of Peirce's Philosophy.* Cambridge, Mass.: Harvard University Press, 1993.

Musselman, Elizabeth Green. *Nervous Conditions: Science and the Body Politic in Early Industrial Britain.* Albany: SUNY, 2006.

Nagel, Thomas. *Stephen Crane and Literary Impressionism.* University Park: Pennsylvania State University Press, 1980.

Nead, Lynda. "'Red Taffeta under Tweed': The Color of Post-War Clothes." *Fashion Theory* 21, no. 4 (2017): 365–89.

"The New Age of Color." *Saturday Evening Post,* 21 January 1928, 28.

Newlin, Keith. *Hamlin Garland: A Life.* Lincoln: University of Nebraska Press, 2008.

Ngai, Sianne. *Ugly Feelings.* Cambridge, Mass.: Harvard University Press, 2005.

Nichols, Herbert. "The Psychological Laboratory at Harvard." *McClure's Magazine,* October 1893, 399–409.

Nicholson, Francis. "Of the Local Colour." In *The Practice of Drawing and Painting Landscape from Nature, in Water Colours,* 13–15. London: John Murray, 1823.

Nielsen, Aldon Lynn. *Reading Race: White American Poets and the Racial Discourse in the Twentieth Century.* Athens: University of Georgia Press, 1988.

Nordau, Max. *Degeneration.* New York: D. Appleton, 1895.

Norris, Frank. "The Green Stones of Unrest." In *Stephen Crane's Career: Perspectives and Evaluations,* edited by Thomas A. Gullason, 87–89. New York: New York University Press, 1972.

North, Michael. *The Dialect of Modernism: Race, Language, and Twentieth-Century Literature.* Oxford: Oxford University Press, 1994.

"A Pane of Blue Glass." *Harper's Bazaar* 10, no. 19 (12 May 1877): 298–99.

Parkhurst, Daniel Burleigh. "Sketching from Nature." *Art Amateur: A Monthly Journal Devoted to Art in the Household* 23, no. 2 (July 1890): 30.

Pastoureau, Michel. *Black: The History of a Color.* Princeton: Princeton University Press, 2008.

———. *Blue: The History of a Color.* Princeton: Princeton University Press, 2001.

———. *Green: The History of a Color.* Princeton: Princeton University Press, 2014.

———. *Red: The History of a Color.* Princeton: Princeton University Press, 2017.

Pater, Walter. *The Renaissance: Studies in Art and Poetry.* 3rd ed. New York: Macmillan, 1888.

Peirce, Charles S. *Collected Papers.* Vols. 1–6. Edited by Charles Hartshorne and Paul Weiss. Cambridge, Mass.: Harvard University Press, 1931–35.

———. *Collected Papers.* Vols. 7–8. Edited by Arthur Banks. Cambridge, Mass.: Harvard University Press, 1958.

———. "[On a Method of Searching for the Categories]." In *The Writings of Charles S.*

Peirce: A Chronological Edition, vol. 1, edited by Max H. Fisch et al., 515–28. Bloomington: Indiana University Press, 1982.

———. "On a New List of Categories." *Proceedings of the American Academy of Arts and Sciences* 7 (1868): 287–98.

Peiss, Kathy. *Hope in a Jar: The Making of America's Beauty Culture.* New York: Metropolitan Books, 1998.

Penn, Jonathon. "A Little Study of Stephen Crane." *Lotus* 2 (October 1896): 208–11.

Phillips, Jennifer. "Relative Color: Baudelaire, Chevreul, and the Reconsideration of Critical Methodology." *Nineteenth-Century French Studies* 33, nos. 3 and 4 (Spring–Summer 2005): 342–57.

Pickering, Andrew. "Decentering Sociology: Synthetic Dyes and Social Theory." *Perspectives on Science* 13, no. 3 (2005): 353–405.

Pike, Benjamin Jr. *Pike's Illustrated Descriptive Catalogue of Optical, Mathematical, and Philosophical Instruments.* New York: Published and sold by the author, 1856.

Piles, Roger de. *Cours de peinture par principes.* Paris: Jacques Estienne, 1708.

———. *The Principles of Painting.* London: J. Osborn, 1743.

Pillsbury, J. H. "A Scheme of Colour Standards." *Nature,* 22 August 1895, 390–92.

Pizer, Donald. *Hamlin Garland's Early Work and Career.* Berkeley: University of California Press, 1960.

———. *Realism and Naturalism in Nineteenth-Century American Literature.* Carbondale: Southern Illinois University Press, 1966.

"A Plea for Color." *Art Digest* 7, no. 10 (15 February 1934): 24.

Porée, Marc. "'Popularity' in Blue." In *The Colours of the Past in Victorian England,* edited by Charlotte Ribeyrol, Cultural Interactions: Studies in the Relationship between the Arts 38, edited by J. B. Bullen, 183–204. Oxford: Peter Lang, 2016.

Posnock, Ross. *Color and Culture: Black Writers and the Making of the Modern Intellectual.* Cambridge, Mass.: Harvard University Press, 1998.

Pound, Ezra. *Gaudier-Brzeska: A Memoir by Ezra Pound.* London: John Lane, the Bodley Head, 1916.

Prang, Louis, Mary Dana Hicks, and John S. Clark. *Color Instruction: Suggestions for a Course of Instruction in Color for Public Schools.* New York: Prang Educational Company, 1893.

Pratt, Alice Edwards. *The Use of Color in the Verse of English Romantic Poets.* Chicago: University of Chicago Press, 1898.

Preyer, William T. *The Mind of the Child.* Part 1, *The Senses and the Will* (1890). Translated by H. W. Brown. New York: D. Appleton, 1898.

Pynchon, Thomas. *Gravity's Rainbow* (1973). New York: Penguin, 2006.

Rancière, Jacques. *The Politics of Aesthetics: The Distribution of the Sensible.* Translated by Gabriel Rockhill. New York: Continuum, 2004.

Reed, Adolph Jr. *W. E. B. Du Bois and American Political Thought: Fabianism and the Color Line.* Oxford: Oxford University Press, 1997.

Rewald, John. *The History of Impressionism* (1946). New York: Museum of Modern Art, 1973.

Ribeyrol, Charlotte. "The Changing Colours of 19th Century Art and Literature." Conference, Ashmolean Museum, Oxford University, 2 June 2017.

———. Introduction to *The Colours of the Past in Victorian England*. Cultural Interactions: Studies in the Relationship between the Arts 38, edited by J. B. Bullen. Oxford: Peter Lang, 2016.

Richards, Graham. "Getting a Result: The Expedition's Psychological Research, 1898–1913." In *Cambridge and the Torres Strait: Centenary Essays on the 1898 Anthropological Expedition,* edited by Anita Herle and Sandra Rouse, 136–57. Cambridge: Cambridge University Press, 1998.

Richardson, Joan. *A Natural History of Pragmatism: The Fact of Feeling from Jonathan Edwards to Gertrude Stein.* Cambridge: Cambridge University Press, 2006.

Rimington, Alexander Wallace. *Colour-Music: The Art of Mobile Colour.* London: Hutchinson, 1912.

Ritter, Gretchen. "Silver Slippers and a Golden Cap: L. Frank Baum's *The Wonderful Wizard of Oz* and Historical Memory in American Politics." *Journal of American Studies* 31, no. 2 (August 1997): 171–202.

Rivers, W. H. R. "Color Vision." In *Reports of the Cambridge Anthropological Expedition to Torres Straits,* vol. 2, *Physiology and Psychology,* part 1, "Introduction and Vision," 48–96. Cambridge: University of Cambridge Press, 1901.

———. "Primitive Color Vision." *Popular Science Monthly* 59, no. 1 (May 1901): 44–58.

Rood, Ogden. *Modern Chromatics, with Applications to Art and Industry.* New York: D. Appleton, 1879.

Rossi, Michael. *The Republic of Color: Science, Perception, and the Making of Modern America.* Chicago: University of Chicago Press, forthcoming.

Ruskin, John. *The Elements of Drawing; In Three Letters to Beginners* (1857). New York: John Wiley and Sons, 1877.

———. *Modern Painters, Vol. 1.* Vol. 3 of *The Works of John Ruskin,* library ed., edited by E. T. Cook and Alexander Wedderburn. London: George Allen, 1903–12.

———. *The Works of John Ruskin.* 39 vols. Library edition. Edited by E. T. Cook and Alexander Wedderburn. London, New York: George Allen, 1903–12.

Sahlins, Marshall. "Colors and Cultures." *Semiotica* 16, no. 1 (1976): 1–22.

Saldívar-Hull, Sonia. "Wrestling Your Ally: Stein, Racism, and Feminist Critical Practice." In *Women's Writing in Exile,* edited by Mary Lynn Broe and Angela Ingram, 181–198. Chapel Hill: University of North Carolina Press, 1989.

Sassi, Maria Michela. "The Sea Was Never Blue." *Aeon,* 31 July 2017. https://aeon.co /essays/can-we-hope-to-understand-how-the-greeks-saw-their-world.

Scarry, Elaine. *Dreaming by the Book.* New York: Farrar, Straus, Giroux, 1999.

Schooling, William. "Color-Music: A Suggestion of a New Art." *Littell's Living Age* 206, no. 2666 (10 August 1895): 349–56.

Schroeder, Jonathan David Shelly. "The Painting of Modern Light: Local Color before Regionalism." *American Literature* 86, no. 3 (September 2014): 551–81.

Schuller, Kyla. *The Biopolitics of Feeling: Race, Sex, and Impressibility in the Nineteenth-Century United States.* Durham, N.C.: Duke University Press, 2017.

Scripture, E. W. "A Test of Safe Color Vision." In *Studies from the Yale Psychological Laboratory,* vol. 7, 1–20. New Haven: Yale University Press, 1900.

See, Sam. "'Spectacles in Color': The Primitive Drag of Langston Hughes." *PMLA* 124, no. 3 (May 2009): 798–816.

Seitler, Dana. *Atavistic Tendencies: The Culture of Science in American Modernity.* Minneapolis: University of Minnesota Press, 2008.

Shea, James J. *It's All in the Game.* New York: Putnam's, 1960.

Shinn, Milicent Washburn. *Notes on the Development of a Child.* Berkeley: University of California Press, 1893.

Shoemaker, Nancy. "How Indians Got to Be Red." *American Historical Review* 102, no. 3 (June 1997): 625–44.

Shuttleworth, Sally. *The Mind of the Child: Child Development in Literature, Science, and Medicine, 1840–1900.* Oxford: Oxford University Press, 2010.

Silverman, Debora L. *Art Nouveau in Fin-de-Siècle France: Politics, Psychology, and Style.* Berkeley: University of California Press, 1989.

Skard, Sigmund. "The Use of Color in Literature." *Proceeding of the American Philological Society* 90, no. 3 (July 1946): 163–249.

Sloane, Patricia. *The Visual Nature of Color.* New York: Design Press, 1989.

Smith, Bruce. *The Key of Green: Passion and Perception in Renaissance Culture.* Chicago: University of Chicago Press, 2008.

Smith, Walter. *Art Education, Scholastic and Industrial.* Boston: James R. Osgood, 1873.

Solomons, Leon. "The Saturation of Colors." *Psychological Review* 3, no. 1 (January 1896): 50–56.

Sorensen, Roy. *Seeing Dark Things: The Philosophy of Shadows.* Oxford: Oxford University Press, 2011.

Sorrentino, Paul. *Stephen Crane: A Life of Fire.* Cambridge, Mass.: Harvard University Press, 2014.

Spencer, Herbert. "The Comparative Psychology of Man" (1876). *Mind* 1, no. 1 (January 1876): 7–20.

———. "The Valuation of Evidence" (1853). In *Herbert Spencer, Collected Writings: Scientific, Political, and Speculative,* vol. 2 (1891), 161–67. Reprint edition. London: Routledge/Thoemmes Press, 1996.

Stallman, R. W. *Stephen Crane: A Biography.* New York: G. Braziller, 1968.

Stankiewicz, Mary Ann. *Roots of Art Educational Practice.* Worchester, Mass.: Davis Publications, 2001.

Stein, Gertrude. *The Autobiography of Alice B. Toklas* (1933). New York: Vintage Books, 1990.

———. *Geographical History of America* (1936). Baltimore: Johns Hopkins University Press, 1995.

———. *Lectures in America* (1935). London: Virago, 1988.

———. "Lipchitz." In *A Stein Reader,* edited by Ulla E. Dydo, 491–92. Evanston, Ill.: Northwestern University Press, 1993.

———. *Narration: Four Lectures* (1935). Chicago: University of Chicago Press, 2010.

———. *Tender Buttons: Objects, Food, Rooms.* New York: Claire Marie, 1914.

———. *Three Lives* (1909). New York: Vintage Books, 1936.

———. *"Three Lives" and "Q.E.D.": Authoritative Texts, Contexts, Criticism.* Edited by Marianne DeKoven. New York: W. W. Norton, 2006.

———. "Transatlantic Interview—1946." In *A Primer for the Gradual Understand-*

ing of Gertrude Stein, edited by Robert Hass, 11–35. Los Angeles: Black Sparrow Press, 1971.

Steiner, Wendy. *The Colors of Rhetoric: Problems in the Relation between Modern Literature and Painting.* Chicago: University of Chicago Press, 1982.

Stengers, Isabelle. *Thinking with Whitehead: A Free and Wild Creation of Concepts.* Translated by Michael Chase. Cambridge, Mass.: Harvard University Press, 2011.

Stephens, Michelle Ann. *Black Empire: The Masculine Global Imaginary of Caribbean Intellectuals in the United States, 1914–1962.* Durham, N.C.: Duke University Press, 2005.

———. *Skin Acts: Race, Psychoanalysis, and the Black Male Performer.* Durham, N.C.: Duke University Press, 2014.

Stetson, Charles Walter. *Charles Walter Stetson: Color and Fantasy.* Edited by Charles C. Eldredge. Lawrence: Spencer Museum of Art and University of Kansas, 1982.

Stetson, Charlotte Perkins [Gilman]. *Women and Economics: A Study of the Economic Relation between Men and Women as a Factor in Social Evolution.* Boston: Small, Maynard, 1898.

Stetson, Elizabeth Mills. "The Management of Details." *Editor* 25, no. 1 (July 1907): 16–20.

Stewart, George R., Jr. "Color in Science and Poetry." *Scientific Monthly* 30, no. 1 (January 1930): 71–78.

St. John, Tom. "Lyman Frank Baum: Looking Back to the Promised Land." *Western Humanities Review* 36 (Winter 1982): 349–60.

Stocking, George. *Race, Culture, and Evolution: Essays in the History of Anthropology.* Chicago: University of Chicago Press, 1968.

Stronks, James B. "A Realist Experiments with Impressionism: Hamlin Garland's 'Chicago Studies,'" *American Literature* 36, no. 1 (March 1964): 38–52.

"The Study of Local Color." *Atlantic Monthly* 90, no. 542 (December 1902): 864–66.

Sully, James. "Child Study and Education." *Current Literature* 30, no. 4 (April 1901): 473–75.

———. "The New Study of Children." *Littell's Living Age* 207, no. 2683 (7 December 1895): 579–89.

Swartz, Mark Evan. *Oz before the Rainbow: L. Frank Baum's "The Wonderful Wizard of Oz" on Stage and Screen to 1939.* Baltimore: Johns Hopkins University Press, 2000.

Symonds, John Addington. *Essays Speculative and Suggestive.* New York: Charles Scribner's Sons, 1894.

———. *In the Key of Blue, and Other Prose Essays.* London: Elkin Mathews and John Lane, 1893.

Taussig, Michael. *Mimesis and Alterity: A Particular History of the Senses.* New York: Routledge, 1993.

———. *What Color Is the Sacred?* Chicago: University of Chicago Press, 2009.

"Textiles: Dyes and Dyers A–Z by Company." Binder 1 of 9. Jay T. Last Collection. Huntington Library, San Marino, Calif.

Thaggert, Miriam. *Images of Black Modernism: Verbal and Visual Strategies of the Harlem Renaissance*. Amherst: University of Massachusetts Press, 2010.

Thomas, Brook, ed. *Plessy v. Ferguson: A Brief History with Documents*. Boston: Bedford Books, 1997.

Thomas, Heather Kirk. "'[A] Kind of "Debased Romanesque" with *Delirium Tremens*': Late-Victorian Wall Coverings and Charlotte Perkins Gilman's 'The Yellow Wall-Paper.'" In *The Mixed Legacy of Charlotte Perkins Gilman*, edited by Catherine J. Golden and Joanna Schneider Zangrando, 189–206. Newark: University of Delaware Press, 2000.

Thompson, Evan. *Color Vision: A Study of Cognitive Science and the Philosophy of Science*. New York: Routledge, 1995.

Thrailkill, Jane F. *Affecting Fictions: Mind, Body, and Emotion in American Literary Realism*. Cambridge, Mass.: Harvard University Press, 2007.

Thurman, Wallace. *The Blacker the Berry* (1929). Mineola, N.Y.: Dover, 2008.

———. *The Collected Writings of Wallace Thurman: A Harlem Renaissance Reader*. Edited by Amritjit Singh and Danial M. Scott III. New Brunswick, N.J.: Rutgers University Press, 2003.

Tompkins, Kyla Wazana. *Racial Indigestion: Eating Bodies in the 19th Century*. New York: New York University Press, 2012.

Toomer, Jean. *Cane* (1923). Edited by Darwin T. Turner. New York: W. W. Norton, 1988.

Torgovnick, Marianna. *Gone Primitive: Savage Intellects, Modern Lives*. Chicago: University of Chicago Press, 1990.

———. *Primitive Passions: Men, Women, and the Quest for Ecstasy*. New York: Alfred A. Knopf, 1997.

Travis, A. S. *The Rainbow Makers: The Origins of the Synthetic Dyestuffs Industry in Western Europe*. Bethlehem, Pa.: Lehigh University Press, 1993.

Turner, Darwin T. Introduction to the 1975 edition of *Cane*, by Jean Toomer, ix–xxv. New York: Liverwright, 1975.

Turner, R. Steven. *In the Eye's Mind: Vision and the Helmholtz-Hering Controversy*. Princeton: Princeton University Press, 1994.

Vanderpoel, Emily Noyes. *Color Problems: A Practical Manual for the Lay Student of Color*. New York: Longmans, Green, 1902.

Van Vechten, Carl. *Nigger Heaven* (1926). Urbana and Chicago: University of Illinois Press, 2000.

Veeder, William. "Who Is Jane? The Intricate Feminism of Charlotte Perkins Gilman." *Arizona Quarterly* 44, no. 3 (Autumn 1988): 40–79.

Véron, Eugène. *Æsthetics*. Translated by W. H. Armstrong. Philadelphia: Lippencott, 1879.

Wall, Cheryl A. *Women of the Harlem Renaissance*. Bloomington: Indiana University Press, 1995.

Wallace, Alfred Russel. *Tropical Nature, and Other Essays*. London: Macmillan, 1878.

Warner, Charles Dudley. "Editor's Study." *Harper's Magazine* 92 (May 1896): 961–62.

Weatherford, Richard M. *Stephen Crane: The Critical Heritage*. New York: Routledge, 1997.

Weber, Nicholas Fox Weber. "Foreword." In *Interaction of Color,* by Josef Albers, 50th anniversary edition, ix–xi. New Haven: Yale University Press, 2013.

Weinberg, Louis. *Color in Everyday Life.* New York: Moffat, Yard, 1918.

Wells, Bridget Germana. "Hamlin Garland's 1887 Travel Notebook: An Edition." Master's thesis, University of North Carolina, 2007.

Wheeler, Candace. "The Philosophy of Beauty Applied to House Interiors." In *Household Art,* edited by Candace Wheeler, 3–35. New York: Harper and Brothers, 1893.

Whitehead, Alfred North. *Science and the Modern World* (1925). New York: Free Press, 1967.

Wilde, Oscar. "The Critic as Artist" (1891). In *The Artist as Critic, Critical Writings of Oscar Wilde,* edited by Richard Ellmann, 341–407. New York: Random House, 1968.

———. *Decorative Art in America: A Lecture by Oscar Wilde together with Letters, Reviews, and Interviews.* Edited and introduced by Richard Butler Glaenzer. New York: Brentano's, 1906.

Williams, William Carlos. *Imaginations.* New York: New Directions, 1970.

Wilson, Harold. "The Relation of Color to the Emotions." *Arena* 19, no. 103 (June 1898): 810–27.

Winch, W. H. "Colour Preferences of School Children." *British Journal of Psychology,* 1909, 42–65.

Wittgenstein, Ludwig. *Culture and Value.* Edited by G. H. von Wright. Translated by Peter Winch. Chicago: University of Chicago Press, 1980.

Woodworth, R. S. "The Puzzle of Color Vocabularies." *Psychological Bulletin* 7, no. 10 (15 October 1910): 325–34.

Woolf, Virginia. "Walter Sickert." In *Collected Essays,* 2: 233–44. London: Hogarth Press, 1966.

Wright, A. E. "Color-Shadows." *Nineteenth Century* 37, no. 219 (May 1895): 819–31.

Young, Helen Binkerd. "Household Decoration." *Cornell Reading Courses* 1, no. 5 (1 December 1911): 43–44.

Zhang, Dora. "Naming the Indescribable: Woolf, Russell, James, and the Limits of Description." *New Literary History* 45, no. 1 (Winter 2014): 51–70.

Zilczer, Judith. "'Color Music': Synaesthesia and Nineteenth-Century Sources for Abstract Art." In *Artibus et historiae* 8, no. 16 (1987): 101–26.

———. "Music for the Eyes: Abstract Painting and Light Art." In *Visual Music: Synesthesia in Art and Music since 1900,* edited by Kerry Brougher, 25–85. London: Thames and Hudson, 2005.

Index

abstract color, 38–39, 79–113, 179–84, 267n61; in Denslow's work, 134–38; interior design and, 92–102. *See also* color music

abstraction: interior designs promoting, 92–102; language as vector of, 30, 177–83, 194; primitive color vision and, 83–92

advertising, 16, 144–45, 165, 169, 176, 240; Baum's trade writing as guidebook for, 145–46; *Oz* as narrative parallel to, 158; race and, 132, 209–10; trade cards, 13, 16, 139. *See also* consumer culture

aesthetics, 20, 31, 99–102; Dewey and McKay on aesthetic education, 230–36; evolution and, 56–68; of the picturesque, 47–51, 57; of pure color, 30

Albers, Josef, 41, 242–49, 277n6, 278n12, 278nn14–15, 278nn18–19; *Interaction of Color,* 41, 242, 244–48; thinking in situations, 242, 246–48

Allen, Grant, 63–64, 88, 89, 260n67, 263n37, 266n30; *The Colour-Sense,* 26, 30, 63; *Physiological Aesthetics,* 63

Allen, James Lane, 263n32; "Local Color," 61

Allen, Judith A., 266n34, 266n54

"American eye, the," 188–89

aniline dyes, 14–21; aniline aesthetic, 40, 168–69, 176, 177, 218; color revolution fueled by, 14, 16–21; language for color expanded by, 34; lurid realism and, 164–65, 168–69, 175–76, 190, 191. *See also* synthetic dyes

anthropology, 88–89; formative role of color in early, 224–26; Rivers's expedition to Torres Strait, 4–5, 21–23, 24, 88–89, 224

Aronowicz, Yaron, 273n61

art: Albers on, 246–47; for art's sake, 39, 79; at Black Mountain, 243–44; Dewey on, 233, 235; nature and, 47–51, 66–67. *See also* impressionism; local color(s); painting; postimpressionism

art education, 122–23. *See also* aesthetics; color education

artificiality: conflation of skin and synthetic colorants, 216–21; decadent and aestheticist obsession with, 19–20. *See also* synthetic dyes

art nouveau, 171; illustrations for Crane's *War is Kind,* 172–74

Austin, Mary, 77, 263n27, 263n33, 264n64; *The Land of Journey's Ending,* 61; *The Land of Little Rain,* 58; "The Pocket Hunter," 58

avant-garde, 38, 40, 80, 163; child's view of color and, 119, 135. *See also* color music; lurid realism; symbolism

Babbitt, Edwin, 86, 265n21; *The Principles of Light and Color,* 85–86

Nicholas Gaskill is associate professor of American literature at the University of Oxford and tutorial fellow at Oriel College. He is coeditor of *The Lure of Whitehead* (Minnesota, 2014).